ADVANCED INTERNET TECHNOLOGIES

ISBN 0-13-759515-8

90000

9 780137 595150

Prentice Hall Series In
Advanced Communications Technologies

Emerging Communications Technologies, 2/E

ATM (Vol I):
Foundation for
Broadband Networks

SONET and T1:
Architectures for
Digital Transport
Networks

Mobile and
Wireless
Networks

ATM (Vol II):
Signaling in
Broadband Networks

ISDN and SS7:
Architectures for
Digital Signaling
Networks

Second Generation
Mobile and Wireless
Networks

ATM (Vol III):
Internetworking
with ATM

Third Generation
Mobile Networks

ATM (Vol IV):
Network
Management

Advanced Internet
Technologies

Residential Broadband:
xDSL, HFC, and Fixed
Wireless Access

The Intelligent Network:
Customizing Telecom-
munication Networks
and Services

Security in the
Internet

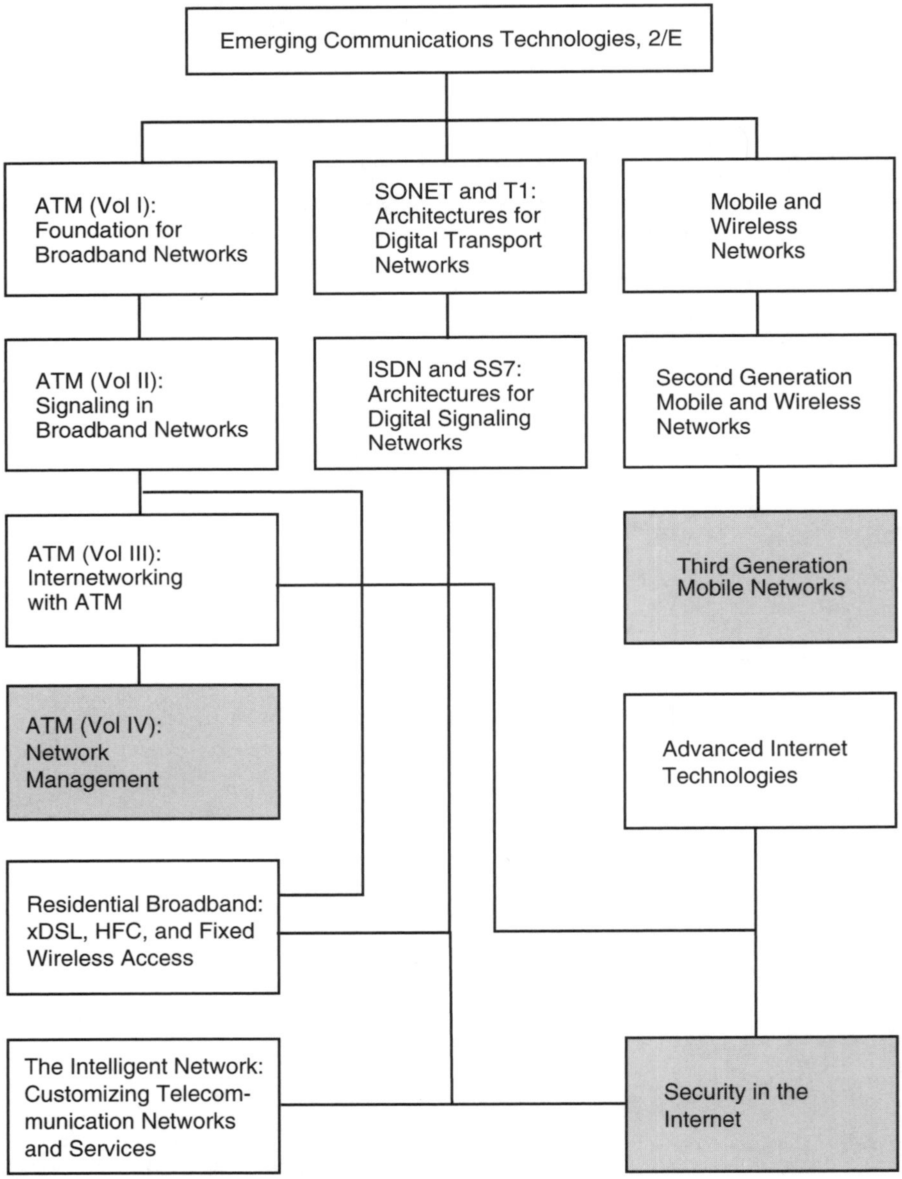

Indicates future books in this Series

Advanced Internet Technologies

UYLESS BLACK

Prentice Hall PTR
Upper Saddle River, New Jersey 07458
http://www.phptr.com

Library of Congress Cataloging-in-Publication Data

Black, Uyless D.
    Advanced internet technologies / Uyless Black.
      p. cm.
    Includes bibliographical references and index.
    ISBN 0–13–759515–8
    1. Internet (Computer network) I. Title.
TK5105.875.I57B55 1998
004.67′8—dc21   98–36914
                                             CIP

Acquisitions editor: Mary Franz
Cover designer: Talar Agasyan
Cover design director: Jerry Votta
Manufacturing manager: Alexis R. Heydt
Marketing manager: Miles Williams
Compositor/Production services: Pine Tree Composition, Inc.

© 1999 by Uyless Black

    Published by Prentice Hall PTR
    Prentice-Hall, Inc.
    A Simon & Schuster Company
    Upper Saddle River, New Jersey 07458

Prentice Hall books are widely used by corporations and government agencies for training, marketing, and resale.

The publisher offers discounts on this book when ordered in bulk quantities. For more information contact:

        Corporate Sales Department
        Phone: 800–382–3419
        Fax: 201–236–7141
        E-mail: corpsales@prenhall.com

        Or write:

        Prentice Hall PTR
        Corp. Sales Dept.
        One Lake Street
        Upper Saddle River, New Jersey 07458

Printed in the United States of America
10 9 8 7 6 5 4 3 2

ISBN: 0-13-759515-8

Prentice-Hall International (UK) Limited, *London*
Prentice-Hall of Australia Pty. Limited, *Sydney*
Prentice-Hall Canada Inc., *Toronto*
Prentice-Hall Hispanoamericana, S.A., *Mexico*
Prentice-Hall of India Private Limited, *New Delhi*
Prentice-Hall of Japan, Inc., *Tokyo*
Simon & Schuster Asia Pte. Ltd., *Singapore*
Editora Prentice-Hall do Brasil, Ltda., *Rio de Janeiro*

I have chosen the chameleon to grace the cover of this book because of its ability to change its color. This change is in response to stimuli such as heat and light. Some scientists believe the chameleon also changes its color due to emotions such as fear, its reactions to a fight with another chameleon, and other feelings. Many researchers think the color changes have survival value.

Like a chameleon, the Internet is trying to change its colors from a data-only shade to a multimedia hue. And in order to survive, the Internet must change. If it remains a data-only network, it will be bypassed by users whose applications demand a network to support the integration of voice, video, and data.

For the public Internet, the task is a challenging one, for its basic architecture is not tuned for the efficient support of synchronous real-time voice and video traffic. For a private internet, the task will be easier because the network manager will have more control over network resources.

But the Internet will (and is) changing. Voice, video, and multimedia conferencing applications are emerging and finding their way into products. And eventually, the final tint of the Interent will be a fully integrated multimedia network.

Contents

CHAPTER 3   **Digital Voice and Video**   **74**

CHAPTER 9   The Point-to-Point Protocol (PPP)   246

CHAPTER 11   Mobile IP 293

Preface

This book is one in a series of books called "Emerging Communications Technologies." As the name of the book implies, the focus is on the Internet and private internets in relation to the support of voice and video traffic, the implementation of hardware-based switches and the ability to achieve mobility of an IP-based machine across multiple internets.

The subject matter of this book is vast and my approach is to provide a system view of the topic. In consonance with the intent of this series, this general survey also has considerable detail, but not to the level of detail needed to design a system. For that, I leave you to your project team and the various specifications that establish the standards.

This book is an intermediate-to-advanced level. As such, it assumes the reader has a background in voice and data communications and the Internet protocol suite. Notwithstanding, for the new reader, I have provided several tutorials and guide you to them in the appropriate parts of the book.

I hope you find this book a valuable addition to your library.

Acknowledgments

I would like to express my appreciation and thanks to several individuals and organizations who have helped me during the time I was doing research on this book. First, British Telecom (BT), Bellcore, and Nortel provided valuable input both in the form of conversations with their engineers as well as information on their R&D efforts on internet, telephony and video systems. The Nortel Lab at Research Triangle Park, North Carolina provided me with many ideas for this book.

I have relied on several Internet Request for Comments (RFCs) in certain chapters in this book. In some cases I have summarized the RFCs with a short tutorial, and in other cases I have extracted key points from the documents. I have so noted these instances in the appropriate parts of the book. In addition, the ITU-T H and G Series Recommendations are explained in this book. However, since these specifications are numerous and wide-ranging, my approach has been to provide tutorials with salient aspects of these Series in relation to the subject matter.

There are many other references cited in this book. Instead of placing these references in the back of the book in a bibliography, I have chosen to credit them in the appropriate chapter. I have been quite selective in the references used and have culled through hundreds of potential sources. Obviously, I recommend these references for further information and I thank these researchers and authors for their contributions. My descriptions of the initial activities that led to Internet we sourced from my own experiences.

1

Introduction

This chapter introduces the reader to the Internet, just in case you have been away for awhile. The first part of this chapter explains the major attributes of the Internet and how it came into being. During this discussion, we learn why the Internet is the way it is. An understanding of the Internet's structure and "behavior" is key to understanding the Internet operations that are described in this book. The second part of the chapter describes the requirements for a network to support multiservice applications (voice, video, data, fax, etc.) from the standpoint of bandwidth and a guaranteed delay. The third and last part of the chapter introduces the key Internet protocols that are used to support a multimedia (voice, video, data) Internet.

BASIC TERMS AND CONCEPTS

The Internet is an association of thousands of user computers that communicate with each other through networks. These user computers are called *hosts*. The networks are connected together through another machine that relays the host computer traffic between user applications (such as email and file transfer) that are running on the hosts. The Internet uses the term *gateway* or *router* to describe the machine that performs the relaying functions between networks. Figure 1–1 shows a gateway/router placed between networks A, B, and C. Routers A, B, and C are said to be internetworking machines, since they connect networks together.

Networks A, B, and C can be called subnetworks. They are full networks unto themselves, but the idea allows a set of subnetworks (subnets) to be associated with one organization or some type of administrative domain, such as an *Internet Service Provider* (ISP). The organization can identify each network with a subnet identifier (ID) and can group these IDs (networks) together (or treat them separately). The grouping concept is called *address aggregation*.

This approach is useful because, like the telephone system, it allows the Internet components to be identified with a hierarchical address. For example, in a telephone system, a person can be reached by dialing first an area code, then an exchange number, and then a subscriber number. In the Internet, addresses are managed by a form of hierarchical aggregation called *address prefixes*, discussed in later chapters.

An internetworking router is designed to remain transparent to the end user application. Since the end user application resides in the host

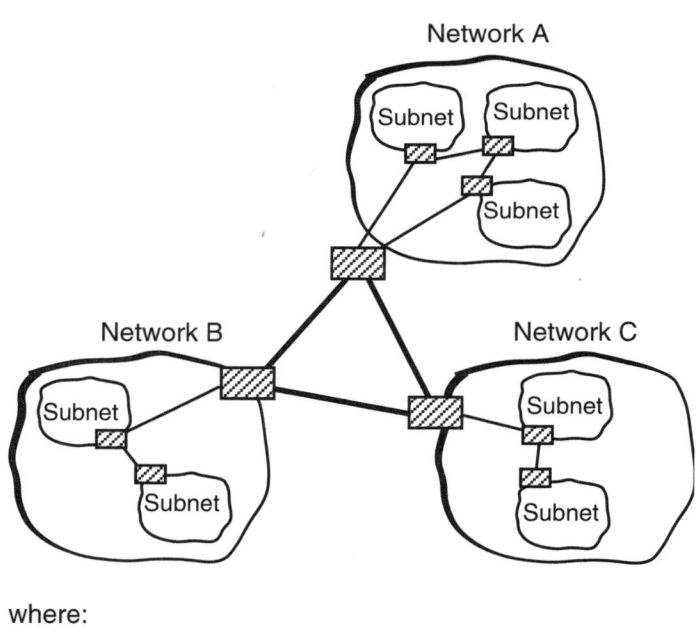

where:

▨▨▨ = Gateway or router

Figure 1–1   Internetworking and internets.

computer, the router need not burden itself with application protocols and can dedicate itself to fewer tasks, such as managing the traffic between networks.

ATTRIBUTES OF THE INTERNET

The Internet was developed to support the transfer of data traffic (packets) between computers and workstations with the use of adaptive routing features (see Table 1–1). Adaptive routing means the traffic may take different routes through the Internet depending on network conditions at a specific time, such as congestion or a failed link. The possible result of adaptive routing is that the destination user may receive the packets out of order. An Internet protocol (the Transmission Control Protocol, TCP) at the receiver can be used to reorder the packets. The other possible result of adaptive routing is that the arrival rate of the packets at the receiver varies in that some packets arrive with little delay and others take longer.

The Internet is designed as a connectionless system. This means that there are no "affiliations" established between the machines in the Internet. As a result, the Internet does not maintain an ongoing knowledge of the user's traffic and does not build a fixed path between the switches from the source and to destination host machines. In effect, the Internet Protocol (IP) that helps in routing traffic is stateless; that is to say, it does not build tables to maintain information about a connection, because there is no connection.

The connectionless aspect of the Internet goes hand-in-hand with the adaptive routing concept. But in the telephone network, the opposite architecture is employed: connection-oriented fixed paths between the calling and called parties. The telephony approach is needed to support the real-time, non-varying delay requirements of speech, whereas the Internet is a data network, and most data applications do not require the real time transport service.

Table 1–1   Attributes of the Internet

Attribute	Consequence(s)
Data applications	Not "tuned" for voice or video.
Adaptive routing	Path may vary during traffic transfer, and packets may arrive out of order.
Connectionless	Circuits are not set up between users.
"Best effort" delivery service	Traffic discarded if problems occur.

The Internet is a "best effort" delivery network. The term best effort means that the Internet will attempt to deliver the traffic, but if problems occur (damaged bits due to noise, congestion at a router, etc.), or the destination host cannot be found, the traffic is discarded. In most instances, TCP residing in the end user host machine can resend the lost or damaged packets.

Internet, internet, and intranet

The term "internet" is used in two separate contexts. If the word has an upper case I, it refers to the public Internet that is used on a commercial basis. In contrast, if the word begins with a lower case i, it refers to a set of networks that do not belong to the public Internet. These internets are usually privately owned. Another term that is used to describe a private internet is an intranet.

CONNECTING INTO THE INTERNET

Most individuals' hosts do not connect directly into the Internet. Rather, a host is first connected to an access node (such as a router). The access system can take several forms. It may be a gateway sponsored by a government agency, a university, a research center, or a commercial company, such as Earthlink. Many service providers for Internet access are competitive companies and price their services based on what they provide to a user. These service providers are called ISPs, or Internet Service Providers.

Figure 1–2 shows some examples of Internet access connections and some typical applications that Internet users run between host computers. Three user applications are depicted in the figure:

- *Rlogin:* A terminal-to-terminal protocol permitting the exchange of small packets of interactive traffic between hosts.
- *FTP:* The File Transfer Protocol (FTP) supporting the exchange of bulk traffic (files, databases).
- *SMTP:* The Simple Mail Transfer Protocol (SMTP) supporting email transfers.

Example of an ISP

Figure 1–3 shows one example of an Internet Service Provider topology. It is MCI's Very High Speed Backbone Network Service (vBNS). As part of the transition to commercialize the Internet, the National Science

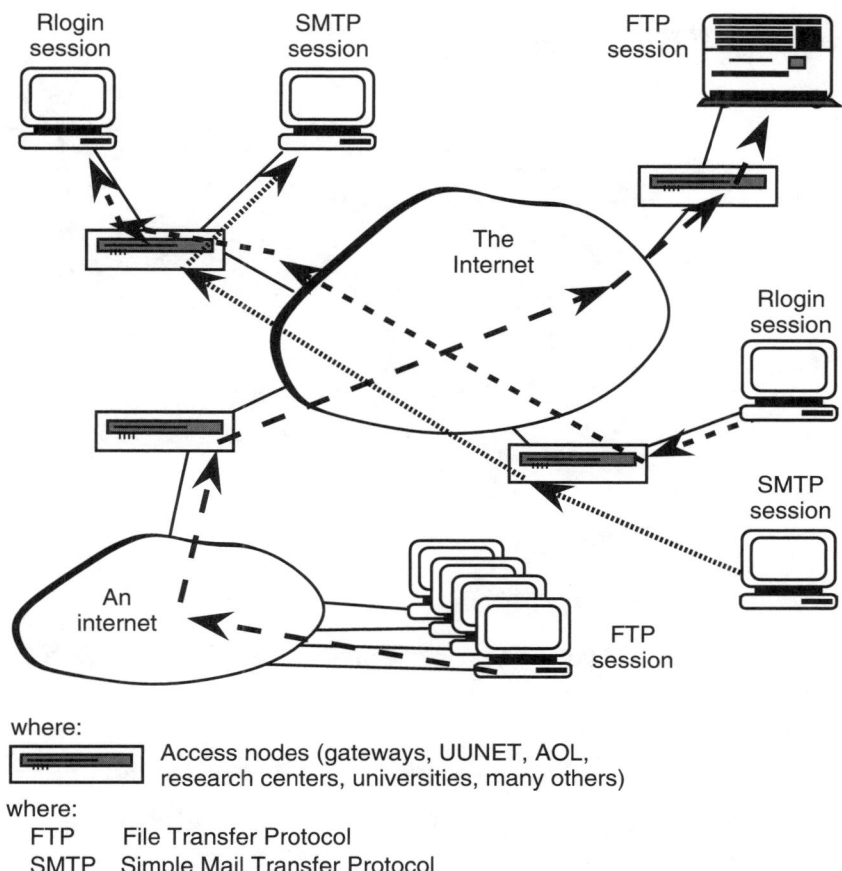

where:

Access nodes (gateways, UUNET, AOL, research centers, universities, many others)

where:
FTP   File Transfer Protocol
SMTP Simple Mail Transfer Protocol

Figure 1–2   Connecting to the Internet.

Foundation (NSF) established a five-year contract with MCI to provide this service.

The network is ATM/SONET based and has four Network Access Points (NAPs) for connecting commercial Internet machines. The backbone operates at the SONET OC 3 (optical carrier) rate of 155 Mbit/s. Plans are underway to upgrade the system to 633 Mbit/s and eventually to 2.2 Gbit/s.

MCI is one of thousands of ISPs that provide Internet access to an end user. The ISPs connect to each other at the NAPs, thus allowing users who subscribe to different ISPs to communicate with each other.

Connection from the user site to the ISP is done with (1) a dedicated link between an ISP router and a router at the user site, (2) a dial-up

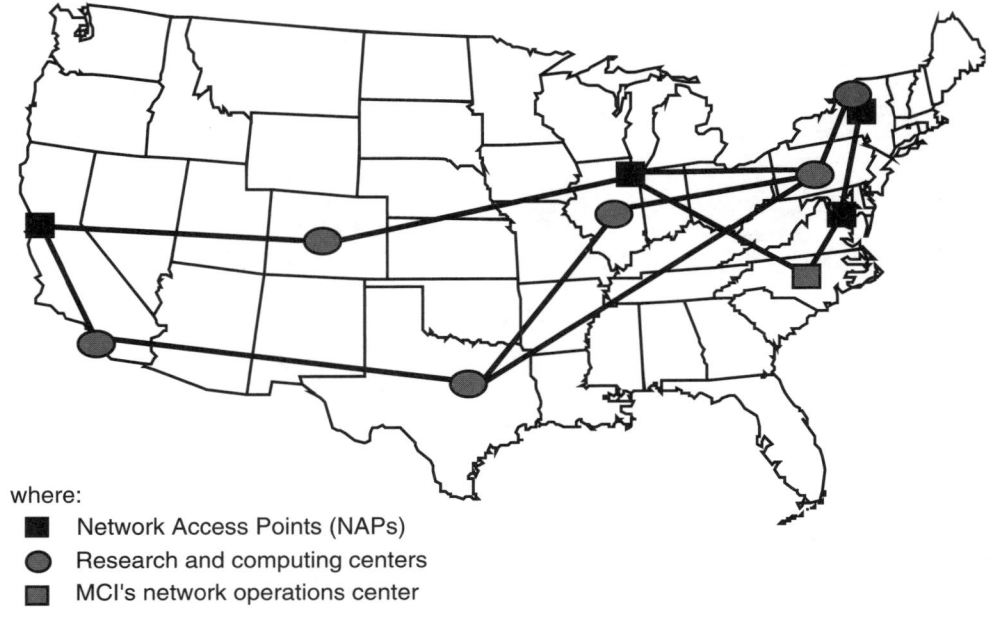

where:
- ■ Network Access Points (NAPs)
- ● Research and computing centers
- ■ MCI's network operations center

Figure 1–3 MCI's Very High Speed Backbone Network Service (vBNS).

link between the ISP and a host, or (3) a wireless link between the ISP and the host.

THE INTERNET LAYERED ARCHITECTURE

Many of the concepts in this book are explained with the layered protocol concept. This section provides a brief review of the Internet layers and Chapter 2 gives more detailed information.

Figure 1–4 provides a review of the Internet protocol suite layers. With some exceptions, the Open Systems Interconnection (OSI) Model layer 6 is not used. Layer 5 is not used at all.

The physical and data link layers are (as a general rule) also not defined. The philosophy is to rely on existing physical and data link systems. One notable exception to this practice is at the data link layer, where the Internet task forces have defined the Point-to-Point Protocol (PPP).

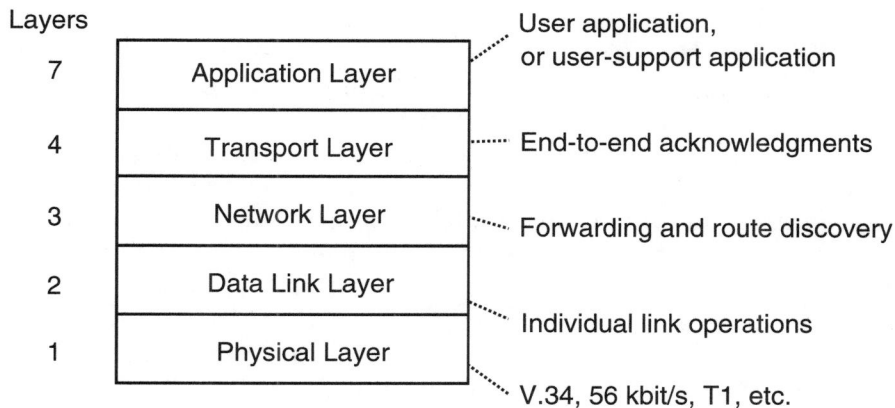

Figure 1–4   Internet Protocol Suite layers.

For the newcomer or for review, here is a summary of the functions of the layers:

- *Physical layer:*   Defines the media, and physical aspects of the signals (voltages, etc.). Defines clocking and synchronization operations. Defines physical connectors. Also identified as layer 1 or L_1.

- *Data link layer:*   Supports the transfer of traffic over one link. May perform error detection and retransmission, depending on the specific link layer protocol. Also identified as layer 2 or L_2.

- *Network layer:*   Performs packet forwarding and route discovery. Supports some limited diagnostic functions, such as status reports. Also identified as network level, layer 3, or L_3.

- *Transport layer:*   Supports end-to-end acknowledgment of traffic, as an option. At a receiving host, supports the identification (with a port number) of the layer 7 protocol to be invoked to support incoming traffic. Also identified as layer 4 or L_4.

- *Application layer:*   Contains the end user application, or another application that directly supports the end user application, such as a file transfer or an email operation. Also identified as layer 7 or L_7.

HOW THE INTERNET CAME INTO EXISTENCE
AND WHY IT IS THE WAY IT IS

The Internet is a good example in our modern world that research counts ... and so do the research dollars. Fortunately, many of the research dollars and resources for the Internet were apportioned wisely. But we should understand that much of the success of what we know today as the Internet came from the very deep pocket of the U.S. taxpayer. This statement is not meant as a criticism, because this writer is in favor of research and research dollars that allow engineers and scientists the ability to explore, make mistakes, throw away, start over, and improve. Nevertheless, I make this point at the initial part in this book to emphasize that the Internet had a very generous benefactor that allowed the development to occur over the period of two decades with, although not limitless funds, some very deep coffers.

Early Activities Leading to the Internet[1]

In order to understand the advanced features of the Internet and its gradual migration to a multiservice environment, it is a good idea to pause for a moment to describe some of the early development operations of the Internet. This approach will allow us to learn why the Internet is organized the way it is, and what challenges it faces to move from a data-only network to a multiservice network.[2]

The Internet owes its origin to some pioneering endeavors performed at the U.S. Department of Defense (DOD) in the mid-1960s. At that time, the Advanced Research Projects Agency (ARPA) of the DOD was tasked with doling out research dollars and coordinating research projects within this agency. During that time, ARPA was a great benefactor to researchers. The U.S. government provided an extensive budget for research and often was in charge of coordinating and providing funds for the various projects.

At this time, it became evident to the ARPA officials that a number of the research sites around the country needed to exchange information with each other. At that time, IBM Selectric typewriters, a Model 33 tele-

---

[1]As stated in the Preface, I have relied on *Where Wizards Stay Up Late,* by K. Hafner and M. Lyon, Prentice Hall (and my early experiences) for my descriptions of the "early Internet."

[2]Multiservice, multiapplication, and multimedia are used interchangeably in this book.

type device, and an ancient IBM Q.32 were installed at the ARPA site in the Pentagon with each machine operating its internal protocols—without regard to each other. The situation was becoming unwieldy because other sites (locations in Boston and California) needed to exchange information with each other and with the ARPA headquarters.

Therefore, the problem dictated a solution. Initial efforts focused on developing some systems to allow these machines to communicate with each other, which eventually led to the system we know today.

A Data-only Network.   There was no consideration for supporting voice or video for this project. After all, the telephone network did a commendable job of supporting voice traffic, and no one could conceive of running video between user machines in those early days. Even if the concept had been surfaced, these primitive machines could not support the video (or voice) traffic.

The Concept of the Router Is Born.   One of the fundamental problems facing the designers of the Internet was that of scaling. Potentially, the DOD's research efforts might result in connecting thousands of machines (although, at that time there was no such thing as thousands of machines). Nonetheless, the designers concocted the notion of networks (perhaps many of them) connected together through homogenous nodes (instead of the disparate machines then in existence). The idea was to allow conventional computers and workstations (hosts) to concentrate on processing their applications and offload communications functions into these specially designed machines (nodes). These nodes would communicate with each other to transfer the user's traffic. Today the nodes are called routers.

This concept was referred to as an *internetwork* or a *subnetwork*. The assumption rests on the notion that all the nodes in the internetwork use the same procedures (the procedure was coined a *protocol*), but the hosts keep running their own systems. After considerable development and experimentation, it was concluded that this approach worked: It allowed the hosts at the various research sites around the country to operate with their own systems, yet use a common internetwork for transporting their traffic to each other. This concept also allowed ARPA to develop its own direct control over the subnetwork without having to worry too much about the characteristics of each host. The individual nodes communicated with the host based on the proprietary protocol of that host (at least at that time).

Another important notion of the initial pioneering efforts was that the exchange of traffic would be solely data. There was no consideration at that time for the transmission of voice or video images. Indeed, the structure of these nascent protocols designed for asynchronous, non-real-time operations to support bursty traffic applications.

In the late 1960s, various research efforts began to culminate in the implementation of some simple systems and at that time (April 7, 1969), the researchers began sending informal correspondence to each other to share their ideas.[3] These pieces of communications were titled, "Request for Comments" (RFCs). This term was coined to connote openness and reception to new ideas.

To re-emphasize a point made earlier, it was envisioned in the initial design that the subnetwork would not be concerned with the nature of traffic emanating from the hosts. The job of the network was to convey the traffic between the hosts without regard to the nature of the traffic. Nonetheless, the emphasis was on the support of data applications. After all, that was the problem being addressed: the interworking of disparate hosts for the exchange of applications traffic.

Development of Host-to-Host Applications. From these efforts the concept of the communications protocols being application-independent was born. Nonetheless, it was also recognized that the researchers needed applications-type protocols that had common formats and conventions. During the late 1960s, several systems were developed for two standard (what now is called layer 7) protocols dealing with file transfers and remote login. Thus, by 1969 specifications had been developed for connecting host computers to each other and to the network nodes that were known as *interface message processors* (IMPs).

Security: The Lack Thereof. Another aspect of these initial pioneering efforts is quite important. The researchers were not overly con-

---

[3]In those early days, I was employed as a programmer in Washington, D.C., and one of the projects assigned to our programming team was an ARPA contract dealing with correcting a badly flawed R&D software package written by another ARPA contractor that simulated submarine and carrier warfare in Asia. We corrected the model by rewriting much of the code, and proudly submitted it to ARPA, who passed it on to a special department in the Navy. Like so many R&D efforts with the DOD, our software was used briefly, then "put on the shelf." In another ARPA office, the architecture that led to the Internet was being created—and we thought our project to be the "plum" of the ARPA largesse!

cerned with security. Indeed, the idea of the initial ARPAnet was based on the idea of openness. After all, many of the researchers knew and trusted each other and their motive was to have a forum for the open communications of their ideas and systems. The ARPAnet was that forum. Consequently, security and privacy were not of paramount importance in this nascent endeavor.

The ARPAnet Comes into Being

By 1969, a simple network configuration was evolving, consisting of two sites, one at UCLA and the other at the Stanford Research Institute (SRI). Shortly afterwards, site number 3 was installed at the University of California Santa Barbara (in November), and then site number 4 was established at a node in Utah (in December).

During this time, the designers were still coming to grips with a host-to-host protocol and finally put together a remote login protocol that they dubbed *Telnet*. They followed this work with an effort that culminated in what is called the *Network Control Protocol* (NCP). By the early 1970s, the hosts were communicating with each other through these four nodes and the designers began to work on tuning the system and making it more robust. Extensive efforts were undertaken at this time to load the simple system to test it for handling congestion and to determine if it could withstand different types of activities and different types of traffic.

Refinement of Applications Support Protocols

Many of these initial efforts focused on connecting users at a host computer through the IMP. However, host computers were quite expensive and not every researcher could afford to install a host computer at his or her site. Thus, another effort was directed toward the provision for logging on to a network through the IMP with a very simple device such as a dumb terminal with nothing more than a keyboard, a printer, and perhaps a CRT. It was believed that this would open up connection opportunities for many researchers throughout the Department of Defense and affiliated institutions. Indeed, instead of having the ARPAnet open to a rather sophisticated engineer or scientist, this approach would allow the layperson to make use of the network.

However, these initial IMPs did not support more than four host connections and none of them could support a conventional teletype connection. Consequently, the next major milestone in the development of the network was the creation of protocols that allowed relatively unintelligent terminal devices to dial into the network and be connected directly. This new device was called the *Terminal IMP* (TIP). This activity was occurring during the early 1970s.

The Pieces Come Together

By the early 1970s a fledging network was in place and the pioneering TIP and Telnet paved the way for users to logon to the network. Indeed, these two protocols served as the avenue for the rapid expansion of the use of the ARPAnet. However, many of the researchers declared the need to send not just message-based traffic but larger units of traffic, typically files and databases. From this effort the *File Transfer Protocol* (FTP) was developed and as the reader probably knows, it is still widely used throughout the world. It was formerly published in July 1972 under Request for Comments (RFC) 354.

By 1972, sites were added between the west coast and east coast and four geographic areas had been connected: Boston, San Francisco, Los Angeles, and Washington D.C. By this time, there were 29 nodes attached to the network which was called ARPAnet or on occasion the *Net*.

During this time, ARPAnet officials on several occasions solicited the telecommunications carriers (i.e., AT&T) to participate in the development of these systems. Since the telecommunications carriers came from the circuit switching world and were accustomed to time division multiplexing (TDM) switches, the concept of small bursty asynchronous packets being shipped through the network (and statistical TDM switches) was foreign to them. These carriers declined to participate in the systems development, thinking it was not feasible. This decision had great consequences on the development of the Internet and its effect on telecommunications carriers. It is still being felt today as we shall explore in more detail in this book.

The Basic Premise of the Internet—Open Systems and Resource Sharing

Once again, it is instructive to note that the ARPAnet was intended for resource sharing and the exchange of information between machines. Indeed, it was not conceived that the ARPAnet would be intended for electronic messaging (the exchange of information between humans), which we know today as email. However, because of the popularity of the system, email in the early 1970s became a dominant part of the traffic on the network.[4]

During 1973, the ARPAnet continued to grow as more nodes were added to the network. This evolving system had the luxury of support from the U.S. Defense Department, the ability to redo things once they did not work, and the lack of any type of monetary, profit-oriented deadline in getting something on-line. No commercial system had (or has) a two-decade window in which to prove itself.

Nonetheless, as the network began to grow, the system started to experience problems, some of which stemmed from the fact that the initial protocols were not designed to scale-up to supporting a large amount of traffic in many nodes. However, the evolution of the software (and the ability to make mistakes and correct them) led to solutions to the problems. Indeed, in the period between 1972 and 1974, a programming staff worked over two years to come up with enhanced routing algorithms—an almost unheard of time latitude in that day's and today's world (except for the pre-divestiture telephone companies, in which some telephone companies sometimes took two to three years to implement a service feature to the customer).

Standards through Trial and Error

Another aspect of the development of the Internet is emphasized once again. The Internet evolved through trial and error and not through the decree of standards. It was really a matter of placing the technology onto the network to see if it worked. If it did not work, it was discarded. If it worked partially, it was improved. If it worked well, it was adopted. The Internet creators were allowed to fail and try again—a vital ingredient in the recipe of a successful technology.

Another interesting aspect to the development of the Internet is that even though it was funded and owned by the federal government, many people considered it to be their own domain. After all, they nurtured it and they contributed to its creation and growth. And they viewed it in some instances as their own private network. Until around the early 1990s, this attitude still existed in certain parts of the Internet.

---

[4]The reader may find it interesting that the well known @ sign was developed at this time to separate a person's name from an overall email address. The idea was to use a character that would not be found in a user's name. In the old-model teletypes, the @ was chosen. It also was useful because it also means "at" in many parts of the world.

By the mid-1970s the ARPAnet was beginning to capture the attention from more than just the community that used it. Some of the telecommunications carriers and the U.S. Postal Service began to examine the adaptation of some of the ideas of the Internet, notably email. Indeed, some of the forward-thinking postmasters in the mid-1970s believed that the nascent email systems would render some of their operations obsolete, which indeed it has.

The Development of ALOHA

In the late 1960s, ARPA set up funding for a radio network at the University of Hawaii. It was designed by Norm Abramson and used packet switching technologies between radios to move traffic back and forth among seven computers stationed over several of the islands in Hawaii. The system was called ALOHA and ALOHAnet. It allowed devices to send packets at any time. If the packets in the traffic interfered with each other (packet collisions), the system simply retransmitted the packets at some random interval. Its attraction was its simplicity and the lack of a master-slave relationship that was inherent in many of the systems at that time (notably many of the IBM systems and the emerging Systems Network Architecture [SNA]). The master-slave protocols used (and use) polling techniques.[5]

As the ALOHA system developed and knowledge was gained from collision networks, it also occurred to several developers that it would make sense to link other networks such as ALOHA into the ARPAnet. However, the systems were different from each other and would require extensive conversion for them to interoperate. Nonetheless, in 1973 an effort was begun called the *interneting project* to develop procedures to connect heterogeneous networks together. Several working groups were formed that began to pursue what became known as the *concatenated network,* which was shortened to *CATENET*. Its principal goal was to interconnect heterogeneous networks in a transparent manner, a vital capability in the world of data communications.

---

[5]Polling techniques entail the master station sending a polling message to the slave. This message "invites" this machine to send traffic, if it indeed has any to send. In a data environment (bursty), the machine often has nothing to send, and precious resources are wasted going through the process of polling and returning a negative response to the poll.

The Birth of the Gateway

Today, the term *gateway* is used in a number of ways to describe different types of machines. The term, as used in computer networks, was created as a result of some of the pioneering work with CATENET. In 1973 several of the Internet designers and planners met in San Francisco to discuss how to connect different networks together, essentially through the ARPAnet. These discussions revolved around the need for a gateway—a machine that would be a routing computer operating between the different networks in order to hand off messages between them and perhaps do some conversion of the formats of the traffic.

Encapsulation and Decapsulation

During these meetings, the concepts of *encapsulation* and *decapsulation* were developed. These terms mean that there would be a common header that operated between all the gateways attaching the networks. The specific traffic indigenous to a network would be encapsulated behind that header with the header used to route the traffic between the networks. Essentially, the gateway contained software that made it appear to be a host to the ARPAnet IMPs, but it also appeared to be a host on the network.

Accounting for Traffic

During these early days, an ongoing problem was how to account for the reliability and integrity of the traffic. Eventually an approach was taken that required the hosts rather than the IMPs (gateways) to be responsible for recovering from errors and problems. This approach essentially shifted a tremendous burden out of the network into the periphery of the network (i.e., the host machines). This clearly had great advantages from the standpoint of simplifying the protocols inside the network and reducing the latency required to process the traffic in the networks as well. This basic concept has found its way into the modern networks that we use today (such as Frame Relay and ATM).

These efforts eventually led in 1973 to a pioneering paper published by Cerf and Kahn, "A Protocol for Packet Network Intercommunication." This paper discussed the concepts of encapsulation and decapsulation of traffic into *datagrams*, with the analogy drawn of the datagram as an envelope to a letter and the traffic as a message inside the envelope. This paper also further explained the concept of a gateway that would be responsible for reading only the header appended to the encapsulation protocol: that is to say, the envelope in our analogy of a mail system.

During this process, the encapsulation protocol was dubbed *Transmission Control Protocol* (TCP). It was responsible for routing, as well as hop-to-hop acknowledgments and retransmitting the traffic in the event of errors.

During this embryonic period, the focus was on a concept that still finds much value today: keeping the IMPs and the routing protocols and the operations within the network as simple and "minimalist" as possible. The designers continually asked themselves, "Is this needed in the network? If not, get rid of it. If it is needed but can be implemented elsewhere, push it out to the host." At the risk of over-hyping the Internet designers, this vision is fundamental to modern systems, such as ATM.

Limit of Responsibility for ARPAnet

During the early 1970s, discussions increased about the responsibility of ARPA (which was renamed DARPA to stand for the Defense ARPA) and its role in operating networks. It was agreed by most parties that the embryonic phases of the network were successful and it was not the role of DARPA to be running networks.

So, who would be a logical candidate for running an increasingly sophisticated and complex network? Certainly, no one would have better credentials than the telecommunications carriers such as AT&T. So, the DARPA officials contacted AT&T to see if they wished to take over the running of ARPAnet. After several weeks of study, AT&T and the Bell Lab staff concluded that the packet technology with asynchronous transmissions was incompatible with the circuit-switched synchronous orientation of the telephone network. Apparently, it did not occur to AT&T or Bell Labs that a data network does not have to follow the same profile as a voice network in its behavior.

But that is history now, and the ARPA people went on to look for other arrangements. Eventually in the summer of 1975, the operation of ARPAnet was transferred to the Defense Communications Agency (DCA) and for a period of time, the DCA took over the operation of the ARPAnet. After DARPA was relieved of the responsibility for running ARPAnet, it was able to concentrate on forward-thinking issues such as the development of other protocols to support the concept of the CATENET.

By this time, in 1975, the initial ideas on TCP were refined further at Stanford University into a more formal specification. Also, during this period the DARPA management established a coordinated policy for managing the various research programs, the ongoing ALOHA systems, and the task of connecting other packet networks together, which was dubbed the *ARPA Internet*. At about this time in 1977, the milestone was finally reached of demonstrating the interconnection of various types of networks through gateways.

The Delineation of Responsibilities between TCP and IP

To this point, the TCP had been responsible for integrity operations as well as routing. During the 1978 period, some of the Internet designers developed a plan to break TCP into two parts. One part, still called TCP, would be responsible for accepting traffic from the user application, breaking it up into small pieces (now called TCP segments) acceptable to the network and reassembling the traffic at the receiving side. It would also be responsible for detecting errors on an end-to-end basis and re-sending traffic that was errored or lost in the network. Conversely, another protocol which became known as the Internet Protocol (IP), would have the relatively simple responsibility of forwarding the datagrams through the network from the source host to the destination host.

Once again, the philosophy was a minimalist approach. If the gateways did not need the information then this information was excluded from gateway operations and would not be passed to the gateway IP for further processing. It should be noted that much of this common-sense design was offered by the engineers at the Xerox Palo Alto Research Center (PARC) who had been working for some time on the PARC Universal Packet Protocol (PUP) from which many of the ideas and concepts of IP (and associated protocols such as Internet Control Message Protocol [ICMP]) were derived. In any event, by 1978 the former TCP had been broken into two parts that became known as TCP/IP.

The Development of Ethernet

As we have learned, the Internet and TCP/IP were developed through a long-range research and collaborative effort coordinated through ARPA for connecting systems together to span over a wide area network (WAN). In the early 1970s, several of the engineers at PARC became involved in developing a new type of network intended to connect computers together over short distances at very high speeds. This effort was led by an engineer at Xerox PARC named Bob Metcalfe. It is interesting to note that much of Metcalfe's pioneering effort occurred while working on his graduate degree at Harvard. The submittal of his dissertation was rejected because it was asserted that Metcalfe's work was not theoretical enough and was too engineering-oriented (alas, too practical!—a similar situation to the rejected graduate work paper by the FEDEX founder that the dissertation committee found to be unrealistic).

Metcalfe drifted away from Harvard and his employment at MIT and moved out to PARC to continue his work. At this time, Metcalfe came upon some of the work being done on ALOHA at the University of Hawaii. Using this system as a research model, he decided that it made some erroneous assumptions and set about to correct it with a new model.

From these activities, the concept of a local area network (LAN) was developed. It was based on the concepts of ALOHA and eliminated the cumbersome store-and-forward, master-slave relationships that were in vogue at that time.

Using the concepts of the ALOHAnet, Metcalfe established the idea of letting the traffic collide with each other on the channel (which in this case was a hardwire channel). But since it was working on a high-speed wire media at short distances, this concept was much faster than the ALOHAnet. Furthermore, techniques were developed to allow the controlled retransmissions onto the channel through timers and retries of the traffic. By May 1973 the system was placed in operation. It worked and was dubbed *Ethernet* in deference to the nineteenth and early twentieth century view of a hypothetical medium that was supposed to transmit light through an empty space.

The reason that we dwell on Ethernet at this point in our discussion is because we shall see in this book that LANs through Ethernet and WANs through TCP/IP developed at about the same time but under different organizations and through different trains of thought. As farsighted as some of these researchers were, there was no inkling that there would be extensive internetworking between what we know today as LANs and WANs.

MORE RECENT EVENTS

This brief history of the development of the Internet gives us information on why the Internet is the way it is, and why it was not designed as a multimedia technology; but, we must move on—I refer you to the Hafner/Lyon book for more details on the history of the Internet development.

For a period of time, the National Science Foundation (NSF) took over the management of the Internet from the DCA and provided the backbone network for the Internet. It was managed by the joint efforts of MCI, Sprintlink, and IBM (by forming Advanced Network Services [ANS]). Access to the Internet was provided at network access points (NAPs), which connected to other networks (private and public).

In November 1994, the NSF informed colleges and other institutions to look for another feed into the Internet, because the U.S. Government was getting out of the public Internet business. Most of the feeds were existing networks that had interconnected into the NSF backbone. NSF announced it would provide some funding for a few more years, and in 1995 it started disconnecting its NAPs.

Today, the Internet is a complex collage of regional and national networks that are interconnected together with routers. The communications links used by the ISPs are leased lines from the telephone system, usually DS1 or DS3 lines, and increasingly, SONET lines. Other lines are provided by competitive access providers (CAPs), and still others are provided by private carriers, such as private microwave and satellite operators.

As the Internet was released from the Department of Defense (DOD) and National Science Foundation (NSF) umbrella, and turned over to private enterprise, it began to "diffuse."[6] By diffuse, we mean that the Internet can no longer be recognized as one backbone with tertiary networks connected to the backbone. Rather, the Internet is a collage of networks that are interconnected together, with about thirty large networks that interconnect with each other and over 4000 North American Internet Service Providers (ISPs).

The "hubs" of the Internet are the public Metropolitan Area Exchanges (MAEs), which are the points where the ISPs interconnect with each other. The large networks, such as Sprint and MCI, have private interfaces (private peering points). Now, some of the mid-size ISPs are following suit and establishing private peering points, which are being administered by the Brokered Private-Peering Group.

There are three major interconnection points or MAEs to which a provider might be connected: (1) MAE-East in Washington, DC, (2) MAE-West in San Jose, CA, and (3) NY NAP in Pennsauken, NJ, and other POPs described (see http://www.digex.net for more information).

---

[6]The term "diffuse" is not mine, but it conveys the idea well. For more information, see Larry Press, "Tracking the Global Diffusion of the Internet," *Communications of the AM, 40* (11), November 1997.

THE CHALLENGE: FROM A DATA CHAMELEON
TO A MULTISERVICE CHAMELEON

As noted in this brief history of the Internet, the intent of the Internet designers was to build a network to support data traffic. And herein lies the challenge for the next few years: to change the Internet chameleon from a data-only network to one that supports all types of traffic, notably voice and video. What are the challenges? We can summarize them by describing the requirements for the support of data, voice, and video applications.

Voice, Data, and Video Requirements

Voice and video transmissions exhibit a high tolerance for errors. If an occasional packet is distorted, the fidelity of the voice or video reproduction is not severely affected. In contrast, data packets have a low tolerance for errors. One bit corrupted likely changes the meaning of the data. Furthermore, voice and video packets can afford (on occasion) to be lost or discarded. In the event of excessive delays in the network, the packets may be discarded because they are of no use if they arrive at the receiver too late. Again, the loss does not severely affect voice fidelity if the lost packets are less than 10% of the total packets transmitted. As discussed before, data packets can ill-afford to be lost or discarded.

Yet another difference between voice, data, and video transmissions deals with network delay. For packetized voice to be translated back to an analog signal in a real-time mode, the two-way delay for voice packets must be constant and generally must be low—usually less than 300–400 milliseconds (ms). Why is low delay important? If it takes a long time for the voice signals to be sent from the speaker (person A) to the listener (person B); when speaker A stops talking, receiver B is still receiving the speech packets. Person B cannot start talking until all the speech signals have arrived. In the meantime, person A hears nothing for a while.

The two-way delay measures how long it takes for: (1) A's speech to reach B, (2) B to hear the speech, (3) B to talk back, and (4) A to hear B's response. If the delay becomes long (say, over 400 or 500 ms), the conversation appears phony, almost like a half-duplex connection where the two people are taking turns talking, but waiting a while before taking the turn. All in all, it can be quite annoying.

For data packets, the network delay can vary considerably. Indeed, the data packets can be transmitted asynchronously through the network, without regard to timing arrangements between the sender and the receiver.

Voice and video transmissions require a short queue length at the network nodes in order to reduce delay, or at least to make the delay more predictable. The short voice packet queue lengths can experience overflow occasionally, with resulting packet loss. However, data packets require longer queue lengths to prevent packet loss in overflow conditions.

Variable Bit Rates (VBRs) and Constant Bit Rates (CBRs)

A useful method to describe the nature of applications traffic is through two concepts known as *variable bit rate* (VBR) and *constant bit rate* (CBR). An application using VBR schemes does not require a constant and continuous allocation of bandwidth. These applications are said to be bursty, which means that they transmit and receive traffic asynchronously (at any time with periods in which nothing is sent or received). Examples of VBR applications are most any type of data communications processes. These applications permit the queuing of traffic in a variable manner from the standpoint of time, and they do not require a fixed timing relationship between the sender and the receiver. Therefore, if traffic is sent from the sender and is buffered (queued) for variable periods of time, the receiver is not disturbed. Typical applications using VBR techniques are interactive terminal-to-terminal dialogues, inquiry/ response operations, client-server systems, and bulk data transfer operations.

It should be emphasized that while VBR permits loose timing and asynchronous operations between the sender and the receiver, most VBR applications do require some type of timing constraint. After all, one cannot wait indefinitely for the arrival of the data.

In contrast, an application using CBR schemes requires constant and continuous (or nearly so) allocation of bandwidth. These applications are said to be non-bursty. The term *non-bursty* has to be used carefully with these applications because some of the applications will tolerate a certain amount of burstyness.

Typical CBR-based applications are voice and video transmission. These applications require guaranteed bandwidth and a constant and continuous timing relationship between the sending and receiving devices. They also require a predictable delay between the sender and the receiver.

Examples of Voice, Video, and Data Applications Requirements

The need to support multimedia traffic requires the Internet to extend its capabilities far beyond what it can do now. It must support the

Table 1–2   Audio Bandwidth and MOS Performance Applications

Coders	Uncompressed Bit Rates in kbit/s	Transmission Mode	Expected Bit Rates in kbit/s**		MOS
			Peak	*Average*	
CD audio	1411.4–1536	CBR	192	192	*
(proprietary algorithm)		VBR	384	192	*
FM stereo audio	1024–1536	CBR	128	128	*
Wideband audio (G.722)	128	CBR	64/ 56/ 48	64/ 56/ 48	*
PCM audio (μ-law, G.711)	64	CBR	64	64	4.3
		VBR	64	32–21	*
ADPCM audio (G.721)	64	CBR	32	32	4.1
LD-CELP audio (G.728)	64	CBR	16	16	4.1

* Expected MOS may be between 4 and 4.5, but is yet to be supported by published results.
** Some of the bit rates are compressed.

where:
ADPCM   Adaptive differential pulse code modulation
CBR   Constant bit rate
CD   Compact disc
CELP   Code excited predictive linear coding
FM   Frequency modulation
LD-CELP   Low delay CELP
MOS   Mean opinion score
PCM   Pulse code modulation
VBR   Variable bit rate

(*Source:* Radhika R. Roy, "Networking Constraints in Multimedia Conferencing and the Role of ATM Networks," *AT&T Technical Journal*, July/August, 1994.)

diverse needs of different types of traffic. As examples, Tables 1–2, 1–3, and 1–4 show the performance requirements for several audio, video, and data applications.[7] Several of the tables show the Mean Opinion Scores (MOS) for the technologies. A MOS of 3.5 is considered to be fair to good.

Table 1–2 shows several audio applications and the ITU-T G Series Recommendations that use devices to code/decode the analog signals to/from digital images. These devices are called *coders, vocoders,* or

[7]Radhika R. Roy, "Networking Constraints in Multimedia Conferencing and the Role of ATM Networks," *AT&T Technical Journal,* July/August, 1994.

Table 1–3   Video Bandwidth and Performance for VBR Codecs

Video Quality, Coding Resolution, and Format	Transmission Mode	Encoder-decoder Delay in Frames**	Compressed Video Bit Rate/s kbit/s*)		
			Peak	*Mean*	MOS*
Low rate videoconferencing quality	VBR with negligible buffer	0	2562	239.6	4.5–5.0
360 × 288 pixels non-interlaced 4:1:1, 8 bits/sample 30 Hz, p × 64 or MPEG-1 standards	VBR with buffer	1	1400	239.6	4.0–4.5
		2	934	239.6	3.5–4.5
		3	847	239.6	3.5–4.5
		4	822	239.6	3.5–4.5

* Estimated
** Delay increases with the increase in buffer size (one frame delay = 33 milliseconds)

   where:

    MOS   Mean opinion score
    MPEG   Motion Pictures Expert Group
    VBR   Variable bit rate

(*Source:* Radhika R. Roy, "Networking Constraints in Multimedia Conferencing and the Role of ATM Networks," *AT&T Technical Journal*, July/August, 1994.)

codecs. The MOS ratings are acceptable, but there is one significant problem: The bit rates are high. The G.722, G.711, G.721, and G.728 coders are not efficient in this regard, and Chapter 3 introduces other coders that are more efficient.

Table 1–3 shows some MOSs for video systems. Notice the requirements for large bandwidth (kbit/s) needed to obtain an acceptable MOS.

Finally, Table 1–4 shows the response time and bandwidth requirements for several data applications. Once again, it is obvious that the support of high-quality images requires considerable capacity. Moreover, for interactive browsing, the network must provide fast response times.

Making the Internet Look Like Telephone and Video Networks

It is clear from the AT&T study that applications' requirements vary, and these variances occur not just between voice, video, and data applications, but within these applications as well. One cannot simply say, "The Internet should change to support voice, video, data." Instead, we must say, "The Internet should change to support the different types of data systems, the different types of video systems, and the different types of voice systems." In other words, the challenge is to make the In-

Table 1-4 Bit Rates Required for Data

Data (text, still images, graphics) Object Size	Uncompressed Object Size in Mbit/s	Typical Compression Ratio	Retrieval & Transfer of Object*	Document Browsing*	Retrieval and Transfer**		Document Browsing**	
					Uncompressed	Compressed	Uncompressed	Compressed
ASCII text, 8.5" × 11" page, (88 char/line × 55 lines × 8 bits/char)	0.029	2–4	2	0.5	0.015	0.008–0.004	0.059	0.029–0.015
8.5" × 11" color page (200 pixels/inch, × 24 bits/pixel)	90	10–20	2	0.5	45	4.5–2.3	180	18–9
Medium resolution, 8.5" × 11" color page (400 pixels/inch, × 24 bits/pixel)	359	10–20	2	0.5	180	18–9	700	70–35
High resolution, 8.5" × 11" color page (400 pixels/inch, × 24 bits/pixel)	1436	10–20	2	0.5	718	72–36	2,872	287–144
Graphics quality, (1600 pixels/inch, × 24 bits/pixel)	5744	10–20	2	0.5	2872	287–144	11,488	1152–575

* Typical response time in seconds
** Peak bandwidth requirements in Mbit/s

(*Source*: Radhika R. Roy, "Networking Constraints in Multimedia Conferencing and the Role of ATM Networks," *AT&T Technical Journal*, July/August, 1994.)

ternet behave more like a telephone network and a CATV system, yet retain its characteristics to support data.

PREVIEW OF THE ADVANCED INTERNET FEATURES

It is time to take turn to the subject of this book, the advanced features of the Internet. This part of the chapter will introduce them to you. Subsequent chapters will explain them in more detail. We start by showing the Internet layers in Figure 1–5, with the emphasis on the multimedia protocols.

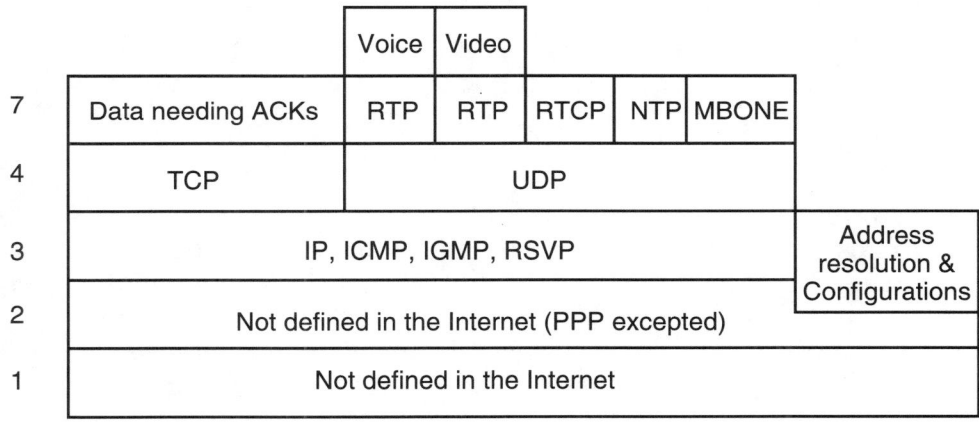

where:

ACK	Acknowledgment
ICMP	Internet Control Message Protocol
IGMP	Internet Group Management Protocol
IP	Internet Protocol
MBONE	Multicasting backbone
NTP	Network Time Protocol
PPP	Point-to-Point Protocol
RSVP	Resource Reservation Protocol
RTCP	Real-time Control Protocol
RTP	Real-time Protocol
TCP	Transmission Control Protocol
UDP	User Datagram Protocol

Figure 1–5   The Internet multimedia protocol stack.

The Internet Protocol (IP)

The Internet Protocol (IP) is essentially a routing protocol.[8] It carries a source IP address and a destination IP address in the IP header. The IP address is examined at each router and is used to access a routing table, which is then used to forward the IP datagram to the next node. One of the IP address formats is used for multicasting. Thus, IP is an important component in the Internet's multicasting operations.

Currently, the industry is running IPv4. IPv6 is new, and it is expected to emerge in the Internet (and internets) in the next few years. IPv4 and IPv6 vary in their ability to support multiservice applications. IPv4 was designed to support data, whereas IPv6 has expanded capabilities for the support of voice, video, or data applications.

The Internet Group Management Protocol (IGMP)

The Internet Group Management Protocol (IGMP) is designed to support multicasting operations. It allows a user machine (a host) to join a multicast group, after which the host receives any multicasting traffic sent within this group. One of the attractive features of IGMP is that it does not require a host to know in advance about all the multicasting groups in an internet. Instead, the routers are knowledgeable of multicast groups and send advertisements to the hosts about their multicasting groups. For example, if an Internet task force is meeting and its proceedings are to be made available to the public, a user machine will receive an advertisement from its router about the conference. In turn, the host can reply with a message stating whether it wishes to join the conference.

The Resource Reservation Protocol (RSVP)

As its name implies, the Resource Reservation Protocol (RSVP) is used to reserve resources for a session in an Internet. This aspect of the Internet is quite different to the underlying design intent of the system, which as we

---

[8]I am swimming against the current by describing IP as a routing protocol, but it is. Many of the Internet engineers use the term "routing protocol" to describe the route advertising or route discovery protocol, such as the Border Gateway Protocol (BGP), etc. Increasingly, routing is defined as forwarding and control. IP is involved in the forwarding operations. Protocols such as the Open Shortest Path First (OSPF) and BGP are involved in the control operations, such as route advertising. Other control operations include the calculations for the route (such as a spanning tree algorithm), resulting in the creation of a routing table. This routing table is used by IP for the forwarding operations.

learned earlier, was established to support only a best effort service, without regard to predefined requirements for the user application.

RSVP is intended to provide guaranteed performance by reserving the necessary resources at each machine that participates in supporting the flow of traffic (such as a video or audio conference). Remember that IP is a connectionless protocol that does not set up paths for the traffic flow, whereas RSVP is designed to establish these paths as well as to guarantee the bandwidth on the paths.

The User Datagram Protocol (UDP)

The User Datagram Protocol (UDP) has long been a mainstay in internets. It is a very important tool for multiservice operations because it is used to manage the Internet ports over which several of the multiservice applications operate. These Internet ports are used to identify each layer 7 application; that is to say, the application that runs on top of UDP.

As Figure 1–5 shows, the Transmission Control Protocol (TCP) is not invoked for most multiservice operations because its many features create excessive delay of the traffic. In addition, TCP has retransmission capabilities as well as retransmission timers that do not work well with real-time traffic. In contrast, UDP is connectionless protocol with no retransmissions, no time outs, no ACKs, and no NAKs.

One might ask why bother to use UDP since it does little. The answer is that the UDP header contains the Internet source and destination port numbers that are required for proper execution of the layer 7 protocols.

The Real-Time Protocol (RTP)

The Real-Time Protocol (RTP) is designed for the support of real-time traffic; that is, traffic that needs to be sent and received in a very short time period. Two real-time traffic examples are (1) audio conversations between two people and (2) playing individual video frames at the receiver as they are received from the transmitter.

RTP is also an encapsulation protocol in that the real-time traffic runs in the data field of the RTP packet, and the RTP header contains information about the type of traffic that RTP is transporting. While RTP can perform this function, not all multiservice applications will use RTP. Each IP telephony or video commercial product should be evaluated to determine the exact "protocol mix" in the offering.

The Real-Time Control Protocol (RTCP)

After a reservation has been established through the use of RSVP, the traffic is then sent between machines with RTP. Next, the Real-Time Control Protocol (RTCP) comes into the picture by providing procedures for the machines to keep each other informed about the quality of services they think they are providing (if they are service providers), and/or the quality of services they are receiving (if they are service clients).

In concept, a server can adjust its quality of service operations depending on the feedback it receives from its clients. However, the manner in which these adjustments are made is not defined by RTCP.

The Multicasting Backbone (MBONE)

The multicasting backbone (MBONE) is another protocol that has been in operation for a number of years. MBONE is the "pioneer" system for Internet audio/video conferences. Originally, MBONE was used to multicast the various standards' groups meetings and its use has been expanded for activities such as viewing the space shuttle launches, video shows in general, and other activities.

MBONE relies on IP multicasting operations and IGMP to convey information. In addition, the term multicasting backbone does not mean that MBONE is actually a backbone network. MBONE is an application that runs on the Internet backbone.

The Network Time Protocol (NTP)

A logical question is, How do machines obtain their timing information? After all, who can say that one node has a more accurate clock than another node? The answer to this question is the Network Time Protocol (NTP).

Clocking information for a network is provided through the NTP primary time server designated as a root. The time server obtains its clocking information from master sources.

These "master clocking sources" are used to derive accurate clocks by the primary time server. Other countries may have their own clocks that are used to provide clocking over large areas. Most of these clocks provide very accurate clocking synchronization on the order of less than 1 millisecond. Local clocks are even more accurate.

The primary time server, upon receiving clocking information from a master clocking source, then uses the NTP protocol to coordinate clocks at the secondary time servers. Secondary time servers may in turn provide clocking for other secondary time servers.

Voice over IP (VoIP)

Running voice over IP (VoIP) is considered by many people to be a novelty, and its use is limited at this time. While it is recognized that the quality of VoIP does not approach the quality found in the telephone network, it is also a very inexpensive way to make long distance calls. Some individuals are using VoIP to make international calls, and saving themselves the expense (often very big) of international telephone rates.

At this time, not many companies have committed in a major way to a full-scale use of the Internet for telephone traffic. So, it remains a niche industry at this time. But the potential for VoIP is enormous. As Netscape has discovered, it is hard to compete with a product that is free.

Figure 1–5 shows the protocol placement of voice over RTP, but it can run directly over IP, or over the User Datagram Protocol (UDP) then IP.

Scores of products are available for VoIP, and the assessment of the service is very mixed: some like it and some do not. One thing is certain. If VoIP becomes a draining factor on the telephone companies' revenue base, the telephone companies will attempt to get VoIP tariffed or get into the VoIP business by becoming Internet Service Providers (ISPs), which they have already begun today.

SUMMARY

The Internet was designed as a research network to support data traffic. Its success stems from its (now) ease-of-use and its low-cost to access and transport traffic. As the need for multiapplications networks grow, the need to "upgrade" the Internet becomes compelling, and much of the multimedia architecture is being put in place today. The ultimate challenge is to change the Internet chameleon from a data-only service to a multimedia architecture.

2

The Internet: Architecture and Traffic Characteristics

This chapter is an introduction to the Internet's architecture and its layered protocol suites. The well-seasoned reader may wish to skip the first part of this chapter or scan through it. The last part of the chapter describes some Internet traffic characteristics, which I recommend all readers review. There are scores of books on the subject matter of this chapter, so my approach is to give you the information you will need to deal with the other chapters in this book.

THE PROTOCOL SUITE

Figure 2–1 is another view of Figure 1–5 (in Chapter 1) and depicts an architectural model of TCP/IP and several of the major related protocols. The choices in the stacking of the layers of this model vary, depending on the needs of network users and the decisions made by network designers. IP is the key protocol at the network layer. Several other protocols are used in conjunction with IP that serve as route discovery and address mapping protocols. The protocols that rest over TCP (and UDP) are examples of the application layer protocols.

The lower two layers represent the data link and physical layers, and are implemented with a wide choice of standards and protocols.

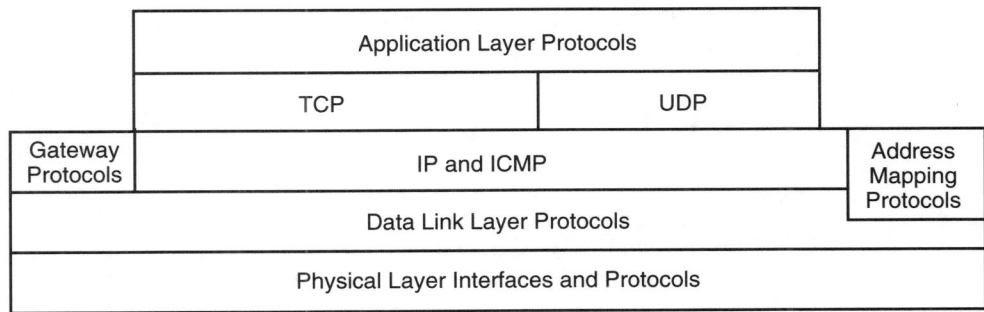

where:
  ICMP   Internet Control Message Protocol
  IP   Internet Protocol
  TCP   Transmission Control Protocol
  UDP   User Datagram Protocol

Figure 2–1   The TCP/IP (Internet model).

The Physical Layer

The lowest layer in the Internet model is called the physical layer, although these standards do not dictate the interfaces and protocols that reside in this layer. The functions within the layer are identical to the OSI Model and are responsible for activating, maintaining, and deactivating a physical circuit between machines. This layer defines the type of physical signals (electrical, optical, etc.), as well as the type of media (wires, coaxial cable, satellite, etc.).

There are many standards published for the physical layer; for example, EIA-232-E, V.34, V.35, and V.90 are physical layer protocols.

The Data Link Layer

The data link layer (layer 2 or L_2) is responsible for the transfer of data across one communications link. It delimits the flow of bits from the physical layer. It also provides for the identity of the bits. It may ensure that the data arrives safely at the receiving DTE.[1] It often provides for flow control to ensure that the DTE does not become overburdened with too much data at any one time. One of its most important functions is to provide for the detection of transmission errors and to provide mechanisms to recover from lost, duplicated, or erroneous data.

---

[1]The term data terminal equipment (DTE) is used to describe an end user device.

Common examples of data link control (DLC) protocols are the High Level Data Link Control (HDLC), published by the ISO; Synchronous Data Link Control (SDLC), used by IBM; and the Point-to-Point Protocol (PPP), an Internet protocol.

The Network Layer

The Internet Protocol (IP) is a simple internetworking protocol operating at the network layer, layer 3, or L_3. It routes traffic between networks. IP is quite similar to the ISO 8473 (the Connectionless Network Protocol or CLNP) specification, which is the OSI counterpart to IP. Many of the ISO 8473 concepts were derived from IP.

IP is an example of a connectionless service. It permits the exchange of traffic between two machines without any prior call setup. It is possible that data could be lost between the two machines. For example, assume an IP gateway enforces a maximum queue length size, and if this queue length is violated, the buffers will overflow. In this situation, the excess datagrams are discarded.

The Internet Protocol has no error-reporting or error-correcting mechanisms. It relies on a module called the Internet Control Message Protocol (ICMP) to report errors in the processing of a datagram and to provide for some administrative and status messages. The ICMP can notify the host if a destination is unreachable. ICMP is also responsible for managing or creating a time-exceeded message in the event that the lifetime of the datagram expires. ICMP also performs certain editing functions to determine if the IP header is in error or otherwise unintelligible.

IP is not a route discovery protocol, but a forwarding protocol. It makes use of the routing tables that are filled in by route discovery protocols; one of which (OSPF) operates directly with the IP header (that is, it does not run on TCP or UDP). The purpose of these protocols is to "find" a good route for the traffic to traverse through an internet. The vast majority of route discovery protocols route traffic based on the idea that it makes the best sense to transmit the datagram through the fewest number of networks and nodes (hops). The newer protocols use other criteria such as finding the route with the best throughput or the shortest delay. These protocols use adaptive, dynamic methods to update the routing tables to reflect traffic and link conditions.

Layer 2 and Layer 3 Address Resolution Operations

The IP stack provides a protocol for resolving addresses. The Address Resolution Protocol (ARP) is used to take care of the translation of

IP addresses to physical addresses and hide these physical addresses from the upper layers.

Generally, ARP works with mapping tables (referred to as the ARP cache). The table provides the mapping between an IP address and a physical address. In a LAN (like Ethernet or an IEEE 802 network), ARP takes an IP address and searches for a corresponding physical address in a mapping table. If it finds the address, it returns the physical address back to the requester, such as a server on a LAN.

Another protocol, called Proxy ARP, allows an organization to use only one IP address (network portion of address) for multiple networks. In essence, Proxy ARP maps a single IP network address into multiple physical addresses.

The ARP protocol is a useful technique for determining physical addresses from network addresses. However, some workstations do not know their own IP address. For example, diskless workstations do not have any IP address knowledge when they are booted to a system. The diskless workstations know only their hardware address. The Reverse Address Resolution Protocol (RARP) works in a manner similar to ARP except, as the name suggests, it works in reverse order: It provides an IP address when given a MAC address.

The Transport Layer

The Transmission Control Protocol (TCP) resides in the transport layer (layer 4 or L_4) of the Internet model. It is situated above IP and below the application layer. It is designed to reside in the host computer or in a machine that is tasked with end-to-end integrity of the transfer of user data.

Since IP is a connectionless protocol, the tasks of reliability, flow control, sequencing, application opens, and application closes are given to TCP. Although TCP and IP are tied together so closely that they are used in the same context —"TCP/IP"—TCP can also support other protocols. In addition, the application protocols, such as the File Transfer Protocol (FTP) and the Simple Mail Transfer Protocol (SMTP), rely on many of the services of TCP.

The User Datagram Protocol (UDP) is classified as a connectionless protocol. It is sometimes used in place of TCP in situations where the full services of TCP are not needed. For example, the Trivial File Transfer Protocol (TFTP) and the Remote Procedure Call (RPC) use UDP.

UDP serves as a simple application interface to the IP. Since it has no reliability, flow control, nor error-recovery measures, it serves principally as a multiplexer/demultiplexer for the receiving and sending of IP traffic.

The Application Layer

The Internet application layer (layer 7 or L_7) protocols serve as a direct service provider to user applications and workstations. Operations, such as electronic mail, file transfer, name servers, and terminal services are provided in this layer.

Some of the more widely used application layer services include:

- *TELNET*: For terminal services
- *Trivial File Transfer Protocol (TFTP)*: For simple file transfer services
- *File Transfer Protocol (FTP)*: For more elaborate file transfer services
- *Simple Mail Transfer Protocol (SMTP)*: For message transfer services (electronic mail)
- *Domain Name System (DNS)*: For name server operations
- *Browsers*
- *Simple Network Management Protocol (SNMP):* For network management operations
- *Several multimedia protocols:* Introduced in Chapter 1

NAMES AND ADDRESSES

A newcomer to data networks is often perplexed when the subject of naming and addressing arises. Addresses in data networks are similar to postal addresses and telephone numbering schemes. Indeed, many of the networks that exist today have derived some of their addressing structures from the concepts of the telephone numbering plan.

It should prove useful to clarify the meaning of names, addresses, and routes. A *name* is an identification of an entity (independent of its physical location), such as a person, an applications program, or even a computer. An *address* is also an identification but it reveals additional information about the entity, principally information about its physical or logical placement in a network. A *route* is information on how to relay traffic to a physical location (address).

A network usually provides a service that allows a network user to furnish the network with a name of something (another user, an application, etc.) that is to receive traffic. A network *name server* then uses this name to determine the address of the receiving entity. This address is then used by a routing protocol to determine the physical route to the receiver.

With this approach, a network user does not become involved and is not aware of addresses and the physical location of other users and network resources. This practice allows the network administrator to relocate and reconfigure network resources without affecting end users. Likewise, users can move to other physical locations but their names remain the same. The network changes its naming/routing tables to reflect the relocation.

In Chapter 1, it was emphasized that the evolution of WANs and LANs occurred separately. Consequently, two different addresses were developed; one to identify WAN entities and another to identify LAN entities. Because these addresses play an important role in this book, they are examined in the next section.

Physical Addresses

Communications between users through a data network requires several forms of addressing. Typically, two addresses are required: a physical address, also called a data link address, and a network address. Other identifiers are needed for unambiguous end-to-end communications between two users, such as upper layer names and/or port addresses (discussed later).

Each device (such as a computer or workstation) on a communications link or network is identified with a physical address. This address is also called the hardware address. Many manufacturers place the physical address on a logic board within the device or in an interface unit connected directly to the device. Two physical addresses are employed in a communications dialogue: one address identifies the sender (source) and the other address identifies the receiver (destination). The length of the physical address varies, and most implementations use singular 48-bit addresses.

The address detection operation on a LAN is illustrated in Figure 2–2. Device A transmits a frame onto the channel. It is received by all other stations attached to the channel, namely stations B, C, and D. We assume that the destination physical address contains the value C. Consequently, stations B and D ignore the frame. Station C accepts it, performs several tasks associated with the physical layer, strips away the physical layer headers and trailers, and passes the remainder of the packet to the next upper layer.

The MAC Address. The IEEE assigns LAN addresses. Previously this work was performed by the Xerox Corporation by administering what were known as block identifiers (Block IDs) for Ethernet addresses. The Xerox Ethernet Administration Office assigned these values, which

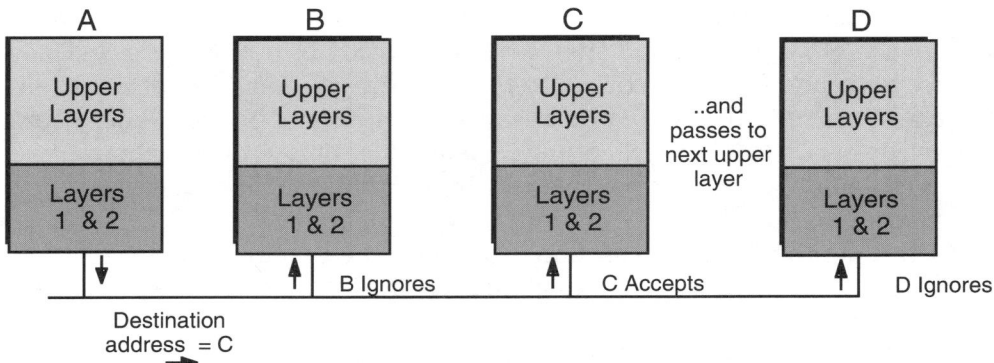

Notes:

For LANs, address is called a MAC address

For non-LAN links, address is called a link address, or some variation of an "HDLC" address

where:
  HDLC   High level data link control
  MAC   Media access control

Figure 2–2   Physical address detection.

were three octets (24 bits) in length. The organization that received this address was free to use the remaining 24 bits of the Ethernet address in any way it chose.

Due to the progress made in the IEEE 802 project, it was decided that the IEEE would assume the task of assigning these universal identifiers for all LANs, not just CSMA/CD types of networks. However, the IEEE continues to honor the assignments made by the Ethernet administration office although it now calls the block ID an *organization unique identifier* (OUI).

The format for the OUI is shown in Figure 2–3. The least significant bit of the address space corresponds to the individual/group (I/G) address bit. The I/G address bit, if set to a zero, means that the address field identifies an individual address. If the value is set to a one, the address field identifies a group address that is used to identify more than one station connected to the LAN. If the entire OUI is set to all ones, it signifies a broadcast address that identifies all stations on the network.

The second bit of the address space is the local or universal bit (U/L). When this bit is set to a zero, it has universal assignment significance—for example, from the IEEE. If it is set to a one, it is an address

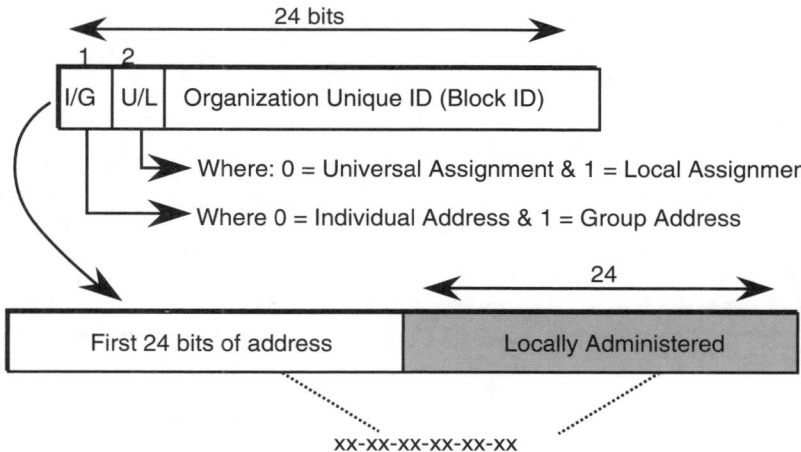

Note: Format of xx represents an octet, with each x 4 bits:
A2-59-ED-18-F5-7C

where:
  MAC   Media access control

Figure 2–3   Universal addresses and IDs: The MAC address.

that is locally assigned. Bit position number two must always be set to a zero if it is administered by the IEEE.

The OUI is extended to include a 48-bit universal LAN address (which is designated as the *media access control* [MAC] address). The 24 bits of the address space is the same as the OUI assigned by the IEEE. The one exception is that the I/G bit may be set to a one or a zero to identify group or individual addresses. The second part of the address space consisting of the remaining 24 bits is locally administered and can be set to any values an organization chooses.

The Network Address

A network address (or network layer address) identifies a network or networks. Part of the network address may also designate a computer, a terminal, or anything that a private network administrator wishes to identify within a network (or attached to a network), although the Internet standards place very strict rules on what an IP address identifies.

A network address is a "higher level" address than the physical address. The components in an internet that deal with network addresses

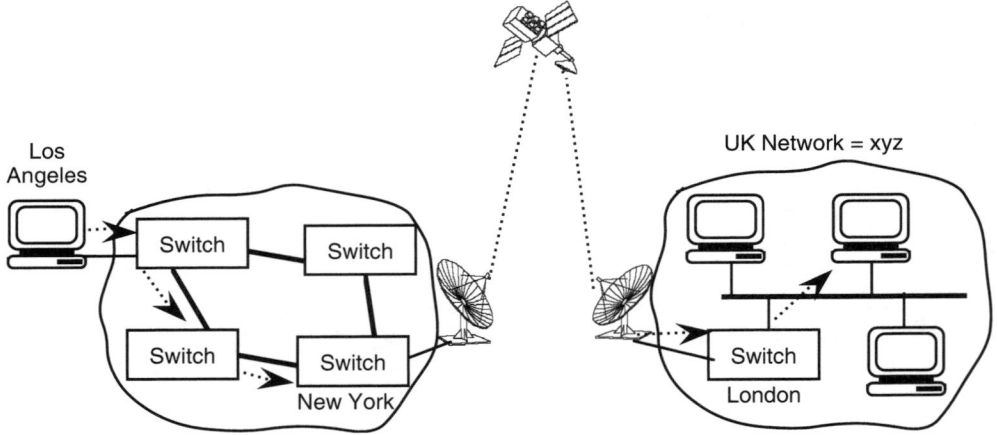

Figure 2–4   Network layer addressing.

need not be concerned with physical addresses until the data has arrived at the network link to which the physical device is attached.

This important concept is illustrated in Figure 2–4. Assume that a user (host computer) in Los Angeles transmits packets to a packet network for relaying to a workstation on a LAN in London. The network in London has a network address of xyz (this address scheme is explained shortly).

The packets are passed through the packet network (using the network's internal routing mechanisms) to the packet switch in New York. The packet switch in New York routes the packet to the gateway located in London. This gateway examines the destination network address in the packet and determines that the packet is to be routed to network xyz. It then transmits the packet onto the appropriate communications channel (link) to the node on the LAN that is responsible for communicating with the London gateway.

Notice that this operation did not use any physical addresses in these routing operations. The packet switches and gateway were only concerned with the destination network address of xyz.

The reader might question how the London LAN is able to pass the packet to the correct device (host). As we learned earlier, a physical address is needed to prevent every packet from being processed by the upper layer network layer protocols residing in every host attached to the network. Therefore, the answer is that the target network (or gateway) must be able to translate a higher layer network destination address to a lower layer physical destination address.

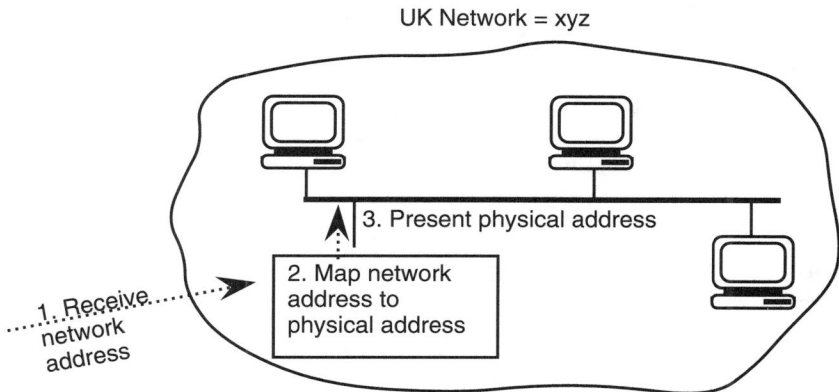

Figure 2–5   Mapping network addresses to physical addresses.

In Figure 2–5, a node on the LAN is a server that is tasked with address resolution. Let us assume that the destination address contains a network address, such as 128.1 *and* a host address, say 3.2. Therefore, the two addresses could be joined (concatenated) to create a full internet network address, which would appear as 128.1.3.2 in the destination address field of the IP datagram.

Once the LAN node receives the datagram from the gateway, it must examine the host address, and either (1) perform a lookup into a table that contains the local physical address and its associated network address, or (2) query the station for its physical address. Then, it encapsulates the user data into the LAN frame, places the appropriate LAN physical layer address in the destination address of the frame, and transmits the frame onto the LAN channel. All devices on the network examine the physical address. If this address matches the device's address, the PDU is passed to the next upper layer; otherwise, it is ignored.

In this manner the two addresses can be associated with each other.

The IP Address.   TCP/IP networks use a 32-bit network layer 3 address to identify a host computer and the network to which the host is attached. The structure of the IP address is depicted in Figure 2–6. Its format is:

IP address = network address + host address

The IP address identifies a host's connection to its network; that is, a point of attachment. Consequently, if a host machine is moved to another

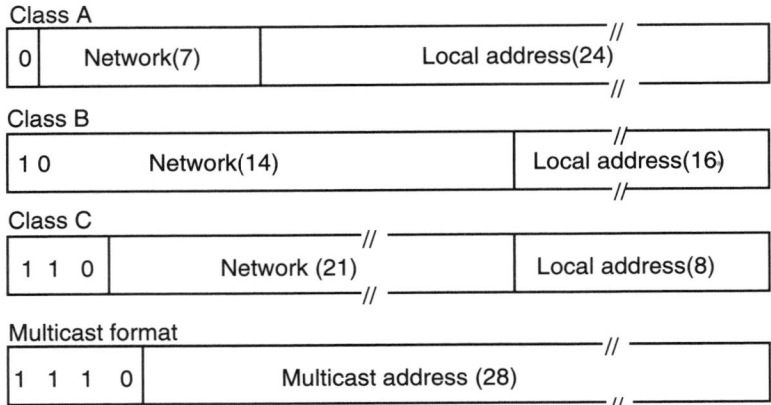

Figure 2–6   Internet Protocol (IP) address formats.

network, its address must be changed. This aspect of the IP address has major implications for mobile systems, discussed in Chapter 11.

In the past, IP addresses have been classified by their formats:[2] class A, class B, class C, or class D formats. As illustrated in Figure 2–6, the first bits of the address specify the format of the remainder of the address field in relation to the network and host subfields. The host address is also called the local address.

The *class A* addresses provide for networks that have a large number of hosts. The host ID field is 24 bits. Therefore, 2^{24} hosts can be identified. Seven bits are devoted to the network ID, which supports an identification scheme for as many as 127 networks (bit values of 1 to 127). *Class B* addresses are used for networks of intermediate size. Fourteen bits are assigned for the network ID, and 16 bits are assigned for the host ID. *Class C* networks contain fewer than 256 hosts (2^{8}). Twenty-one bits are assigned to the network ID. Finally, *class D* addresses are reserved for multicasting, which is a form of broadcasting but within a limited context.

The IP address space can take the following forms, as shown in Figure 2–7, and the maximum network and host addresses that are available for the class A, B, and C addresses are also shown.

---

[2]I say, "in the past," but this system still prevails. Yet, it is being replaced by a concept called classless addresses, a topic explained in Chapter 7.

Network Address Space Values

A	from: 0.0.0.0	to: 127.255.255.255*
B	from: 128 .0.0.0	to: 191.255.255.255
C	from: 192.0.0.0	to: 223.255.255.255
D	from: 224.0.0.0	to: 239.255.255.255
E	from: 240.0.0.0	to: 247.255.255.255**

* Numbers 0 and 127 are reserved
** Reserved for future use

	Maximum Network Numbers	Maximum Host Numbers
A	126 *	16,777,124
B	16,384	65,534
C	2,097,152	254

* Numbers 0 and 127 are reserved
The addresses set aside for private allocations:

Class A addresses:	10.x.x.x – 10.x.x.x (1)
Class B addresses:	172.16.x.x – 172.31.x.x (16)
Class C addresses:	192.168.0.x – 192.168.255.x (256)

Figure 2–7   IP addresses.

There are instances when an organization has no need to connect into the Internet or another private intranet. Therefore, it is not necessary to adhere to the IP addressing registration conventions, and the organization can use the addresses it chooses. It is important that it is certain that connections to other networks will not occur, since the use of addresses that are allocated elsewhere could create problems.

In RFC 1597, several IP addresses have been allocated for private addresses, and it is a good idea to use these addresses if an organization chooses not to register with the Internet. Systems are available that will translate private, unregistered addresses to public, registered addresses if connections to global systems are needed.

Figure 2–8 shows examples of the assignment of IP address in more detail (examples use IP class B addresses). A common backbone (Common Net) connects three subnetworks: 176.16.2, 176.16.3, and 176.16.4. Routers act as the interworking units between the legacy (conventional) LANs and the backbone. The backbone could be a conventional Ethernet, but in most situations, the backbone is a Fiber Distributed Data Interface (FDDI), a Fast Ethernet node, or an ATM hub.

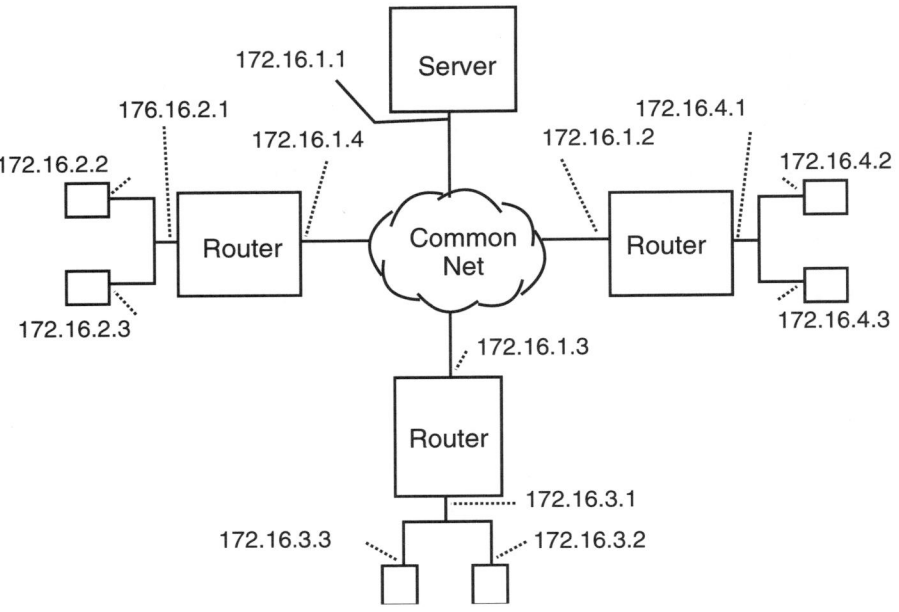

Figure 2–8   Examples of IP addressing.

The routers are also configured as subnet nodes and access servers are installed in the network to support address and naming information services.

ARP

Earlier discussions in this chapter covered the need to correlate a host's MAC and IP addresses and the IP protocol stack provides a protocol to support this operation. The Address Resolution Protocol (ARP) is used to take care of the translation of IP addresses to physical addresses and hide these physical addresses from the upper layers.

Generally, ARP works with mapping tables (which we referred to as the ARP cache in earlier discussions). The table provides the mapping between an IP address and a physical address. In a LAN (like Ethernet or an IEEE 802 network), a requester takes an IP address and searches for a corresponding physical address in a mapping table. If it finds the address, it returns the 48-bit address, such as a workstation or server on a LAN. If the needed address is not found in the ARP cache, the ARP module sends a broadcast onto the network.

The broadcast is called the *ARP request*. The ARP request contains an IP address. Consequently, if one of the machines receiving the broadcast recognizes its IP address in the ARP request, it will return an ARP reply to the inquiring host. This datagram contains the physical hardware address of the queried host. Upon receiving this datagram, the inquiring host places this address into the ARP cache. Thereafter, datagrams sent to this particular IP address can be translated to the physical address. The ARP system thus allows an inquiring host to find the physical address of another host by using the IP address.

The concepts of ARP requests and replies are shown in Figure 2–9. Host A wishes to determine C's physical address. It broadcasts datagrams (all 1s in the MAC destination address) to B, C, and D. Only C responds because it recognizes its IP address in the incoming ARP request datagram. Host C places its address into an IP datagram in the form of the ARP reply. The other hosts, B and D, do not respond.

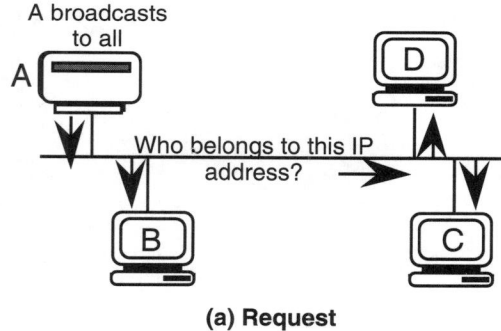

(a) Request

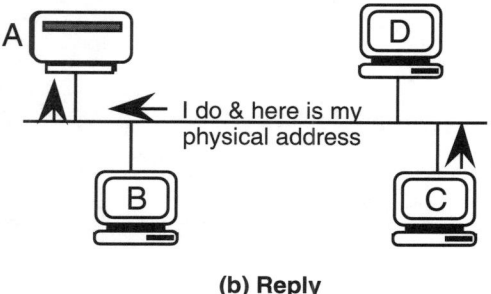

(b) Reply

Figure 2–9 The ARP request and reply.

A BRIEF LOOK AT IP

I mentioned that it is not the intent of this book to describe in detail the current Internet Protocols. So, a productive approach to a general analysis of IP is to examine the fields in the IP datagram (PDU) depicted in Figure 2–10.

The *version* field identifies the version of IP in use. Most protocols contain this field because some network nodes may not have the latest release available of the protocol. The current version of IP is 4, or IPv4.

The *header length* field contains four bits that are set to a value to indicate the length of the datagram header. The length is measured in 32-bit words. Typically, a header without QOS options contains 20 octets. Therefore, the value in the length field is usually 5.

The *total length* field specifies the total length of the IP datagram. It is measured in octets and includes the length of the header and the data. IP subtracts the header length field from the total length field to compute the size of the data field. The maximum possible length of a datagram is 65,535 octets. Routers that service IP datagrams are required to accept any datagram that supports the maximum size of a PDU of the attached networks. Additionally, all routers must accommodate datagrams of 576 octets in total length.

Each 32-bit value is transmitted in this order: (1) bits 0–7, (2) bits 8–15, (3) bits 16–23, and (4) bits 24–31. This is known as *big endian byte ordering*.

0	1-2	3	4	5-6	7	8	9-15	15	16	17-22	23	24	25-30	31
Version			H-Length			Type of Service (TOS)				Total Length				
Identifier									Flags			Fragment Offset		
Time to Live				Protocol					Header Checksum					
Source Address (32)														
Destination Address (32)														
Options and Padding (Variable)														
Data (Variable)														

where:
  H-Length   Header Length

Figure 2–10   The IP datagram.

Type of Service (TOS)

The *type of service* (TOS) field can be used to identify several QOS functions provided for an Internet application. Transit delay, throughput, precedence, and reliability can be requested with this field.

The TOS field contains five entries consisting of 8 bits. Bits 0, 1, and 2 contain a precedence value that is used to indicate the relative importance of the datagram. Values range from 0 to 7, with 0 set to indicate a *routine precedence*. The precedence field is not used in most systems, although the value of 7 is used by some implementations to indicate a network control datagram. However, the precedence field could be used to implement flow control and congestion mechanisms in a network. This would allow gateways and host nodes to make decisions about the order of "throwing away" datagrams in case of congestion.

The next three bits are used for other services and are described as follows: Bit 3 is the *delay bit* (D bit). When set to 1 this TOS requests a short delay through an internet. The aspect of delay is not defined in the standard and it is up to the vendor to implement the service. The next bit is the *throughput bit* (T bit). It is set to 1 to request high throughput through an internet. Again, its specific implementation is not defined in the standard. The next bit used is the *reliability bit* (R bit), which allows a user to request high reliability for the datagram. The last bit of interest is the *cost bit* (C bit), which is set to request the use of a low-cost link (from the standpoint of monetary cost). The last bit is not used at this time.

The *TOS field* is not used in some vendors' implementation of IP. Nonetheless, it will be used increasingly in the future as the internet capabilities are increased. For example, it is cited in the Open Shortest Path First (OSPF) protocol. Consequently, a user should examine this field for future work and ascertain a vendor's use or intended support of this field.

Fragmentation Fields

The IP protocol uses three fields in the header to control datagram fragmentation and reassembly. These fields are the *identifier*, *flags*, and *fragmentation offset*. The identifier field is used to uniquely identify all fragments from an original datagram. It is used with the source address at the receiving host to identify the fragment. The flags field contains bits to determine if the datagram may be fragmented, and if fragmented, one of the bits can be set to determine if this fragment is the last fragment of the datagram. The fragmentation offset field contains a value that specifies the relative position of the fragment to the original datagram. The value is initialized as 0 and is subsequently set to the proper number if/when an IP node fragments the data. The value is measured in units of eight octets.

Time-to-Live (TTL) Field

The *time-to-live* (TTL) field is used to measure the number of hops a datagram has transversed in the internet. Each router is required to check this field and discard the datagram if the TTL value equals 0. The node is also required to decrement the volume in this field in each datagram it processes. In actual implementations, the TTL field is a number of hops value. Therefore, when a datagram proceeds through a hop, the value in the field is decremented by a value of one. Some implementations of IP use a time-counter in this field and decrement the value in one-second decrements.

The time to live (TTL) field is used not only to prevent endless loops, it can also be used by the host to limit the lifetime that datagrams have in an internet. Be aware that if a host is acting as a "route-through" node, it must treat the TTL field by the router rules. The reader should check with the vendor to determine when a host throws away a datagram based on the TTL value.

Protocol Field

The *protocol* field is used to identify the next protocol that is to receive the datagram at the final host destination. It is similar to the Ethertype field found in the Ethernet frame, but identifies the payload in the data field of the IP datagram. The Internet standards groups have established a numbering system to identify the most widely used protocols that "reside" in the IP datagram data field.

Header Checksum

The *header checksum* is used to detect an error that may have occurred in the header. Checks are not performed on the user datastream. Some critics of IP have stated that the provision for error detection in the user data should allow the receiving node to at least notify the sending host that problems have occurred. (This service is indeed provided by a companion standard to IP [the ICMP.]) Whatever one's view on the issue, the current approach keeps the checksum algorithm in IP quite simple. It does not have to operate on many octets, but it does require that a higher level protocol at the receiving host must perform some type of error check on the user data if it cares about its integrity.

The checksum is computed as follows (and this same procedure is used in TCP, UDP, ICMP, and IGMP):

- Set checksum field to 0
- Calculate 16-bit ones complement sum of the header (header is treated as a sequence of 16-bit words)
- Store 16-bit ones complement in the checksum field
- At receiver, calculate 16-bit ones complement of the header
- Receiver's checksum is all ones if the header has not been changed

Address Fields

IP carries two addresses in the datagram. These are labeled *source* and *destination addresses* and remain the same value throughout the life of the datagram. These fields contain the Internet addresses, described earlier in this chapter.

Options Field

The *options* field is used to identify several additional services[3] (see Figure 2–11). The options field is not used in every datagram. The majority of implementations use this field for network management and diagnostics.

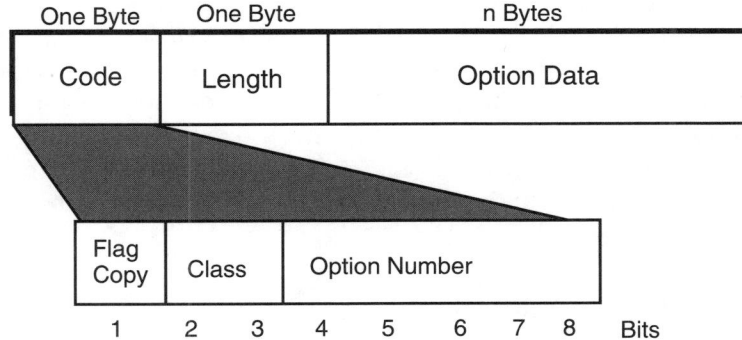

Figure 2–11   The IP option field and option codes.

---

[3]The option field has fallen into disuse by some routers, because of the processing overhead required to support the features it identifies. The concepts of this field are well-founded, and a similar capability is found in IPv6, discussed in Chapter 8.

The options field length is variable because some options are of variable length. Each option contains three fields. The first field is coded as a single octet containing the option code. The option code also contains three fields. Their functions are as follows:

- *Flag copy (1 bit)*: 0 = Copy option into only the first fragment of a fragmented datagram

    1 = Copy option into all fragments of a fragmented datagram
- *Class (2 bits)*:   Identifies the option class
- *Option Number*:   Identifies the option number

The option class can be set to the following values:

- *0:* A user datagram or a network control datagram
- *1:* Reserved
- *2:* Diagnostics purposes (debugging and measuring)
- *3:* Reserved

The next octet contains the length of the option. The third field contains the data values for the option. The *padding* field may be used to make certain that the datagram header aligns on an exact 32-bit boundary.

IP provides two options in routing the datagram to the final destination. The first, called *loose source routing*, gives the IP nodes the option of using intermediate hops to reach the addresses obtained in the source list as long as the datagram traverses the nodes listed. Conversely, *strict source routing* requires that the datagram travel only through the networks whose addresses are indicated in the source list. If the strict source route cannot be followed, the originating host IP is notified with an error message. Both loose and strict routing require that the route recording feature be implemented.

An Overview of Fragmentation

An IP datagram may traverse a number of different networks that use different frame sizes, and all networks have a maximum frame size, called the *maximum transmission unit* (MTU). Therefore, IP contains procedures for dividing (fragmenting) a large datagram into smaller datagrams. It also allows the ULP to stipulate that fragmentation may or may not occur. Of course, it must also use a reassembly mechanism at the final destination that places the fragments back into the order originally transmitted.

When an IP gateway module receives a datagram that is too big to be transmitted by the transit subnetwork, it uses its fragmentation operations. It divides the datagram into two or more pieces. Each of the fragmented pieces has a header attached containing identification, addressing, and as another option, all options pertaining to the original datagram. The fragmented packets also have information attached to them defining the position of the fragment within the original datagram, as well as an indication if this fragment is the last fragment. The flags (the 3 bits) are used as follows:

- *Bit 0* = reserved
- *Bit 1; 0* = fragmentation and 1 = don't fragment
- *Bit 2 (M bit)*; 0 = last fragment and 1 = more fragments

Interestingly, IP handles each fragment operation independently. That is to say, the fragments may traverse different paths to the intended destination, and they may be subject to further fragmentation if they pass through networks that use smaller data units. The next node uses the offset value in the incoming fragment to determine the offset values of fragmented datagrams. If further fragmentation is done at another node, the fragment offset value is set to the location that this fragment fits relative to the original datagram and not the preceding fragmented packet.

A BRIEF LOOK AT TCP AND UDP

The Transmission Control Protocol (TCP) and the User Datagram Protocol (UDP) operate at layer 4 of the Internet protocol stack. TCP is a connection-oriented protocol and is responsible for the reliable transfer of user traffic between two hosts. Consequently, it uses sequence numbers and acknowledgments to make certain all traffic is delivered safely to the destination end point.

UDP is a connectionless protocol and does not provide sequencing or acknowledgments. It is used in place of TCP in situations where the full services of TCP are not needed. For example, telephony traffic, the Trivial File Transfer Protocol (TFTP), and the Remote Procedure Call (RPC) use UDP. Since it has no reliability, flow control, or error-recovery measures, UDP serves principally as a multiplexer/demultiplexer for the receiving and sending of traffic into and out of an application.

The packets exchanged between two TCP modules are called segments. Figure 2–12 illustrates the format for the segment.

The first two fields of the segment are identified as *source port* and *destination port*. These 16-bit fields are used to identify the upper layer application programs that are using the TCP connection.

The next field is labeled *sequence number*. This field contains the sequence number of the first octet in the user data field. Its value specifies the position of the transmitting module's byte stream. Within the segment, it specifies the first user data octet in the segment.

The sequence number is also used during a connection management operation. If a connection request segment is used between two TCP entities, the sequence number specifies the *initial send sequence* (ISS) number that is to be used for the subsequent numbering of the user data.

The *acknowledgment number* is set to a value that acknowledges data previously received. The value in this field contains the value of the sequence number of the next expected octet from the transmitter. Since this number is set to the next expected octet, it provides an inclusive acknowledgment capability, in that it acknowledges all octets up to and including this number, minus 1.

The *data offset* field specifies the number of 32-bit aligned words that comprise the TCP header. This field is used to determine where the data field begins.

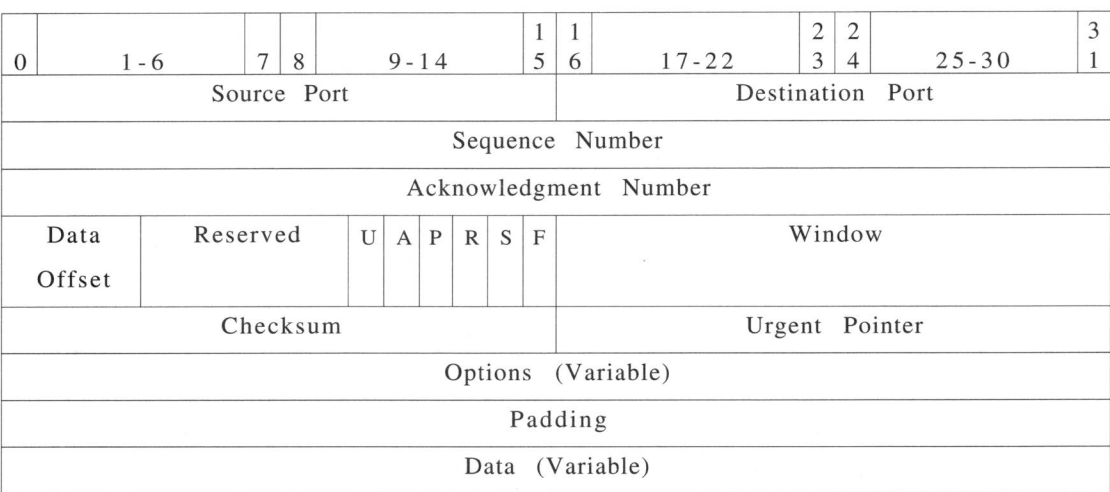

Figure 2–12   The TCP segment (PDU).

As the reader might expect, the *reserved* field is reserved. It consists of 6 bits that must be set to zero. These bits are reserved for future use.

The next six fields are called *flags*. They are labeled as control bits by TCP and they are used to specify certain services and operations that are to be used during the session. Some of the bits determine how to interpret other fields in the header. The six bits are used to convey the following information:

- *URG (U):* This flag signifies if the urgent pointer field is significant.
- *ACK (A)*: This flag signifies if the acknowledgment field is significant.
- *PSH (P)*: This flag signifies that the module is to exercise the push function. Some systems do not support the push function, but rely on TCP to "push" the traffic efficiently.
- *RST (R)*: This flag indicates that the connection is to be reset.
- *SYN (S)*: This flag is used to indicate that the sequence numbers are to be synchronized; it is used with the connection-establishment segments as a flag to indicate handshaking operations are to take place.
- *FIN (F)*: This flag indicates that the sender has no more data to send and is comparable to the end-of-transmission (EOT) signal in other protocols.

The next field is labeled *window*. This value is set to a value indicating how many octets the receiver is willing to accept. The value is established based on the value in the acknowledgment field (acknowledgment number). The window is established by adding the value in the window field to the value of the acknowledgment number field.

The *checksum* field performs a 16-bit ones complement of the ones complement sum of all the 16-bit words in the segment. This includes the header and the text. The purpose of the checksum calculation is to determine if the segment has arrived error-free from the transmitter.

The next field in the segment is labeled the *urgent pointer*. This field is only used if the URG flag is set. The purpose of the urgent pointer is to signify the data octet in which urgent data follows. Urgent data is also called *out-of-band* data. TCP does not dictate what happens for urgent data. It is implementation specific. It only signifies where the urgent data is located. It is an offset from the sequence number and points to the octet following the urgent data.

The *options* field was conceived to provide for future enhancements to TCP. It is constructed in a manner similar to that of IP datagrams option field, in that each option specification consists of a single byte containing an option number, a field containing the length of the option, and last the option values themselves.

Presently the option field is limited in its use, but options are available dealing with size of the TCP data field, window size, a timestamp for an echo, and some others under consideration. The options field in the TCP header can contain a number of options, and the original specification included only the maximum segment size (MSS) option. This option is almost universal and is found in practically all TCP SYN segments. The MSS value permits the two TCP entities to inform each other about the size of their traffic units, and to reserve buffer of their reception. The other options are relatively new, and their implementation will depend upon the TCP product. For more information, see RFCs 793 and 1323.

Finally, the *padding* field is used to insure that the TCP header is filled to an even multiple of 32 bits. After that, as the figure illustrates, user *data* follows.

The TCP Open Operation

Figure 2–13 illustrates the major operations between two TCP entities to establish a connection.

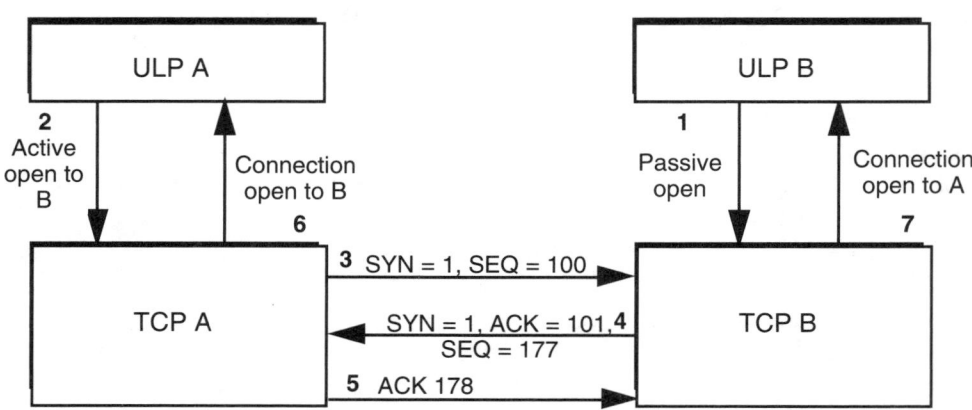

Figure 2–13   TCP open operations.

TCP A's user has sent an active open primitive to TCP. The remote user has sent a passive open to its TCP provider. These operations are listed as events **2** and **1** respectively, although either event could have occurred in either order.

The invocation of the active open requires TCP A to prepare a segment with the SYN bit set to 1. The segment is sent to TCP B and is depicted in the figure as **3** and coded as: SYN SEQ 100. In this example, sequence (SEQ) number 100 is used as the ISS number although any number could be chosen within the rules discussed earlier. The SYN coding simply means the SYN bit is set to the value of 1.

Upon receiving the SYN segment, TCP B returns an acknowledgment with the sequence number of 101. It also sends its ISS number of 177. This event is labeled as **4**.

Upon the receipt of this segment, TCP A acknowledges with a segment containing the acknowledgment number of 178. This is depicted as event **5** in the figure.

Once these handshaking operations have occurred with events **3**, **4**, and **5** (which is called a three-way handshake), the two TCP modules send opens to their respective users as in events **6** and **7**.

TCP Data Transfer Operations

Figure 2–14 shows the TCP entities after they have successfully achieved a connection. In event **1**, ULP A sends data down to TCP A for transmission with a function call. We assume 50 octets are to be sent. TCP A encapsulates this data into a segment, sends the segment to

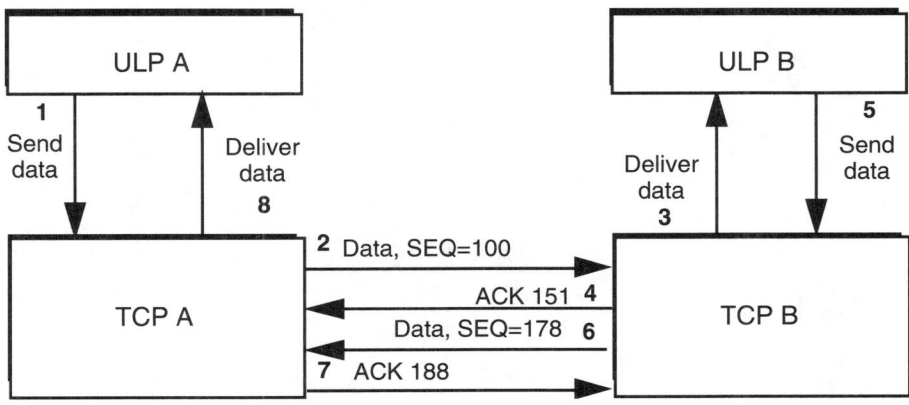

Figure 2–14   TCP data transfer operations.

TCP B with sequence number = 101, as depicted in event **2**. Remember that this sequence number is used to number the first octet of the user datastream.

At the remote TCP, data is delivered to the user (ULP B) in event **3**, and TCP B acknowledges the data with a segment acknowledgment number = 151. This is depicted in event **4**. The acknowledgment number of 151 acknowledges inclusively the 50 octets transmitted in the segment depicted in event **2**.

Next, the user connected to TCP B sends data in event **5**. This data is encapsulated into a segment and transmitted as event **6** in the diagram. This initial sequence number from TCP B was 177. Therefore, TCP begins its sequencing with 178. In this example, it transmits 10 octets.

TCP A acknowledges TCP B's 10 segments in event **7** by returning a segment with acknowledgment number = 188. In event **8**, this data is delivered to TCP A's user.

Figure 2–15 shows a close operation. Event **1** illustrates that TCP A's user wishes to close its operations with its upper peer layer protocol at TCP B. The effect of close is shown in event **2**, where TCP A sends a segment with the FIN bit set to 1. The sequence number of 151 is a continuation of the operation shown in the previous figure. This is the next sequence number the TCP module is required to send.

The effect of this transmitted segment is shown as event **3** from TCP B, which acknowledges TCP A's FIN SEQ 151. Its segment contains ACK = 152. Next, it issues a closing call to its user, which is depicted as event **4**.

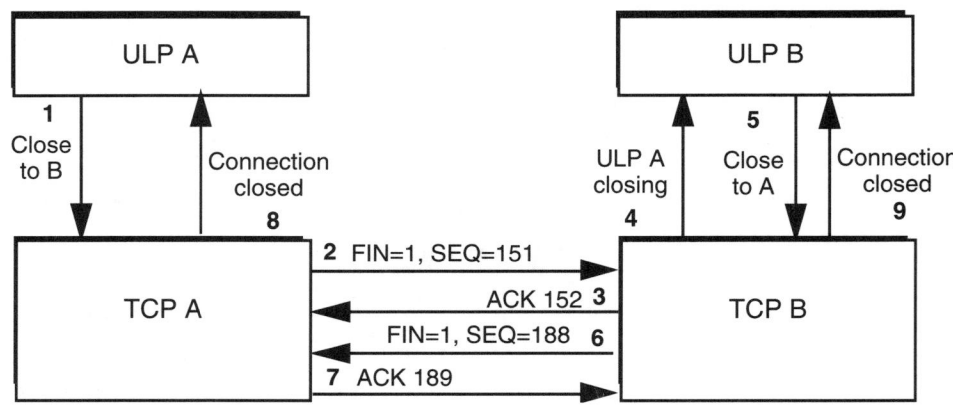

Figure 2–15   TCP close operations.

In this example, the user application acknowledges and grants the close in event **5**. It may or may not execute the close depending on the state of its operations. However, for simplicity, we assume the event depicted in **5** does occur. The information in this function is mapped to event **6**, which is the final segment issued by TCP B. Notice that in event **6**, the FIN flag is set to 1 and SEQ = 188. Finally, TCP A acknowledges this final segment with event **7** as ACK = 189.

The result of all these operations is shown in events **8** and **9**, where connection closed signals are sent to the user applications.

HOW TRAFFIC IS TRANSPORTED ACROSS THE INTERNET

Figure 2–16 shows a typical internet layered architecture for both a public and private network. This analysis is presented in a general way here and in more detail later.

At the bottom part of the figure, we find router A and three hosts attached to an Ethernet. Two of the hosts are running the IP protocol family (hosts A and C) and host B is running IBM's Systems Network Architecture (SNA) protocol suite. The notation ULPs connotes that the hosts are running IP-specific or SNA-specific upper layer protocols. At host B, IBM's layer 3 is the Path Control Protocol (labeled in this figure as IBM Path). Router A is running multiple protocol families. While this example shows only two protocol families (IP and SNA), routers typically support several other protocol families such as DECnet, AppleTalk, and X.25.

Notice that all four machines (router A, and hosts A, B, and C) are running Ethernet's layer 1 (L_1) layer 2 (L_2: media access control [MAC]). At router A, the outbound links to routers B and C are configured with T1 at the physical layer. At the data link layer (L_2), the point-to-point protocol (PPP) is used for the IP link and IBM's Synchronous Data Link Control (SDLC) is used on the SNA link.

When the traffic is passed to either router B or router C, these routers examine the destination address in the layer 3 header to make forwarding decisions. This operation is depicted in router B with the IP module (at an ISP) and in router C with the IBM Path module. When the layer 3 protocols make their forwarding decisions, the layer 3 header and the upper layer traffic is passed to the outgoing links L_2 protocol which (once again) is PPP in the internet-based router and SDLC in the SNA-based router.

Next, the traffic is placed in a layer 1 (L_1) protocol data unit to be sent across either the public Internet or the private SNA network. As the

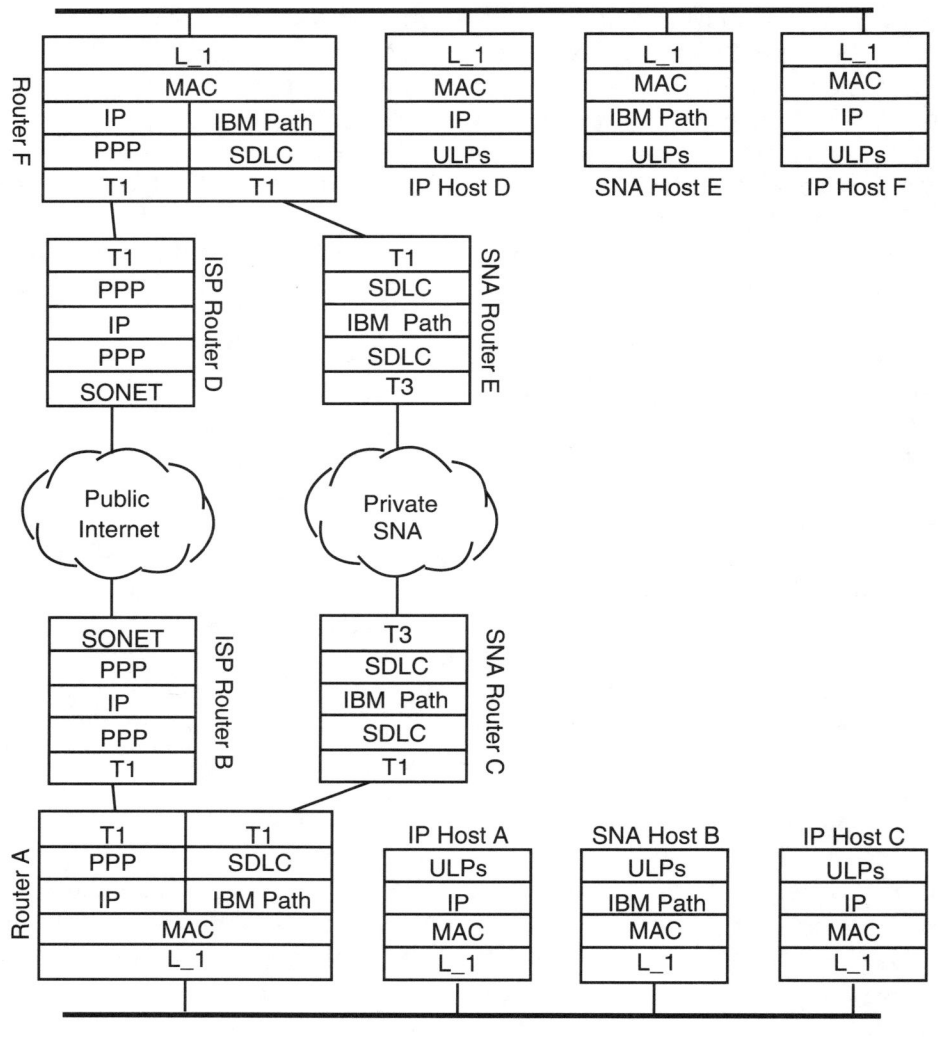

where:

IP	Internet Protocol (layer 3 of the Internet protocol suite)
MAC	Media access control (layer 2 of Ethernet)
PPP	Point-to-Point Protocol (layer 2 of many IP interfaces)
SDLC	Synchronous Data Link Control (layer 2 of SNA)
ULPs	Upper layer protocols (typically layers 4 through 7)
SNA	Systems Network Architecture (IBM's data communications system)
ISP	Internet service provider

Figure 2–16   Typical topology for an internet.

figure shows, the Internet traffic is transported by SONET at layer 1 and the SNA traffic is transported by the T3 carrier system. There is no restriction on the choice of the physical layers; they are used here to illustrate two options.

At routers D and E, and subsequently at router F and hosts D, E, and F, the processes just described are reversed, with the traffic placed on the receiving Ethernet and sent to the specific host on this network at the top of the figure.

Thus, the complete transmissions in these examples traverse through different types of networks as well as different transmission media. This example is sufficient to demonstrate the relationships of local and wide area networks and their corresponding layers. The next discussions will focus in more detail on how these operations come about.

To continue this analysis, Figure 2–17 shows the format of the Ethernet frame that is transmitted across the Ethernet link. We stated that two different protocol "families" are supported on this Ethernet LAN, the

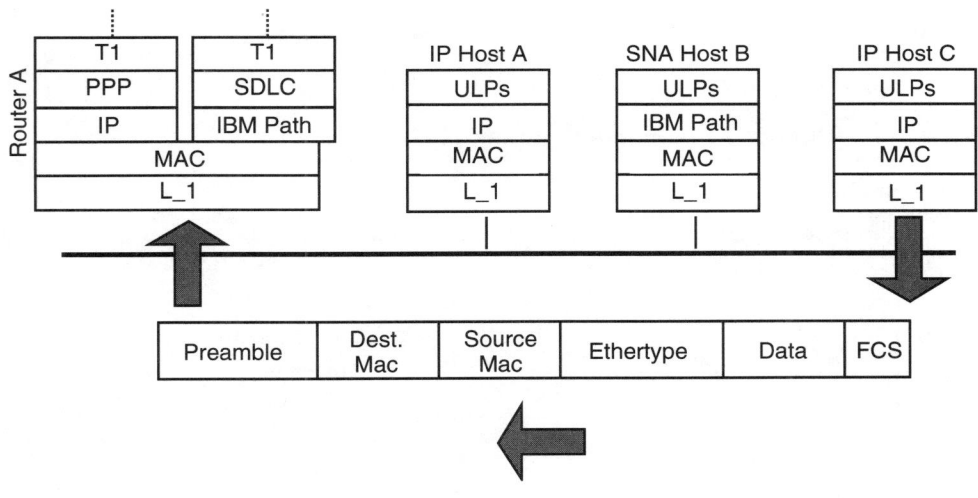

where:
  FCS   Frame check sequence
  IP   Internet Protocol
  MAC   Media access control
  PPP   Point-to-Point Protocol
  SDLC   Synchronous Data Link Control
  ULPs   Upper layer protocols

Figure 2–17   An internet LAN.

Internet Protocol (IP) and the Systems Network Architecture (SNA). The addresses in the Ethernet frame are conventional MAC addresses. The Ethertype field in Ethernet is used to identify the different protocol families that are running on the network.

The preamble is transmitted first to achieve medium stabilization and synchronization. The destination address can identify an individual workstation on the network or a group of stations. A cyclic redundancy check (CRC) value is contained in the frame check sequence (FCS) field for error detection operations.

The IEEE specifies values to identify Ethertype assignments. Some of the codes are contained in Table 2–1. Their purpose is to identify the upper layer protocol (ULP) that is running on the LAN, typically at L_3.

After the local router processes the IP datagram and makes routing decisions regarding the next node that is to receive the datagram, this datagram is passed to this next node (see Figure 2–18).

It is possible that the next node is on the same network as the sending host. In this situation, the router relays the datagram back onto the LAN from which the datagram originated. For this example, the figure highlights the routers involved in transporting the datagram through a wide area network (or networks) to the final destination.

Table 2–1   Ethertype Assignments (Examples)

Ethernet Decimal	Hex	Description
2048	0800	DoD Internet Protocol (IP)
2049	0801	X.75 Internet
2051	0803	ECMA Internet
2053	0805	X.25 level 3
2054	0806	Address Resolution Protocol (ARP)
2055	0807	XNS compatibility
4096	1000	Berkeley Trailer
21000	5208	BBN Simnet
24579	6003	DEC DECnet Phase IV
24580	6004	DEC LAT
32773	8005	HP Probe
32821	8035	Reverse ARP
32824	8038	DEC LANBridge
32823	8098	AppleTalk

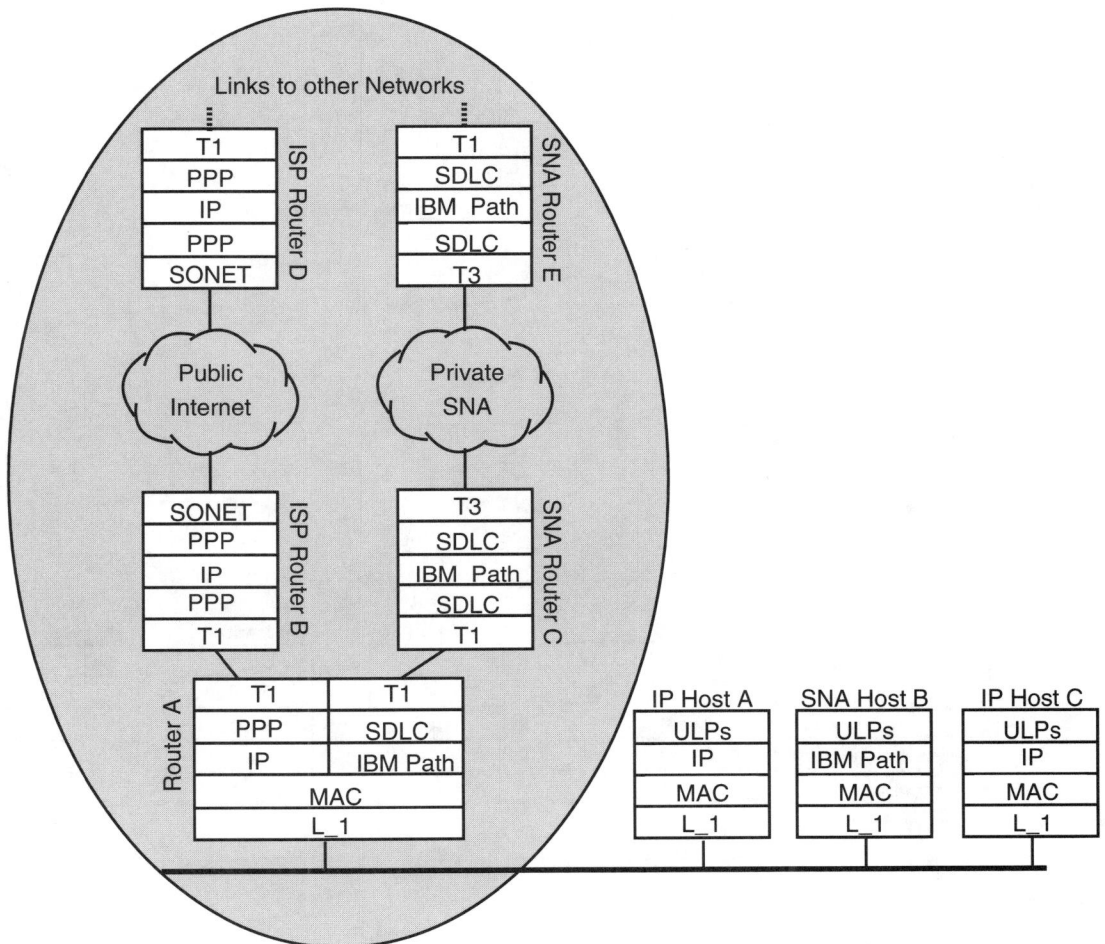

Figure 2–18   An internet WAN.

Notice that routers B, C, D, and E are not configured with the LAN interfaces. They perform the function of wide area network relay systems. In most installations, these routers have LAN interfaces but they are not germane to this discussion.

Figure 2–19 depicts the operations on the outgoing link of the router that received the Ethernet frame across a local interface. Notice that the protocol data unit on the left side of the figure differs from the protocol data unit originally sent to the router. This protocol data unit is an example of a Point-to-Point Protocol (PPP) frame.

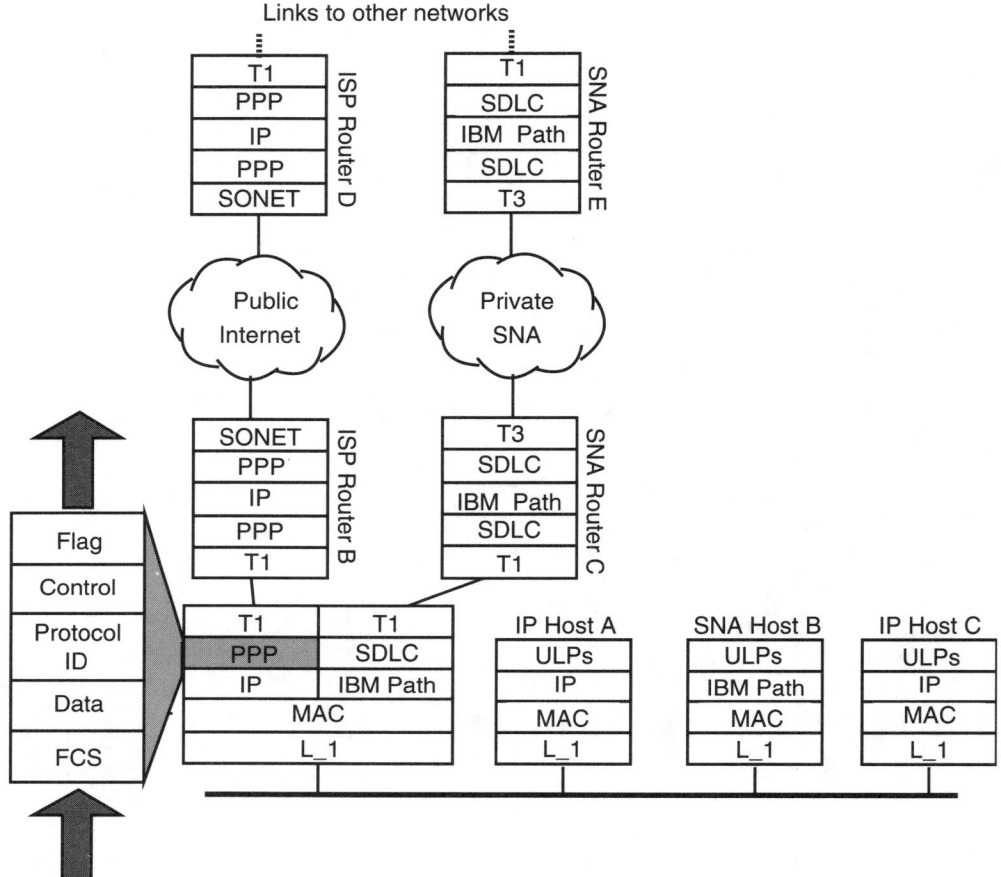

Figure 2–19   Presenting the traffic to the WAN.

The specific contents of each field in the PPP frame are beyond this discussion. The relevant aspects of the frame contents are the protocol ID field and the data field. The protocol ID field provides the same function as the Ethernet Ethertype field. It identifies the type of traffic residing in the data field. The router's task is to map the Ethertype value to the PPP protocol ID field, since the LAN L_2 Ethernet headers and trailers are stripped away and replaced with the WAN L_2 PPP headers and trailers.

Figure 2–20 shows that the traffic is now passed to a T1 link. At this stage of the operation, the PPP frame is placed into a T1 DS0 channel (or channels). The traffic is shipped across the T1 link to a network service provider, and in this example, the ISP's router B.

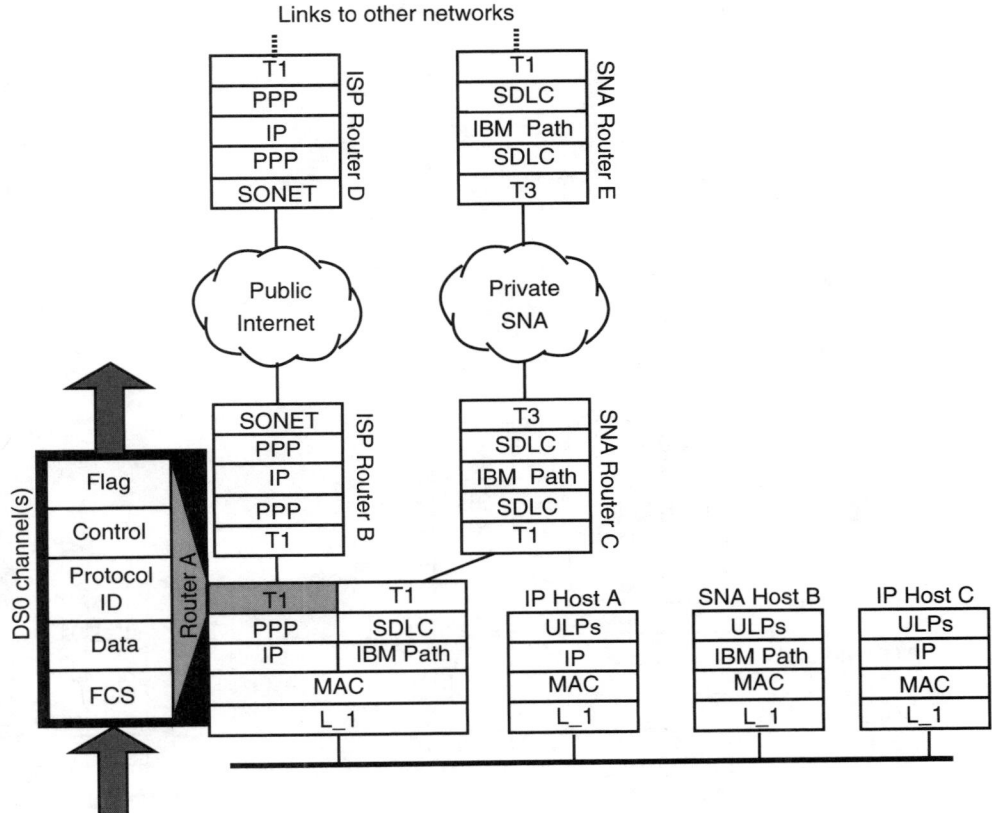

Figure 2–20   Relaying the traffic onto the outgoing link.

The manner in which T1 supports data communications varies and the reader should check the specific vendor implementations. In some systems, the data traffic is not slotted into discrete DS0 channels. In others, it is placed precisely into the DS0 slots on a periodic basis.

We now find the datagram being processed by router B in Figure 2–21.[4] Notice that the PPP headers and trailers have been stripped away and the router examines the IP datagram header that resides in the data field of the arriving protocol data unit.

The router compares the destination IP address in this datagram to IP addresses stored in a routing table. Following various rules on IP ad-

---

[4]Obviously, I am not taking you through each and every layer, but I trust you can fill-in these other operations.

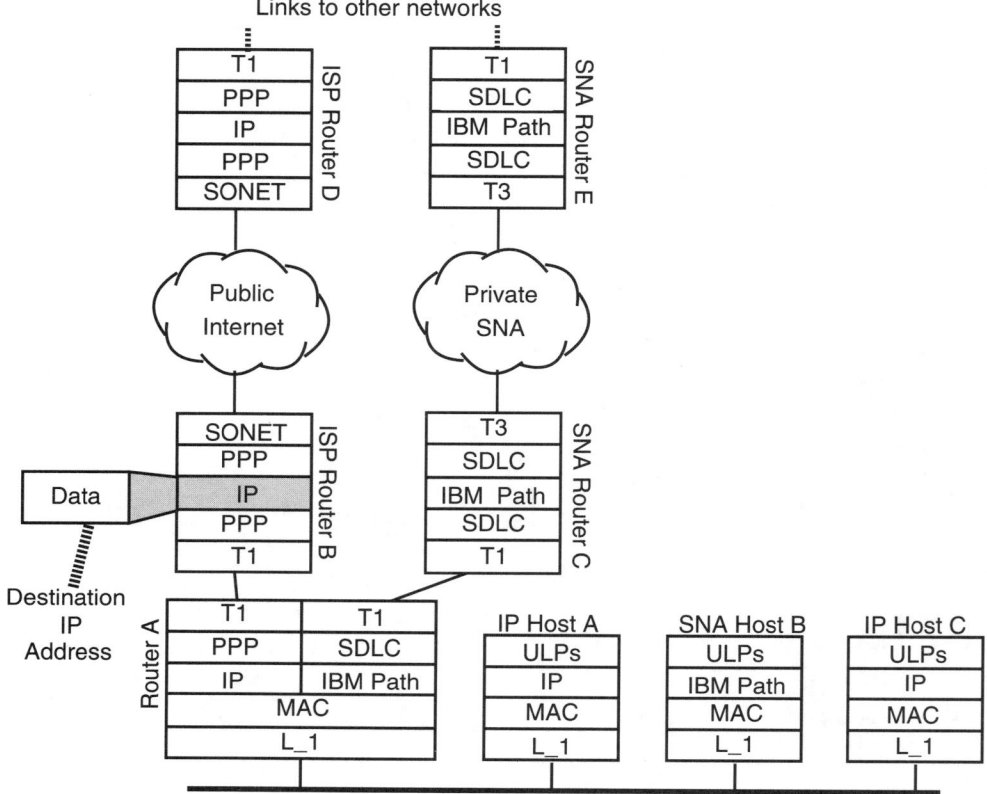

Figure 2–21   At an intermediate router.

dress searching operations (discussed later), a match will reveal the next node that is to receive the datagram. If a match occurs successfully, the router (in this example) places the data field inside a layer 2 frame (PPP in this case) and sends the frame to the outgoing physical layer, which in this example is a SONET (Synchronous Optical Network) link. In effect, the traffic is encapsulated into a SONET frame.

In many of the high-capacity links in the Internet, SONET has replaced the T1/T3 trunks, as shown in Figure 2–22. The SONET OC-3 rate (optical carrier) of 155 Mbit/s is more attractive than the slower 1.5 Mbit/s T1 and 45 Mbit/s T3 trunks. In addition, SONET has other significant advantages over the T1 technology.

First, SONET is built on fiber optic standards that provide for superior performance vis-à-vis the copper-cable systems. SONET also provides the ability to combine and consolidate traffic from different loca-

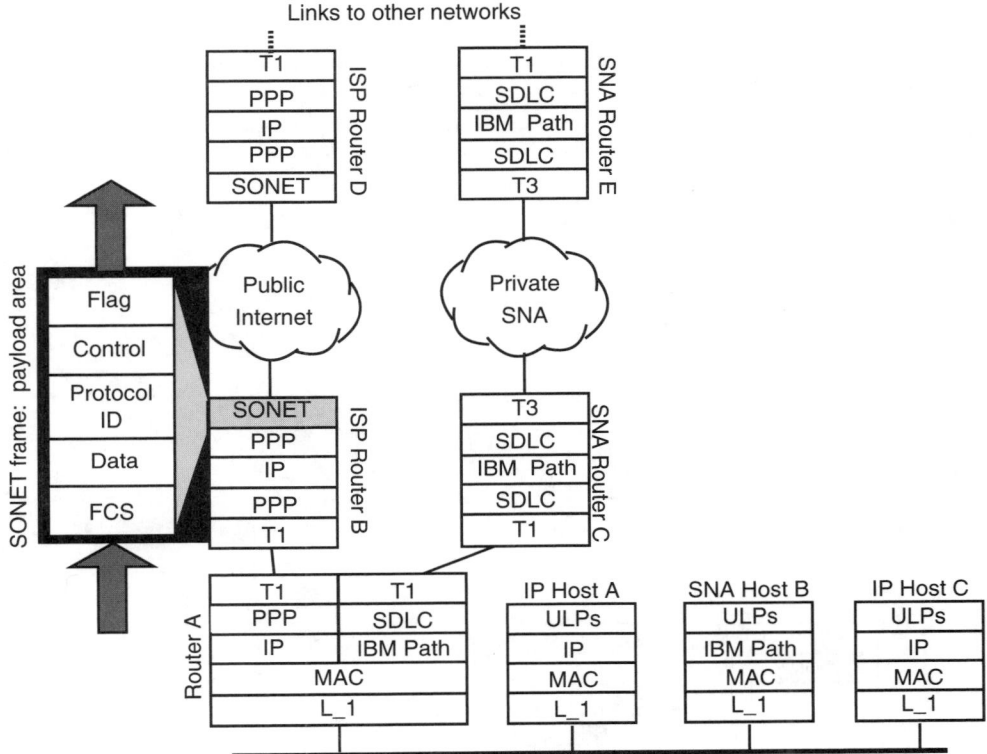

Figure 2–22   Using SONET.

where:
  SONET   Synchronous Optical Network

tions through one facility. This concept, known as *grooming,* eliminates inefficient techniques that are part of the T1 operation.

SONET has notably improved network management features relative to current technology and uses extensive headers to provide information on diagnostics, configurations, and alarms. In addition, SONET can be configured with a number of topologies, some of which can provide for robustness in the form of backup links, and the ability to divert traffic around problem nodes or links.

The datagram continues its journey through the Internet, through the terminating IP node (router D in Figure 2–23) and to the local router that services the destination host's network (router F in this example). The process depicted by the arrows in this figure is identical to the opera-

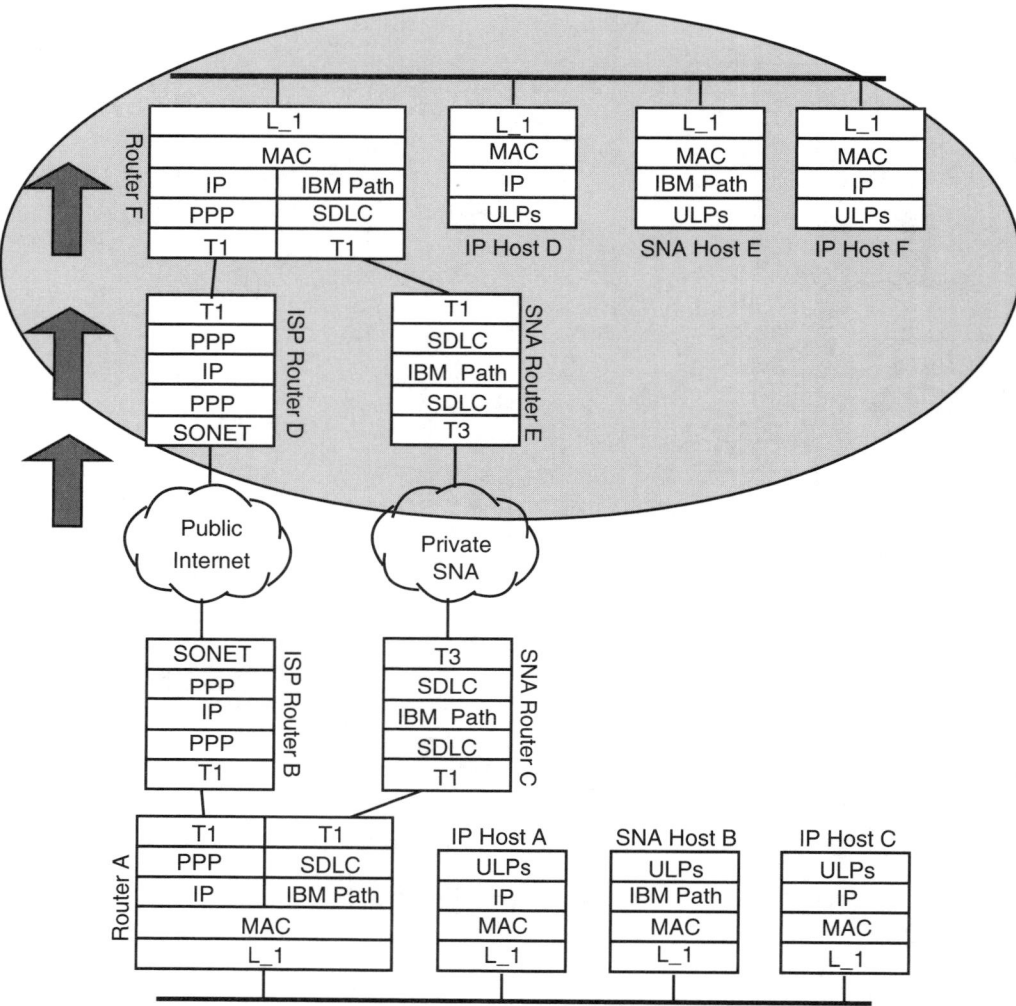

Figure 2–23   Delivery to the receiving network.

tions that occurred at the originating nodes except in reverse order. Therefore, we shall not revisit them here.

In Figure 2–24, after the datagram has arrived at router F (which has demultiplexed the IP traffic from the T1 frame and has processed the PPP frame as well), it examines the destination IP address in the IP datagram header to determine the recipient of this datagram. Once this determination has been made, router F: (1) resolves the destination IP

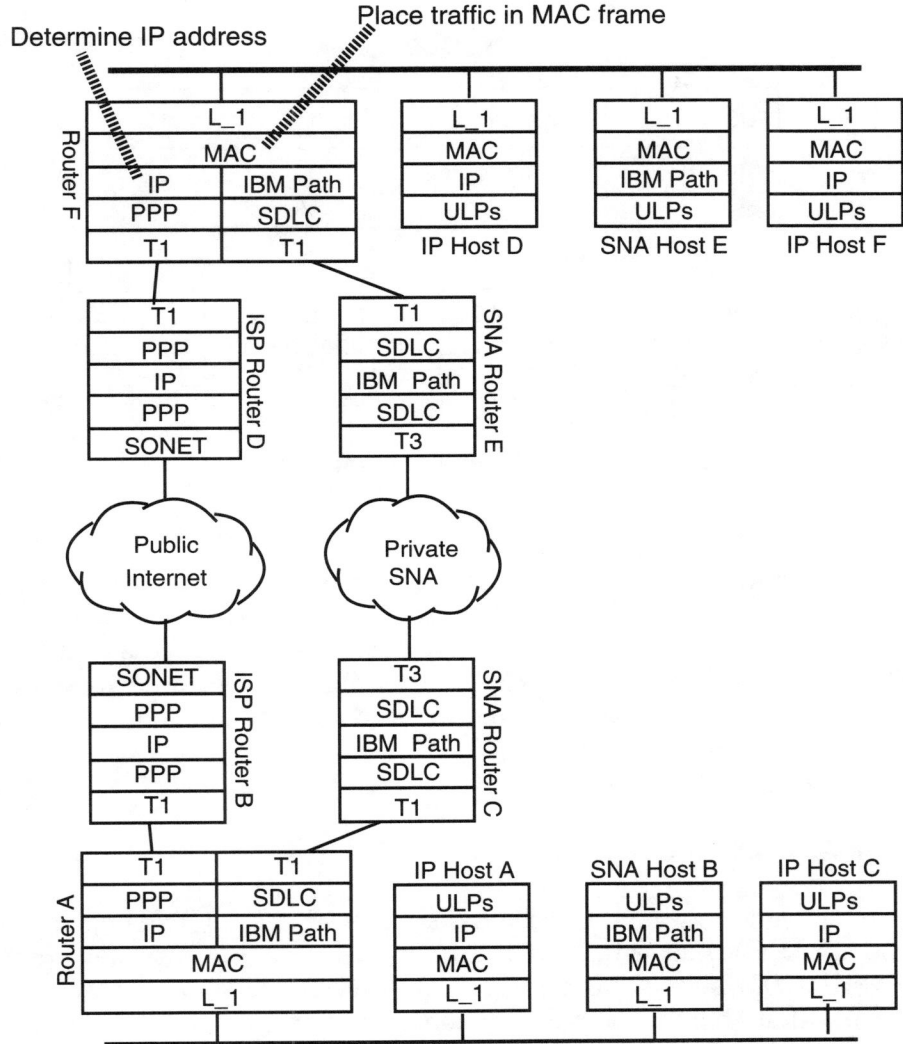

Figure 2–24 Address determination, Ethernet encapsulation.

address to the destination MAC address, (2) encapsulates the data field into an Ethernet MAC frame, and (3) maps the PPP protocol ID field into the Ethernet Ethertype field. The traffic is then sent out onto the local network in the Ethernet frame.

To conclude this overview, in Figure 2–25 we now see the Ethernet frame being sent from router F to IP host F. Inside the data field resides the

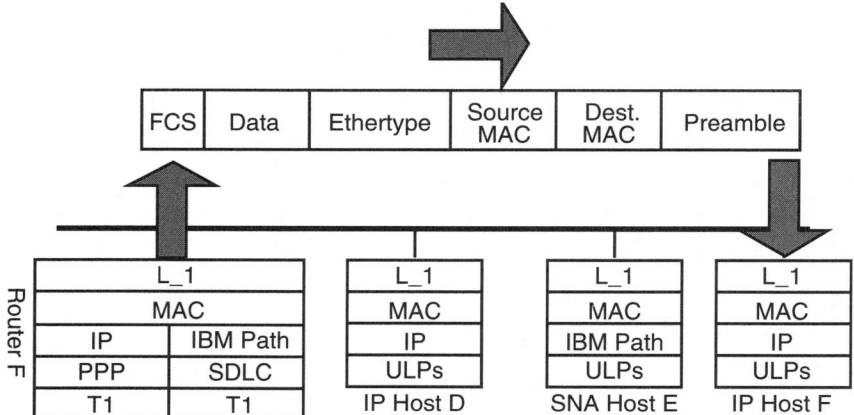

Figure 2–25   The final transmission.

IP datagram, which (among other values) contains the IP source address and IP destination address. The MAC addresses identify the source MAC address that is router F and the destination MAC address that is host F.

This completes our analysis of the traffic flow between local and wide area networks. It is a general view and further analyses will provide more details on these operations.

THE DOMAIN NAME SYSTEM

This section examines the Domain Name System (DNS) specification and its UNIX-based implementation, the Berkeley Internet Name Domain (BIND) system. These systems provide name server operations. This means that their principal function is to map (or correlate) a user-friendly email name to a routable address.

This type of service is quite helpful to a user, because the user is not tasked with remembering an abstract address of a person (or application) with whom the user wishes to communicate. Rather, the sending user need only know an easy-to-remember text-oriented value (a name) of the recipient . This name is keyed in during a session and relayed to a name server, which looks up an associated address.

So, DNS and BIND are similar to ARP. They correlate (map) one identifier to another. But the correlations are different. ARP maps layer 2 addresses to/from layer 3 address, or layer 2/3 addresses to/from virtual circuit identifiers, whereas DNS correlates names to/from addresses.

The Internet Protocol (IP) address structure (consisting of 32 bits) is somewhat awkward to use by humans. Indeed, instead of using the IP address, many users have adapted the use of acronyms and meaningful terms to identify a numeric address. This practice presents an interesting problem if a network user is using acronyms and so on as an address and must internetwork with a network that uses the numeric IP addresses. How is the non-IP identifier mapped to an IP address?

One could say that the user should conform and learn to use the IP addresses. Yet, we cannot expect an end user to remember all the values on these addresses, much less to key-in these addresses at the workstation. The solution is to devise a naming scheme wherein an end user can employ a friendly, easy-to-remember name to identify the sending and receiving entities.

In order for this idea to be implemented, procedures must first be established to provide a framework for establishing user friendly names and conventions for mapping the names to IP addresses.

In the Internet, the organization and managing of these names was provided originally by the SRI Network Information Center. It maintained a file called HOST.TXT, which listed the names of networks, gateways, and hosts and their corresponding addresses.

The original structure of *flat name* spaces worked well enough in the early days of internet. This term describes a form of a name consisting merely of characters identifying an object without any further meaning or structure. As stated earlier, the Internet Network Information Center was responsible for administering name spaces and assigning them to new objects that were identified in internet.

Figure 2–26 shows the approach used today. In event 1, a person enters a domain name for Uyless Black: ublack@infoinst.com. The name server software in the host forms a query to a local name server (event 2). In effect, this query asks the name server to look up the name in the DNA database and find an associated address. In event 3, the name server responds with a reply that associates ublack@infoinst.com to address 38.146.104.234.

In event 4, this address is placed into the destination IP address field of the IP datagram and in event 5, it is sent to a local router. The router receives the datagram (event 6), and finds a match in its routing table with the identification address in the datagram (event 7), which reveals the node to receive the datagram, as well as the outgoing physical

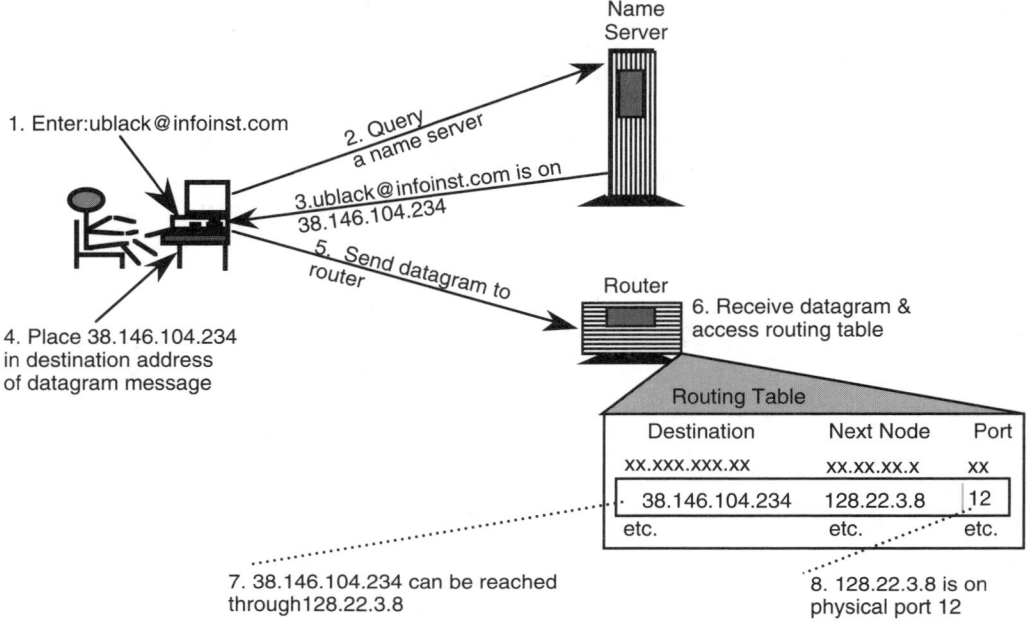

Figure 2–26   Operations with name servers.

port (interface) through which the datagram is transported to the next node (event 8).

UPPER LAYER IDENTIFIERS

Physical and network level addresses are insufficient to move the packet to its final "destination" on the host machine, and other higher layer identifiers are needed. For example, a packet may be destined for a specific software application, such as an email or a file transfer system. Since both these applications reside in the same upper layer (the application layer), some means must be devised to identify the application that is to process the packet. An identifier is used by the host machine to determine which application receives the data.

The upper layer names are identified by a variety of terms. The Internet convention is to use the terms *port* and *socket*. The OSI convention is to use the term service access point (SAP) (see Figure 2–27.)

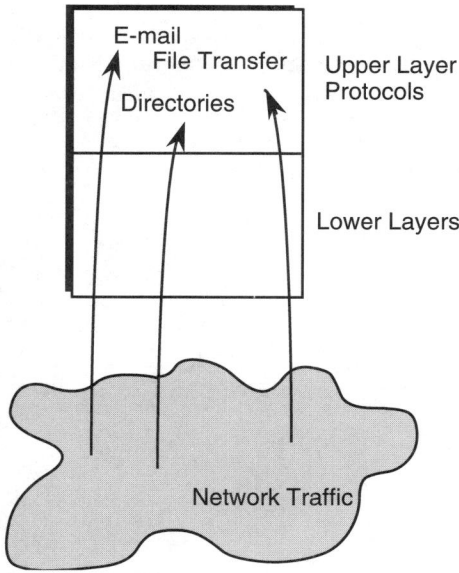

Figure 2–27   Upper layer identifiers.

INTERNET TRAFFIC CHARACTERISTICS

Originally, the Internet was designed for terminal-to-terminal traffic and file transfer traffic. The Internet still supports this traffic, but the types of traffic have become more diverse.

Table 2–2 compares the different types of traffic flows in the Internet. The four major flows are compared: (1) Web traffic, server-to-client, (2) Web traffic, client-to-server, (3) MBONE traffic, and (4) Domain Name System (DNS) traffic.

The first two columns describe the percentage of the application's flows (sessions) to the total flows and the number of bytes sent by each application to the total number of bytes sent. The last two columns cite the number of units (packets) and the average number of bytes for the applications.

The information in this table is of no surprise. MBONE traffic entails the use of considerable bandwidth, which would be expected of an application that is audio- and video-based.

Given that fixed routing is a desirable feature for real-time traffic, one can ask: Is it needed? That is, does an internet (or more precisely, the Internet) shuffle traffic around frequently, with the routers altering routes often? If so, routing headers are important for real-time traffic.

Table 2–2   Internet Traffic Characteristics

Flow Type	% of Flows	% of Bytes	Average Number of Units	Average Number of Bytes
Web S to C	20.0	34.0	16.5	8270
Web C to S	23.3	3.3	12.5	710
MBONE	0.01	20.0	10,088	6,344,202
DNS	32.0	3.2	—	—
Others	25.7	35.4	—	—

Source: Antonio Rodriquez-Moral, "LIBRA." *Bell Labs Technical Journal,* 2(2): 42–67, Spring 1997.
where:
  C   Client
  DNS Domain Name System
  S   Server

Studies conducted on the routing behavior of the Internet reveal that most of the traffic between two or more communicating parties remains on the same physical path during the session. In fact, route alteration is more an exception than the rule.

One study on Internet "routing persistence" is summarized in Table 2–3. This information represents a small part of the study that is available from IEEE/ACM *Transactions on Communications,* "End-to-End Routing Behavior in the Internet," by Vern Paxson, Vol. 5, No. 5, October 1997. Paxson defines routing persistence as how long a route endures be-

Table 2–3   Routing Persistence

Time	% of Total	Comments
Seconds	NA	Used in load balancing
Minutes	NA	In tightly coupled routers
10s of minutes	9	Changes usually through different cities or Autonomous Systems
Hours	4	Usually intranetwork changes
6+ hours	19	Usually intranetwork changes
Days	68	(a) 50% of these routes persist for < 7 days (b) Other 50% persist for > 7 days

Source: Vern Paxson, "End-to-End Routing Behavior in the Internet," IEEE/ACM *Transactions on Communications,* 5(5), October 1997.

fore changing. Even though routing changes occur over a wide range of time, most of the routes in the Internet do not change much.

A point should be emphasized in Paxson's study. The "not applicable" (NA) entries in this table represent situations in which frequent routing fluctuations do occur in parts of the Internet. While they are not a factor in the "big picture," if your traffic flows through that part of the Internet, it will be affected by these changes.

Notwithstanding, in most cases, the routing header is not needed. But it is still a valuable tool when used in conjunction with other protocols discussed later. At the least, it is insurance against wavering routes.

Other statistics that are pertinent to the deployment of voice and video over the Internet are summarized in Table 2–4.

Round trip time (RTT) is a measure of the time it takes to send a packet to a node and receive a reply from that node. RTT includes the transmission time in both directions and the processing time at the far-end node. Most RTTs in the Internet are within the range of 70 to 160 ms, although large variations to RTT do occur. Due to the asynchronous nature of the Internet, the user has no assurance that RTT will be consistent.

The ITU-T G.114 Recommendation limits RTT to 300 ms or less. This performance factor is based on many studies and observations that longer delays in a telephone-based conversation leaves the impression on the conversationalists that they are using a half-duplex circuit. However, other surveys show some people tolerate large RTTs of up to 800 ms. But this tolerant population is in the minority.

Table 2–4 Internet Traffic Characteristics

- *Round Trip Delay (RTT)*
    - Most RTTs are within 70–160 ms
    - ITU-T G.114: limit RTT to 300 ms or less
    - However . . .
        - Surveys show some people tolerate large
        - RTTs of 800 ms
- *Packet Loss*
    - Very bursty
    - Affects contiguous packets
- *Order of Packet Arrival*
    - Studies underway, but . . .
    - Paxson study shows out-of-sequence arrival not unusual

Another Internet characteristic that is important to audio and video applications is packet loss. These factors are involved: how often packet loss occurs and when the loss occurs, and how many successive (contiguous) packets are affected. Packet loss is masked in the data application by using TCP to resend the lost TCP segments. Certainly, the loss of many segments and their retransmissions will affect the application's performance, but on the whole, the end-user data application is not concerned (or aware) of packet loss.

Packet loss is quite important in audio and video applications, since the loss may affect the outcome of the decoding process at the receiver and be detected by the end-user's ears or eyes. Notwithstanding, today's voice coders can produce high-quality audio signals in the face of about 10% loss of the voice packets (G.723.1 as the example), *if* the packet losses are random and independent. G.723.1 compensates for this loss by using the previous packet to simulate the characteristics of the vocal signal that was in the lost packet.

Traffic loss in the Internet is bursty: Large packet losses occur in a small number of bursts. In effect, the losses are not random or independent. This characteristic of internet behavior complicates the support of telephony; as we just learned, packetized voice works best if the packet loss is random and independent.

The effect of packet loss can be alleviated somewhat by the use of forward error correction (FEC) schemes, and studies have been conducted to compensate for loss bursts (see M. S. Borella et al., "Analysis of End-to-End Internet Packet Loss: "Dependence and Asymmetry," *IEEE Network*, Preprint, 1997). These schemes add extra delay to the process and may result in the loss of the packet because it is made available to the user in a time domain that is too late to be useful.

The FEC approach borrows from the tried-and-true mobile wireless technology: Repeat the signal more than once. With mobile wireless systems, this operation interleaves successive copies of the coded voice image across multiple packets (slots in the mobile wireless terminology). With Internet telephony, experiments are underway to send copies of the packet 1 to n times. But if one copy is lost, say copy n, it can be recovered from the other copies. However, this operation is only effective if a copy arrives safely, and therefore implies that one of the copies survives the burst error. But if the copies are spaced out too far in time to survive the error, they may arrive too late to be useful.

The subject of the order of the arrival of packets at the receiver is not of keen interest to the data application if it is supported by TCP, because TCP can reorder the TCP segments and present the traffic to the application in the correct order. TCP is not used for voice and video, so the order of packet arrival is an important subject to these applications. As of this writing, studies are underway to capture statistics and discover the incidences of misordered packet arrival. The Paxson study (cited earlier) shows that out-of-sequence arrival is not unusual.

Once again, it is obvious that the Internet is not set up to gracefully accommodate voice and video traffic. Subsequent chapters will explain how the Internet multimedia protocols deal with these traffic characteristics.

SUMMARY

The architecture of the Internet retains its basic composition as envisioned by the original Internet designers. IP is the datagram forwarding entity operating in a sparse connectionless mode. TCP, operating on the host, is responsible for traffic integrity with the use of retransmissions.

Other key protocols include ARP to correlate L_2 and L_3 addresses and DNS to correlate L_3 addresses and domain names.

Analysis of Internet traffic reveals that (1) delay is often high and variable, (2) traffic often arrives out of order, and (3) traffic may be lost or discarded. These factors must be taken into account when upgrading the Internet to support a multimedia environment.

3

Digital Voice and Video

The manner in which speech is encoded/decoded for transmission in a data network is the subject of the first part of this chapter. We follow this discussion with a review of a video coder based on the ISO standard, MPEG-2 (named for the Motion Pictures Experts Group-2).

VOICE DIGITIZATION STANDARDS FOR VoIP

VoIP vendors use several ITU-T specifications on the coding, formatting, and decoding of the voice traffic with their coders. Table 3–1 lists the common ITU-T G Series Recommendations that may be used in VoIP. I say "may" because all organizations that belong to the International Media Teleconferencing Consortium (IMTC) have selected G.723.1 for their basic vocoder, and this chapter explains the operations of G.723.1.[1]

In addition to the G Series Recommendations, the H Series also play an important role in internet telephony. H.323 is being used (by few vendors, since it is new) to define the internet telephony architecture, and by the time this book is published, several vendors will have their H.323 products on the market. H.323 is discussed in Chapter 5.

---

[1]While G.723.1 will be the choice for current systems, G.729 or G.728 may be a better alternative in some networks. More information is provided on this subject later.

Table 3–1   The G Series Recommendations

Reference	Description
ITU G.729/ITU G.729, Annex A	Coding of Speech at 8 kbit/s using Conjugate Structure-Algebraic code Excited Linear Predictive (CS-ACEP) Coding, March 1996
ITU G.711	Pulse Code Modulation (PCM) of Voice Frequencies, 1988
ITU G.726	40, 32, 24, 16 kbit/s Adaptive Differential Pulse Code Modulation (ADPCM), March 1996
ITU G.727	5-, 4-, 3-, and 2-bit Sample Embedded Adaptive Differential Pulse Code Modulation, November 1994
ITU G.764	Voice packetization—Packetized voice protocols, December 1990
ITU-T G.722	Wideband Coder
ITU G.728	Coding of Speech at 16 kbit/s Using Low-Delay Code Excited Linear Prediction (LD-CELP), November 1994
ITU G.723.1	Dual Rate Speech Coder for Multimedia Communications Transmitting at 5.3 & 6.3 kbit/s, March 1996
ITU G.723.1, Annex A	Silence Compression Scheme, March 1996
ITU G.723.1, Annex B	Alternative Specification Based on Floating Point Arithmetic, March 1996
ITU G.723.1, Annex C	Scalable Channel Coding Scheme for Wireless Applications, March 1996

The 64 kbit/s G.711 PCM coder is used throughout the world in digital telephone networks. The G.728 coder is employed in private networks, undersea cable, and on satellite links. The G.722 and G.728 coders are employed in video conferencing applications that operate over ISDN or frame relay links. The G.723.1 and G.729 coders are the subject of interest in this book, because they are the primary coders being used for internet telephony.

Other documents are important as well. For mobile operations, Table 3–2 provides a summary of the voice coders.

Table 3–2   Cellular Coders

Reference	Description
IS-54	7.95 kbit/s VSLEP
Japan RCR	6.7 kbit/s VSLEP
IS-95	8.5/4.0/2.0/0.8 kbit/s QCELP
Japan RCR	3.45 kbit/s PSI-CELP
GSM	13 kbit/s RPE-LTP

A REVIEW OF ANALOG-TO-DIGITAL CONVERSION

The subject of analog-to-digital conversion (A/D) (and vice versa, D/A) is well treated in scores of books and other references. This section of the chapter will provide an overview of the subject for the uninitiated reader.

The Conventional Telephony Approach

Several methods are used to change an analog signal into a representative string of digital binary images. Even though these methods entail many processes, they are generally described in three steps: *sampling, quantizing,* and *encoding.* These steps form the basis of the G.711 Recommendation, which is the coding method used in the telephone network (see Figure 3–1).

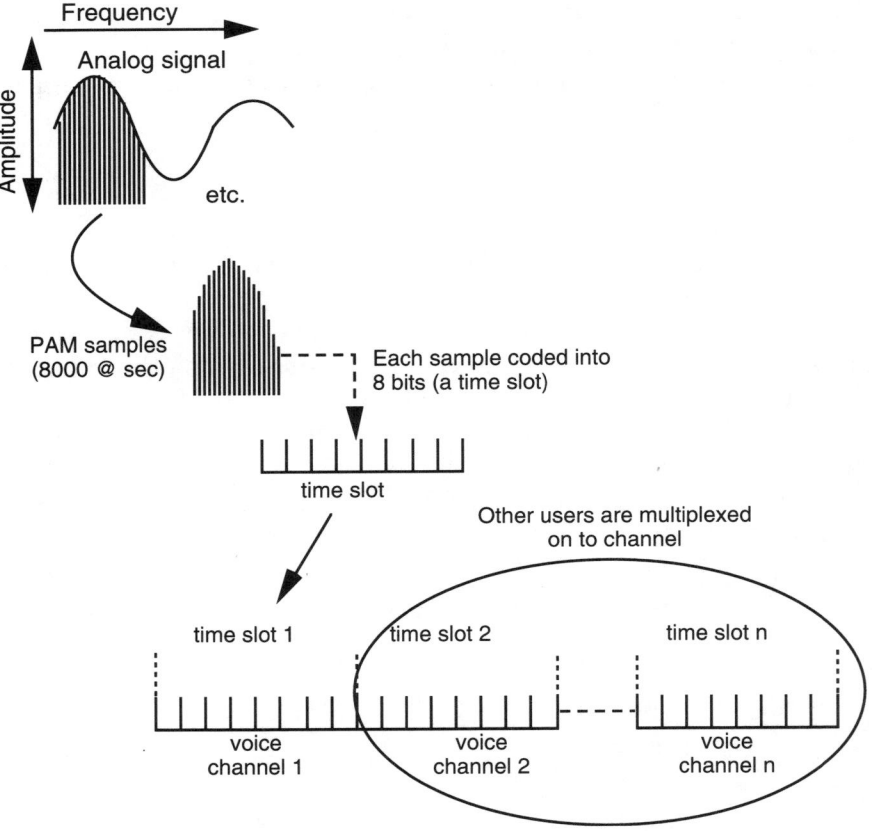

Figure 3–1   Conventional telephony digitization.

The devices performing the digitizing process are called voice coders (vocoders). They have two basic functions: (1) converting analog signals to digital signals, and (2) vice versa at the other end. In the telephone network, the coder is embedded into another device called a channel bank, which is responsible for combining (multiplexing) the digital signals into a single time division multiplexed (TDM) datastream (and demultiplexing them at the other end).

Sampling takes place at 8000 times a second using an analog-to-digital conversion process based on Nyquist sampling theory. The Nyquist sampling theorem states that when a signal is sampled instantaneously at the transmitter at regular intervals and at a rate at least twice the highest frequency in the channel, then the samples will contain sufficient information to allow an accurate reconstruction of the signal at the receiver. The voice bandwidth is 300 Hz to 3400 Hz. The accepted sampling rate in the industry is 8000 samples per second.

The signal f(t) can be reconstructed from the samples by a low pass filter. Theoretically and ideally, the sampling provides an amplitude value at a specific time and the continuous signal is reconstructed by applying the samples to the low pass filter. Practically speaking, sampling is done over a finite time and the reconstruction filters are not ideal. Nonetheless, the process is sufficient to provide adequate reproduction at the receiver.

In 1933, Harry Nyquist defined the minimum sampling frequency needed to convey all information in an analog waveform:

$$fs > 2BW$$

where: fs = sampling frequency; BW = bandwidth of the input signal.

The 8 kHz sampling rate results in a sample pulse train of signals with a 125 microseconds (µsec) time period between the pulses (1 second/8000 = .000125). Each pulse occupies 5.2 µsec of this time period. Consequently, it is possible to interleave sampled pulses from other signals within the 125 µsec period. The most common approach in North America utilizes 24 interleaved channels, which effectively fills the 125 µsec time period (.0000052 ∗ 24 = .000125). The samples are then multiplexed using TDM and put into a digital TDM frame. TDM provides an efficient and economical means of combining multiple signals for transmission on a common facility, and is examined in a later chapter. As shown in this simplified picture in Figure 3–2, each sample is assigned a binary value. This process is called quantizing.

The A/D process uses a compression technique, called *companding*, to compensate for errors in the assignment of values to each sample. It is

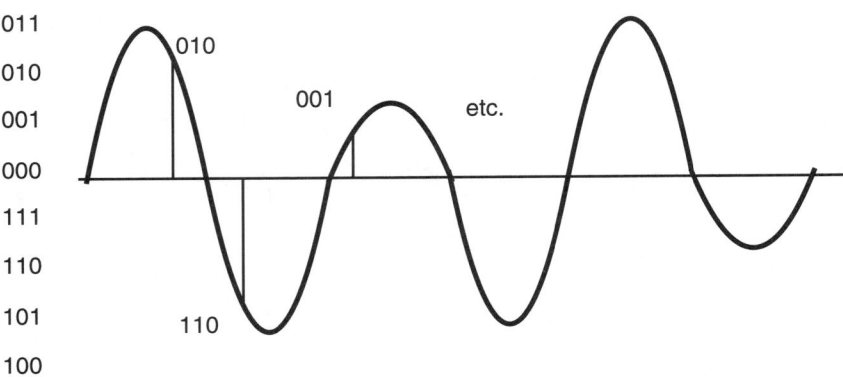

Note: Actual sampling: 8,000 times a second x 8 bits per sample = 64, 000 kbit/s

Figure 3–2   Signal sampling and quantizing.

this assignment process that is called companding. Errors occur because the sampled signal may not correlate exactly to a quantizing value.

The distortion in the quantization is a function of the differences between the quantized steps. Ideally, one would like to use many quantizing steps in order to reduce the quantizing "noise." Studies show that 2048 uniform quantizing steps provide sufficient "granularity" to represent the voice signal accurately. However, 2048 steps require an 11-bit code (2^{11}), which translates to 88000 bit/s (8000×11). Since the voice signals in a telephone system can span 30 dB of variation, it makes sense to vary the distribution of the quantization steps. The variable quantizing levels reduce the quantizing noise.

The nonlinear companding is implemented in a stepwise linear process (see Figure 3–3). For the μ law, the m = 255 is used and the companding value is coded by a set of eight straight-line segments that cut across the compression curve (actually eight for negative segments and eight for positive segments; since the two center segments are collinear, they are considered one).

Figure 3–3 shows the segment approximation. With this approach, each segment is double the amplitude range of its preceding segment and each segment is also one-half the slope of the preceding segment. In this manner, the segments representing the low range of PAM signals are more accurately encoded than the segments pertaining to the high range of PAM signals.

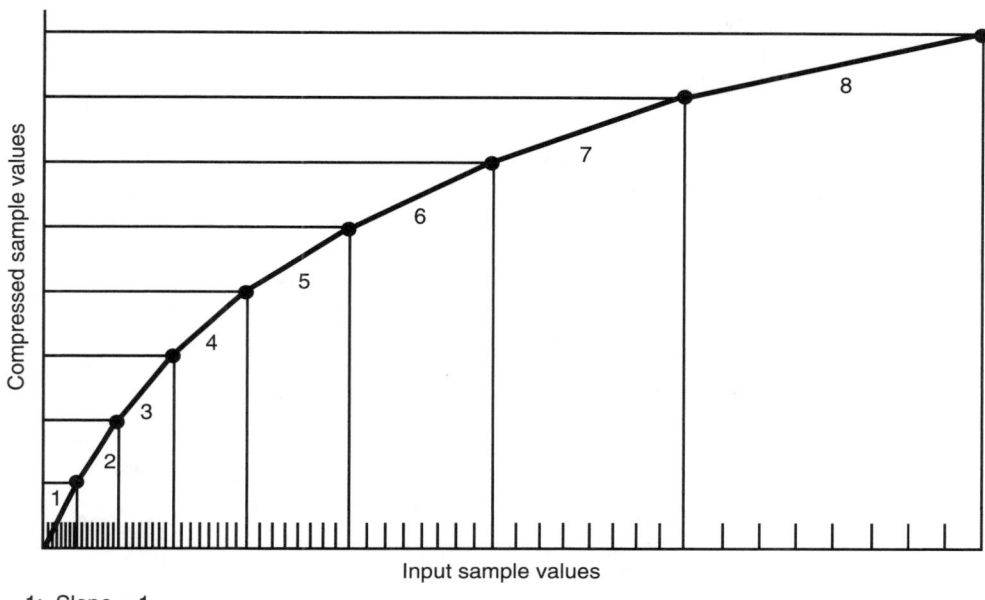

Input sample values

1: Slope = 1
2: Slope = 1/2
3: Slope = 1/4
4: Slope = 1/8
5: Slope = 1/16
6: Slope = 1/32
7: Slope = 1/64
8: Slope = 1/128

Figure 3–3   Companding with 8-segment approximation.

The A law functions similarly to the µ law characteristic. Eight positive and eight negative segments exist as in the µ law characteristic, but it is described as the 13-segment law.

The code of µ 255 PCM consists of: (1) a 1-bit polarity where 0 = positive sample value and 1 = negative sample value; (2) a 3-bit segment identifier(s); and, (3) a 4-bit quantizing step identifier. The use of the segment and step values is similar to the representation of a floating point number, with one part representing the linear part and another representing the exponent.

We learned that, if an acceptable S/D performance of the signal distribution is to be maintained, a logarithmic compression law must be used. Two common methods of modifying a true logarithmic law are described herein.

Table 3–3   Comparison of μ-law and A-law

Coded Numerical Value	Bit Number		
	μ-Law *12345678*	*A-Law* *12345678*	
+127	10000000	11111111	The left-most bit (bit 1) is transmitted first and
+96	10011111	11100000	is the most significant bit (MSB). This bit is
+ 64	101111111	11000000	known as the "sign" bit and is a 1 for positive
+32	11011111	10100000	values and a 0 for negative values (both PCM
0	11111111	10000000	types).
0	01111111	00000000	
−32	01011111	00100000	Bits 2 through 8 are inverted between A-Law
−64	00111111	01000000	and μ-Law PCM.
−96	00011111	01100000	
−126	00000001	01111110	In A-Law, all even bits (2, 4, 6, . .) are inverted
−127	00000000	01111111	prior to transmission. The zero-energy code of
			00000000 is actually sent as 01010101 (hex 55).

The coding process to modify companding to make it near-linear for low sound levels is defined in:

μ-law:

$$F_m^{-1}(y) = sgn(y) \frac{1}{m} [(1 + m)^{|y|} - 1]$$

where: y = the compressed value = $F_m(x)$ ($-1 \leq x \leq 1$); sgn (y) = the polarity of y; m = the companding parameter.

A law:

$$F_A(x) = sgn(x) \frac{A |x|}{1 + ln(A)} \qquad 0 \leq x \leq 1/A$$

$$F_A(x) = sgn(x) \frac{1 + ln |A x|}{1 + ln(A)} \qquad 1/A \leq x \leq 1$$

Table 3–3 shows the bit and byte patterns for these systems.

THE G.711 PCM CODER

The G.711 PCM coder has been used in telephone networks for many years. It is simple, provides high-quality signals, and yields low delay (one sample). However, its high bit rate of 64 kbit/s is not attractive for use on bandwidth limited data links. Also, G.711 has no error detection or correction mechanism and would not be a good choice to operate for error-prone links. Consequently, other coders are used for IP telephony.

A REVIEW OF OTHER METHODS

The other methods that are used in IP telephony and other data networks are summarized here. This part of the chapter provides a summary of these methods.[2] I place particular emphasis on G.723.1, G.729, and G.729A, because G.723.1 is the coder being implemented in the majority of internet telephony products today, and G.729/G.729A are likely competitors in the very near future. Overall, G.728 may be the best choice of the G series coders, so it is also highlighted.

Wideband Speech Coder G.722

The G.722 wideband speech coder operates at 64, 56, or 48 kbit/s. It is designed to transmit voice or music for a 7-kHz bandwidth. The quality is not transparent to the person receiving the information, especially for music, because the upper band (4–7 kHz) is quantized using 2 bits/sample ADPCM. But for teleconferencing, G.722 is preferred to G.711.

G.722 does not have any packet-loss concealment strategy. Moreover, most of the delay in G.722 is due to a filter used in both the encoder and decoder to divide the speech into two bands, which results in a delay of 1.5 ms. The authors of the paper cited in footnote 2 state that a project is underway by the ITU to standardize a second wideband speech coder operating at bit rates of 16, 24, and 32 kbit/s.

Backward ADPCM G.726 and G.727

Speech coders G.726 and G.727 are backward ADPCM coders. They operate on a sample-by-sample basis by predicting the value of the sample and then quantizing the difference between the actual value and the predicted value.

A linear predictor is used based on the two previous output values and the six previous quantizer values. The predictor functions are updated on a sample-by-sample basis in a backward adaptive fashion. The levels of the quantizer are also updated in a backward adaptive fashion. Both coders can operate using 2, 3, 4, or 5 bits/sample, corresponding to rates of 16, 24, 32, and 40 kbit/s.

---

[2]An excellent paper on multimedia technologies (from which this discussion is abstracted, plus my own views) is: R. V. Cox, B. G. Hassle, A. Lacuna, B. Shahraray, and L. Rabiner, "On the Applications of Multimedia Processing to Communications," *Proceedings of the IEEE*, *86*(5), May 1998.

G.727 uses embedded quantizers, while G.726 uses individually optimized quantizers for each of the four bit rates. The principal rate for both coders is 32 kbit/s. The quality at 32 kbit/s is almost equivalent to that of G.711 PCM. The embedded quantizer feature allows the least significant bits to be dropped if there is network congestion, an operation examined later in this chapter. These coders perform well for speech and they also can pass most modem signals below 4800 bit/s with their 32-bit/s rates.

Linear Prediction Analysis-by-Synthesis (LPAS) Coders

The most popular class of speech coders for bit rates between 4.8 and 16 kbit/s are model-based coders that use an LPAS method. A linear prediction model of speech production is excited by an appropriate signal in order to model the signal over time. The parameters of both the speech model and the excitation are estimated and updated at regular time intervals (e.g., every 20 ms) and used to control the speech model. Two LPAS coders are discussed next: the forward adaptive and backward adaptive LPAS coders.

Forward Adaptive LPAS coders—8-kbit/s G.729 and 6.3- and 5.3-kbit/s G.723.1. In a forward adaptive analysis-by-synthesis coder, the prediction filter coefficients and gains are explicitly transmitted. To provide toll-quality performance, these two coders rely on a source model for speech. The excitation signal, in the form of information on the pitch period of the speech, is transmitted as well. The linear predictive coding (LPC) filter is tenth order and is augmented by a pitch predictor. This provides a good model for a speech signal but is not an appropriate model for some noises or for most instrumental music. Thus, the performance of LPAS coders for noisy backgrounds and music is poorer than G.726 and G.727 coders.

For this discussion, please refer to Table 3–4. The information from this table is derived from *IEEE Network*, January/February 1998, and is

Table 3–4   Comparison of G.723.1, G.729, and G.729A

Codec	G.723.1	G.729	G.729A
Bit rate	5.3 / 6.4 kbit/s	8 kbit/s	8 kbit/s
Frame size	30 ms	10 ms	10 ms
Processing delay	30 ms	10 ms	10 ms
Lookahead delay	7.5 ms	5 ms	5 ms
Frame length	20 / 24 bytes	10 bytes	10 bytes

Source: IEEE Network, January/February 1998.

discussed in more detail in Chapter 4. For this discussion, the following definitions are used:

- Bit rate: This parameter is the output rate of the coder.
- Frame size: This parameter represents the length of the voice traffic measured in time. This traffic is placed in voice packets and sent to the receiver.
- Processing delay: This factor represents the delay incurred at the coder to run the voice and coding algorithm on one frame.
- Lookahead delay: Lookahead delay occurs when the coder examines a certain amount of the next frame to provide guidance in coding the current frame. The idea of lookahead is to take advantage of the close correlations existing between successive voice frames.
- Frame length: This value represents the number of bytes resulting from the encoding process (the value excludes headers).

G.723.1 provides toll-quality speech at 6.4 kbit/s.[3] A lower quality speech coder operating at 5.3 kbit/s is also included. G.723.1 was designed with low-bit-rate video telephony in mind. For this application, the delay requirements are less stringent because the video coding delay is usually so much larger than that of speech. The G.723.1 coder has a 30 ms frame size and a 7.5 ms lookahead. When combined with processing delay to implement the coder, it is estimated that the coder would contribute 67.5 ms to the one-way delay. Additional delays result from the use of network and system buffers.

The G.723.1 coder is designed to perform conventional telephone bandwidth filtering (based on G.712) of the voice signal, sample the signal at the conventional 8000 Hz rate (based on G.711), and convert the 16-bit linear PCM code for input to the encoder. The decoder part of the vocoder performs a complementary operation on the output to reconstruct the voice signal.

The vocoder encodes the voice signal into frames-based LPAS coding. A coder is capable of producing two rates of voice traffic: (1) 6.3 kbit/s for the high rate, and (2) 5.3 kbit/s for the low rate. The high rate coder is based on Multipulse Maximum Likelihood Quantization (MP-MLQ), and the low rate coder is based on Algebraic-Code-Excited Linear-Prediction

---

[3]Some of my clients would not agree with this statement. They find G.723.1's speech signals "tinny." I have found some systems that are good and some that are poor.

(ACELP). A coder and decoder must support both rates, and the coder/decoder can switch between the rates between frame boundaries. Music and other audio signals are compressed and decompressed as well, but the coder is optimized for speech.

The encoder operates on frames (blocks) of 240 samples each to support the 8000 kHz sampling rate. Further operations (a high pass filter to remove the DC component) result in four sub-frames of 60 samples each. A variety of other operations occur, such as the computation of an LPC filter and unquantized LCP filter coefficients, resulting in a packetization time of 30 ms. For every subframe, a tenth order LPC filter is calculated using the unprocessed input signal. The filter on the last subframe is quantized with a predictive split vector quantizer (PSVQ). Q.923.1 uses LPC predictor coefficients and a forward estimation of the signals, which avoids the older backward estimation of the vocal tract (the latter is not as accurate as the vocal signal changes rapidly). As stated earlier, the lookahead takes 7.5 ms, so the coding delay is 37.5 ms. This delay is a significant factor in evaluating coders, especially for transporting speech through a data network, since less delay in the coding (and decoding) process means more latitude to deal with the inevitable delay (and variable delay) found in internets.

The decoder operates also on a frame basis. The decoding process occurs as follows (a general summary of G.723.1):

- The quantized LPC indices are decoded.
- The LPC synthesis filter is constructed.
- On each subframe, the adaptive codebook excitation and fixed codebook excitation are decoded and input to the synthesis filter.
- The excitation signal is input into a pitch postfilter, and then into a synthesis filter.
- This is input into a formant postfilter, which uses a gain scaling unit to maintain the energy at the input level of the formant postfilter.

Silence compression.   Silence compression has been used for a number of years to exploit the fact that silent periods in a voice conversation occupy about 50% of the total time of the conversation. The idea is to reduce the number of bits sent during these silent intervals and save in the overall number of bits transmitted.

For many years in the telephony network, selected analog speech signals have been processed through time-assigned speech interpolation

(TASI). This technology places other speech or data signals into the silent periods of a conversation, which provides additional capacity on multichannel links. Today, the concepts of TASI are applied to digital signals and tagged with new names—one example is TDMA. To review briefly, TDMA breaks down the conventional signals into small digitized segments (slots). These slots are time division multiplexed with other slots into one channel.

G.723.1 uses silence compression by executing discontinuous transmission operations, which means that artificial noise (at reduced bit ates) is inserted into the bit stream during silent periods. In addition to conserving bandwidth, this technique keeps the transmitter's modem in continuous operation, and avoids the tasks of switching the carrier on and off.

G.729 is designed for low-delay applications, with a frame size of only 10 ms, a processing delay of 10 ms, and a lookahead of 5 ms. This yields a 25-ms contribution to end-to-end delay and a bit rate of 8 kbit/s. These delay performances are important in an internet, because we have learned that any factor decreasing delay is important.

G.729 comes in two versions: G.729 and G.729A. The original version is more complex than G.723.1, while the Annex A version is less complex than G.723.1. The two versions are compatible but their performance is somewhat different, the lower complexity version (G.729) having slightly lower quality. Both coders include provision for dealing with frame erasures and packet-loss concealment, making them good choices for use with voice over the Internet. Cox and colleagues (see footnote 2) state that the G.729 performance for random bit errors is poorer and do not recommend them for use on channels with random bit errors unless there is a channel coder (forward error correction, and convolutional coding, discussed in the wireless section of this book) to protect the most sensitive bits.

Backward Adaptive LPAS Coding—16 kbit/s G.728 Low Delay Code Book Excitation Linear Prediction (LD-CELP). G.728 is a hybrid between the lower bit rate linear predictive analysis-by-synthesis coders (G.729 and G.723.1) and the backward ADPCM coders.

G.728 is an LD-CELP coder, and operates on five samples at a time. It uses LPC analysis to create three different linear predictors. The first is a fiftieth-order prediction filter for the next sample values. The second is a tenth-order prediction filter that guides the quantizer step size. The third is a perceptual weighting filter that is used to select the excitation signal.

CELP is speech-coding technique in which the excitation signal is selected from a set of possible excitation signals through an exhaustive search. While the lower rate speech coders use a forward adaptation scheme for the sample value prediction filter, LD-CELP uses a backward adaptive filter that is updated every 2.5 ms. There are 1024 possible excitation vectors. These vectors are further decomposed into four possible gains, two possible signs (+ or −), and 128 possible shape vectors.

G.728 is a suggested speech coder for low-bit-rate (56–128 kbit/s) ISDN video telephony. Because of its backward adaptive nature, it is a low-delay coder, but it is more complex than the other coders, because the fiftieth-order LPC analysis must be repeated at the decoder. It also provides an adaptive postfilter that enhances its performance.

Although LPC analysis is widely associated with speech, the fiftieth-order LPC filter can capture the underlying redundancy in music. G.728 exhibits very high quality and is considered equivalent in performance to 32-kbit/s G.726 and G.727 ADPCM. Because of the adaptive postfilter, there is a frame- or packet-loss concealment strategy for G.728 that is under consideration by the ITU-T. G.728 is quite robust to random bit errors, more so than any other speech coder. Moreover, the sensitivity to bit errors is roughly equal for all ten bits in a code word.

Parameter Speech Coders—2.4-kbit/s Mixed-Excitation LPC (MELP)

Parametric speech coders assume a generic speech model with a simplified excitation signal and thus are able to operate at the lowest bit rates. All of the speech coders discussed previously can be described as *waveform following*. Their output signals are similar in shape and phase to the input signal.

Parametric speech coders are different, and they do not exhibit waveform following. They are based on an analysis-synthesis model for speech signals that can be represented using relatively few parameters. These parameters are extracted and quantized, usually on a regular basis from every 20–40 ms. At the receiver, the parameters are used to create a synthetic speech signal. Under ideal conditions, the synthetic signal sounds like the original speech. Under harsh enough background noise conditions, any parametric coder will fail because the input signal is not well modeled by the inherent speech model. The 2.4 kbit/s MELP was selected as the U.S. government's new 2.4 bit/s speech coder for secure telephony.

For multimedia applications, the study from Cox and colleagues states that parametric coders are a good choice when there is a need for low bit rates. For example, parametric coders are often used for single user games. This keeps down the storage requirements for speech. For the same reason, they also are a good choice for some types of multimedia messaging. They tend to be lower in absolute quality for all types of speech conditions and particularly noisy background conditions. This shortcoming can be overcome when the speech files can be carefully edited in advance. At the present time, most of the parametric coders being used in such applications are not standards. Rather, they are proprietary coders that have been adapted to work for such applications.

G.721.3 SCALABLE CODING FOR WIRELESS APPLICATIONS

Annex C of G.723.1 specifies a channel coding scheme that can be used with a triple rate speech codec. The channel codec is scalable in bit rate and is designed for mobile multimedia applications as a part of the overall H.324 family of standards.

A range of channel codec bit rates is supported ranging from 0.7 kbit/s up to 14.3 kbit/s. The channel codec supports all three operational modes of the G.732.1 codec, namely high rate, low rate and discontinuous transmission modes.

The channel codec uses punctured convolutional codes. Based on the subjective importance of each class of information bits, the available channel codec bit rate is allocated optimally to the bit classes. This allocation is based on an algorithm that is known by the encoder and decoder. Each time the system control signals either a change in the G.723.1 rate or in the available channel codec bit rate, this algorithm is executed to adapt the channel codec to the new speech service configuration.

If a low channel codec bit rate is available, the subjectively most sensitive bits are protected first. When increasing the channel codec bit rate, the additional bits are used first to protect more information bits and second to increase the protection of the already protected classes.

Prior to the application of the channel encoding functions, the speech parameters are partly modified in a channel adaptation layer to improve their robustness against transmission errors.

COMPARISON OF SPEED CODERS

To conclude the discussion on standardized coders, Table 3–5 compares several coders with regard to bit rate, Mean Opinion Score (MOS), complexity (with G.711 as the base), and delay (frame size and look-ahead time).

Table 3–5   Speech Coding Standards

Standard	Coding Type	Bit Rate kbit/s	MOS	Complexity	Delay (ms)
G.711	PCM	64	4.3	1	0.125
G.726	ADPCM	32	4.0	10	0.125
G.728	LD-CELP	16	4.0	50	0.625
GSM	RPE_LTP	13	3.7	5	20
G.729	CSA-CELP	8	4.0	30	15
G.729A				15	
G.723.1	A-CELP	6.3	3.8	25	37.5
	MP-MLQ	5.3			
US Dod FS1015	LPC-10	2.4	synthetic	10	22.5

Source: S. Rudkin, A. Grace, M. W. Whybray, "Real-Time Applications on the Internet." *BT Journal, 15*(2), April 1997.

PROPRIETARY CODERS

The G series coders are lagging behind the industry (as does most any standard). Today, proprietary coders are available that provide high MOS with very low bit rates. I cite one of these coders in this section, the Digital Voice System, Inc. coder.[4] This coder has been chosen for use on the satellite-based Iridium system. The following description is abstracted from DSI's technical documents.

Most CELP speech coders make a single determination as to whether each speech segment is a periodic (voiced) signal or a noise-like (unvoiced) signal. One difference between CELP coders and the DSI speech coder is that the DSI coder divides each segment of speech into distinct frequency bands and makes a voiced/unvoiced (V/UV) decision for each frequency band. This allows the excitation signal for a particular speech segment to be a mixture of periodic (voiced) and noise-like (unvoiced) energy. This added degree of freedom in the modeling of the excitation signal allows the DSI speech model to generate higher quality speech than conventional speech models. In addition, it allows the DSI speech model to be robust in the presence of background noise.

A problem with linear-prediction based speech coders is that the linear prediction model does not yield high quality speech (or robustness-to-background noise) without the addition of a prediction residual. The pre-

[4]DSI can be reached at www.http://dusinc.com.

diction residual can be viewed as an error signal which corrects for inaccuracies in the linear prediction model. Elimination of this residual, as is
done in the U.S. government standard 2.4 kbit/s LPC-10 system, results
in a harsh, mechanical quality in the speech. Consequently, all high
quality linear predictive speech coders transmit a residual.

The primary difference between these systems is the manner in
which they accomplish this task. The favored method used in linear predictive speech coding at rates below 8 kbit/s is to divide the residual into
small pieces or vectors and to then search through a codebook to find the
code vector that is the closest match. Searching through a reasonable-
sized codebook is a computationally complex task. Furthermore, a particular codebook is designed to operate at a fixed date rate and is not easily
scalable to other data rates.

The DSI speech coders are not based upon linear prediction. Instead, they use the Multi-Band Excitation speech model to produce
speech without the need for a residual signal. They maintain speech in-
telligibility and naturalness at rates as low as 2.4 kbit/s. In addition, the
DSI speech coders do not require the use of codebooks. Consequently,
this system requires fewer computations than either CELP or VSELP.
The speech coders can be scaled to data rates above 2.4 kbit/s.

I refer you to the web site in footnote 4 for more information. DSI
states that its 4.8 coder rated a 3.849 MOS in a test with an 8 kbit/s
G.729 coder (MOS 3.63), a 32 kbit/s G.726A coder (MOS 3.589), a 13 kbit/
GSM coder (MOS 3.182), and so on.

TRANSPORT OF THE TRAFFIC

Assuming the use of a VoIP gateway, as shown in Figure 3–4, after
the digitized frames are created by the coder, they are encapsulated into
the Real Time Protocol (RTP). They are transported through the IP net-

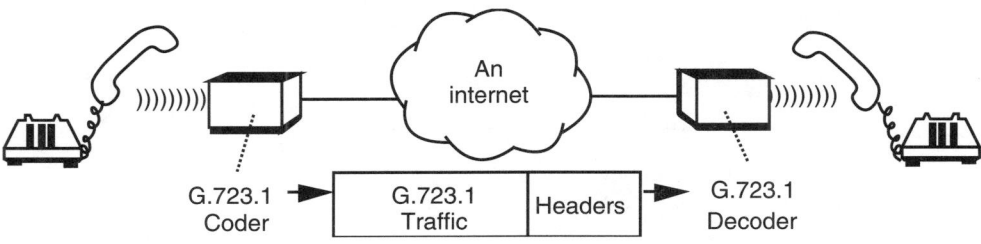

Figure 3–4   Transport of G.723.1 traffic.

work and passed to the decoder. The decoder converts the digital images to the output voice signal, which is played out to the receiver. G.723.1 is used as the example here, but other coders may be employed.

PACKETIZED VOICE

All digitized speech is encapsulated into "packets" for transmission across the communications links. The term *packet* is used here in a generic sense. Some implementations call the packet a frame, others a block, and others a cell. Whatever the term used, the digital speech bits have header information added to them for the purpose of managing the speech payload, and delivering it to the end user.

This part of the chapter explains one method of packetized voice, published in ITU-T G.764. While G.764 is "old" (it was published in 1990), it provides a good model to allow us to explore some additional issues about transporting voice through data networks, such as the playback of noise and selective discards.

Previous discussions in this book have explained that a certain amount of traffic loss (packet discard, misrouting, etc.) for voice is tolerable and acceptable. The amount of loss that can occur is quite variable, ranging from 1% to 10%, depending on (1) how the voice images are sampled, (2) how they are compressed and coded in the packet, and (3) how they may be discarded. For systems that do not selectively discard traffic,

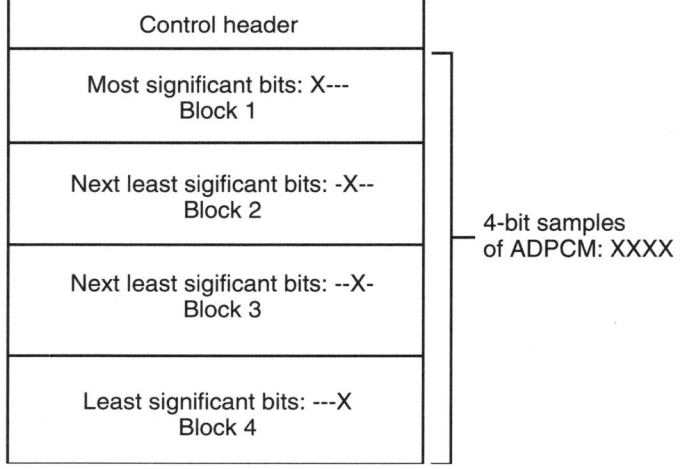

Figure 3–5   Grouping the bits of the samples.

the tolerable loss is lower; for systems that selectively discard traffic, the tolerable loss is higher.

To explain the rationale for these three suppositions, we will use an example of a digitized voice image of 32 kbit/s. This technique carries 4 bits per sample (4 * 8000 samples per second = 32,000). As Figure 3–5 shows, the voice samples for a 32 kbit/s image are placed into a packet with the 4 bits of each sample grouped together based on the arithmetic significance of each bit in each sample. That is, the least significant bits (---X) are grouped together, followed by the next least significant bits (--X-), and so on. Since ADPCM (adaptive pulse code modulation) uses 4 bits per sample, the packet contains 4 blocks, one for each bit of the 4-bit sample, and a control header, which is explained shortly.

Let us assume two of the samples in the packet of 4 bits are coded as: (1) 15_{10} or 1111_2 and (2) 7_{10} or 0111_2. Of course, if a full sample is discarded, all 4 bits of the sample are not available for the digital-to-analog conversion process at the receiver. However, since the bits are not encoded in the packet on a sample-by-sample basis, but rather on the arithmetically significant positions of the bits in the samples, the selective discarding of bits is not so severe.

To see why, consider that a router (an advanced router, to be sure) is experiencing congestion and determines that it must shed traffic. The packet header contains a block dropping indicator field to track the status of the blocks. (This indicator is explained shortly.) So, the block in the packet containing the least significant bits is dropped. The effect of the samples is (where x is the discarded bit of the samples):

$$15_{10} \text{ or } 1111_2 \text{ is now } 14_{10} \text{ or } 111x_2$$

$$7_{10} \text{ or } 0111_2 \text{ is now } 6_{10} \text{ or } 011x_2$$

This slight change in the sample translates to a different PAM pulse at the receiver, but the distortion is not severe.

Figure 3–6 shows the speech stream is coded into the packet in 16 ms time slots. Each packet contains 128 4-bit samples. This coding convention results in a 32 kbit/s transmission stream, based on the following calculations (and depicted graphically in the figure):

$$1 \text{ second } / 8000 \text{ samples per second} = \text{a } .000125 \text{ sample interval}$$
$$.000125 \times .016 = .016 \text{ packet interval}$$

The packet in the figure is 64 octets in length (512 bits). Therefore, the 32 kbit/s transmission stream is derived by:

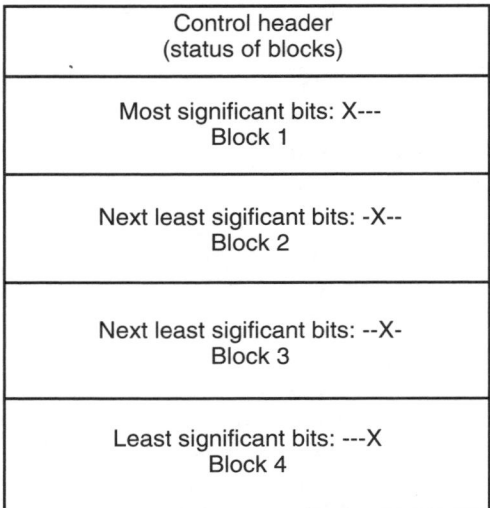

Packet interval: 1 sec./8000 = .000125; .000125 × 128 = .016
Bit rate: 1 sec. / .016 × 512 bits (64 byte packet) = 32,000

Figure 3–6   Voice packet interval and bit rate.

$$1 \text{ second} / .016 = 62.5$$
$$62.5 \times 512 \text{ bits} = 32,000$$

The number of blocks in the 16 ms interval depends upon the type of coding used. For example, if 8 bits were carried per sample, then 8 blocks would be needed, and a 64,000 bit rate is required. Table 3–6 shows the number of blocks collected during the 16 ms interval based on the coding type used.

Most voice packet systems also employ digital speech interpolation (DSI), which does not generate packets during periods of silence in a voice conversation. This allows more voice channels to be multiplexed on any given media. Thus, a system such as AT&T's Integrated Access and Cross-Connect System (IACS) uses a combination of ADPCM and DSI to multiplex 96 voice channels onto a DS1 1.544 Mbit/s channel and 120 voice channels onto a CEPT1 2.048 Mbit/s channel.

Furthermore, block dropping decreases the bursty aspect of digitized voice by smoothing the queues. It has also been demonstrated that this process increases the system capacity by some 20 to 25%.

Table 3–6   Blocks Collected During the Packetization Interval

Coding Type	Number of Blocks
8 bit/sample	8
1 bit/sample	1
2 bit/sample	2
3 bit/sample	3
4 bit/sample	4
5 bit/sample	5
6 bit/sample	6
7 bit/sample	7
8 bit PCM (A-law or μ-law)	8
2 bit/sample ADPCM	2
3 bit/sample ADPCM	3
4 bit/sample ADPCM	4
5 bit/sample ADPCM	5
(4,2) embedded ADPCM	4
(5,2) embedded ADPCM	5
(8,6) embedded ADPCM	8

The ITU-T G.764 Voice Packet Format

The format for the ITU-T G.764 voice packet is shown in Figure 3–7. To simplify this discussion, the octet and bit positions are not shown. The packet is encapsulated into a High Level Data Link Control (HDLC) type header, which contains an address field, a command/response bit (not used), and a frame type field. The address field is a conventional data link connection identifier (DLCI). The frame type is an HDLC unnumbered information type (UI), and can also be coded to indicate if a cyclic redundancy check (CRC) with the frame check sequence is performed on the frame header and packet header or on the entire frame. The former is called the unnumbered information with header check (UIH).

This option does not protect the voice bits because the dropping of blocks does not require the recalculation of the CRC, and retransmissions in the event of an error are not performed due to the sensitivity of voice traffic to delay.

The *protocol discriminator* is preset to 01000100. The *block dropping indicator* contains several fields. One field contains two bits, labeled as C1 and C2. These bits are set to indicate how many blocks are droppable as follows: 00 = no droppable blocks; 01 = one droppable block; 10 = two droppable blocks; 11 = three droppable blocks. C1 and C2 are changed

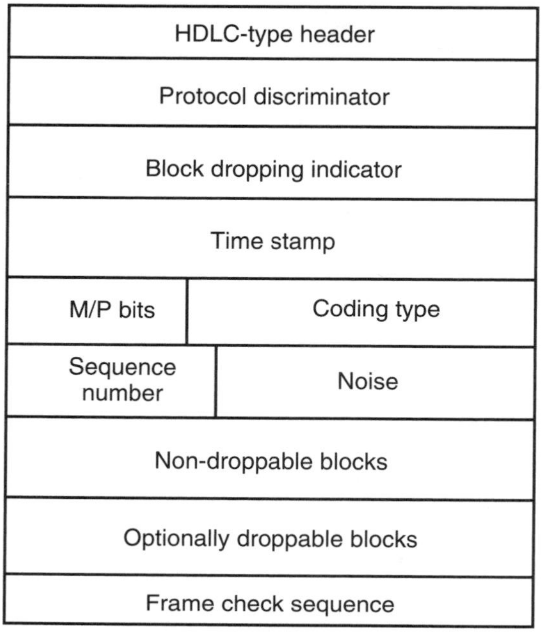

HDLC-type header
Protocol discriminator
Block dropping indicator
Time stamp

M/P bits	Coding type
Sequence number	Noise

Non-droppable blocks
Optionally droppable blocks
Frame check sequence

where:
  M/P   More/Poll bits

Figure 3–7   Format of G.764 voice packet.

when a block is dropped to indicate how many blocks are still available for dropping.

The *timestamp* field records the cumulative delay encountered as the packet makes its journey through the network. Its value is not to exceed 200 ms.

The *coding type* field indicates the specific analog-to-digital technique used. The coding of this field must adhere with the ITU-T conventions shown in Table 3–6.

The *M bit* (more data bit) is set to 1 for all packets of a voice burst, except the last packet in the burst. The receiver uses this bit to learn that all samples have arrived. The *P bit* (poll bit) is not used and is set to zero.

The *SN* is used at the receiver during the building of the voice burst. It is used to note the first packet in the burst, and also to note if a packet has been lost. The value is incremented by 1 for each subsequent packet in the signal. The SN is used with the time stamp to assure that variable delay is removed for the process.

Since this technique uses DSI, a *noise field* indicates the level of background noise that is to be played in the absence of packets. These bits must be coded in accordance with the ITU-T specifications, shown in Table 3–7.

Packet Decoding and Voice Playout

To properly decode voice packets, they must arrive at the receiver (terminating endpoint) experiencing almost non-variable delay. However, since variable delay is inevitable due to queuing and switching operations in the network, the receiver masks the variability of the delay through the use of the timestamp (TS) value in the packet header.

For this operation to work correctly, the system must define a maximum allowable delay. This can be defined when a permanent virtual circuit is provisioned, when a connection VC is created on demand, or in any manner deemed appropriate by the network administrator. Additionally, the terminating endpoint must check the TS value in the packet as part of this operation, compare it to a predefined constant delay value (CDV),

Table 3–7   Noise Field Format

Bit Number	Noise Level
4321	(dBmc0)
0000	Idle code
0001	16.6
0010	19.7
0011	22.6
0100	24.9
0101	26.9
0110	29.0
0111	31.0
1000	32.8
1001	34.6
1010	36.2
1011	37.9
1100	39.7
1101	41.6
1110	43.8
1111	46.6

and determine if the packet is to be buffered, released to the decoding application, or discarded.

Figure 3–8 shows four possible scenarios that may occur when voice packets reach the receiver. After the cell headers are processed, the terminating endpoint compares the timestamp to the CDV (100 ms in this example). In scenario 1, the packet has arrived with TS = 80 ms, which means it took 80 ms to traverse the network from the originating endpoint to the terminating endpoint. Since 100 – 80 = 20, the packet is held for 20 ms before being given to the decoding application.

In scenario 2, the endpoint has no packets to play out. So, it examines the M bit of the previous packet for this speech signal (which it must buffer). If M = 0, the gap is legitimate, and the noise field in the previous packet is used to play out appropriate background noise.

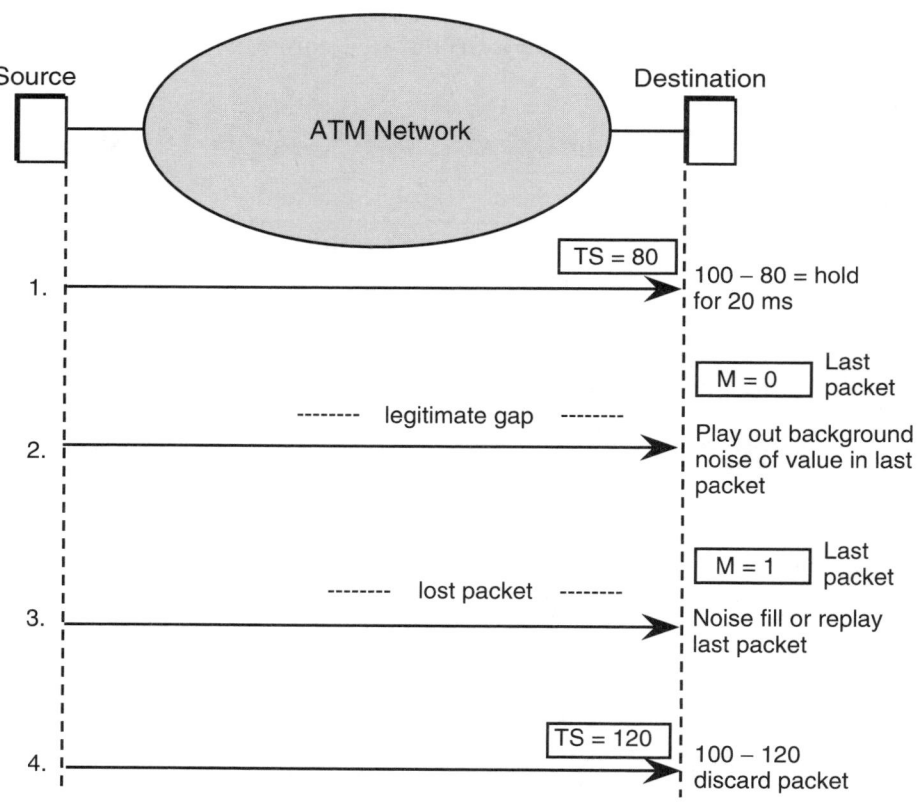

Figure 3–8   Build-out operations at the receiver.

Scenario 3 is the same as scenario 2 in that the endpoint has no packets to play out. In this case, the M bit of the previous packet is 1. Therefore, a packet is lost, and the terminating endpoint creates a noise fill, replays the previous packet, and so on. This interpolation procedure has not yet been defined in any of the standards, and the ITU-T cites it as for "further study."

In scenario 4, the packet arrives later than the CDV (120 ms in the timestamp), and the packet is discarded.

ONCE AGAIN: SYNCHRONOUS VERSUS ASYNCHRONOUS AND CBR VERSUS VBR

My explanations of packetized voice once again emphasize the involved machinations needed to support CBR, synchronous telephony traffic in a VBR, asynchronous data network.

Yet, the voice/data network is inevitable. Moreover, we know how to create the multimedia network to support all applications. Given enough bandwidth and processing power, the problems are solved with "brute force"! But, I digress. Let us finish the chapter by seeing how packetized video can be supported in the Internet.

DIGITIZED VIDEO: THE MPEG-2 STANDARDS

The ISO Motion Pictures Experts Group-2 (MPEG) standard, named MPEG-2, is a recent standard for high-quality audio and video applications. Originally, MPEG-1 was developed to standardize monaural sound systems. Now, MPEG-2 provides stereo and multichannel capabilities.

The MPEG-2 standards are viewed by some people to define video compression and the coding of the compressed video images into messages. While compression is an important component in MPEG-2, it is only one component. MPEG-2 defines other components besides video compression. Certainly one of the important parts of a video image (or most of them) is the associated audio, and MPEG-2 defines the use of audio as well.

Table 3–8 lists the MPEG-2 standards, as published by ISO (The International Standards Organization), which obviously encompass considerably more than video.

Table 3–8   MPEG-2 Standards

ISO Standard	Purpose
13818–1	System description
13818–2	Video operations
13818–3	Audio operation
13818–4	Compliance statements
13818–5	Software simulation
13818–6	Digital storage media
13818–9	Real-time interface for decoders
13818–10	Digital storage media script format

BASIC OPERATIONS OF MPEG-2

Figure 3–9 shows the basic operations of a packetized (digitized) video system using the MPEG-2 specification. The audio and video images are converted to digital streams and packetized by an encoder. Several headers are appended to the traffic in order to identity it and provide guidance to the decoder at the receiving end as to how to reassemble the images and play them back to the user.

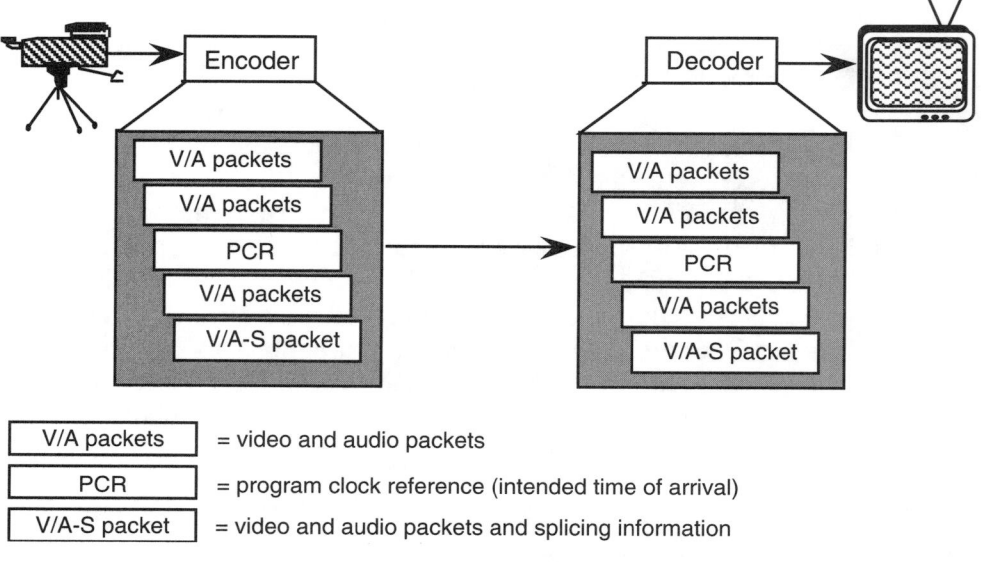

V/A packets	= video and audio packets
PCR	= program clock reference (intended time of arrival)
V/A-S packet	= video and audio packets and splicing information

Figure 3–9   MPEG-2: The basic operations.

MPEG-2 contains fields in these headers to instruct the decoder on the proper timing of the playback. The program reference clock (PCR) is used for time base recovery and contains the value indicating the intended time of arrival of the traffic. The decoder uses this clock to establish a synchronous relationship with the encoder. Splicing information is also provided, which directs the decoder how to place the packets together and splice together the video and audio streams.

Examples of MPEG-2 Operations

MPEG-2 supports a wide variety of operations. Two examples in Figure 3–10 will give you an idea of these operations. For the first example, refer to Figure 3–10a. It is possible that a system may lose its time base; that is, the system clock may fail. A more probable situation is when a link goes down that was sending the clock information to a device. Whatever the failure may be, the MPEG-2 encoder notifies the MPEG-2 decoder when such a situation arises by sending a packet containing a discontinuity indicator. When the decoder receives this information, it knows that there is a problem with the incoming time stamps. How the decoder handles the problem is up to the decoder. It may resort to an internal clock, or continue to use the clock references in the incoming stream of traffic.

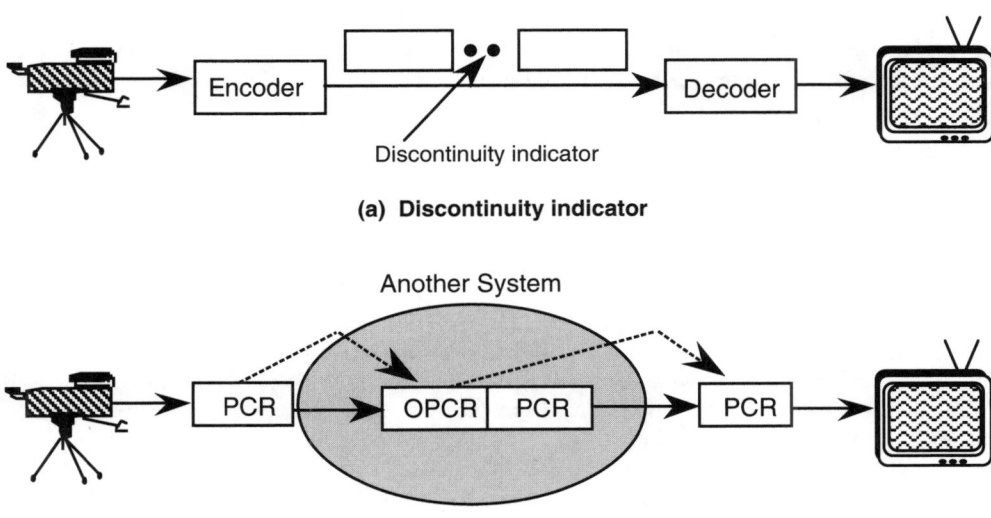

(a) Discontinuity indicator

(b) Original program clock reference (OPCR)

Figure 3–10   Other operations of MPEG-2.

For the second example, refer to Figure 3–10b. In some systems, a real-time image, such as voice or video, may be processed by an another system that has a different timing reference than the originating system. If this situation arises in an MPEG-2 environment, the sender's program reference clock (PCR) is transported through the intervening network by mapping the PCR into another field, called the original PCR (OPCR). The intervening network uses its own PCR for its operations. At the egress point of the intervening network, the OPCR is mapped back into the PCR for the encoder's use. In this manner, clocking is preserved between the encoder and the decoder.

MPEG-2 Compression

Notwithstanding the fact that MPEG-2 is more than a compression technique, the compression aspect of the specification is one key to its effectiveness. A brief review of MPEG-2's compression operations is provided here. Figure 3–11 provides a general view of the MPEG-2 operations.

MPEG-2 takes advantage of the fact that the human eye and brain are less sensitive to color than to black and white images.[5] Moreover, the eye and brain are less sensitive to color changes, so MPEG-2 performs compression by reducing the amount of information per image, which is based on a human's audio and video perception capabilities.

In essence, MPEG-2:[6] (1) removes information that is less sensitive to the eye. A code carries an approximation of the image (and through quantization, part of the information is lost and cannot be recovered); (2) uses variable length codes to represent information, with short codes for patterns that occur often, and long codes for patterns that occur less frequently; (3) uses motion estimation between frames to find closely correlated movements and inserts codes to show the difference in movements between frames (and not the absolute movement itself).

---

[5]Two different kinds of receptors are located in the eye, rods and cones. Rods (about 120 million on the retina) are concerned with black and white, and cones (about 8 million on the retina) distinguish between different colors. The cones are sensitive to red, green, and blue colors. Rods are more sensitive to light intensity. The center of the retina contains cones, and farther away from the center of the retina is a higher distribution of rods. Viewing objects directly in the center of the eye lens means that more cones are used, and that direct viewing (focusing on an object) allows us to distinguish color better. Viewing peripheral objects are perceived more as black and white (at least with less color).

[6]For more information on this technique, refer to the standards cited in this material. In addition, see: M. Orzessek and P. Sommer, *ATM and MPEG-2,* Hewlett-Packard Professional Books, ISBN 0-13-243700-7.

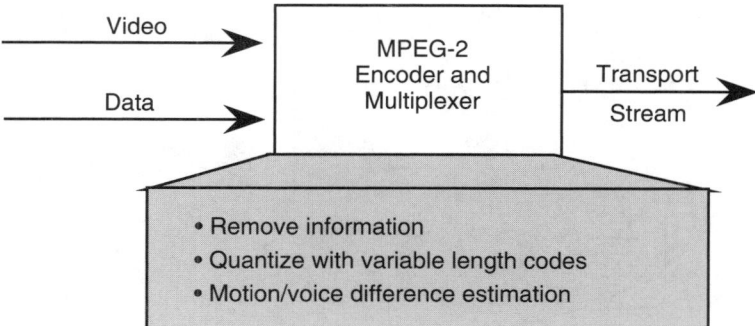

Figure 3–11   The major components of MPEG-2 operations.

For audio traffic, MPEG-2 uses some of the same techniques. For example, reducing the bits per sample by carrying the differences between successive samples instead of the absolute value of the sample. The video compression operations are based on the audio compression techniques, which have been used in the industry for many years.

MPEG-2 assumes that a constant, nonvariable delay is needed on an end-to-end basis between the video sender and the video receiver. Even though variable delay will be experienced, the system must be able to compensate for this variability by removing the variable delay (jitter) at the receiver.

The delay buildup occurs in buffers at the sender, the receiver, and any nodes in between that perform buffering operations. Even with circuit-switched systems, there is some delay (although very small) at the circuit switch, as the traffic is moved from the ingress port across the time slot interchange (TSI) switching fabric to the egress port. However, once the connection is set up, this delay is constant at each node. In addition, the delay on the communications link is, for all purposes, constant. Very slight deviations may occur at repeaters, but this delay is not considered significant enough to factor into the delay model, shown in Figure 3–12.

However, for systems that buffer traffic, such as IP, the delay is not constant. Since the cells that arrive at a node are held in a buffer (even if for a very short time) jitter will accumulate. Therefore, the support of real-time voice and video traffic requires the network reduce the variable delay as much as possible. It also requires that the receiving node be able to compensate for these timing variations.

For Internet-based systems, the delay at the nodes is variable since buffers hold the traffic while awaiting for an available egress port and its

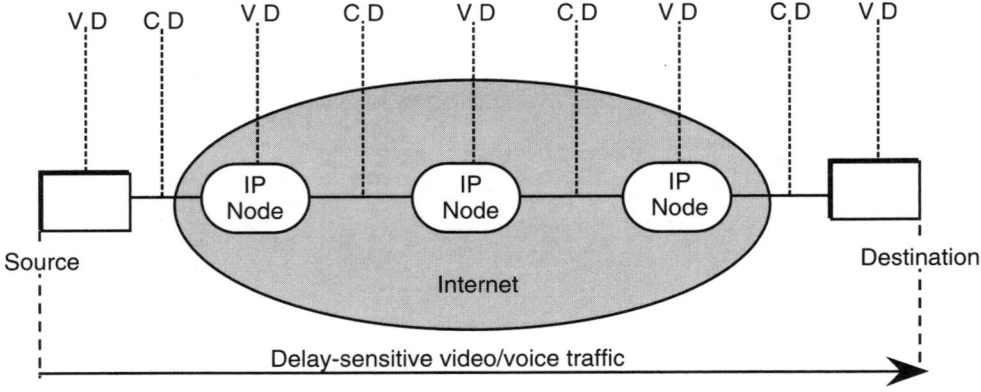

where:
   CD   Constant delay
   VD   Variable delay

Figure 3–12   The timing model.

output buffer. Granted, the variability of this delay is small, but it does exist, and builds more variability into the traffic flow as more intermediate nodes are traversed from the sender to the receiver.

The approach used by MPEG-2 is to manage the buffer delay with timestamps (see Figure 3–13). The timestamps, which are called the program reference clock (PCR), are placed into the MPEG-2 packets by the encoder and used at the decoder to smooth the traffic into a constant

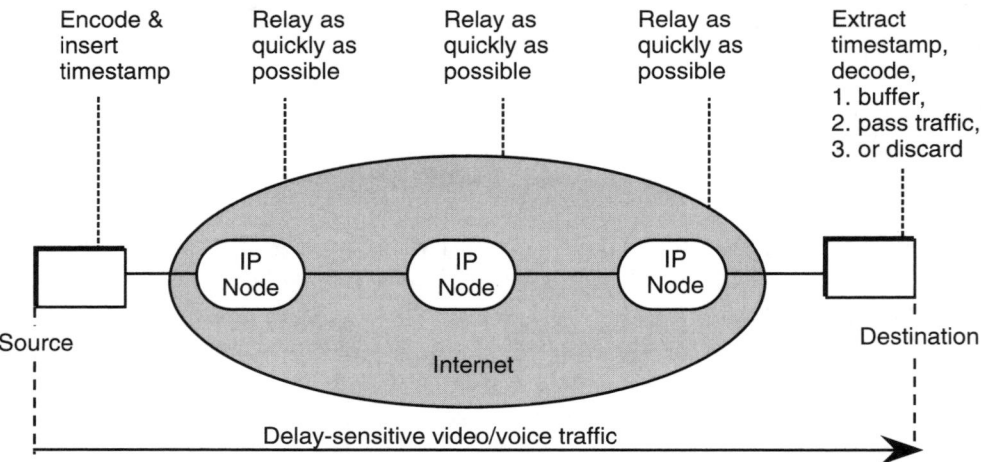

Figure 3–13   MPEG-2 timestamps.

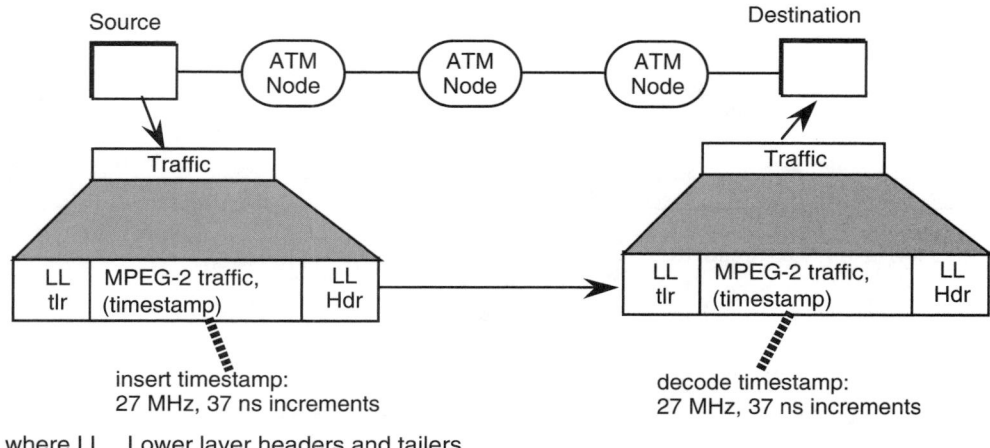

where LL   Lower layer headers and tailers

Figure 3–14   Operations between sender and receiver.

delay. If the traffic arrives experiencing excessive jitter, the decoder may discard the traffic. If it arrives early, it will be held in a buffer, then played out to the application in a manner that creates a constant delay stream from the sender to the receiver.

Excessive jitter can lead to unacceptable video images or audio sound at the receiving application. To combat this problem, MPEG-2 defines a clock that is accurate within 30 ppm (parts per million). The timestamp is used at the decoder to regenerate the system time clock (STC) that was used at the encoder.

This recovered STC can contain some inaccuracies, but not much. The program clock reference (PCR) operates at 27 MHz, and the recovered STC can vary plus or minus by 810 Hz from the 27 MHz at the encoder. The 27 MHz frequency means the clock is incremented every 37 ns. To accommodate a 24-hour day, the timestamp is 42 bits in length. Figure 3–14 depicts the timestamp process.

MPEG-2 Streams

As Figure 3–15 illustrates, MPEG-2 transmissions are "packaged" into streams. The first package is an elementary stream (ES), which consists of compressed video, voice, data, or control traffic. Each of these streams is a separate stream, but they are placed into a packetized elementary stream (PES), which contains a variable number of bits of a specific ES. Each PES contains fields used at the receiving decoder to recover the clock. More on these fields shortly.

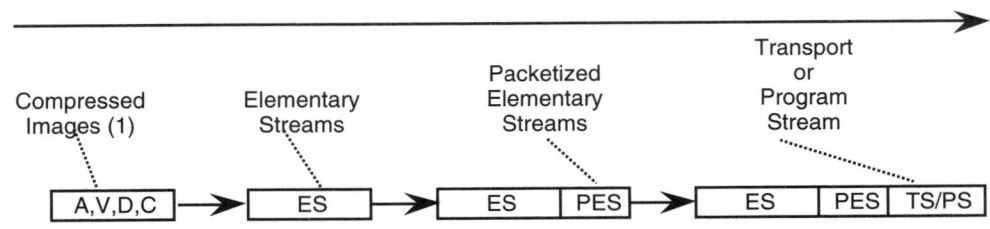

(1): Some data (D) or control (C) images may not be compressed

(a) Flow of operations

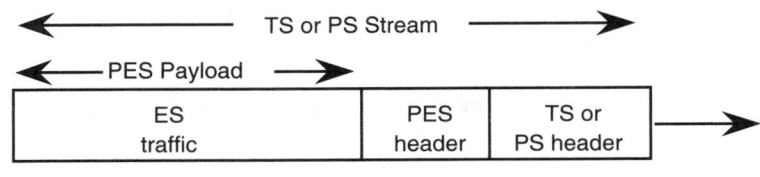

(b) The TS and PS streams

where:

A	Audio
C	Control
D	Data
ES	Elementary stream
PES	Packetized elementary streams
PM	Program stream
TS	Transport stream
V	Video

Figure 3–15   MPEG-2 stream multiplexing.

The PES is packaged into either a transport stream (TS) or a program stream (PS). These units are the output from a multiplexer and are composed of all related PESs (audio, video, data) for a specific program.

Program streams are used in an error-free environment and are appropriate for non-networked applications, because each PS carries a single program, which is variable in length and may be long. Program streams are similar to MPEG-1 streams (the earlier version of MPEG-2). Transport streams are used in an environment with a higher bit error rate (BER) than program streams and are used when traffic is transported over a network.

I introduced the concept of streams in the previous discussion. MPEG-2 distinguishes between two kinds of bit streams: program streams (PS) and transport streams (TS), which were introduced in the previous discussion. Program streams are designed to be used in a relatively error-free environment, such as CD-ROM applications and hard disks. Each program stream is long, and each PS carries a single program. The long data structure is possible since errors are rare, and the probability of losing traffic is small. Program streams can carry timing information that is generated during the multiplexing process from a system clock reference.

Transport streams are designed for use in an environment that is more error-prone, such as communications links and networks. The transport stream is a fixed-length unit of 188 bytes. Transport streams are used to carry MPEG-2 programs between MPEG-2 users.

Figure 3–16 shows how MPEG-2 accepts different programs (audio, video, etc.), processes them into elementary streams (ESs), then packetized elementary streams (PESs), then into TSs or PSs.

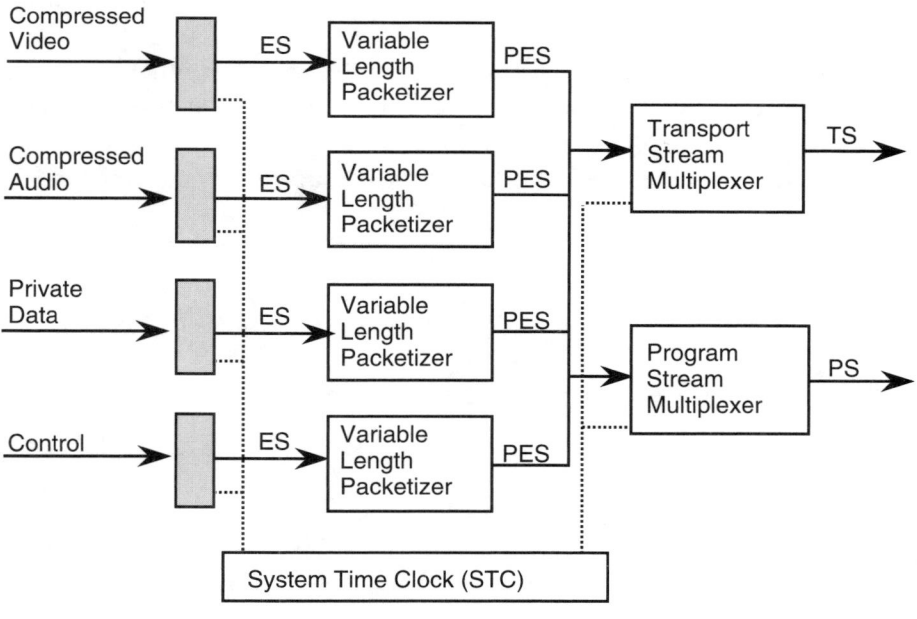

where:

ES	Elementary streams
PES	Packetized elementary streams
PS	Program stream
TS	Transport stream

Figure 3–16   Stream multiplexing.

Figure 3–17 shows the packet format of the transport stream. It consists of a 4-byte header and an 188-byte payload. The contents of the header are as follows:

- *Sync byte:* Preset to hexadecimal 47 to identify the beginning of the transport unit.
- *Transport error indicator:* Set to connote an error in the transport unit.
- *Payload unit start indicator:* Indicates if the first byte in the payload is the beginning of a payload unit.
- *Transport priority:* If set to 1, indicates that this packet is a higher priority than others with the same PID
- *Packet identifier:* Unique identifier of the elementary stream.
- *Transport scrambling control:* Identifies the scrambling method used in the payload.
- *Adaptation field control:* Indicates whether the TS packet contains an adaptation field.
- *Continuity header:* A counter that is incremented with the creation and sending of each packet with the same packet identifier. Used to ascertain packet loss.
- *Adaptation field:* An optional adaptation field, discussed next.

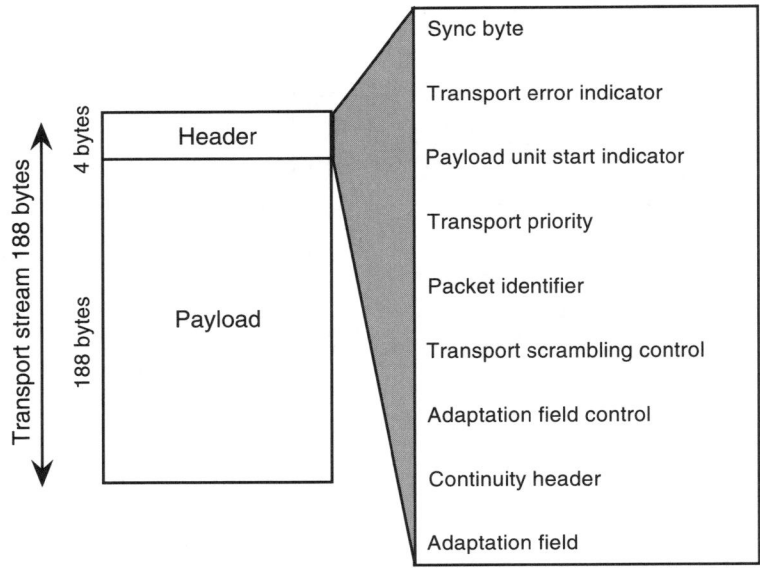

Figure 3–17   The MPEG-2 header.

Figure 3–18 shows the format of the adaptation field. The contents of this field are as follows:

- *Length:* Length of the field.
- *Discontinuity indicator:* Indicates two types of discontinuities. System time-base discontinuities are used for a PID designated as a PCR PID to indicate that the next PCR for the associated program represents a sample of a new system time clock. The continuity_counter discontinuity is used to indicate a problem with the continuity counter (not continuous from one transport stream to the next).
- *Random access indicator:* A field that is set (to 1) to indicate that the current transport stream packet (with the same PID) contains some information to aid in locating specific types of traffic in the payload (first byte of a video frame, first byte of an audio frame).
- *ES streams indicator:* Set to 1 to indicate that the elementary stream carried within the transport stream is of a higher priority than other payloads in the stream.
- *Flags:* Indicate which of the optional fields are in the packet.
- *Optional fields:* Discussed next.
- *Stuffing byte:* An 8-bit value that can be inserted by the encoder, and discarded by the decoder.

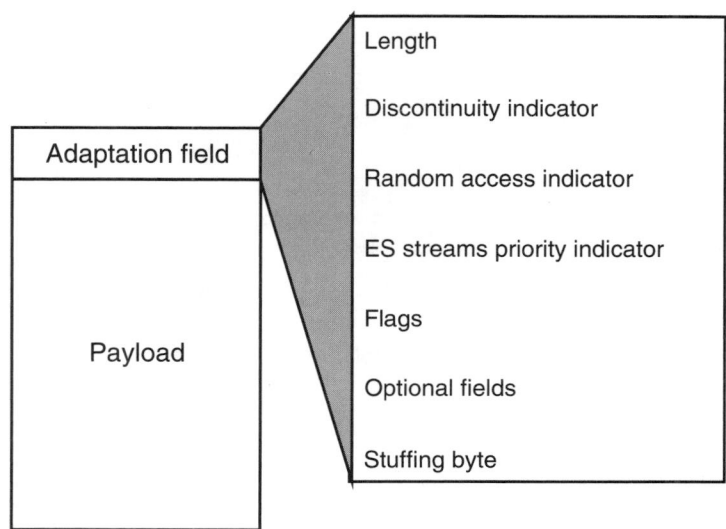

Figure 3–18   The Adaptation field.

Figure 3–19 shows the format of the optional fields. The contents of these fields are as follows:

- *Program clock reference (PCR):* The PCR used for time base recovery at the decoder. Contains the value indicating the intended time of arrival of the byte containing the last bit of the PCR at the input of the decoder.
- *Original program clock reference:* Used to reconstruct a single transport stream for another transport stream. This field is copied into the program clock reference during the reconstruction. It allows the original clock to be carried through another system (tunneled) and then used at the end-point.
- *Splice countdown:* Shows where in the stream a splicing point is reached. Splicing is used to reassemble a set number of packets at the decoder in order to play out the video, audio, data, or control streams to the user.
- *Private transport data:* Private user data that is defined by user application.
- *Adaptive field extension:* Indicates an optional adaptive field follows.

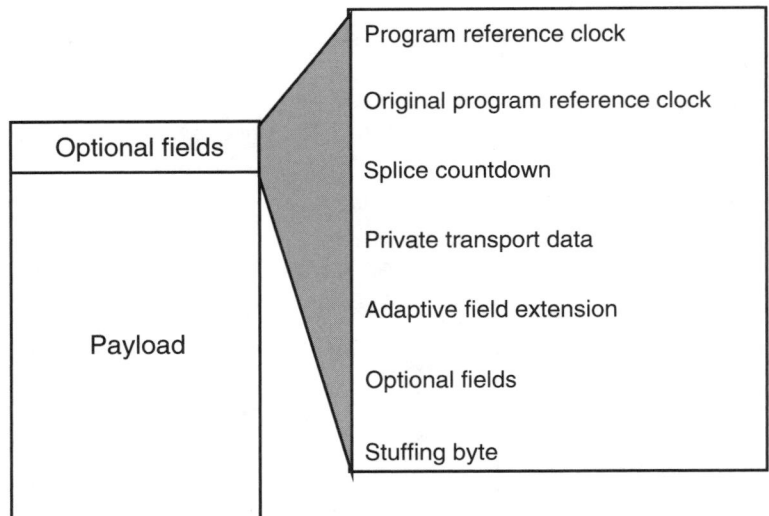

Figure 3–19   Optional fields.

MPEG-4

ISO MPEG-4 is an emerging multimedia coding standard that, in addition to higher compression, aims to support new content-based tools for communication, access, and manipulation of digital audiovisual data.

Work requirements for MPEG-4 identified eight key functionalities which are not well supported by existing or other emerging standards. These were grouped into three fundamental categories of: content-based interactivity, compression functionality, and universal access functionality, see Table 3–9.[7]

The MPEG-4 standard will consist of six parts, of which systems, audio, and visual are the most advanced at this time. Other parts include a conformance testing specification, a technical report on reference software implementations, and a multimedia integration framework definition. The systems, audio, and visual parts are currently at working draft (WD) status and are expected to progress to full international standard (IS) status in January 1999. Audio (WD 14496-3) and visual (WD 14496-2) will define a standardized coded representation of audio and visual content, both natural and synthetic, called, "audio visual objects" or AVOs. Systems (WD 14496-1) will standardize the composition of these objects together to form compound AVOs (e.g., an audiovisual scene) and multiplex and synchronize the data associated with individual objects, so that they can be transported over networks at appropriate quality of service levels.

Table 3–9 MPEG-4 Video Categories

Categories	Functionalities
Content-based interactivity	• Content-based multimedia data access tools • Content-based manipulation and bitstream editing • Hybrid natural and synthetic data coding • Improved temporal random access
Compressing functionality	• Improved coding efficiency • Coding of multiple concurrent datastreams
Universal access functionality	• Robustness in error-prone environments • Content based scalability

[7]See M. W. Whybray, D. G. Morrison, and P. J. Mulroy, "Video Coding-Techniques, Standards and Applications." *BT Journal*, 15(4), October 1997, from which I have abstracted this summary.

For highest efficiency in video compression, the video specification is building on the work of ITU-T Recommendation H.263. Extensions have already been made to the core coder, which will be capable of coding video at rates from 10 kbit/s to more than 4 Mbit/s. Transcoding between MPEG-4 and MPEG-1/H.263 elementary bit streams should be straightforward.

MPEG-7

The title of the MPEG-7 activity is "Multimedia Content Description Interface." The focus of this work is no longer that of efficient compression of audio/visual content, but rather its representation for searching and browsing purposes, including sound and images on the Web, video-on-demand systems, and corporate image databases.

According to BT (Whybray et al.) the standard will have many application domains but a major one is likely to be Web search engine functionality on audio, video, and still pictures. Nearly all Web searching is currently done on a text basis, although image-based searching is starting to appear in a basic form. MPEG-7 is currently in a requirements capture phase of development but is scheduled to reach "International Standard" status in the year 2000.

SUMMARY

The industry has yet to settle on one voice coder, and a variety of standards are being used in commercial products. However, the best performances are being achieved with proprietary coders, and it is certain that these higher-quality/lower-bit rate coders will find their way into the ITU-T Recommendations.

MPEG-2 is the latest technology for high-quality video traffic; other MPEG versions will surely find their way into the multimedia Internet.

4

Voice over IP (VoIP)

The length of this chapter does not reflect the importance of its subject. Chapter 3 established the groundwork for voice over IP (VoIP) with a discussion of voice coders, and Chapter 5 is devoted to the H Series, the specifications used to support VoIP on LANs. The focus of this chapter is on VoIP configuration options, performance issues, and an evaluation of several VoIP gateways.

MARKET PROJECTIONS FOR VoIP

Figure 4–1 shows a forecast prepared by Frost and Sultan that projects the internet telephony revenue through the year 2001. It is evident that beginning in 1997 the market has been and is growing rapidly, and in some of the projected years, it will grow exponentially.

The reader who has used voice-over-Internet connections may question the predicted sharp rise in the Internet telephony market as published in this study. Internet telephony quality is far from toll quality.[1] However, there appears to be a fairly large population that is will-

---

[1]Toll quality is a term used in telephony to describe the quality of voice traffic. It is associated with the 64 kbit/s G.711 technology.

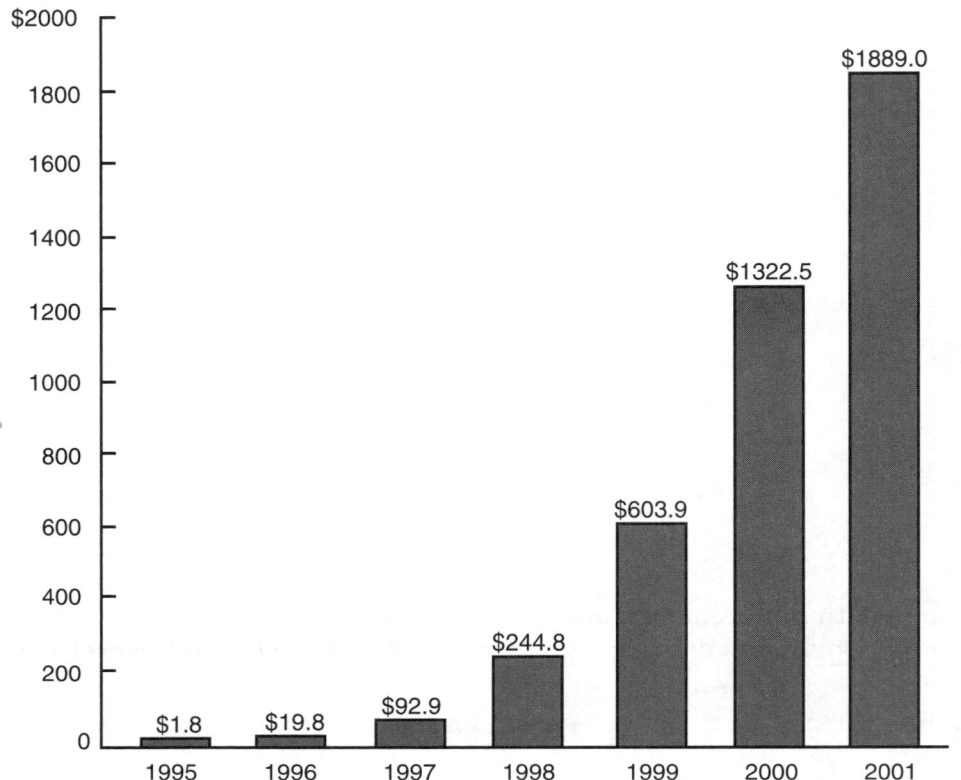

Figure 4–1   Revenue forecast of Internet telephony market.
(*Source:* Frost and Sultan Study, "The Time is Now—Swim
and Swim Fast," by Richard Sewell, *Telephony,* February 16,
1998.)

ing to experience less than toll quality service if they can obtain internet telephony at an inexpensive rate.

Of course, in most situations today, the internet telephony rates
are no more expensive than the cost to hook up with an ISP. Moreover,
people are starting to recognize that they can make international calls
and incur relatively modest cost for these calls—certainly in relation to
a conventional international call over the telephony backbone.

In addition, when an entrepreneur recognizes a potential market
for a service, the technology that supports that service is examined
carefully with the aim to capture that potential market as quickly as
possible. For this to occur in the internet telephony market requires

that many of the products built to run voice over IP must be improved (in fairness, some of the products perform quite well).

The problem is not so much the quality of the vendors' products as it is the Internet architecture, a topic discussed in Chapters 1 and 3. Without question, the Internet itself must be upgraded to provide for less delay, less delay-variability, and better reliability if high-quality telephony is to be realized.

My view is that it is only a matter of time that the Internet is so upgraded. As stated earlier, the Internet was not designed for the real-time low-delay synchronous traffic such as voice. But the thrust is to move the Internet in that direction, and the study cited in Figure 4–1 suggests a market exists for such a system.

THE THREE KEY FACTORS

In evaluating how to place audio and video on the Internet, a designer must carefully evaluate three key factors: (1) packet delay, (2) bandwidth requirements, and (3) computational effort.

Packet delay describes two aspects of delay. The first aspect is how long it takes to send the traffic from the sender to the receiver. The second aspect is the variation in time of the arrivals of the packets at the receiver, which is called jitter.

Studies (the ITU-T G.114 Recommendation) show that one-way end-to-end delay for a telephone conversation should be below 150 ms in order to maintain a conversation between the parties. A round trip delay of 300 ms is not discernible to even the most sensitive listener.[2] This aspect of telephony requirements is a big challenge, since the Internet experiences longer delays in its normal operations.

The second factor deals with how much bandwidth is required to support the audio transmission. The bandwidth calculation must factor in the bits required to represent the audio or video signal as well as the overhead headers that are used to support the signals.

The third major factor is the computational effort needed to support the coding, transport, and decoding of the audio images in each machine in the network. The term computational effort refers to the expense and complexity involved in supporting the service to the audio or video appli-

---

[2]Round trip delays of about 500 ms result in a loss of conversational efficiency of about 25%. Most users will not accept round trip delays of greater than 800 ms.

cation. In simple terms, it refers to the millions of instructions per second (MIPs) required to support the operation, as well as the amount of memory needed.

The Telephony Approach

The traditional telephone approach to supporting the three factors just described is obviously to support voice traffic. The delay for real time voice traffic must be very low. Likewise, jitter must be low (and for telephone networks, jitter is practically nonexistent).

The bandwidth requirements in legacy telephony systems is quite large. Typically, most systems use pulse code modulation (PCM), which requires a 64 kbit/s transmission rate.

The computational effort to support digital voice is low primarily because the network is tailored specifically for voice and uses time division multiplexing (TDM) and time slot interchange (TSI) hardware-based operations.

The Internet (Ideal) Approach

Achieving these goals using the Internet to support telephony is a challenging operation. Obviously, the delay factor is the same as in telephony. The amount of delay must be low as well as the variation in the delay.

The bandwidth requirements for Internet video and telephony must be as low as possible. While this statement is somewhat self-evident, it must be pointed out that it is desirous from the user's standpoint to have only one local loop line to the user's telephone and computer. Consequently, the telephony images should allow sufficient capacity on that line to support other traffic such as data applications.

If an internet cannot provide low-delay and low-bandwidth support to an audio or video application then it will not be used. Therefore, from a practical standpoint, it makes sense to concentrate on a high-computational effort to achieve low delay in a coder. In so many words, put the efforts and money into processors that produce the performance needed to meet the delay and bandwidth requirements for Internet audio and video.

We restate Moore's Law here: The cost of computation and storage decreases by a factor of two every 18 months. And for the past twenty years, integrated circuit development has followed Moore's Law. Therefore, it is clear that the efforts to enhance IP telephony should concentrate on the computational effort.

Notwithstanding the above statements, it is equally clear that the main impediment to high-quality Internet telephony is not the voice coder's delay but the delay that is (presently) inherent in the Internet.

VoIP CONFIGURATIONS

Several configuration options are available to affect the VoIP operations. Figure 4–2 shows four examples (others are variations of these basic configurations). In Figure 4–2a, conventional telephones are employed as well as the telephone network. The VoIP gateway provides the translation functions for the voice/data conversions. The gateway may coexist with the ISP's facilities, but wherever it is located, this gateway is designed to support multiple users. This idea is shown in Figure 4–2a with the notations N:1 and 1:N, where N signifies the number of voice connections. On the transmit side, the VoIP gateway codes, compresses, and encapsulates the voice traffic into data packets. At the receiving VoIP gateway, the process is reversed.

Figure 4–2b shows the use of a personal computer (PC) and the employment of a router. With this operation, the encoding, compression, and encapsulation operations are performed at the personal computers. The router's job is to examine the destination IP address in the datagram and route the traffic accordingly.

The use of a PC poses a problem with background noise and echo. Since the speaker is speaking into a PC microphone (an "open microphone"), the signal is subject to speaker-to-microphone echo, room echoes, and ongoing background noise. Many PC-based systems now provide facilities to ameliorate these problems, but you are well advised to check the product carefully.

The VoIP layout depicted in Figure 4–2c eliminates the echo and noise problems cited in Figure 4–2b by using a telephone instead of an open microphone. Like the configuration in Figure 4–2b, the PC is tasked with A/D and D/A operations.

A simple and low-cost approach to VoIP is the 1:1 VoIP gateway, shown in Figure 4–2d. The 1:1 ratio means that only one voice connection is supported by the gateway. This layout is the simplest of all the layout alternatives depicted in Figure 4–2.

The 1:1 gateway sits beside the telephone. It accepts the speech analog signals and performs a G-Series operation (at this time, typically G.723.1) on the signals. At the receiver, the reverse operation takes place.

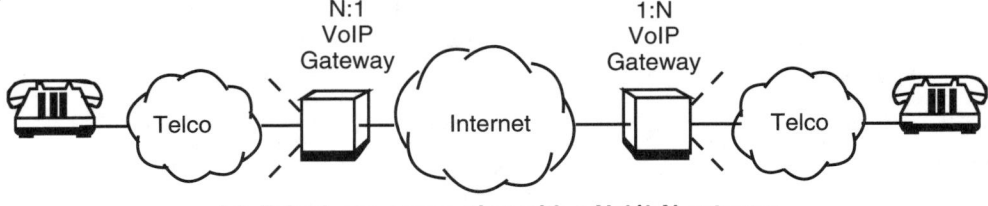

(a) Telephone connection with a N:1/1:N gateway

(b) PC connection with router

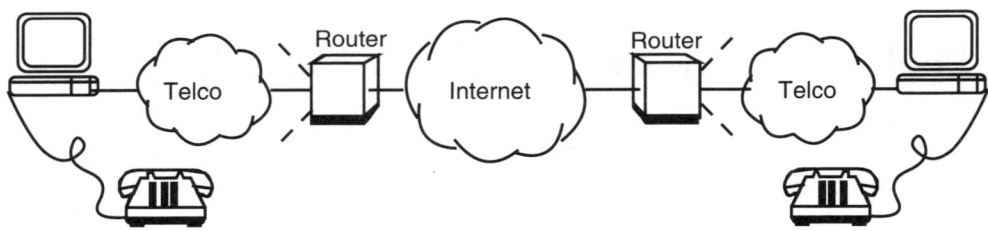

(c) Telephone-to-PC connection

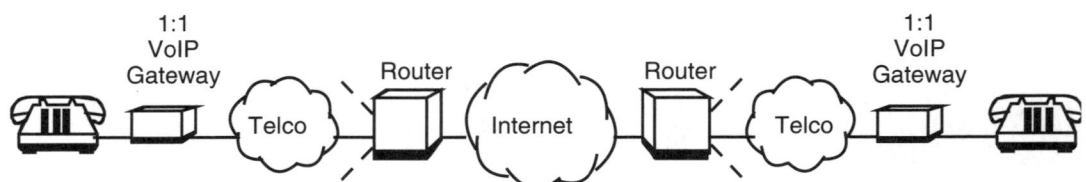

(d) Telephone connection with a 1:1 gateway

Figure 4–2   Typical VoIP layouts.

These systems are designed not only for voice coding/decoding (e.g., G.723.1) but for supporting operations such as (1) V.42/V.42 bis, (2) MNP 2-10 error correction and compression, and (3) Point-to-Point Protocol (PPP) operations.

EVALUATION CRITERIA

In evaluating the performance of coders for the VoIP gateway or PC, several factors come into play; some were introduced in Chapter 3. This part of the chapter provides a summary of these factors:

- *Frame size:* Frame size represents the length of the voice traffic measured in time. This traffic is placed in voice packets and sent to the receiver.
- *Voice bit rate*: This parameter is the output rate of the codec when its input is standard pulse code modulation voice images (at 64 kbit/s).
- *Processing delay*: This factor represents the delay incurred at the codec to run the voice and coding algorithm on one frame.
- *Lookahead delay*: Lookahead delay occurs when the coder examines a certain amount of the next frame to provide guidance in coding the current frame. The idea of lookahead is to take advantage of the close correlations existing between successive voice frames.
- *Frame length*: This value represents the number of bytes resulting from the encoding process (the value excludes headers).
- *DSP MIPS*: This value specifies the minimum speed for the DSP processor to support the specific encoder. Be aware that DSP MIPS does not correlate to MIPS ratings of other processors. These DSPs are designed specifically for the task at hand, in contrast to general purpose processors that operate in work stations and personal computers. Consequently, to achieve the operations discussed in this analysis requires a much greater MIPS capability from a general processor than from a specially designed DSP.
- *Required RAM*: This value describes the amount of RAM needed to support a specific encoding process.

A key evaluation factor is the time required for the encoder to do its work. This time is referred to as "one way latency." It is computed as the sum of frame size + processing delay + look ahead delay. Obviously, decode delays are important as well. In practice, the decode delays are about one-half the time of the encode delays.

Table 4–1 reflects a study conduced at 3COM[3] using the evaluation factors described earlier. As the table shows, three codecs were evalu-

---

[3]T. J. Kostas, M. S. Borella, I. Sidhu, G. M. Shuster, J. Grabiec, and J. Mahler, "Real-Time Voice over Packet-Switched Networks." *IEEE Network,* January/February, 1998.

Table 4–1   Codec Performance Parameters

Codec	G.723.1	G.729	G.729A
Bit rate	5.3 / 6.4 kbit/s	8 kbit/s	8 kbit/s
Frame size	30 ms	10 ms	10 ms
Processing delay	30 ms	10 ms	10 ms
Look ahead delay	7.5 ms	5 ms	5 ms
Frame length	20 / 24 bytes	10 bytes	10 bytes
DSP MIPS	16	20	10.5
RAM	2200	3000	2000

Source: *IEEE Network*, January/February 1998.

ated: G.723.1, G.729, and G.729A. The study reveals that G.723.1 supports the lowest bit rate but exhibits the largest delay. In contrast, G.729 exhibits a higher bit rate (and a more complex operation), but there is a marked decrease in delay. G.729A is not as complex as G.725 and yet provides about the same performance.

G.729 and G.729A have very small frame sizes that allow for low latency operations. But these small frame sizes can be a detriment if the Real Time Protocol packet (RTP) carries only one frame. Consequently, the larger frame size exhibited with G.723.1 is more attractive for users with bandwidth-limited channels. Those users with access to leased T1 lines and local area networks may find G.729A attractive because of its low-delay operations.

Other Factors in the Delay Equation

In addition to the coding and decoding delays just explained, three other delay factors must be examined. They are (1) the delay encountered at each machine (routers, switches, etc.) to process the traffic, (2) the number of hops or hop distance (number of machines on the path between the communicating parties), and (3) the physical distance between the two parties. Since the telephone conversation is two-way, the delay factors must be evaluated for the transmission in both directions.

Processing Delay in the Machines.   The delay at the machines on the path is a function of the speed at which the traffic is passed through the machine. The longest delays encountered in studies so far are found in the personal computer (if it is used). The reason is that the PC's generalized architecture is not designed for the coding and decoding of voice signals. For this reason, VoIP gateways use digital signal processing (DSPs) for coding and decoding operations.

Hop Distance.   Hop distance is more of a factor than physical distance. Hop distance must also factor-in the link speeds (bit/s) between the hops. Each hop adds delay because each hop (usually a router) must execute forwarding operations to determine the next node that is to receive the packet. In some situations, route determination may entail the checking of very large routing tables, which translates into increased delay.

Physical Distance.   The physical (geographical) distance, and its effect on delay, depends on the link distance between the sender and receiver, and on the speed (measured in bit/s) between these two parties. The link distance is not a major variable in the delay equation because the signal travels at the speed of light across the link (or links). The speed of the link(s) is an important consideration, because higher-speed links result in lower delay, since more bits per second are being pumped through the links.

ANOTHER VIEW OF EVALUATION CRITERIA

Table 4–2 shows a more detailed study on delay sources for Internet telephony.[4] The BT study provides additional information on the issue and recommends using a low delay codec (of course) and the following:

- Use pre-emptible priority scheduling and use a protocol processing architecture that allows the timing of the protocol processing to be under the control of the application.
- Use header compression to reduce the transmission delays.
- Use an internal modem (to avoid communicating with the modem via a serial link).
- Turn off modem's error checking, compression, and block transmission.
- Use priority scheduling in the network (this minimizes queuing delay and the need to buffer to account for jitter arising from any variation in network queuing delay).

---

[4] See P. Cordell, M. Courtenay, and S. Rudkin, "Conferencing on the Internet," *BT Journal*, *15*(4), October 1997.

Table 4–2   Sources of Delay in Internet Telephony

Source of Delay	Calculation	Typical Current Delay	Achievable Delay
Frame size (sampling time)	Determined by codec	30 ms (G.723.1*)	10 ms (G.729A)
Additional sound card/API/OS latency (over and above sampling time)		~30 ms	~ 5 ms (pre-emptible priority scheduling and real-time protocol processing)
Encode/decode	Lookahead + 2 x 'frame size' x required_MIPs/available_MIPs	< 67.5 MS (G.723.1)	< 25 MS (G.729A)
Packet header	Add 42 bytes	24 bytes becomes 66 bytes	10 bytes becomes 14 bytes (use header compression)
Serial link at transmitter	10/8 x packet size/line_speed	20 ms	0 (use internal modem)
Modem tx processing	53 symbols @ 3200 symbols/s	17 ms	17 ms
Modem waiting time	50 ms	50 ms	0 (turn off compression, error checking, transmission of blocks)
Modem transmission	packet/modem_speed	18 ms	4 ms (fewer bytes)
Modem rx processing	103 symbols @ 3200 symbols/s	32 ms	32 ms
Propagation delay	5 ms per 1000 km	25 ms	25 ms

Table 4–2 has some interesting information. The BT study (from which I abstract the following summary) reveals that for the chosen number of bytes of data, header compression has minimal effect on delay. The transmission/serialization delays are masked by the modem processing delays. In the case of an internal modem, the size of the packet makes no difference until the transmission delay for a packet is at least 32 ms, that is, the packet is at least 115 bytes long. Then each additional byte adds $2 \times 0.28 = 0.56$ ms delay one way (@ 28.8 kbit/s).

In the absence of an internal modem, the size of the packet starts making an impact for packets with transmission delay of at least 17 ms (when the packet is at least 61 bytes long). Then every additional byte adds 0.28 ms delay one way. Above 115 bytes every additional byte adds a delay of 3×0.28 ms = 0.86 ms one way. So, when used with 28.8 kbit/s modems as in this scenario, header compression is only useful for any re-

Table 4–2   (Continued)

Source of Delay	Calculation	Typical Current Delay	Achievable Delay
Router queuing delay	~ 10 ms per router	~ 100 ms	~ 10 ms (priority scheduling)
Modem tx processing	53 symbols @ 3200 symbols/s	17 ms	17 ms
Modem waiting time	50 ms	50 ms	0 (turn off compression, error checking, transmission of blocks)
Modem transmission	packet/ modem_speed	18 ms	4 ms (fewer bytes)
Modem rx processing	103 symbols @ 3200 symbols/s	32 ms	32 ms
Serial link at receiver	10/8 x packet size/ 38.4 ms	20 ms	0 (internal modem)
Buffer for network jitter, etc.	2 x mean variance in queuing delay	~ 200 ms	~ 20 ms (priority scheduling)
Buffer for os latency		30 ms	~ 5 ms pre-emptible priority scheduling
Total		~ 700 ms one way ~ 1.4 s both ways	~ 200 ms one way ~ 400 ms both ways

* The speech coding schemes G.723.1 and G.729(a) have the following delay characteristics:

	Lookahead	Frame
G.729(A)	5 ms	10 ms
G.723.1	7.5 ms	30 ms

Source: *BT Journal*, *15*(4), October 1997.

duction in packet size it has above 61 bytes and is especially useful for the reduction it has above 115 bytes.

This is in absolute terms. In relative terms, the longer the packet, the less significant is the saving of about 38 bytes. Also, above a certain packet size, the audio sampling time will no longer be hidden by the operating system latency in the application programming interface (API) calls to the sound system.

For data interactions, the sound card and encode/decode delays are not relevant. However, playout delay would have to be increased to at least 15 ms. This would give a saving of about 20 ms in each direction resulting in a round-trip delay of around 360 ms.

Unlike audio frames (which describe the audio signal over a period of around 20 ms), each video frame represents the video signal at a particular instant in time. Consequently, the coding schemes do not impose a minimum delay. In practice, most software implementations have coding delays of around 100 ms. This is only significant for frame rates above 10 frames per second. Below this rate each frame can be processed before receiving the next frame. With improved PC performance, the video coding delay can be expected to decline steadily.

By the way, I recommend to you the entire issue of the *BT Journal* (October 1997) as well as *BT Journal, 15*(2) (April 1997), which deals with the Internet in general.

UNIDIRECTIONAL DELAYS

To return to the 3COM study, Figure 4–3 shows a summary of its findings. Based on the two alternatives of (1) use of the telephone and VoIP gateways, and (2) use of PCs and routers, the study reveals that the telephone/gateway approach provides significantly better performance than the PC/router approach.

Under ideal conditions, option (1) meets the 300 ms round trip delay established by the ITU-T specifications. Option (2) does not meet these requirements, but comes close. During less-than-ideal conditions, neither

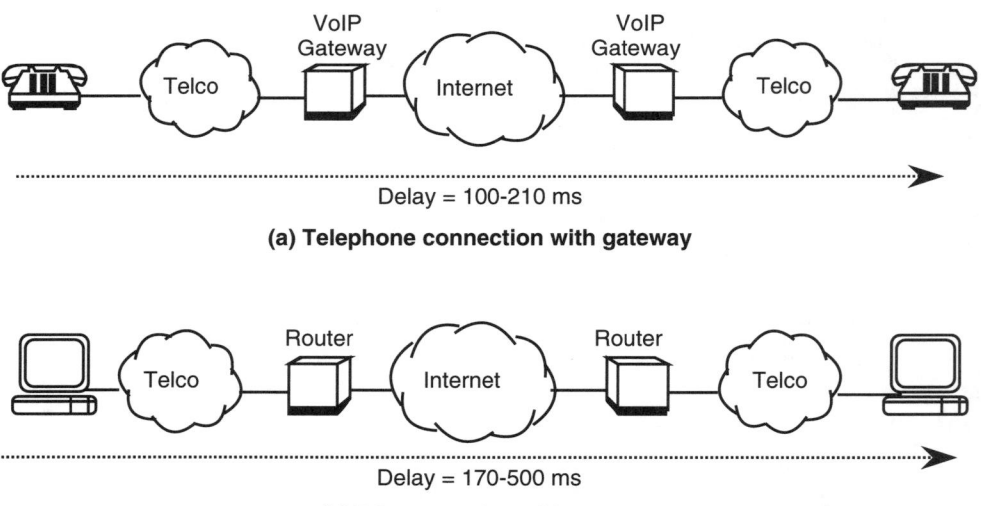

Figure 4–3 Expected unidirectional delays with G.729A. (*Source: IEEE Network,* January/February 1998.)

approach meets the requirements, but a large segment of the population would likely find the performance acceptable for option (1). Option (2) is pushing the envelope of acceptable quality.

So, is Internet telephony feasible? Yes, but under the present Internet environment, it is acceptable to some people and is not acceptable to others. Nonetheless, given the attractive features of Internet telephony (one link to the home, integrating voice and data, and low costs), it will surely succeed.

THE MISSING INGREDIENT: A HIGH CAPACITY LOCAL LOOP

One other aspect of this subject bears examination: the deployment of high-speed (1) ADSL modems, (2) cable modems, or (3) fixed wireless access technologies on the local loop. Once the customer has these technologies available, the equation changes.

First, overhead (headers and trailers) is not as significant a factor, since the increased bandwidth can support this overhead. Second, new PCs will be upgraded to support faster voice coders to take advantage of the higher-speed local loop. Third, the increased capacity of the links into and out of the Internet will force an upgrading of the Internet's capacity. Fourth, the increase of voice (and video) traffic will also force the Internet to look more and more like the telephone network, but with significantly enhanced multi-application capabilities. I have more to say on this subject in Chapter 12.

COMPARISON OF FOUR VoIP GATEWAYS

Our focus for this part of the chapter is to examine a study conducted by Meir Communications Inc. on four voice over IP products.[5]

Figure 4–4 shows the topology layout and configuration for the study conducted by Meir Communications. The voice traffic was exchanged between two Cisco 7000 routers over an unchannelized T1 link. The voice traffic was created through a simulated analog line and fed into a T1 mux where it was digitized into 64 kbit/s DS0 slots. This

---

[5]The general results of this study are available in the *Business Communications Review* (February 1998) and the principal authors of the study are R. Smithers and T. Scavo. You can reach these individuals at (609) 275-7311 if you need more detailed information about the study.

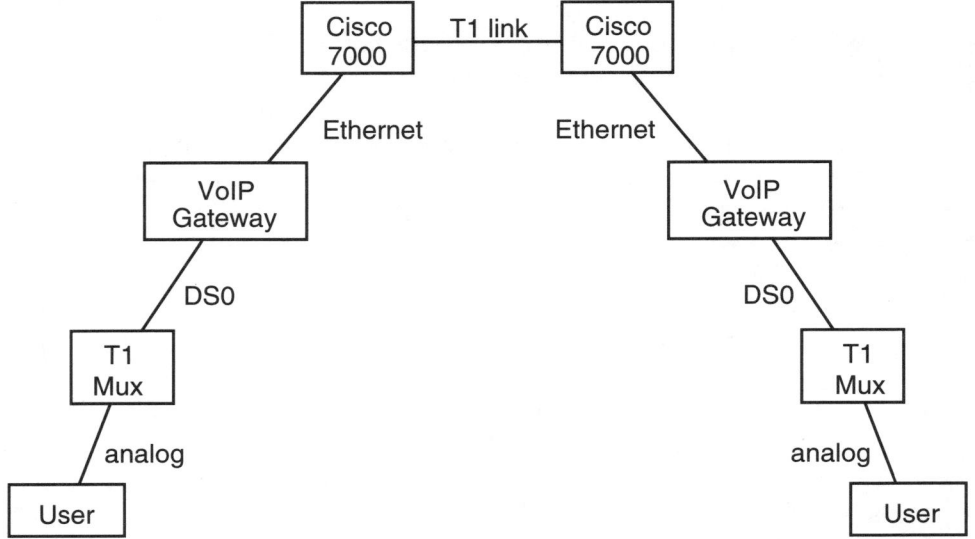

Figure 4–4   Topology layout for the study.

signal was fed into the VoIP gateway (the products under test) where they were then input into the Cisco router across an Ethernet 10 Mbit/s channel. The signals were then transported across the unchannelized T1 link to the receiving router where the signal then was sent through an Ethernet interface to the receiving VoIP gateway, then via a DS0 slot to a T1 mux. The mux converted the signal back to analog and transported the signal to the user at either a telephone handset or a speaker.

The study was performed with various voices (female speakers, male speakers, etc.). All speakers recited common voice images such as do, re, mi, and so on.

Keep in mind that this study did not test voice quality over the Internet. The test was run over the T1 link between the routers. Consequently, you should not infer that these tests state anything about the performance of the Internet in supporting telephony. But the study does provide an interesting and useful assessment of VoIP products. As we shall see, the test reveals that high-quality products are available to run voice over what are essentially data-based protocols.

Several tests were performed on four products. According to Meir Communications, all four products performed well and provided high-quality telephony images to the end user. The four products tested were

Lucent Technologies, Micom (now part of Nortel), Nuera Communications, and Selsius Systems.

Figure 4–5 reflects the assessment of the quality of these systems when operating under ideal network conditions. The definition of ideal network conditions is a fully available T1 channel that is then unchannelized (not restricted to DS0, TDM slots). In addition, the media operated under relatively error-free conditions without adding delay or latency across the system. That is to say, any latency or delay in the test was introduced as a result of the components in the topology and the operations of the VoIPs.

Obviously, the evaluation of the tests is subjective, but the evaluation of voice quality on the telephone network is subjective as well. Notwithstanding, as Figure 4–5 shows, all products were evaluated as exceeding a minimum quality for the signal. The scale of 0 to 10 was devised with the expectation that a score between 7 and 8 represented the current "toll quality" exhibited in the telephone network. The evaluation of 10 would reflect the best possible telephone voice connection wherein the analog loop is terminated into a digital system one time only, sent a very short distance, and then converted back to an analog signal.

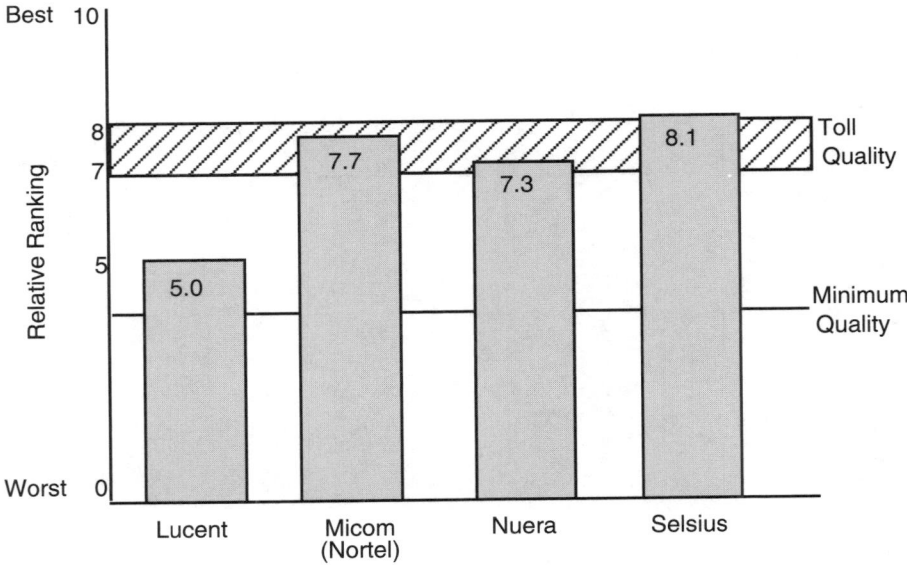

Figure 4–5   Voice quality under ideal network conditions.

Next, the test was conducted in an environment that exhibited poor quality conditions. To simulate these poor conditions, Meir Communications applied burst errors to the T1 line. The approach was to cycle: a 5 ms burst of random errors at a rate of 1×10^2, followed by 50 ms of transmissions with a bit error rate of 1×10^6. The 1×10^6 value is a reasonable assumption for BER performance on a typical local loop. The result of this operation is the introduction of errors in about 10% of the IP telephony datagrams.

As Figure 4–6 shows, Micom and Nuera continue to exhibit high-quality performance and Lucent and Selsius still exhibited acceptable quality.

Figure 4–7 shows the bandwidth utilization of the four tested products working under relatively error-free conditions and on a full-unchannelized T1 link. The Nuera system scored the highest with a bandwidth requirement of 14 kbit/s followed by Micom with 18 kbit/s. The Nuera performance approaches that of the sophisticated mobile/wireless vocoders that operate in a range of 13 kbit/s.

Not shown in this figure is the underlying fact that voice quality improved with those systems that used smaller protocol data units (with one exception). Micom's packet size is 91 bytes and Nuera's packet size is

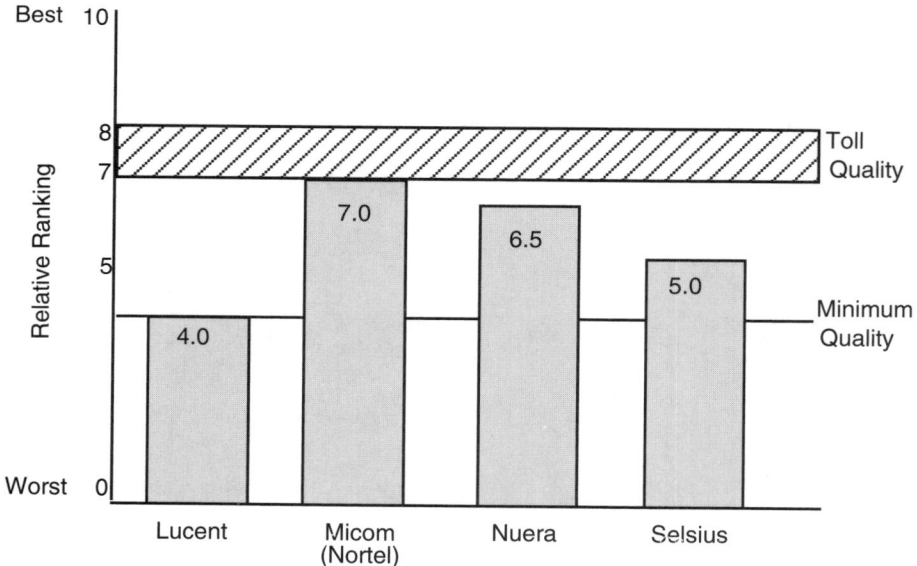

Figure 4–6 Voice quality under poor network conditions.

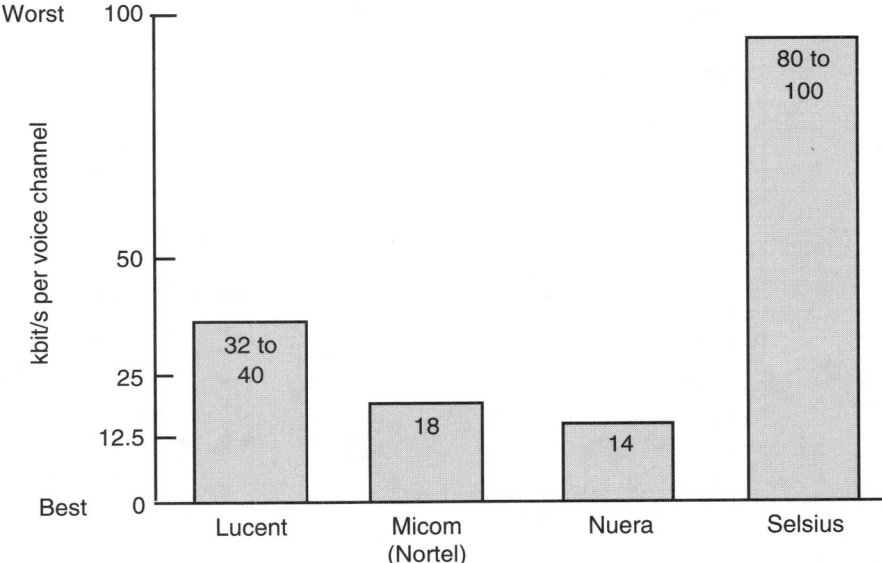

Figure 4–7 Bandwidth used under ideal network conditions.

93 bytes. The Lucent's packet size is 77 bytes and Selsius system uses 300 bytes.

In fairness it should be stated that the performance of Nuera and Micom is attributable to the fact that they are using proprietary vocoding techniques, whereas Lucent employs the ITU-T G.723.1 and Selsius uses ITU-T G.711. All organizations that belong to the VoIP and the International Media Teleconferencing Consortium (IMTC) have all selected G.723.1 for their basic vocoder.

It is reasonable to assume that the Lucent and Selsius performance would improve with proprietary schemes.

The tradeoff of proprietary versus standardized schemes pertains to the fact that private systems might opt for proprietary schemes because of their superior performance. But if different vendor systems are to interoperate with each other, the standards must be used.

Figure 4–8 shows the latency introduced by the tested systems. All operated within the 250 ms threshold (which is not considered very good performance), and none operated in accordance with the telco standard for one-way latency of 100 ms. The 250 ms delay is considered in this test to be the threshold at which it becomes noticeable and disturbing to the users of the system.

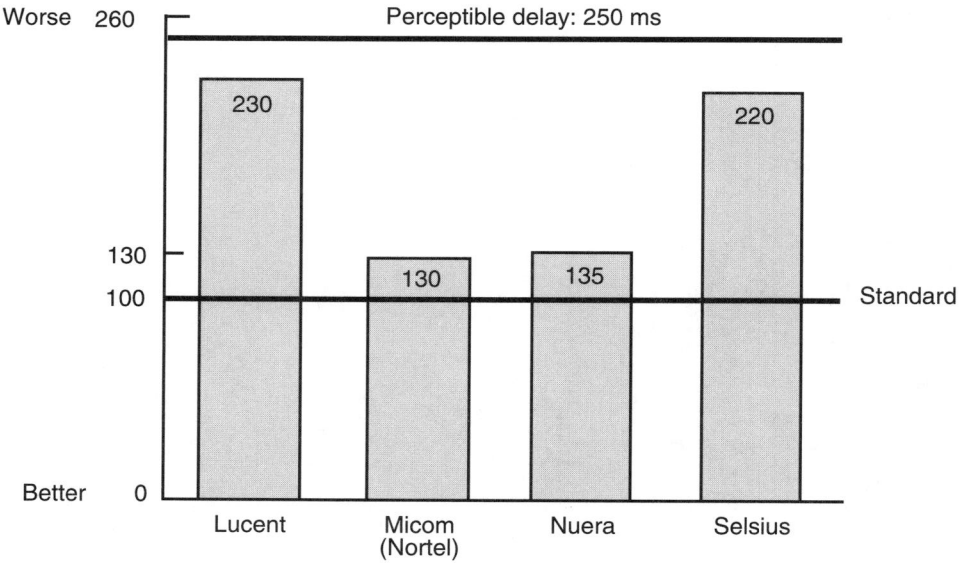

Figure 4–8   Latency: One-way delay.

In addition, the general study did not focus on where the delay was encountered. Recent tests with voice over telephony in some products (not those cited in the study), indicate that significant delay is occurring in the line card located at the customer premises equipment. Therefore, a clear analysis must focus on the specific components that are creating the delay.

SUMMARY

Several alternatives exist for the deployment of VoIP. All entail the use of a voice coder/decoder designed for low-bandwidth links. The difference in performance lies in where these machines are placed and how effectively they are designed and configured.

While the efficiency of the coders is important, as is the VoIP layout, the quality of VoIP is determined also by the behavior of the Internet, or an internet.

5

The H Series: Audiovisual and Multimedia Systems

T his chapter provides an analysis of the ITU-T H.323 Recommendation. Several VoIP vendors are using H.323 (or a subset) in their products. It is too early to know if H.323 will become a dominant audiovisual protocol. But its initial interest and implementations in VoIP warrant an explanation in this book.

H.323 encompasses considerably more than one H.323 specification. Other H-Series Recommendations come into play, such as H.225.0 and H.245. The focus of attention for the first part of this chapter is H.323, but the other pertinent H-Series Recommendations are also explained.

Some people believe H.324 will have a broader impact in the marketplace than H.323. H.324 is explained in the last part of the chapter.

The H Series use Abstract Syntax Notation.1 (ASN.1) to describe the messages that are exchanged between machines. From previous experience, I know that few readers understand ASN.1. So, I have kept the ASN.1 examples to a minimum, and I explain each element (field) in the ASN.1 code that is shown in this chapter.

ARCHITECTURE OF H.323

The H.323 Recommendation assumes the transmission path between the telephony users passes through at least one local area network

(LAN), such as an Ethernet or a token ring. It is further assumed that the LAN may not provide a guaranteed quality of service (QOS) needed to support the telephony traffic. As shown in Figure 5–1, the H.323 encompasses end-to-end connection between H.323 terminals and other terminals and through different kinds of networks. To gain an understanding of the scope and architecture of H.323, the entities in Figure 5–1 are explained in more detail here.

The H.323 Terminal

The H.323 terminal provides real-time, two-way audio, video, or data communications with another H.323 terminal. The terminal can also communicate with an H.323 gateway or a Multipoint Control Unit (MCU). While I cite the ability to support voice, video, and data, the terminal need not be configured for all those services, and H.323 does not require the terminal to be multiservice-capable.

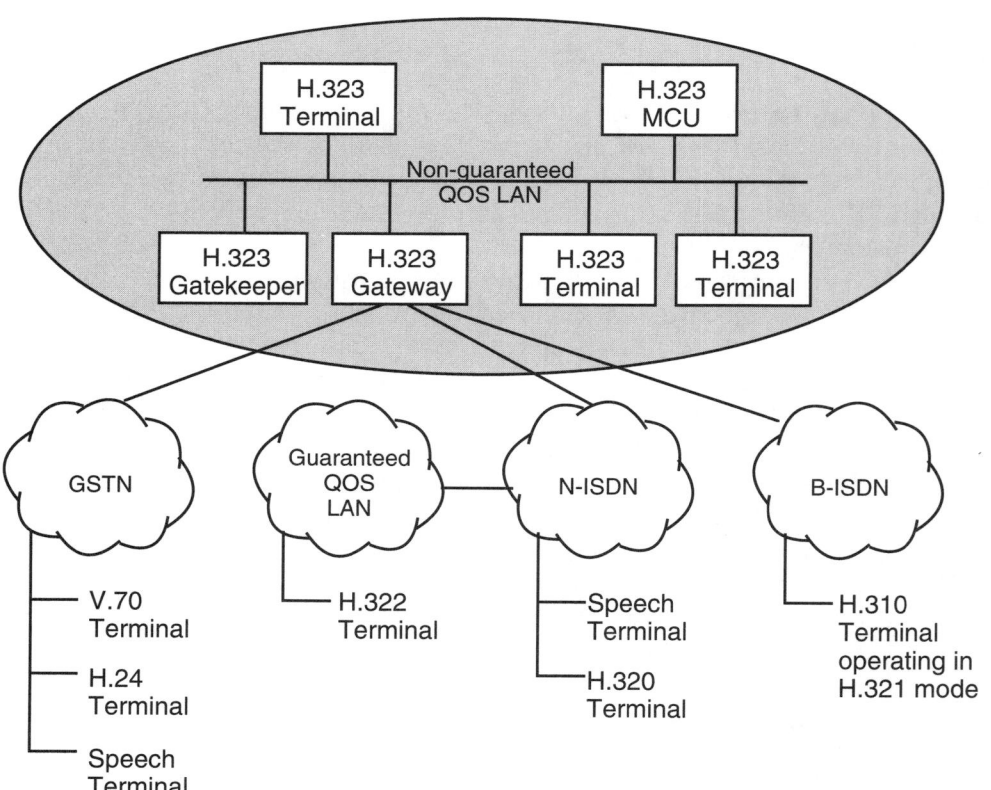

Figure 5–1   H.323 architecture.

The H.323 Gateway

The H.323 gateway is a node on a LAN that communicates with the H.323 terminal or other ITU-T terminals attached to other networks. If one of the terminals is not an H.323 terminal, the gateway performs translation of the transmission formats between the terminals. One H.323 gateway can interwork with another H.323 gateway. In addition, the gateway can operate with other ITU switched circuit networks (SCNs): (1) the General Switched Telephone Network (GSTN), (2) the narrowband-ISDN (N-ISDN), and (3) the broadband-ISDN (B-ISDN, an ATM-based network). Also, the gateway can operate as an H.323 Multipoint Control Unit (MCU), discussed next.

The gateway can set up and clear calls on the LAN and SCN. In effect, it reflects the LAN characteristics to the H.323 terminal on the LAN side and the SCN terminal characteristics on the SCN side. Under certain conditions, the gateway can be used to bypass a LAN router or a low bandwidth communications link.

The Multipoint Control Unit (MCU)

The Multipoint Control Unit (MCU) supports multiconferencing between three or more terminals and gateways. A two-terminal point-to-point conference can be expanded to a multipoint conference. The MCU consists of a mandatory multipoint controller (MC) and optional multipoint processor (MP).

The MC supports the negotiation of capabilities with all terminals in order to insure a common level of communications. It can also control the resources in the multicast operation. The MC is not capable of mixing or switching audio, video, or data traffic. However, the MP can perform these services (under the control of the MC). The MP is the central processor of the audio, video, and data streams for a multipoint conference.

MCU Multipoint Conference Control. The MCU may (or may not) control three types of multipoint conferences (see Figure 5–2):

- *Centralized multipoint conference:* All participating terminals communicate with the MCU point-to-point. The MC manages the conference, and the MP receives, processes, and sends the audio, video, or data streams to and from the participating terminals.
- *Decentralized multipoint conference:* The MCU is not involved in this operation. Rather, the terminals communicate directly with each other through their own MCs. If necessary, the terminals as-

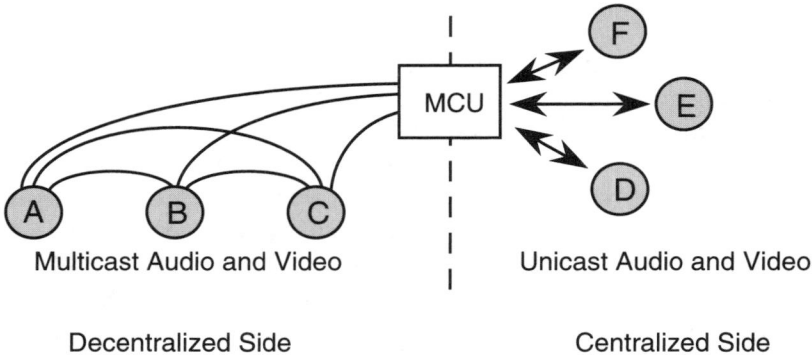

Multicast Audio and Video   Unicast Audio and Video

Decentralized Side   Centralized Side

Figure 5–2   Multipoint conferences.

sume the responsibility for summing the received audio streams and selecting the received video signals for display.

* *Mixed multipoint conference:* As the name suggests, this conference is a mix of the centralized and decentralized modes. The MCU keeps the operations transparent to the terminals.

The H.323 Gatekeeper

The H.323 gatekeeper provides address translation and call control services to H.323 endpoints. It also is responsible for bandwidth control, a set of operations that allow endpoints to change their available bandwidth allocations on the LAN.

A single gatekeeper manages a collection of terminals, gateways, and MCUs. This collection is called a *zone*. A zone is a logical association of these components and may span multiple LANs.

CODEC REQUIREMENTS

H.323 establishes the requirements for speech codecs; the video codec is optional. A summary of the requirements follows.

Speech (Audio) Codecs

All H.323 terminals must have an audio codec. The minimum requirement is the support of Recommendation G.711 (the A-law and μ-law). Other speech encoding/decoding standards cited by H.323 are G.722, G.728, G.729, G.723, and MPEG-1 audio.

H.245 is used during an initial handshake between the machines to determine the audio encoding algorithm. The terminal should be capable of sending and receiving different audio streams. After H.245 has completed the agreements on the terminal's capabilities, H.225 is used to format the audio stream.

Video Codecs

If video is supported, the H.323 terminal must code and decode the video streams in accordance with H.261 Quarter Common Intermediate Format (QCIF). Options are available, but they must use the H.261 or H.263 specifications.

Audio Mixing

In a multipoint conference, terminals may be sending different simultaneous audio streams to a terminal. The H.323 terminal must be able to present a composite audio signal to the user, so it must support an audio mixing function.

THE H.323 PROTOCOL STACK

H.323 consists of several standards and cites the use of others, as shown in Figure 5–3. For audio applications, G.711 is required, and other G Series Recommendations are options. However, the preference in recent commercial products is not G.711, because of its 64 kbit/s bandwidth requirement.

The video standards are H.261 and H.263. Data support is through T.120, and the various control, signaling, and maintenance operations are provided by H.245, Q.931, and the gatekeeper specification.

The audio and video packets must be encapsulated into the Real-Time Protocol (RTP) and carried on a UDP socket pair between the sender and the receiver. The Real-Time Control Protocol (RTCP) is used to assess the quality of the sessions and connections as well as to provide feedback information among the communicating parties. The data and support packets can operate over TCP or UDP.

H.323 was released in late 1996 and, as we just learned, is organized around four major facilities: (1) terminals, (2) gateways (which can perform protocol conversions), (3) gatekeepers (bandwidth managers), and (4) multipoint control units (MCUs), responsible for multicasting.

H.323 is a rich and complex specification. As of this writing, user and vendor groups are meeting to define a subset of H.232 to be used in internets.

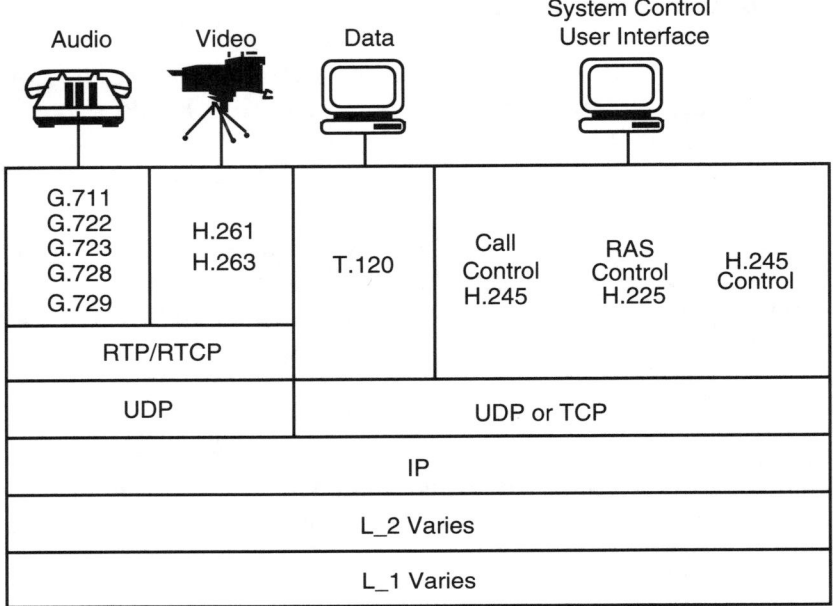

Figure 5–3   H.323 protocol stack.

REGISTRATION, ADMISSIONS, AND STATUS (RAS) OPERATIONS

The approach in this section is to describe the H.323 functions pertaining to gatekeeper discovery, endpoint registration, call management, and other key H.323 operations. I also explain the role of H.225 and H.245. These examples are not all-inclusive, but represent a sampling of the RAS function.

H.323 uses a logical channel on the LAN to manage overall signaling activities. This channel is the Registration, Admissions, and Status (RAS) channel. The RAS signaling function uses H.225.0 messages for a variety of support operations, discussed next.

Gatekeeper Discovery Procedures

The gatekeeper discovery is a very straightforward procedure used by an endpoint to determine with which gatekeeper it should register. The process is automatic and does not require manual configuration, and allows the association between the endpoint and its gatekeeper to change over time.

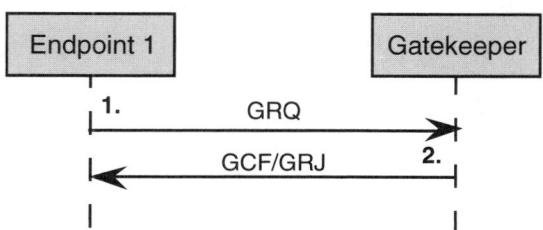

Figure 5–4   Auto discovery.

Figure 5–4 shows the messages exchanged for the gatekeeper discovery operation, which starts in event 1 with endpoint 1 sending a Gatekeeper Request (GRQ) message on the LAN. This message is examined by one or more gatekeepers who may (or may not, depending on the implementation) respond with a Gatekeeper Confirmation (GCF) message. This message contains the transport address of the gatekeeper's RAS channel.

The transport address is implemented with a Transport Service Access Point (TSAP) and allows the multiplexing of multiple connections on a TSAP.[1] The transport address is a LAN MAC address and a TSAP.

An alias address can be used as an alternate method for identifying an endpoint. An example of an alias address is E.164 (the ISDN telephony address). If alias addresses are used, they must be unique within a zone; also, gatekeepers, MCs, and MUs cannot use alias addresses.

The endpoint starts a timer upon issuing the GRQ message. If it does not receive a response, the timer expires and another GRQ can be issued. If auto discovery fails, the network administrator must do troubleshooting to determine the problem.

Alternatively, the gatekeeper may return a Gatekeeper Reject (GRJ) message if it chooses not to be the endpoint's gatekeeper.

H.323 defines the GRQ, GEF, and GRJ messages in a general way. It is left to the H.225.0 to define the contents of these messages using Abstract Syntax Notation.1 (ASN.1). The ASN.1 coding for these three messages is listed below and Box 5–1 describes a few simple rules to help you understand the code.

---

[1]The TSAP is an OSI transport layer SAP. It is equivalent to an Internet socket number. An Internet socket consists of a port number and an IP address.

```
GatekeeperRequest                ::=SEQUENCE---(GRQ)
{
    requestSeqNum                RequestSeqNum,
    protocolIdentifier           ProtocolIdentifier,
    nonStandardData              NonStandardParameter OPTIONAL,
    rasAddress                   TransportAddress,
    endpointType                 EndpointType,
    gatekeeperIdentifier         GatekeeperIdentifier OPTIONAL,
    callServices                 QseriesOptions OPTIONAL,
    endpointAlias                SEQUENCE OF AliasAddress
                                 OPTIONAL,

    ...

}

GatekeeperReject                 ::=SEQUENCE---(GRJ)
{
    requestSeqNum                RequestSeqNum,
    protocolIdentifier           ProtocolIdentifier,
    nonStandardData              NonStandardParameter OPTIONAL,
    gatekeeperIdentifier         GatekeeperIdentifier OPTIONAL,
    rejectReason                 GatekeeperRejectReason,
    ...
}

GatekeeperRejectReason           ::=CHOICE
{
    resourceUnavailable          NULL,
    terminalExcluded             NULL, --permission failure, not a
                                     resource failure
    invalidRevision              NULL,
    undefinedReason              NULL,
    ...
}

GatekeeperConfirm                ::=SEQUENCE---(GRF)
{
    requestSeqNum                RequestSeqNum,
    protocolIdentifier           ProtocolIdentifier,
    nonStandardData              NonStandardParameter OPTIONAL,
    gatekeeperIdentifier         GatekeeperIdentifier OPTIONAL,
    rasAddress                   TransportAddress,
    ...
}
```

Box 5–1   Rules for Reading ASN.1 Code

::=	Means defined as.
SEQUENCE	Means a sequence of ASN.1 elements. H.325 uses the SEQUENCE statement to explain the fields in the packet, typically each line in the code represents a field in the packet.
Words beginning with an upper case	This word describes a field in the packet and somewhere in the code; it must be defined by another ASN.1 descriptor called the "type." A type could be integer, Boolean, etc. In fact, SEQUENCE is a type.
Word beginning with a lower case	This word is supposed to be a user friendly description of the associated upper case word. An ASN.1 compiler does not act upon these words.
OPTIONAL	The entry is not required in a message.
CHOICE	One and only one of the fields is present in the message.
NULL	A type stating that information may not be available and therefore not provided.
---	Comments in the code.
{ }	Proclaims the start and end of a part of the code.
, after the field	Signifies the continuance of the code.
Words all in CAPS	ASN.1 reserved words.
Other concepts	A word is a string of words without spaces in which the initial letter determines its status by being either a capital letter or lower case letter. The individual words in the string are capitalized to aid the reader in understanding the string but do not have any other significance.

The contents of these messages are used primarily for identification purposes and contain the following information:

- *requestSeqNum:* A number unique to the sender, returned by the receiver in any messages associated with this message.
- *protocolIdentifier:* Used to determine version/vintage of implementation.
- *nonStandardData:* An optional parameter whose contents are not defined.
- *rasAddress:* The transport address that this endpoint uses for registration and status messages.
- *endpointType:* Specifies the type(s) of the terminal that is registering.
- *gatekeeperIdentifier:* Identifies the gatekeeper that the terminal would like to receive permission to register. A missing or null string *gatekeeperIdentifier* indicates that the terminal is interested in any available gatekeeper.
- *callServices:* Provides information on support of optional Q-Series protocols to the gatekeeper and called terminal.
- *endpointAlias:* Contains external address (if used), such as E.164.
- *rejectReason:* Codes for why the GRQ was rejected by this gatekeeper.

Endpoint Registration Procedures

Once the discovery process has taken place, registration procedures are undertaken. These administrative operations define how an endpoint joins a zone and provides the gatekeeper with its transport (and alias) address(es). Figure 5–5 shows the message exchange, with an endpoint 1 sending the Registration Request (RRQ) message to the gatekeeper, who was discovered with the auto-discovery operation. Of course, the connect transport address is used in the RRQ message. In event 2, the gatekeeper responds with the Registration Confirmation (RCF) message or the Registration Reject (RRJ) message.

Either the endpoint or the gateway can cancel the registration and end the association between the two entities. The operations in events 3 and 4 show the registration cancellation emanating from the endpoint with the Unregister Request (URQ) message. The gatekeeper can respond with the Unregister Confirm (UCF) message or the Unregister Reject (URJ) message. The gatekeeper starts the registration cancellation

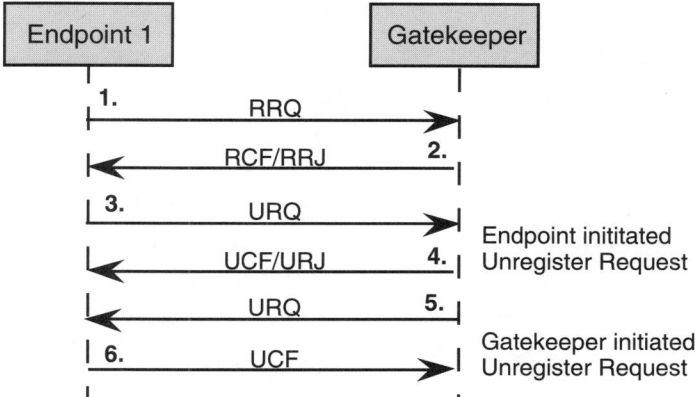

Figure 5–5   Registration.

process with the URQ message and the endpoint must respond with the UCF message.

The ASN.1 coding for the terminal and gateway registration messages is:

```
RegistrationrRequest          ::=SEQUENCE---(RRQ)
{
    requestSeqNum             RequestSeqNum,
    protocolIdentifier        ProtocolIdentifier,
    nonStandardData           NonStandardParameter OPTIONAL,
    discoveryComplete         BOOLEAN,
    callSignalAddress         SEQUENCE OF TransportAddress,
    rasAddress                SEQUENCE OF TransportAddress,
    terminalType              EndpointType,
    terminalAlias             SEQUENCE OF AliasAddress
                              OPTIONAL,
    terminalIdentifier        GatekeeperIdentifier OPTIONAL,
    endpointVendor            VendorIdentifier,
    ...
}

RegistrationConfirm           ::=SEQUENCE---(RFC)
{
    requestSeqNum             RequestSeqNum,
    protocolIdentifier        ProtocolIdentifier,
    nonStandardData           NonStandardParameter OPTIONAL,
    callSignalAddress         SEQUENCE OF TransportAddress,
```

```
        terminalAlias              SEQUENCE OF AliasAddress
                                   OPTIONAL,
        gatekeeperIdentifier       GatekeeperIdentifier OPTIONAL,
        endpointVendor             VendorIdentifier,
        ...
    }

    RegistrationReject             ::=SEQUENCE---(RRJ)
    {
        requestSeqNum              RequestSeqNum,
        protocolIdentifier         ProtocolIdentifier,
        nonStandardData            NonStandardParameter OPTIONAL,
        rejectReason               RegistrationRejectReason,
        gatekeeperIdentifier       GatekeeperIdentifier OPTIONAL,
        ...
    }

    RegistrationRejectReason       ::=CHOICE
    {
        discovery required         NULL, -- registration permission
                                        has aged
        invalidRevision            NULL,
        invalidCallSignalAddress NULL
        invalidRASAddress          NULL, -- supplied address is invalid
        duplicateAlias             SEQUENCE OF AliasAddress,
                                   --alias registered to another end
                                     point
        invalidTerminalType        NULL,
        undefinedReason            NULL,
        transportNotSupported      NULL, --permission failure, not a
                                   resource failure
        ...
    }

    UnregistrationRequest          ::=SEQUENCE---(URQ)
    {
        requestSeqNum              RequestSeqNum,
        callSignalAddress          SEQUENCE OF TransportAddress,
        endpointAlias              SEQUENCE OF AliasAddress
                                   OPTIONAL,
        nonStandardData            NonStandardParameter OPTIONAL,
        endpointIdentifier         EndpointIdentifier OPTIONAL,
        ...
    }

    UnregistrationReject           ::=SEQUENCE---(URJ)
    {
        requestSeqNum              RequestSeqNum,
        rejectReason               UnregRejectReason,
```

```
        nonStandardData            NonStandardParameter OPTIONAL,
        ...
}

UnregRejectReason              ::=CHOICE
{
        notCurrentlyRegistered    NULL,
        callInProgress            NULL,
        undefinedReason           NULL,
        ...
}
```

The contents of these messages are as follows:

- *requestSeqNum:* A number unique to the sender. It is returned by the receiver in any response associated with this specific message.
- *protocolIdentifier:* Identifies the H.225.0 vintage of the sending terminal.
- *discoveryComplete:* Set to TRUE if the requesting endpoint has preceded this message with the gatekeeper discovery procedure; set to FALSE if registering only.
- *callSignalAddress:* The call control transport address for this endpoint. If multiple transports are supported, they must be registered all at once.
- *rasAddress:* The registration and status transport address for this endpoint.
- *terminalType:* Specifies the type(s) of the terminal that is registering.
- *gatekeeperIdentifier:* The type(s) of the terminal that is(are) registering.
- *terminalAlias:* A list of external addresses.
- *gatekeeperIdentifier:* Identifies the gatekeeper that the terminal wishes to register with.
- *endpointVendor:* Information about the endpoint vendor.
- *callSignalAddress:* An array of transport addresses for H.225.0 call control messages, one for each transport address that the gatekeeper will respond to. This address includes the TSAP identifier.
- *endpointIdentifier:* A gatekeeper-assigned terminal identity string that is echoed in subsequent RAS messages.

- *callServices:* Provides information on support of optional Q-Series protocols to gatekeeper and called terminal.
- *endpointAlias:* Contains external address (if used), such as E.164.
- *rejectReason:* Codes for why the GRQ was rejected by this gatekeeper.

Admission Procedures

H.323 defines the use of a modified Q.931 signaling protocol. An example of how Q.931 is used with RAS is shown in Figure 5–6 to support the admission procedures. Notice that the RAS messages are used between the terminals (Endpoint 1 and Endpoint 2) and the Gatekeeper—which of course is the purpose of RAS. The Q.931 messages are exchanged between the H.323 terminals.

In events 1/2 and 5/6, the terminals and the gatekeeper exchange these messages:

- *ARQ:* The Admission Request message
- *ACF:* The Admission Confirmation message
- *ARJ:* The Admission Reject message (perhaps)

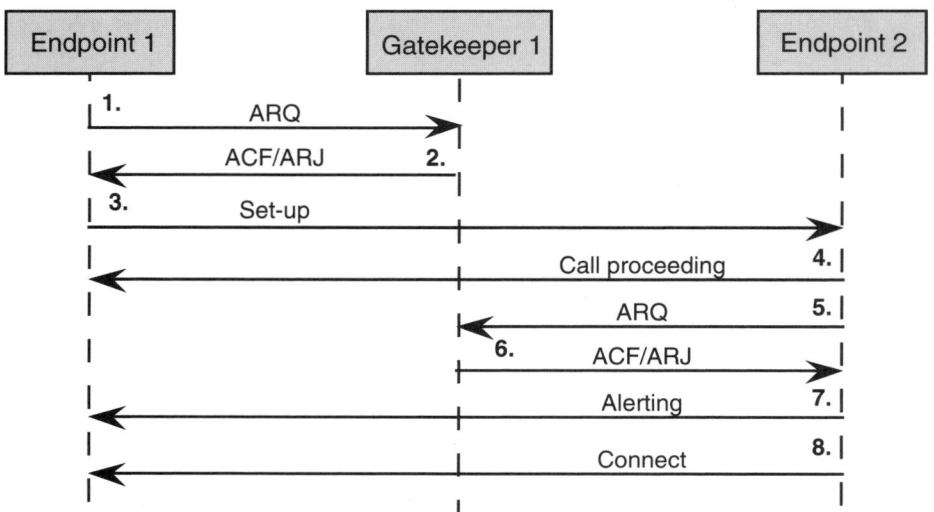

Figure 5–6   The Admission procedures.

Let us examine the content of these messages first and then look at the Q.931 messages. Keep in mind: To this point, the RAS operations have been concerned with discovery and registration procedures. Thus far, there have been no requests for bandwidth or other services.

The ASN.1 coding for the Admission messages are:

```
AdmissionRequest              ::=SEQUENCE---(ARQ)
{
    requestSeqNum             RequestSeqNum,
    callType                  CallType,
    callModel                 CallModel OPTIONAL,
    endpointIdentifier        EndpointIdentifier,
    destinationInfo           SEQUENCE OF AliasAddress OPTIONAL,
    destCallSignalAddress     TransportAddress OPTIONAL,
    destExtraCallInfo         SEQUENCE OF AliasAddress OPTIONAL,
    srcInfo                   SEQUENCE OF AliasAddress,
    srcCallSignalAddress      TransportAddress OPTIONAL,
    bandWidth                 BandWidth,
    callReferenceValue        CallReferenceValue,
    nonStandardData           NonStandardParameter OPTIONAL,
    callServices              QseriesOptions OPTIONAL,
    conferenceID              ConferenceIdentifier,
    activeMC                  BOOLEAN,
    answerCall                BOOLEAN, --answering a call
    ...
}

CallType                      ::=CHOICE
{
    pointToPoint              NULL, --Point-to-point
    oneToN                    NULL, --no interaction(FFS)
    nToOne                    NULL, --no interaction (FFS)
    nToN                      NULL, --interactive (multipoint)
}

CallModel                     ::=CHOICE
{
    direct                    NULL,
    gatekeeperRouted          NULL,
}

AdmissionConfirm              ::=SEQUENCE---(AFC)
{
    requestSeqNum             RequestSeqNum,
    bandWidth                 BandWidth,
    callModel                 CallModel,
    destCallSignalAddress     TransportAddress,
    irrFrequency              INTEGER (1..65535) OPTIONAL
```

```
    nonStandardData           NonStandardParameter OPTIONAL,
    ...
}

AdmissionReject               ::=SEQUENCE---(ARJ)
{
    requestSeqNum             RequestSeqNum,
    reject Reason             AdmissionRejectReason,
    nonStandardData           NonStandardParameter OPTIONAL,
    ...
}

AdmissionRejectReason         ::=CHOICE
{
    calledPartyNotRegistered NULL,  --cannot translate address
    invalidPermission        NULL,  --permission has expired
    requestDenied            NULL,  --no bandwidth available
    undefinedReason          NULL,
    callerNotRegistered      NULL,
    routeCallToGatekeeper    NULL,
    invalidEndointIdentifer  NULL,
    resourceUnavailable      NULL,
    ...
}
```

The contents of these messages are as follows:

- *requestSeqNum:* A number unique to the sender. It is returned by the receiver in any response associated with this specific message.
- *callType:* The gatekeeper uses this parameter to determine bandwidth usage. The default value if *pointToPoint* for all calls.
- *callModel:* If direct, the endpoint is requesting the direct terminal to terminal call model. If *gatekeeperRouted*, the endpoint is requesting the gatekeeper-mediated model.
- *endpointIdentifier:* An endpoint identifier that was assigned to the terminal by RCF, probably the E.164 address or H323_ID. It is used as a security measure to help ensure that this is a registered terminal within its zone.
- *destinationInfo:* Sequence of external addresses for the destination terminal, such as E.164 addresses or H323_IDs.
- *destCallSignalAddress:* Transport address used at the destination for call signaling.
- *destExtraCallInfo:* Contains external addresses for multiple calls.

- *srcInfo:* Sequence of external addresses for the source terminal, such as E.164 address or H323_IDs.
- *srcCallSignalAddress:* Transport address used at the source for call signaling.
- *bandWidth:* The number of 100 bit/s requested for the bidirectional call. For example, a 128 kbit/s call would be signaled as a request for 256 kbit/s. The value refers only to the audio and video bit rate excluding headers and overhead.
- *callReferenceValue:* The CRV from Q.931 for this call; used by a gatekeeper to associate the ARQ with a particular call.
- *nonStandardData:* An optional value whose contents are not defined.
- *irrFrequency:* The frequency, in seconds, that the endpoint shall send information request response (IRR) messages to the gatekeeper while on a call, including while on hold. The IRR message is discussed shortly.
- *requestSeqNum:* The same value that was passed in the ARQ.
- *rejectReason:* Reason the bandwidth request was denied.
- *callServices:* Information on support of optional Q-Series protocols to gatekeeper and called terminal.
- *conferenceID:* Unique conference identifier.
- *activeMC:* If TRUE, the calling party has an active MC; otherwise FALSE.
- *answerCall:* Used to indicate to a gatekeeper that a call is incoming.

The Q.931 messages are similar to the conventional ISDN L_3 messages. The setup message is explained here. First, the ASN.1 code is listed, followed by a description of the fields in the message.

The ASN.1 coding for the Q.931 Setup message is:

```
Setup_UUIE              ::=SEQUENCE
{
    protocolIdentifier      ProtocolIdentifier,
    h245Address             TransportAddress OPTIONAL,
    sourceAddress           SEQUENCE OF AliasAddress OPTIONAL,
    sourceInfo              EndpointType,
    destinationAddress      SEQUENCE OF AliasAddress OPTIONAL,
    destCallSignalAddress   TransportAddress OPTIONAL,
    destExtraCallInfo       SEQUENCE OF AliasAddress OPTIONAL,
```

```
destExtraCRV              SEQUENCE OF CallReferenceValue
                          OPTIONAL,
activeMC                  BOOLEAN,
conferenceID              ConferenceIdentifier,
activeMC                  CHOICE
{
        create            NULL,
        join              NULL,
        invite            NULL,
                          ...
}
callServices              QseriesOptions OPTIONAL,
callType                  CallType,
...
}
```

The contents of the Setup message are as follows:

- *protocolIdentifier:* Set by the calling endpoint to the version of H.225.0 supported.
- *h245Address:* A specific transport address on which the calling endpoint or gatekeeper handling the call would like to establish H.245 signaling.
- *sourceAddress:* Contains the H323_IDs for the source; the E.164 number of the source is in the Q.931 part of SETUP.
- *sourceInfo:* Contains an EndpointType to allow the called party to determine whether the call involved a gateway.
- *destinationAddress:* The address the endpoint wishes to be connected to.
- *destCallSignalAddress:* Informs the gatekeeper of the destination terminal's call signaling transport address.
- *destExtraCallInfo:* Needed to make possible additional channel calls, for example, for 2×64 kbit/s call on the WAN side.
- *destExtraCRV:* CRVs for the additional SCN calls specified by *destExtraCallInfo*. Their use is for further study.
- *activeMC:* Indicates that the calling endpoint is under the influence of an active MC.
- *conferenceID:* Unique conference identifier.
- *conferenceGoal:* Indicates a desire to join an existing conference, start a new conference, or to invite a party to join an existing conference.

- *callServices:* Provides information on support of optional Q-Series protocols to gatekeeper and called terminal.
- *callType:* The gatekeeper uses this parameter to determine bandwidth usage. The default value is *pointToPoint* for all calls.

OTHER RAS PROCEDURES

As mentioned earlier, all the RAS procedures are not discussed in this overview. So, here is a brief description of the others.

Terminal Gatekeeper Requests for Changes in Bandwidth

These messages are exchanged for this procedure:

- *BRQ:* Bandwidth Change Request, contains the bandwidth parameter, discussed earlier.
- *BCF:* Bandwidth Change Confirmation, confirms the change request with the bandwidth parameter.
- *BRJ:* Bandwidth Change Reject, rejects the request and provides the reason for the reject.

Location Requests

This procedure is not an actual location request, but a service that the gatekeeper provides a requester. The service translates an address (say E.104) to transport address (a port or socket).

The location request procedure uses two messages:

- *LRQ:* Location Request, contains the endpoint identifier and destination info parameters.
- *LCF:* Location Confirm, contains the call signal address and the ras address.

Disengage Procedures

This procedure is invoked by an endpoint to notify the gatekeeper that an endpoint is being dropped. If the gatekeeper invokes the procedure, it forces a call to be dropped. These messages are exchanged for this procedure:

- *DRQ:* Disengage Request, contains the identifiers associated with this endpoint, the ID of the call (endpoint ID, conference ID), and the reason for the disengage.
- *DCF:* Disengage Confirmation.
- *DRJ:* Disengage Reject.

Status Request Procedures

These procedures are used to obtain status information between terminals and gatekeeper, including information about a call. These messages are exchanged for this procedure:

- *IRQ:* Information Request, contains the call reference value in order to identify the call.
- *IRR:* Information Request Response, contains information about the terminal or gatekeeper as well as information about the call. The call information provides fields for identifying (a) RTP data, (b) type of call (video, audio), (c) bandwidth usage, and so on.

SOME COMMENTS ON H.323 AND H.225.0

You may have noticed that the only RAS/Q.931 information pertaining to bandwidth or QOS is in the bandwidth parameter of the RAS ARQ and ACF messages. This parameter is coded in 100 bit/s increments for a symmetrical two-way call.

By an examination of Figure 5–5, it can be seen that the Gatekeeper *and* the endpoints know about bandwidth, but the endpoints' knowledge of each other's bandwidth requirements is made available by the Gatekeeper with the ACF message.

It would seem reasonable for the bandwidth field in the ACF message in event 2 to be used in the Setup message in event 3 to inform the called party of the bandwidth requirements of the calling party. But, the Setup message has no such field. So, Endpoint 2 receives a Setup message without any knowledge of the calling party's bandwidth needs. It sends its bandwidth information to the Gatekeeper in event 5 and receives a reply in event 6. I assume the bandwidth field in the ACF message in event 6 is a reflection of the bandwidth field in the ACF message in event 2. However, H.323 does not discuss this situation. Thus, the gateway acts as the agent between the endpoints, and we can only assume that the bandwidth fields in events 1 and 2 are made available to the messages in events 5 and 6.

T.120

The T.120 specifications define the data (document) conferencing part of a multimedia conference. IMTC[2] describes T.120 as a protocol that distributes files and graphical information in real-time during a multipoint multimedia meeting. The objective is to assure interoperability between terminals without either participant assuming prior knowledge of the other system. T.120 permits data sharing among participants in a multimedia teleconference, including white board image sharing, graphic display information, image exchange, and protocols for audiographic or audiovisual applications.

The T.120 series governs the audiographic portion of the H.320, H.323, and H.324 series and operates either within these or by itself. The T.120 suite consists of a series of recommendations, which are summarized in Table 5–1.

H.245

I made a few comments about H.245 earlier. Its purpose is to specify the syntax of terminal information messages and the procedures to use those messages. It is a "generic" protocol in that it is used by H.222.0, H.223, and H.225.0.

H.245 provides some features that are similar to RTCP, such as the calculation of round trip delay between two terminals. However, the H Series Recommendations provide no guidance on how to (or how not to) interwork H.245 and RTCP. The Recommendations contain "informative" appendices describing RTCP but (unfortunately) not in relation to the H Series operations.

I have not shown any H.245 message flows in this chapter (just RAS and Q.931 messages have been shown). Notwithstanding, H.323 de-

---

[2]International Teleconferencing Corsortium, Inc. (IMTC)   HTTP://www.imtc. org/main.html.

Table 5–1   ITU T.120 Recommendations

Recommendation	Description
T.120	Data protocols for multimedia conferencing: This provides an overview of the T.120 series.
T.121	Generic Application Template: This provides a guide for development of T.120 application protocols.
T.122	Multipoint Communication Service (MCS) Description: This describes the multiport services available to developers.
T.123	Protocol stacks for audiographic and audiovisual teleconference applications: This specifies transport protocols for a range of networks.
T.124	Generic Conference Control (GCC): This defines the application protocol supporting reservations and basic conference control services for multipoint teleconferences.
T.125	Multipoint Communication Service (MCS) Protocol specification: This specifies the data transmission protocol for multipoint services.
T.126	Multipoint still image and annotation protocol: This defines collaborative data sharing, including &quot, white board&quot, image sharing, graphic display information, and image exchange in a multipoint conference.
T.127	Multipoint Binary File Transfer Protocol: This defines a method for applications to transmit files in a multipoint conference.
T.130	Real-time architecture for multimedia conferencing: Provides an overview description of how T.120 data conferencing works in conjunction with H.320 videoconferencing.
T.131	Network-specific mappings: Defines how real-time audio and video streams should be transported across different networks (i.e., ISDN, LAN, ATM) when used in conjunction with T.120 data conferencing.
T.132	Real-time link management: Defines how real-time audio and video streams may be created and routed between various multimedia conferencing endpoints.
T.133	Audio visual control services: Defines how to control the source and link devices associated with real-time information streams.
T.RES	Reservation services: This is an overview document that specifies how terminals, MCUs, and reservation systems need to interact and that defines the interfaces between each of these elements.

scribes several scenarios for using the H.245 protocol. If you wish more information on the relationship of H.323 and H.245, I refer you to Section 8 of the H.323 Specification.

H.324

H.324 defines the operations of terminals for low-bit-rate multimedia communication using V.34/V.34+ modems operating over the telephone network. H.324 terminals can carry real-time voice, data, and video, or any combination, including video-telephony.

The H.324 suite consists of five Recommendations: H.324, H.223, H.245, H.263, and G.723.1. H.261 Video Compression and T.120 operations are also included. Table 5–2 summarizes these Recommendations.

H.324 terminals may be integrated into personal computers or implemented in stand-alone devices such as videotelephones. The ability to use a specified common mode of operation is required, so that all terminals supporting that media type can interwork.

H.324 uses the logical channel signaling procedures of H.245. Procedures are provided for expression of receiver and transmitter capabilities, so transmissions are limited to what receivers can decode, and so that receivers request a particular desired mode from transmitters. According to the ITU-T, since the procedures of Recommendation H.245 are also planned for use by Recommendation H.310 for ATM networks, and Recommendation H.323 for non-guaranteed bandwidth LANs, interworking with these systems should be straightforward.

Table 5–2   H.324 and Supporting Recommendations

Recommendation	Description
H.324	Terminal for low bit-rate multimedia communications. It includes T.120 and V.34.
H.263	Speech coding at rates less than 64 kbit/s.
H.223	Multiplexing protocol for two-bit-rate multimedia terminals.
H.245	Control of data communications between multimedia terminals.
G.723.1	Speech coding for multimedia telecommunications transmitting at 5.3/6.3 kbit/s.

SUMMARY

The H Series Recommendations are relatively new to the industry and vendors are now placing these protocols into their products. H.323 is attracting considerable interest because it essentially makes a data-only LAN a multimedia LAN.

H.324 is viewed by many people as the preferred protocol stack for POTS multimedia services. While this claim may hold true, cable modems and the ADSL protocols must be factored into the H Series operations. Thus far, there has been no such effort.

6

Routing, Route Discovery, and Traffic Integrity Operations

T his chapter is a tutorial on several basic operations found in data communications networks and sets the stage for Chapters 7 and 8. The focus is on (1) labels and addresses, (2) routing, (3) route discovery, and (4) traffic integrity operations. The experienced reader can skip this chapter.

CONNECTION-ORIENTED AND CONNECTIONLESS NETWORKS

Most data communications networks today are designed to operate as either connection-oriented or connectionless systems. The Internet (and most internets) is connectionless in that IP operates in a connectionless mode. However, many of the transport protocols that are deployed in internets are connection-oriented, such as Frame Relay and ATM. (In an internet, IP, Frame Relay, and ATM may be required to interwork with each other. This subject is covered in the *ATM Volume III* to this series, so we will not rehash it here.)

As illustrated in Figure 6–1, a connection-oriented network is one in which no connection exists *initially* between the user device (we use the common term, DTE, for data terminal equipment to describe a user device) and the network. The connection between the network and network user is in an idle or disconnected state.

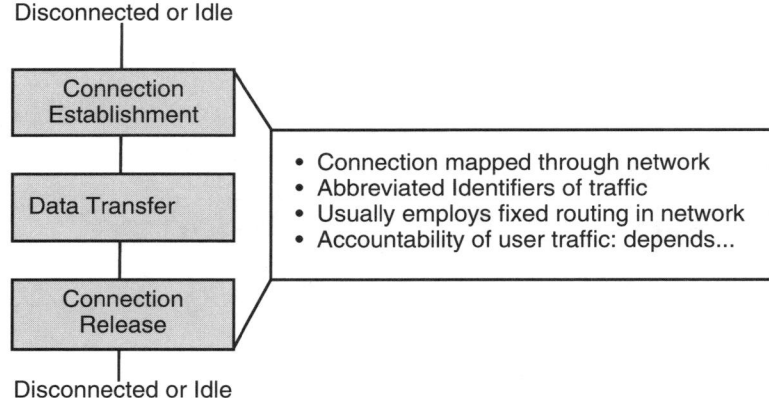

(a) Connection-oriented networks

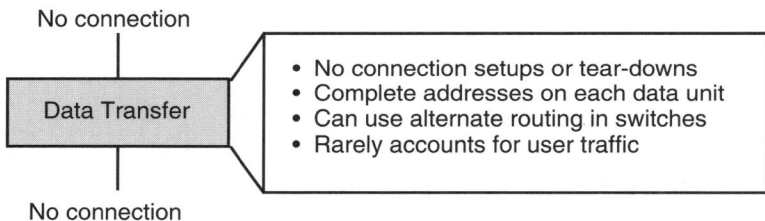

(b) Connectionless networks

Figure 6–1   Connecting into data networks.

In order for the DTEs to communicate through a connection-oriented network, they must go through a handshake, also called connection establishment. During this process, the users and the network may negotiate the services that are to be used during the session. Once the connection is established, data are exchanged in accordance with the negotiations that occurred during the connection-establishment phase. Eventually, the DTEs perform a connection release, after which they return to the idle or disconnected state.

The connection-oriented network usually provides a substantial amount of care for the user's signaling traffic (the traffic that sets up and tears down the connection). The procedure requires an acknowledgment from the network and the responding user that the connection is established; otherwise, the requesting DTE must be informed as to why the connection request was not successful. The network must also maintain an awareness of the end-to-end DTE/DTE connection. Flow control (i.e., making certain that all the data arrives in order, and does not saturate the user DTE) may be required of the network.

It can be seen that the connection-oriented network takes care of *its* traffic: the signaling traffic. But what about the user traffic that is transported after the signaling traffic sets up the connection? Well, it depends on the specific implementation.

In the past, error checking and error recovery of user traffic were performed by connection-oriented networks. They were designed to recover from lost traffic, misrouted traffic, and out-of-sequence traffic. However, the newer data communications networks do not perform these functions; therefore, if the user wishes to have these operations performed, they must be performed in the user's computer.

Another point should be made about the connection-oriented network. It is controlled by software or hardware modules operating in the user and network nodes that execute state diagrams (they are called state machines). These state diagrams govern the behavior of the network. For example, a state diagram controls how a connection to a network proceeds, from an idle connection, to an in-progress connection, to an active connection, and so on. These states are governed by timers, and if the timers expire without an action being completed, the state "machines" define remedial actions, such as trying again, or aborting the attempt to connect.

The connectionless (also called datagram) network goes directly from an idle condition to the data transfer mode, followed later by the idle condition. The major difference between this network and the connection-oriented network is the absence of the connection establishment and release phases. There are no state machines governing the behavior of the connectionless network (it is known as a stateless network). Moreover, a connectionless network (in most instances) has no acknowledgments, flow control, or error recovery of the user's traffic.

LABELS AND ADDRESSES

Connection-oriented networks usually identify each user's traffic with a label placed in the header of the user's traffic unit. This value is simply a number chosen from a table of numbers. They are managed so that they provide unambiguous identification of the user traffic. For connectionless traffic, the identifiers are not arbitrarily chosen numbers, but specific addresses that have some type of topological significance, such as

Table 6–1   Examples of Labels and Addresses.

Labels:

- Logical channel number (LCN): Used in X.25 packet header
- Data link connection identifier (DLCI): Used in Frame Relay frame header
- Virtual channel ID/virtual path ID (VPI/VCI): Used in ATM cell header

Addresses:

- Internet Protocol (IP): Used in IP datagram headers
- Telephone numbers: Used in some data systems
- X.121: Used in older X.25 packets during a connection setup
- E.164: Standard for ISDN addresses (supports telephone numbers)
- OSI: Used in ATM systems during connection setup

---

where:
  ATM   = Asynchronous Transfer Mode
  OSI   = Open Systems Interconnection

an IP address, a country id, an network id, a DTE id, and so on. With these addresses, the connectionless network can easily be one that supports dynamic routing by using topologically significant addresses, in contrast to the connection-oriented network that tends to use static routing because of the non-topologically significant labels.

Table 6–1 provides some examples of widely used labels and addresses. Labels are usually associated with layer 2 or layer 3 virtual circuits. In this example, the X.25 logical channel number (LCN) identifies the user traffic in the X.25 packet header. Likewise, the data link connection identifier (DLCI) identifies user traffic in a Frame Relay frame header and the same function is provided in an ATM cell header by the virtual channel identifier/virtual path identifier (VPI/VCI).

Quoting the old saying, "A rose by any other name is still a rose," a virtual circuit identifier by any other name is still a virtual circuit identifier.

The bottom part of this table shows examples of widely used addresses. Note that some of these addresses were designed for telephony systems but they are also employed in data communications systems.

TAKING CARE OF THE USER TRAFFIC

Some people in the industry confuse connection management with that of payload integrity management. The latter operation entails taking care of the user traffic; that is, instituting procedures to assure that the traffic is delivered safely to the destination host. Connection management and payload integrity management are completely separate from each other in how they operate in a network. However, this confusion exists because in the past, most connection-oriented protocols also provided payload integrity management with features such as the acknowledgment (ACK) of traffic for correctly received traffic, the negative acknowledgment (NAK) for incorrectly received traffic, and other features such as flow control operations. Notwithstanding, you should understand that even though a system may offer a user connection-oriented services, these services do not imply that the network will be responsible for the user payload being delivered correctly through the network.

Link Layer Operations

Figure 6–2 shows how payload integrity management is provided at the link layer (layer 2), wherein each node on a link performs operations to ensure the safe delivery of the traffic from one node to the other.

In order to account for the user traffic, rather extensive operations may be performed on behalf of the user. For example, error checking can occur at each node where the traffic is received. The sender then is sent either an ACK or NAK by the receiving node. In effect, a link layer proto-

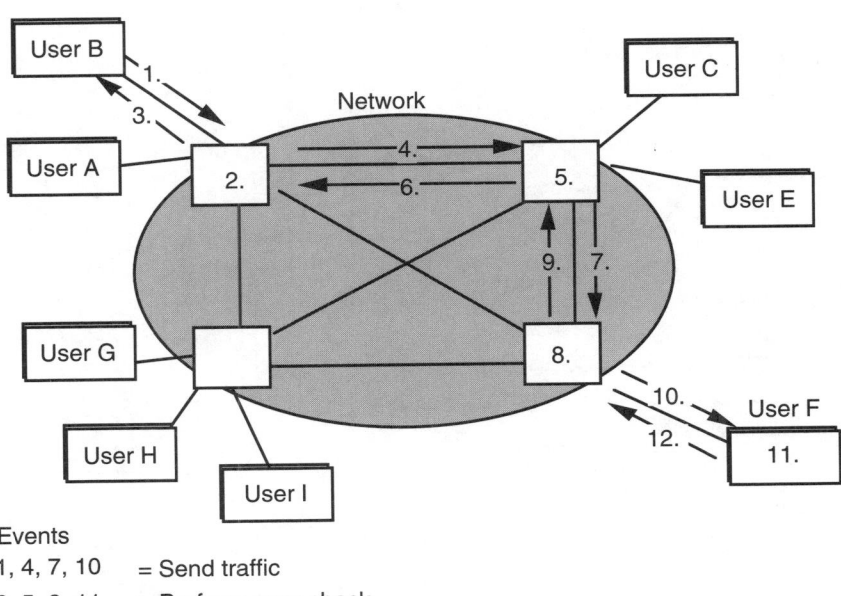

Events
1, 4, 7, 10   = Send traffic
2, 5, 8, 11   = Perform error check
3, 6, 9, 12   = ACKs or NAKs

Figure 6–2   Payload integrity management: Link level.

col that provides traffic integrity requires that the user payload be sent from the source on the link to the destination on the link with assurance that it will arrive safely and correctly at that destination. But be aware that link layer operations only insure that the traffic is delivered safely across one link. In Figure 6–2, four link layer operations are invoked to deliver traffic from user B to user F. Each link operation is separate from the others. For example, events 1, 2, and 3 are not known on the other links. The idea is to keep the link operations separated so that (if necessary) different link protocols can be placed onto each link.

The link layer does not insure the traffic is delivered safely end-to-end (from one user host machine to another). It insures the safe delivery across one link only. End-to-end delivery is left to the transport layer, discussed shortly.

Network Layer Operations

Some data communications systems provide for payload integrity management at the user-to-network interface (UNI) at the network layer (L_3). The prime example of this approach is the X.25 packet interface specification. In Figure 6–3, event 1 depicts the user sending packets to

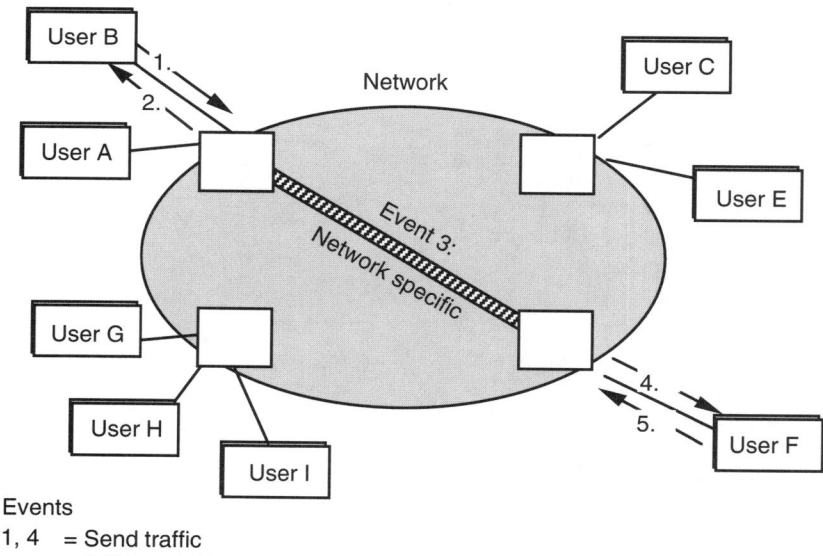

Events

1, 4 = Send traffic

2, 5 = ACKs or NAKs

Figure 6–3   Payload integrity management: Network interface.

the network where they are checked with a layer 3 protocol. This protocol does not perform bit error checks, but implements a routine to check for proper sequencing into the network. If the packets are sent to the network in the proper sequential order, the network acknowledges these packets by returning a packet to user B, as shown in event 2. Otherwise, the connection is reset (with the loss of packets).

The operations depicted in event 3 have traditionally not been defined in data communications networks. Consequently, these operations vary depending on the network specific implementations. Some data networks implement event 3 by providing a wide array of network integrity management operations while others provide very few features.

Finally, the operations just discussed in events 1 and 2 at the transmitting UNI are mirror images of the events 4 and 5 at the receiving UNI.

The layer 3 operations discussed here assume that layer 2 has performed an error check on the bits in the packet to determine if they have not been damaged during transferral. The error checks at layer 3 are primarily concerned with proper sequencing—have the packets arrived in order? So, if layer 2 cannot recover from an error, layer 3 will detect an out-of-sequence packet, and take remedial action.

Transport Layer Operations

Figure 6–4 shows yet another option for taking care of the user payload. It is called end-to-end traffic management because the end users are responsible for the operations. The figure shows two events occurring for this procedure. In event 1, user B sends traffic through the network to user F. In event 2, user F returns an acknowledgment of this traffic to user B.

In the data communications systems that have evolved in the last fifteen years, the operations shown in this figure are performed at layer 4 of the OSI Model, the transport layer. In most systems today, the protocol that provides these services is the Transmission Control Protocol (TCP), an Internet specification.

The dashed arrows in Figure 6–4 depict the traffic flowing through the network, and this layer 4 traffic is carried through the network via the invocation of lower layer protocols. Generally speaking, the network and these lower layer protocols are not aware of the layer 4 operations. Their job is to pass the layer 4 traffic safely between users B and F.

By the use of end-to-end payload integrity management procedures, the network implementor may be able to eliminate integrity and management operations at the lower layers. We say "may" because in some

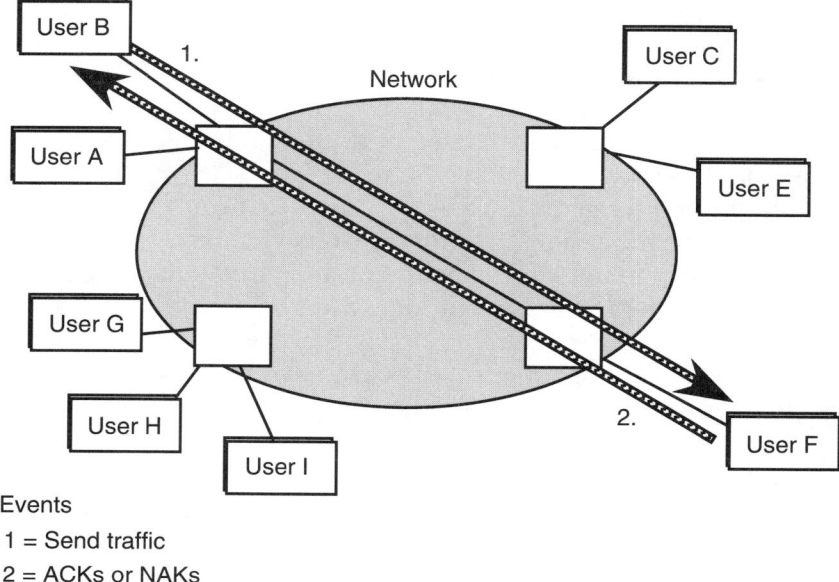

Events
1 = Send traffic
2 = ACKs or NAKs

Figure 6–4 Payload integrity management: User end-to-end.

situations, the use of layer 3 and/or layer 2 integrity management procedures may still be desirable. For example, if the network is using error-prone links, the use of layer 2 retransmission procedures provides a faster and more efficient way to recover from errors than the use of end-to-end integrity procedures.

Notwithstanding, the trend is toward the elimination of L_2 and L_3 retransmission operations. With the use of relatively error-free optical fibers, it makes little sense to perform L_2 retransmissions. Additionally, the L_3 sequencing checks are slowly but surely falling into disuse as X.25 is replaced with other user network interfaces such as Frame Relay and ATM.

RELAYING TRAFFIC THROUGH THE NETWORK

We now move to the subject of how data traffic is relayed through the network to the receiving user. Several methods are employed, and we start this analysis with a description of circuit switching, the principal time division multiplexing (TDM) technology employed in telephony systems.

Circuit Switching

Circuit switching provides a direct connection between two components or the "illusion" of a direct connection with a switch that provides almost nonvariable delay through the switching fabric. The direct connection of a circuit switch serves as an open "pipeline," permitting the two end-users to utilize the facility as they see fit—within bandwidth and tariff limitations. Many telephone networks use circuit switching systems.

Circuit switching only provides a path for the sessions between data communications components. Error checking, session establishment, frame flow control, frame formatting, selection of codes, and protocols are the responsibility of the users. Little or no care of the data traffic is provided in the circuit switching arrangement, although circuit-switched networks are built to be very reliable. Consequently, the telephone network is often used as the basic foundation for a data communications network, and additional facilities are added by the value-added carrier, network vendor, or user organization.

Message Switching

In the 1960s and 1970s, the pervasive method for switching data communications traffic was message switching. The technology is still widely used in certain applications, such as electronic mail, but it is not the architecture for a "backbone" network.[1] The switch is typically a specialized computer. It is responsible for accepting traffic from attached terminals and computers. It examines the address in the header of the message and switches (routes) the traffic to the receiving station.

Message switching is a store-and-forward technology: The messages are stored temporarily on disk units at the switches. The traffic is not considered to be interactive or real-time. However, selected traffic can be sent through a message switch at very high speeds by establishing levels of priority for different types of traffic.

The message switches were originally designed with a star topology: only one switch existed in the network. The reason? . . . The switches were too expensive to warrant the purchase of multiple switches.

---

[1]An example of the deployment of message switches in modern networks is the airlines' reservation systems. They use message switches as interfaces to a backbone Frame Relay, ATM, or X.25 network. The message switches readily adapt to variant workloads into/out of the reservation applications (holidays, etc.) that are attached to the message switches.

Packet Switching

Because of the problems with message switching and the development of large scale integration (LSI) and cheaper switches, the industry began to move toward a different data communications switching structure in the 1970s: packet switching. Packet switching distributes the workload to more than one switch, reduces vulnerability to network failure, and provides better utilization of the communications lines than does message switching.

Packet switching is so named because user data (for example, messages) are divided into smaller pieces. These pieces, or packets, have protocol control information (headers) placed around them and are routed through the network as independent entities.

The topology permits the traffic to be routed to alternate switches in case a particular switch encounters problems, such as congestion or a faulty link. Thus, packet switching provides for a very robust network. In addition, the small packets can be processed more quickly than longer data units, which translates to less delay for the traffic transfer.

Today's Internet is based on packet switching. Adaptive routing is used in the event of problems, and variable length frames are permitted, with some limitations.

Frame Relay

The best way to think of the Frame Relay technology is that it is a scaled down version of X.25. Like X.25, it is a fast relay, hold and forward technology. Unlike X.25, it provides fewer value-added features. The idea of eliminating features is to reduce delay and increase throughput of the user's traffic. Typically, the Frame Relay's topology is similar to a conventional packet switching system in that the architecture allows the distribution of workload and diversion of traffic around problem areas.

Frame Relay is designed specifically for transporting data traffic, although there is increasing interest in the industry for enhancing Frame Relay to support voice traffic. Frame Relay is also distinguished by its use of variable length protocol data units (PDUs) which are called frames.

Cell Relay

Cell relay represents an evolution from circuit switching and packet/frame switching. In essence, it combines some of the attributes of all the relay/switching technologies we have just discussed.

In relation to these other technologies, cell relay is distinguished by its use of fixed length protocol data units (called cells). In addition, the Asynchronous Transfer Mode (ATM), a cell-relay technology, is designed to support voice, video, and data traffic. Also, the ATM technology provides for extensive quality of service (QOS) operations for the user.

Once again, the topology of cell relay is distributed but the routing is fixed. This last statement may seem to be contradictory but the intent of the cell relay network is to provide for alternate paths in the event of severe problems in the network. But, it keeps the same path for each virtual circuit unless unusual problems occur.

EVOLUTION OF SWITCHING AND ROUTING TECHNIQUES

Data communications came along well after the voice communications technology was entrenched in the marketplace. Indeed, compared to telephony, data communications is an infant. Consequently, when data communications systems were first employed in the 1960s and 1970s, they used the circuit-switched telephone infrastructure for data communications traffic.

However, the circuit switch was never designed to support variable bit rate bursty asynchronous traffic. To meet this need, the message switch was developed. The message switch was widely deployed in the late 1960s and early 1970s.

At about this time, a new technology appeared in the data market, the local area network (LAN). This technology uses a broadcast approach on a shared media, so it does not need switches.

As depicted in Figure 6–5, the data networks diverged at this point into wide area networks (WANs) and local area networks (LANs). Let us move to the left side of the figure to trace the development of the WANs. As discussed earlier, due to the slow store-and-forward aspect of message switching as well as its star topology, the industry migrated to packet switches in the early 1970s. It was at this time that the concept of L_3 switching was implemented. Packet switches and L_3 switching remain a dominant technology today, but their progeny, the router, has taken over much of the marketplace from the conventional packet switch. The conventional router still employs L_3 relay operations, but it is designed with more data-specific features than can be found in the conventional X.25-based packet switch. In addition, it uses the term routing instead of switching (more on this subject later).

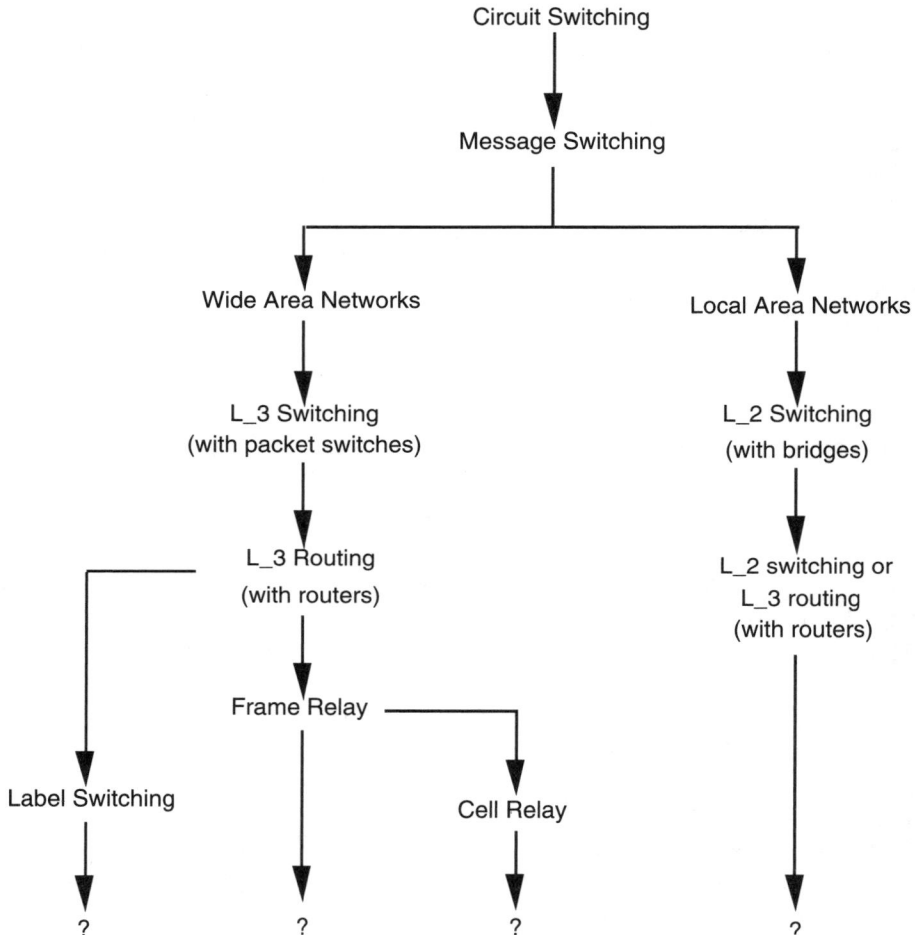

Figure 6–5   Evolution of data communications networks.

The figure shows a divergence at L_3 routing to label switching, Frame Relay, and cell relay. It should be emphasized that high-end routers can be configured to support all these functions. The point of this figure is to emphasize that conventional L_3 routing is different from label switching, Frame Relay, and cell relay. As we shall learn in Chapter 7, these three newer technologies are designed to increase the throughput and decrease the delay at the router.

Now let us take a look at the taxonomy in Figure 6–5 dealing with local area networks. LANs became prominent in the data communications industry in the early 1980s with the development and implementation of Ethernet. The LAN networks were distinguished from wide area packet switches through the use of a special machine called a bridge. The bridge connects LANs together and performs the same functions as a layer 3 switch except that its operations occur at layer 2. This concept is known in the industry as L_2 switching and uses the L_2 48-bit MAC destination address in a frame to make its switching decisions.

Routers are also placed in local area networks, as suggested in Figure 6–5. These routers are quite versatile and are capable of either L_2 switching or L_3 routing.

So, what is the difference between the terms switching and routing? As a general definition, routing has meant making L_3 relaying decisions in software, whereas switching has meant making L_3 or L_2 relay decisions in hardware. Be aware that vendors have different definitions of the terms switching and routing. In fact, the old X.25-based packet *switches* perform their operations in software.

To conclude this brief analysis, the bottom part of the picture shows the evolution to question marks. This depiction is meant to convey that the future of how data communications networks are constructed has not been decided. The components of cell relay hold that cell relay is the best answer. The proponents of label switching back their technology, and so on. In all likelihood, the future data communications networks will be hybrids of label switching, Frame Relay, cell relay, and bridging.

COMPARISON OF ROUTING AND SWITCHING PROTOCOLS

Frame Relay and cell relay (also called cell switching) evolved from packet switching. The three technologies are similar in some of their characteristics, but do have differences. Table 6–2 provides a summary of their similarities and differences, as well as the Internet Protocol (IP). For packet switching, the X.25 specification is used. For cell relay, the ATM specification is used. Frame Relay assumes the use of the Frame Relay specification.

BRIDGES AND ROUTERS

Networks were originally conceived to be fairly small systems consisting of relatively few machines. As the need for data communications services has grown, it has become necessary to connect networks to-

Table 6–2 Data Communications Technology Comparisons

Attribute	IP	Packet Switching (X.25)	Frame Relay	Cell Relay (ATM)
Application support?	Asynchronous data (not designed for voice)	Asynchronous data (not designed for voice)	Asynchronous data (voice use is emerging)	Asynchronous, synchronous voice, video, data
Connection mode?	Connectionless	Connection-oriented	Connection-oriented	Connection-oriented
Congestion management?	None, performed by TCP	A receive not ready packet (RNR)	Congestion notification, traffic tagging, and possibly traffic discard	Congestion notification, traffic tagging, and possibly traffic discard
Identifying traffic?	IP address	Virtual circuit id: The LCN and an X.121 or an OSI address	Virtual circuit id: The DLCI and an E.164 address	Virtual circuit id: The VPI/VCI and an OSI address
Congestion notification?	None, performed by TCP	A receive not ready packet (RNR)	The BECN and FECN bits in the header	The CN bits in the PTI field
Traffic tagging?	None	None	The discard eligibility bit (DE)	The cell loss priority (CLP) bit
PDU size?	Variable (a datagram)	Variable (a packet)	Variable (a frame)	Fixed at 48 bytes plus header (a cell)
Sequence numbers	None	Yes	No	Cell header, no; for payload, depends on payload type
ACKs/NAKs/ Resends?	None, performed by TCP	Yes, at layer 2	No	Only for signaling traffic (SVCs)
Position in industry	Quite prevalent	Quite prevalent	Quite prevalent	Not prevalent, but growing in use

where:

BECN = Backward explicit congestion notification
CN   = Congestion notification
FECN = Forward explicit congestion notification

gether for the sharing of resources, the distribution of functions, and administrative control. In addition, some LANs, by virtue of their restricted distance, often need to be connected together through other devices, such as bridges and routers.

Figure 6–6 shows the relationships of these devices vis-à-vis a layered model. A *repeater* is used to connect the media on a LAN, typically called media segments. The repeater has no upper layer functions, its principal job is to terminate the signal on one LAN segment and regenerate it on another LAN segment.

The *bridge* operates at the data link layer (always at the MAC sublayer and sometimes at the LLC sublayer). Typically, it uses MAC physical addresses to perform its relaying functions. As a general rule, it is a fairly low-function device and connects networks that are homogeneous (for example, IEEE-based networks).

A *router* operates at the network layer because it uses network layer addresses (for example: IP, X.121, E.164 addresses). It usually contains more capabilities than a bridge and may offer flow control mechanisms as well as source routing or non-source routing features.

The term *gateway* is used to describe an entity (a machine or software module) that not only performs routing capabilities but may act as a protocol conversion or mapping facility (also called a convergence function). For example, such a gateway could relay traffic and also provide conversion between two different types of mail transfer applications.

To avoid any confusion about these terms, some people use the term *internetworking unit* (IWU). An IWU is a generic term to describe a router, a gateway, a bridge, or anything else that performs relaying functions between networks.

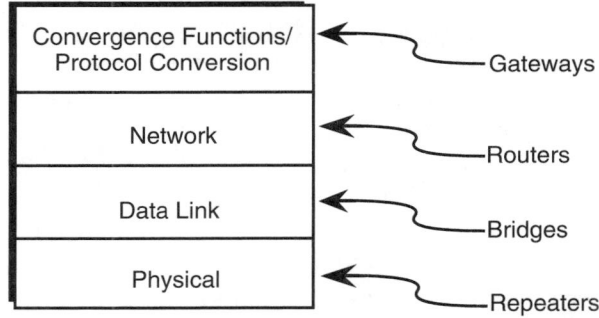

Figure 6–6   Placement of internetworking units.

ROUTE ADVERTISING

There are two types of route advertising protocols used in the data communications industry: distance-vector and link state metric.

The distance-vector protocol is more commonly known as a minimum hop protocol, which means the protocol searches for a path between a sending and receiving machine that has the fewest number of intermediate machines (hops) between them. The term "distance" refers to number of hops, to a "vector" (an address).

The link state metric protocol assigns a value (metric) to each link in the system. Each node advertises its links by sending messages to its neighbors. These messages contain the link's metric (or metrics, if advertising is done on more than one metric criterion). The path chosen between the machines is the one in which the metrics of all the links making up the path are summed to a lower value than any other contending path.

Distance vector operations rely on each neighbor informing its neighbor(s) about their knowledge of the topology of downstream or upstream nodes. In Figure 6–7, F informs E that it is directly attached to G on the same network. Since E is aware that it is next to G, it informs C that it is one hop away from G.

C then knows that it is two hops away from G and so C informs A. Since A knows that it is one hop away from C, and has received an advertisement of C's two hops to G, A can make the inference that it is three hops away from G.

The advertisements of D and B also reach A. It is not unusual for a node to receive multiple advertisements about an address. A makes comparisons of the two alternative routes (one through C and one through B). Obviously A would make the choice using C, since B's advertisements would reveal that it is more hops away from G.

The link state metric approach is shown in Figure 6–8. Note that A continues to receive two advertisements about host G. These advertisements contain the sum of the metrics associated with each link connected to the nodes that created the advertisements. The single advertisement begins with node F advertising a "distance" of 2 to host G. This advertisement is conveyed to node E. Previously, nodes F and E have ascertained that the link state metric on the link between them has a value of 1. Consequently, node E adds 1 to the value of 2 it received from node F's advertisement and creates a route advertisement message to send to node C. Since this advertisement is transmitted across the link between nodes

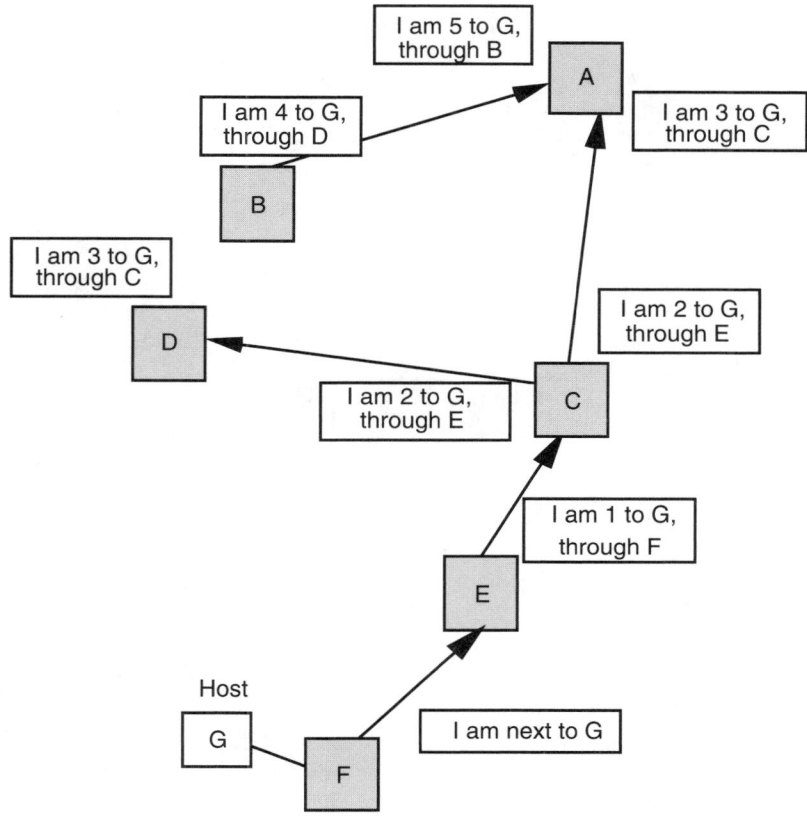

Figure 6–7 Exchanging information: Minimum hop advertising.

E and C, node C adds the metric associated with this link to the advertised value of 3 coming from E and creates two advertising messages. One message is sent to node A and the other is sent to node D.

The messages find their way to node A, where the final link state sum is 10 on one path and 9 on the other. Consequently, if node A receives traffic destined for host G, it will relay this traffic to node B. Even though C represents the shortest path in number of hops, the path emanating from node B represents the shortest path in relation to the metric count. This situation can occur if (for example) the link between nodes C and A is congested or operating at lesser capacity than the links on the alternate path.

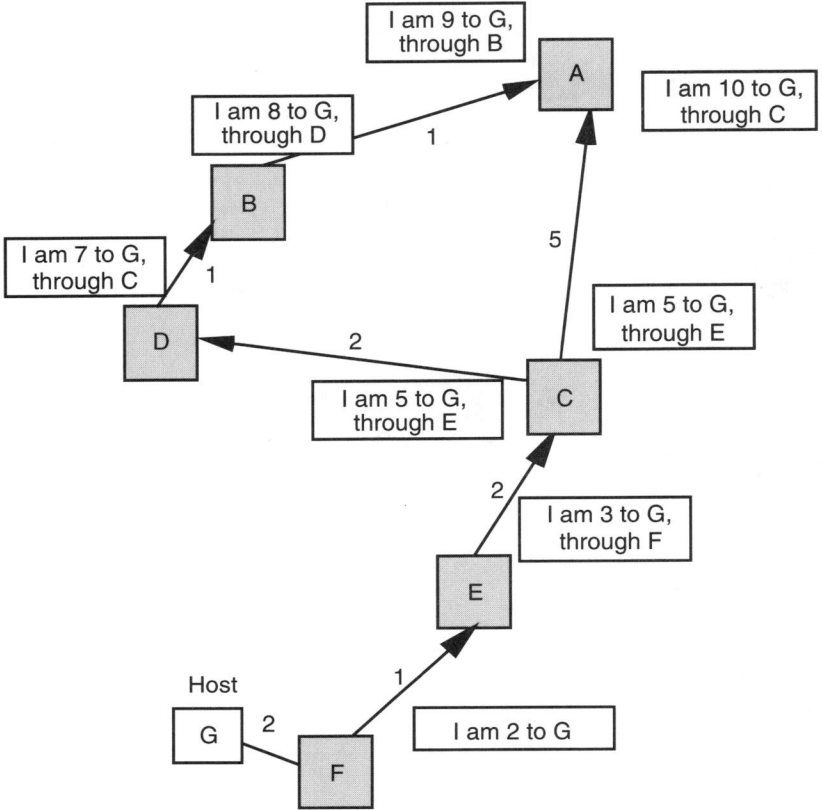

Figure 6–8   Exchanging information: Link state advertising.

SUMMARY

This chapter has served to acquaint the newcomer with several basic operations found in data communications networks. With this information in mind, we expand this discussion in Chapter 7 and examine a relatively new technique called label switching.

7

IP Routing and Label Switching

$$T$$his chapter explores how IP and companion processes route and switch IP datagrams. The initial emphasis on the chapter is to describe how IP routing occurs in traditional internet operations. Next, the concepts of classless routing and route aggregation are explored as well as the variable length subnet mask. Then the chapter describes some of the problems associated with traditional IP routing and explores alternatives, which are called "label switching" (LS).[1]

CLARIFICATION OF TERMS

The term *port* has been used in the past to identify a physical port on a machine connected to a communications link or a logical port associated with a software module. The former (older) use of the term is being replaced with the term physical interface or just interface.

---

[1]The term "label switching" is chosen because terms such as IP switching, tag switching, cell switching routing, etc. are often associated with a specific solution (and specific vendor). Therefore, the term label switching is used to describe an overall concept whose implementations can vary. I thank the authors of *Switching and IP Networks* for their clarification on these terms (B. Davie, P. Doolan, and Y. Rekhter offer this distinction. Their text is published by Morgan Kaufmann Publishers Inc., San Francisco, CA).

The term *interface* is used in this chapter as a physical interface. The term *port* means a software port.

To aid in reading this chapter, interfaces are identified with a character, such as a, b, c, and so on. Labels are identified with numerals, such as 0, 14, and so on. In practice, interfaces are usually identified with a numeral.

IP ROUTING OPERATIONS

To set the stage for this chapter, we first examine how an IP datagram is processed by a router. Figure 7–1 shows the operations at a router on an incoming IP datagram.[2] The incoming datagram is stored in a queue to await processing.

In L3 routing, the operations are divided into two major procedures: forwarding and control. Forwarding is responsible for the actual placement of the datagrams through the router from the input interface to the output interface. The forwarding process uses the routing table and the addresses in the incoming IP datagram. The control operation entails the route discovery protocols introduced in earlier parts of this book. Recall that their job is to advertise (exchange) routing information among

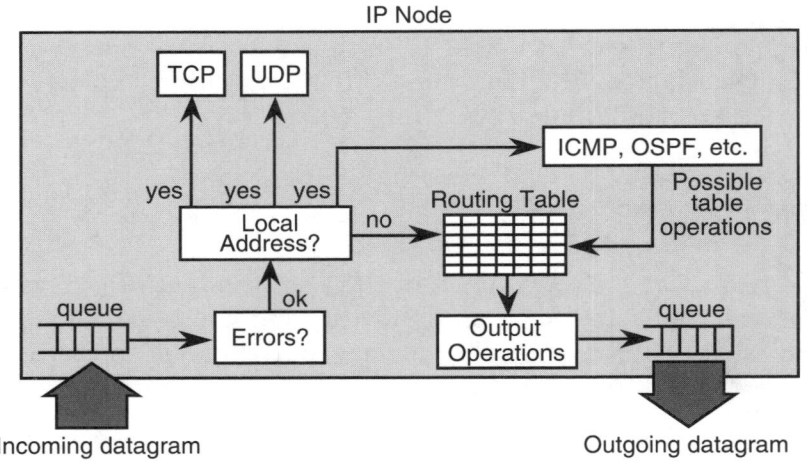

Figure 7–1   Processing the datagram.

---

[2]See W. R. Stevens, *TCP/IP Illustrated*, p. 112, published by Addison-Wesley. Mr. Steven's figure does not contain the error check operation, which I have added in this figure.

the routers in the subnet or subnets. The examples cited earlier in Chapter 2 are OSPF, RIP, BGP, and so on. We return to the concepts of forwarding and control later in this chapter when we pick up the topic of label switching in more detail.

Once processing begins, the routing decisions take place depending on how the router is set up and if the routing is unicast or multicast traffic. For unicast traffic, the router performs a longest match check on the destination address. For unicast traffic with types of services (TOS), the longest match check is performed, plus an exact match on the TOS field in the datagram header. (The longest match is explained later in this chapter.)

For multicast traffic, a longest match is performed on the source address, and an exact match is performed on the source and destination address in regard to incoming interfaces. The source address must be checked to ensure efficient distribution of multicast datagrams. For example, a multicast router might receive more than one copy of the datagram from different incoming interfaces. It must quietly discard the datagrams arriving over a "non-preferred" route.

Initially, the datagram header is checked for any modifications (distortions of the bits) that may have occurred to its contents during its journey on the link from the sending IP node to this IP node. Next, it is determined if the IP address is local; if so, the IP protocol ID field in the header is used to pass the bits in the data field to the next module, such as TCP, UDP, and ICMP.

An IP node can be configured to forward or not forward datagrams. If the node is a forwarding node, the IP destination address in the IP datagram header is matched against a routing table to calculate the next node (next hop) that is to receive the datagram. If a match in the table to the destination address is found, the datagram is forwarded to the next node. Otherwise, it is sent to a default route, or it is discarded.

AN IP ROUTING TABLE

Figure 7–2 is an example of a typical routing table found in a router. Individual systems differ in the contents of the routing table; for example, the table in a Cisco router differs from a Bay router, but they all resemble this example. Each row of the table contains an IP address and associated information about that address. The column entries in the table are:

• *Destination:* IP address of the destination node for this row entry. The entry is 172.16.8.231.

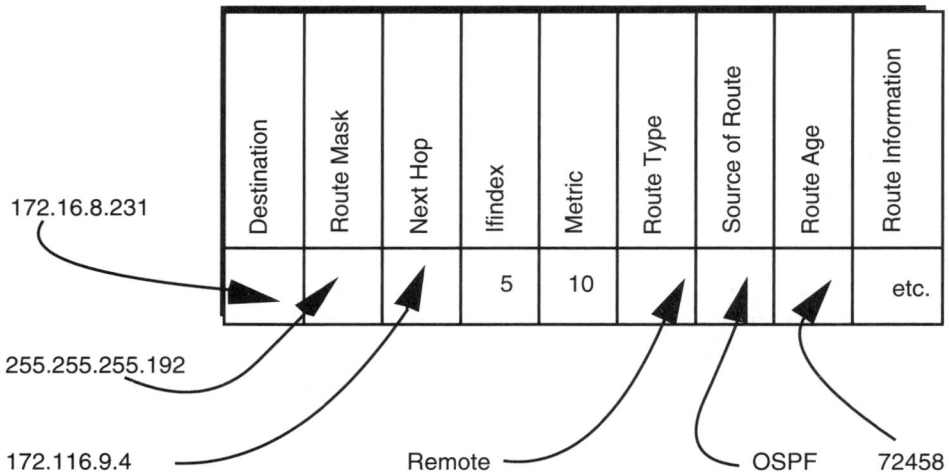

Figure 7–2 Typical routing table.

- *Route Mask:* Mask that is used with destination address in IP header and destination address in the table to identify bits pertaining to the prefix part of an address. The entry is 2.55.255.255.192.
- *Next Hop:* IP address of the next hop (next node) in the route, which is 172.116.9.4.
- *Ifindex:* Output interface on the router to reach the next hop address.
- *Metric:* "Cost" to reach the destination address, such as a hop count or metric (described in Chapter 6).
- *Route Type:* Directly attached to router (DIRECT), or reached through another router (REMOTE).
- *Source of Route:* How the route was discovered, by OSPF, RIP, and so on.
- *Route Age:* In seconds, since the route was last updated.
- *Route Information:* Miscellaneous information.

NETWORK MASKS

At first glance, it might appear that the IP addressing scheme is flexible enough to accommodate the identification of a sufficient number of networks and hosts to service almost any user or organization. But this is not the case. The Internet designers were not shortsighted; they simply failed to account for the explosive growth of the Internet as well as the rapid growth of TCP/IP in private networks.

The problem arises when a network administrator attempts to identify a large number of networks and/or computers (such as personal computers) attached to these networks. The problem becomes onerous because of the need to store and maintain many network addresses and the associated requirement to access these addresses through large routing tables. The use of the address advertising to exchange routing information requires immense resources if they must access and maintain big addressing tables.

The problem is compounded when networks are added to an internet. The addition requires the reorganization of routing tables and perhaps the assignment of additional addresses to identify the new networks.

To deal with this problem, the Internet task forces established a scheme whereby multiple networks are identified by one address entry in the routing table. Obviously, this approach reduces the number of network addresses needed in an internet. It also requires a modification to the routing algorithms and the use of a subnet mask, but the change is minor in comparison to the benefits derived.

Figure 7–3 shows how a subnet mask is interpreted. Assume a class B IP address of 128.1.17.1, with a mask of 255.255.240.0. At a router, to discover the subnet address value, the mask has a bitwise Boolean *and* operation performed on the destination address as shown in the figure. The mask is also applied to the destination address in the datagram.

	128.	1.	17.	1
IP address	10000000	00000001	0001|0001	00000001
Mask	11111111	11111111	1111|0000	00000000
Result	10000000	00000001	0001|	don't care
Logical address	128	1	1	don't care
	network		sub net	host

Note: "don't care" means router doesn't care at this time (the router is looking for subnet matches)

Figure 7–3 Address masking operations.

The notation "don't care" means that the router is not concerned at this point with the host address. It is concerned with getting the datagram to the proper subnetwork. So, in this example, it uses the mask to discover that the first 4 bits of the host address are to be used for the subnet address. Further, it discovers that the subnet address is 1.

As this example shows, when the subnet mask is split across octets, the results can be a bit confusing if you are "octet-aligned." In this case, the actual value for the subnet address is 0001_2 or 1_{10}, even though the decimal address of the "host" space is 17.1. However, the software does not care about octet alignment. It is looking for a match of the destination address in the IP datagram to an address in a routing table, based on the mask that is stored in the routing table.

ADDRESS AGGREGATION

The class address scheme (A, B, C) described in Chapter 2 has proved to be too inflexible to meet the needs of the growing Internet. For example, the class A address of 47 means that three bytes are allocated to identify hosts attached to network 47, resulting in 2^{24} hosts on the single network! . . . clearly not realistic. Moreover, the network.host address does not allow more than a two-level hierarchical view of the address. Multiple levels of hierarchy are preferable, because they permit using fewer entries in routing tables and the aggregation of lower-level addresses to a higher-level address.

The introduction of subnets in the IP address opened the way to better utilize the IP address space by implementing a multilevel-level hierarchy. This approach allows the aggregation of networks to reduce the size of routing tables.

Figure 7–4 is derived from Halabi,[3] and shows the advertising operations that occur without route aggregation (without Classless Interdomain Routing [CIDR], discussed later). The ISPs are ultimately advertising all their addresses to the Internet to a NAP. Four addresses are shown here, but in an actual situation, thousands of addresses might be advertised.

In contrast to the above example where each address is advertised to the Internet, the use of masks allows fewer addresses to be advertised. In Figure 7–5, ISP1 and ISP2 are using masks of 16 bits in length

---

[3]B. Halabi, *Internet Routing Architectures*, published by Cisco Press, 1997.

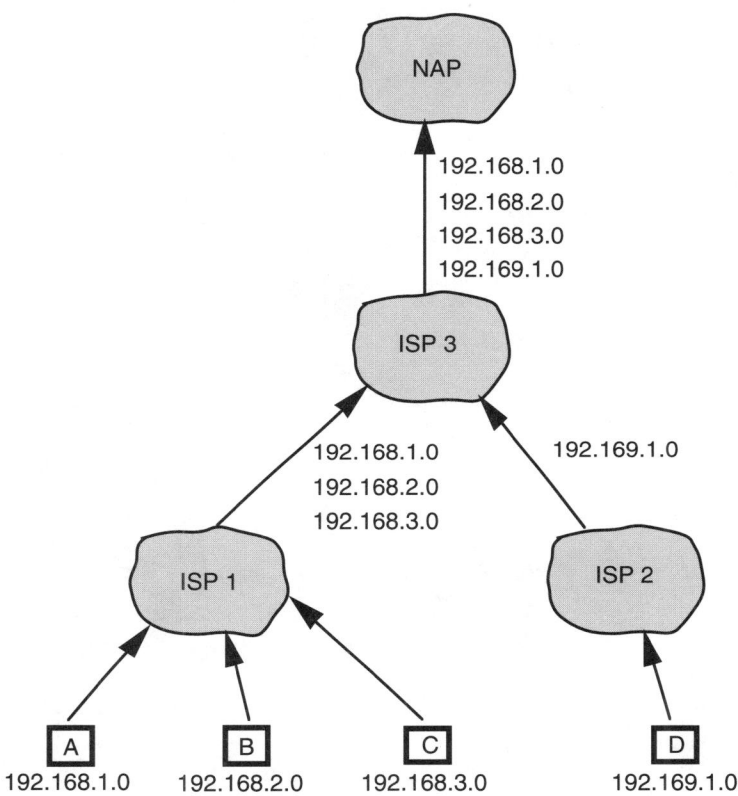

Figure 7–4   **Without aggregation.** (*Source:* **B. Halabi,** *Inter-*
net Routing Architectures, **published by Cisco Press, 1997.)**

(255.255.0.0), and ISP1 need only advertise address 192.168.0.0 with the
16-bit mask to inform all interested nodes that all addresses behind this
mask can be found at 192.168.x.x. ISP1 uses the same mask to achieve
the same goal.

ISP3 uses a mask of 8 bits (255.0.0.0), which effectively aggregates
the addresses of ISP1 and ISP2 under the aggregation domain of ISP3.
Thus, in this simple example, one address is advertised to the NAP instead of four.

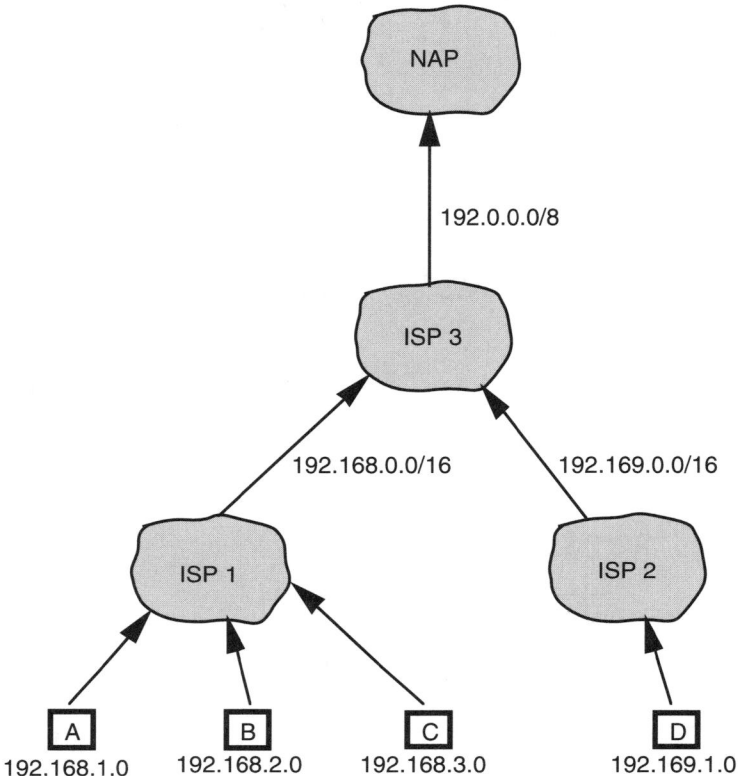

Note: The notations /16 and /8 refer to the lengths of masks

where:
NAP   Network Access Point
ISP   Internet service provider

Figure 7–5   With aggregation. (*Source:* B. Halabi, *Internet Routing Architectures*, published by Cisco Press, 1997.)

The Longest Match Rule

Address aggregation requires that routes are selected by using the longest match rule. A router must use a longer mask if the same network is advertised with more than one prefix.

Figure 7–6 shows one reason for using the longest match rule. ISP2 has two ways to get to the MAP: One way is through ISP3 and the other is directly to the NAP. ISP3 has aggregated addresses 192.169.1.0 and 192.169.2.0 (and others) to an 8-bit prefix. ISP2 has a more specific mask being advertised to the NAP with a 16-bit prefix. It so happens that by

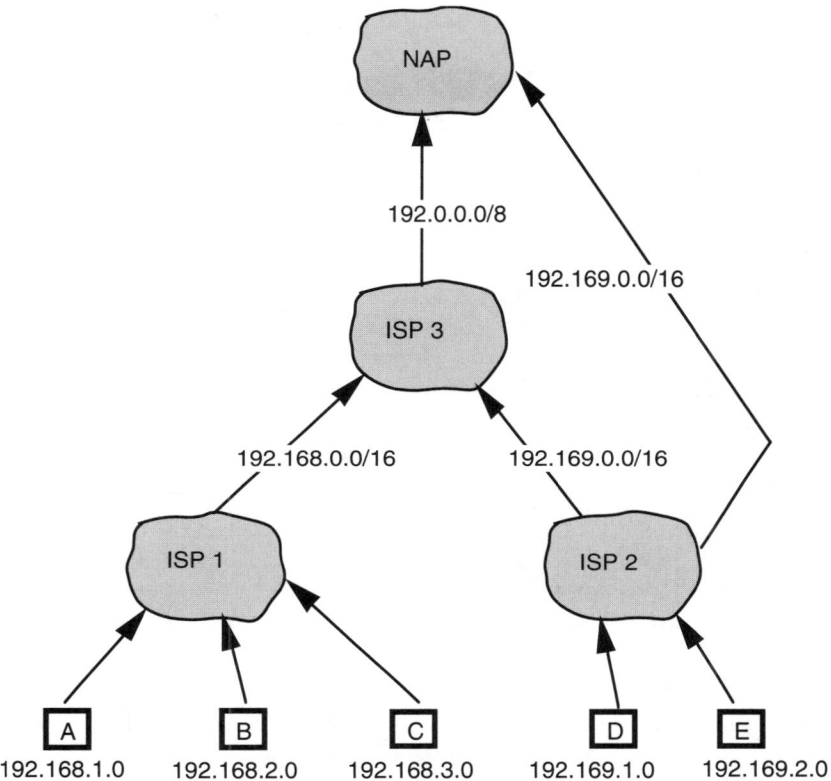

Note: The notations /16 and /8 refer to the lengths of masks

where:
NAP   Network access point
ISP   Internet service provider

Figure 7–6   Longest match.

using the longest match rule, the NAP will route traffic for these addresses to ISP2 and avoid extra hops of going through ISP3.

CLASSLESS INTERDOMAIN ROUTING (CIDR)

In order to extend the limited address space of an IP address, Classless Interdomain Routing (CIDR) is now used in many systems. It permits networks to be grouped together logically and to use one entry in a routing table for multiple class C networks.

Here is how the concept works. The first requirement for CIDR is for multiple networks to share a certain number of bits in the high-order part of the IP address. In this example, assume the first 7 bits in the address are the same. Thus, by using the mask of 254.0.0.0 (11111110.00000000.00000000.00000000), all addresses between say 194.0.0.0 and 195.255.255.255 can be identified by a single entry in the routing table.

Additional information on CIDR is available in RFCs 1518, 1519, 1466, and 1447.

VARIABLE LENGTH SUBNET MASKS

Subnet masks are useful in internetworking operations, especially the variable length subnet mask (VLSM). Figure 7–7 (which is a summary of a more detailed example from the Halabi reference) shows the idea of VLSM.

We assume an organization is using a class C address of 192.168.1.x. The organization needs to set up three networks (subnets) as shown in this figure. Subnet A has 100 hosts attached to it, and subnets B and C support 50 hosts each.

Recall from our previous discussions that the subnet mask is used to determine how many bits are set aside for the subnet and host addresses. This figure shows the possibilities for the class C address. (The resultant numbers in the table assume that the reserved numbers are used, which is possible, since 192.168.1.x is from a pool of private addresses, and can be used as the organization chooses.)

The use of one mask for the three subnets will not work. A mask of 255.255.255.128 yields only 2 subnets, and a mask of 255.255.255.192 yields only 64 hosts.

Fortunately, different subnetwork masks can be used on each subnet. As the figure shows, subnet A uses subnet mask 255.255.255.128, and subnets B and C use subnet mask 255.255.255.192.

Not all route discovery protocols support subnetwork masks. So, check your product before you delve into this operation.

THE HIGH OVERHEAD OF IP ROUTING

With the advent of subnet operations, the routing operations to support diverse topology and addressing needs are greatly enhanced. As an added bonus, the 32-bit IP address space is utilized more effectively.

Class C Address of 192.168.1.x is used by an organization

Organization needs the following topology:

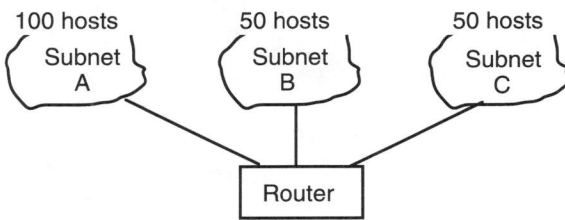

Possible Masks:

Subnet Mask	Resultant Subnets*	Resultant Hosts*
255.255.255.128	2	128
255.255.225.192	4	64
255.255.225.224	8	32
255.255.225.240	16	16
255.255.225.248	32	8
255.255.225.252	64	4

* Assumes use of reserved bits

Use .128 yields 2 subnets with 128 hosts each: Won't work
Use .192 yields 3 subnets with 64 hosts each: Won't work

Answer? Use both (Variable length subnet mask):

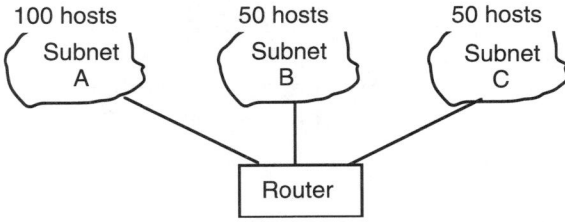

Subnet A mask = 255.255.255.128
Subnet B mask = 255.255.255.192
Subnet C mask = 255.255.255.192

**Figure 7–7   Managing the IP addresses. (*Source:* B. Halabi,
Internet Routing Architectures, Cisco Press, 1997.)**

However, these features translate into a more complex set of operations at the router. Moreover, as the Internet and internets continue to grow, the router may be required to maintain large routing tables. In a conventional routing operation, the processing load to handle many addresses in combination with subnet operations can lead to serious utilization problems for the router.

Part of the overhead stems from the fact that a network can be configured with different subnet masks. The router must check each entry in the routing table to ascertain the mask, even though the table addresses may point to the same network. This concept provides considerable flexibility in configuring different numbers of hosts to different numbers of subnets. For example, a class C address could use different subnet masks to identify different numbers of hosts attached to different subnets in an enterprise: say 120 hosts at one site and 62 at another.

To route traffic efficiently, the router must prune (eliminate) table entries that do not match the masked portion of the table entry and the destination IP address in the datagram. After the table is pruned, the remaining entries must be searched for the longest match, and "more general" route masks are discarded.

After all these operations, the router has to deal with the type of service (TOS) (in practice, TOS may not be implemented), the best metric, and perhaps special procedures dealing with routing policies.

To show how the router performs the operations described in the previous section, Figure 7–8 shows a routing table that is stored in the router. The table is quite abbreviated, showing just a few entries, and is a summary of a more detailed example in the Buck Graham reference.[4] The figure depicts how the table is pruned down to the two entries shown at the bottom of the figure. This example does not include the table entries on default routes. This type of route is identified with a mask of all 0s.

For high-end routers that are placed in the Internet to interwork between the large internet service providers, the routing table could contain several thousand entries. To execute the operations of masking, table pruning, and longest mask matching requires extensive computational resources.

Notice that the first match prunes the table to four entries. The first match follows these rules. Rule 1: Prune (eliminate) all entries in the table in which the masked part of the destination address (172.16.8.66) is not identical to the masked part of the destination address in the table.

---

[4]B. Graham, *TCP/IP Addressing*, AP Professional. I highly recommend this book to the reader, as well as the Halabi text, cited in footnote 3.

• Destination Address is: 172.16.8.66:

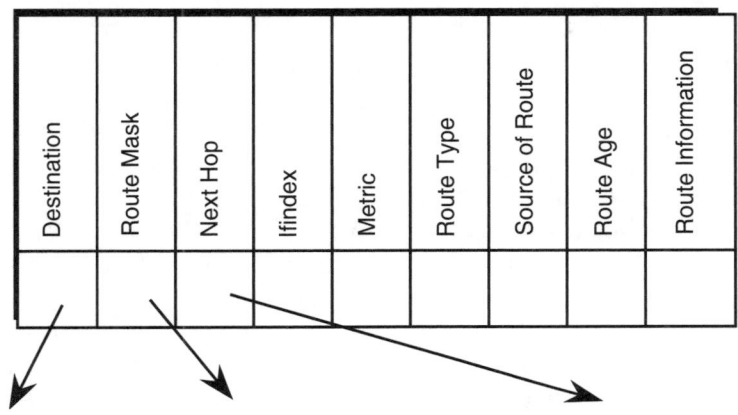

The Basic Match:

172.16.0.0	255.255.0.0	172.16.3.65	match 1
172.16.3.0	255.255.255.192	172.16.3.1	no match a
172.16.8.0	255.255.255.0	172.16.3.65	match 2
172.16.8.0	255.255.255.192	172.16.3.65	no match b
172.16.8.64	255.255.255.192	172.16.3.65	match 3
172.16.8.64	255.255.255.192	172.16.3.62	match 4
172.16.25.192	255.255.255.192		no match c

...and many others..

After the Basic Match:

172.16.0.0	255.255.0.0	172.16.3.65
172.16.8.0	255.255.255.0	172.16.3.65
172.16.8.64	255.255.255.192	172.16.3.65
172.16.8.64	255.255.255.192	172.16.3.62

After Longest Match:

172.16.8.64	255.255.255.192	172.16.3.65
172.16.8.64	255.255.255.192	172.16.3.62

Figure 7–8   An example of how IP routing occurs. (*Source*: Buck Graham, *TCP/IP Addressing*, AP Professional, 1998.)

So, the mask for each destination IP address in the table is applied to the destination IP address in the datagram and the destination address in the table. Rule 2: Keep the remaining entry (entries) in the pruned table that has (have) the longest mask (the most specific mask). After the longest match, two entries remain for consideration in this example. If more than one entry remains, the route taken may depend on metrics, or the network administration's policy. The next part of this explanation will explain how the rules were executed.

Figure 7–9 shows how the routing table was pruned, and how the route was chosen. First, for match 1, the 255.255.0.0 mask for this table entry address covers the first 16 bits of address 172.16.0.0, and 172.16 is equal to the first 16 bits of the destination IP address in the datagram.

The no-match labeled (a) uses a mask of 255.255.255.192, or 26 bits (including the first two bits of the fourth octet of table address 172.16.3.0). Obviously, address 172.16.3. (and first 2 bits in octet 4) does not equal 172.16.8. (and first 2 bits in octet 4).

For match 2, the mask of 255.255.255.0 covers 24 bits of the table address 172.16.8.0. So, this is another exact match to the datagram address.

The no-match labeled (b) also uses mask 255.255.255.192. So, this no-match occurs because the table address of 172.16.8. (and first 2 bits of octet 4) does not equal the datagram address. The no-match labeled (c) also yields an unequal match.

For matches 3 and 4, the mask of 255.255.255.192 again covers 26 bits. Thus, the IP datagram address matches these two addresses because:

$$x.x.x.64 = x.x.x.01000000$$
$$x.x.x.66 = x.x.x.01000010$$

The binary equivalents of 64 and 66 are not equal, but the mask ends at bit 26, so bits 27–32 are not examined.

Finally, the routing candidates are matches 3 and 4 because they meet Rule 2. They have the longest route mask in comparison to the entries shown as matches 1 and 2.

SOURCE ROUTING

IP uses a mechanism called source routing as part of its routing algorithm.[5] Source routing allows an upper layer protocol (ULP) to deter-

---

[5]Source routing is not used much in the Internet. I introduce it here because it will become more important in the Internet and internets to support fixed path routing for delay-sensitive traffic.

Destination address in the datagram: 172.16.8.66, or
    10101100.00010000.00001000.01000010:

For match 1:
    Mask: 11111111.11111111.00000000.00000000
    Table address   10101100.00010000.00000000.00000000
    Datagram address   10101100.00010000.00001000.01000010

For no-match (a):
    Mask: 11111111.11111111.11111111.11000000
    Table address   10101100.00010000.00000011.00000000
    Datagram address   10101100.00010000.00001000.01000010

For match 2:
    Mask: 11111111.11111111.11111111.00000000
    Table address   10101100.00010000.00001000.00000000
    Datagram address   10101100.00010000.00001000.01000010

For no-match (b):
    Mask: 11111111.11111111.11111111.11000000
    Table address   10101100.00010000.00001000.00000000
    Datagram address   10101100.00010000.00001000.01000010

For match 3:
    Mask: 11111111.11111111.11111111.11000000
    Table address   10101100.00010000.00001000.01000000
    Datagram address   10101100.00010000.00001000.01000010

For match 4:
    Mask: 11111111.11111111.11111111.11000000
    Table address   10101100.00010000.00001000.01000000
    Datagram address   10101100.00010000.00001000.01000010

For no-match (c):
    Mask: 11111111.11111111.11111111.11000000
    Table address   10101100.00010000.00011001.11000000
    Datagram address   10101100.00010000.00001001.01000010

Figure 7–9 How the routes were chosen. (*Source:* Buck
Graham, *TCP/IP Addressing,* AP Professional, 1998.)

mine how the IP nodes route the datagrams. The ULP has the option of passing a list of internet addresses to the IP module. The list contains the intermediate IP nodes that are to be transited during the routing of the datagrams to the final destination. The last address on the list is the final destination of an intermediate node.

When IP receives a datagram, it uses the addresses in the source routing field to determine the next intermediate hop. As illustrated in Figure 7–10, IP uses a pointer field to learn about the next IP address. If a check of the pointer and length fields indicate the list has been completed, the destination IP address field is used for routing. If the list is not exhausted, the IP module uses the IP address indicated by the pointer.

The IP module then replaces the value in the source routing list with its own address. It must then increment the pointer by one address (4 bytes) in order for the next hop to retrieve the next IP address in the route. With this approach, the datagram follows the source route dictated by the ULP and also records the route along the way.

In the first step, in Figure 7–10, IP uses the pointer to locate the next address in the route data field. In this example, it locates address 128.2.3.4 and makes a routing decision based on this address. In step 2, it places its own address in the route data field in the same location of the current destination address. In the third step, it increments the pointer value to enable the next IP module to determine the next (or final) hop in the route.

COMPARISON OF ROUTING AND LABEL SWITCHING

Figure 7–11 shows two methods of relaying traffic through a network. At the top of the figure is an example of conventional routing. The router receives an IP datagram and examines the destination address in the datagram header. It accesses its routing table and searches for matches described earlier. If it finds a match, the routing table contains an entry of the next hop (the next node) that is to receive the datagram. If it cannot find a match, it will use a default route. Else, it will discard the datagram.

It is clear that this operation can be very time consuming because (1) the address is large and requires resources to examine each bit in the address, (2) the routing tables are large and require resources to search them, and/or (3) the matches occur on a "closest match" that entails a lot of CPU-intensive bit comparisons.

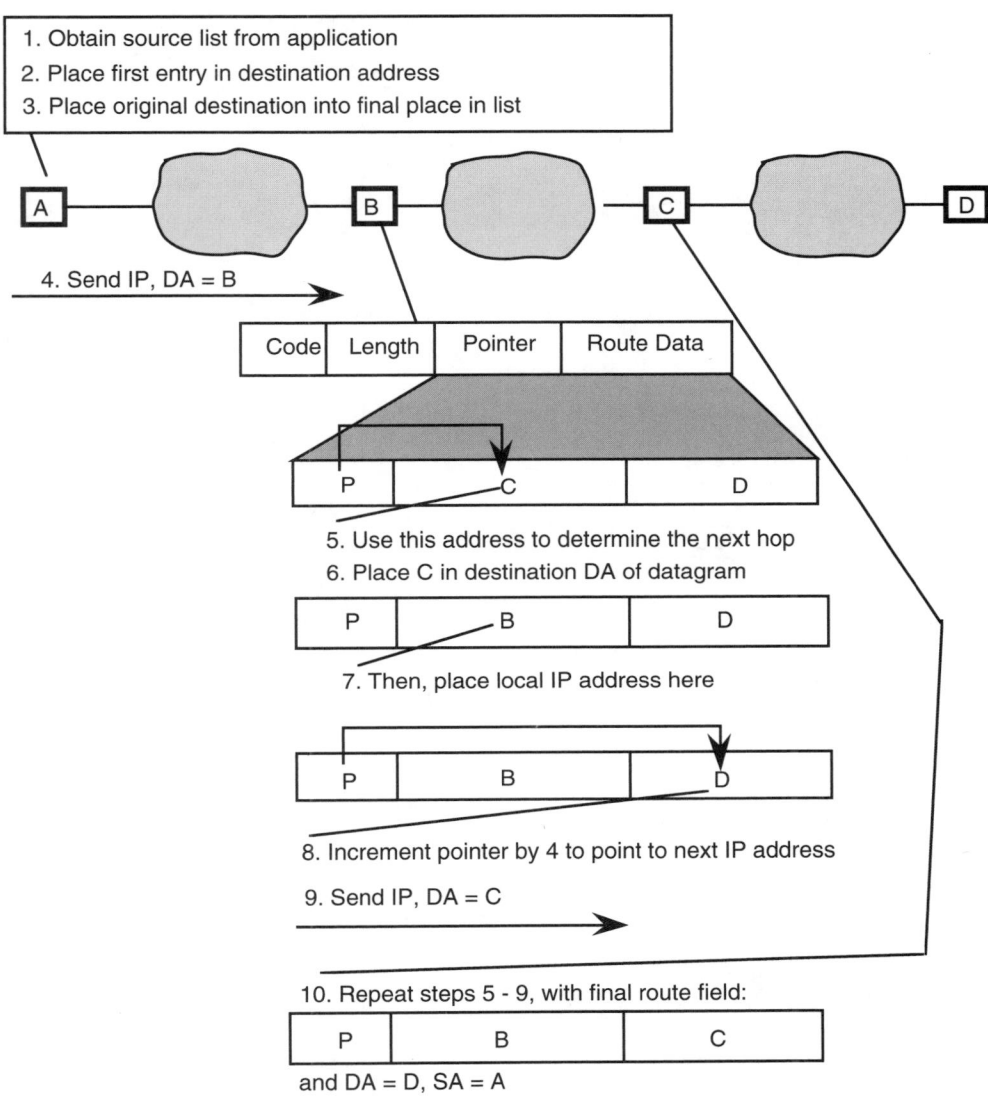

1. Obtain source list from application
2. Place first entry in destination address
3. Place original destination into final place in list

4. Send IP, DA = B

Code	Length	Pointer	Route Data

P	C	D

5. Use this address to determine the next hop
6. Place C in destination DA of datagram

P	B	D

7. Then, place local IP address here

P	B	D

8. Increment pointer by 4 to point to next IP address

9. Send IP, DA = C

10. Repeat steps 5 - 9, with final route field:

P	B	C

and DA = D, SA = A

Figure 7–10   Source routing.

Label-based routing (IP label switching) uses another identifier to route the traffic. The most common name for this identifier is a tag. The tag is a value of a few bits, and it is used in place of the IP address for routing. It is examined on a complete value, and not on a bit-by-bit clos-

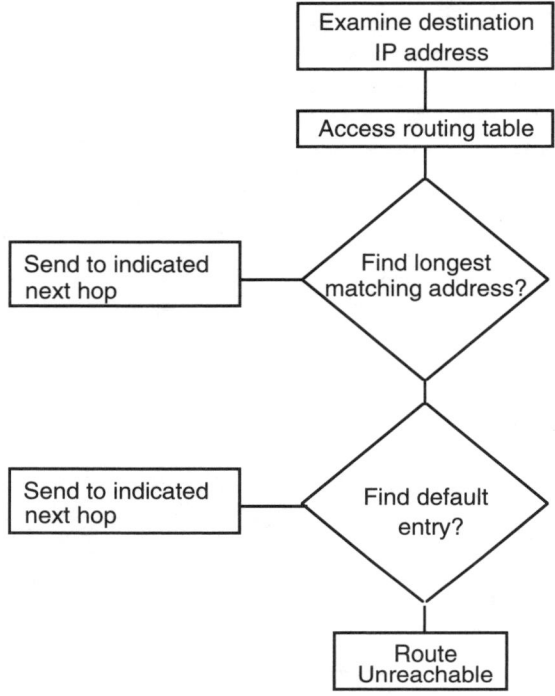

(a) Traditional IP routing

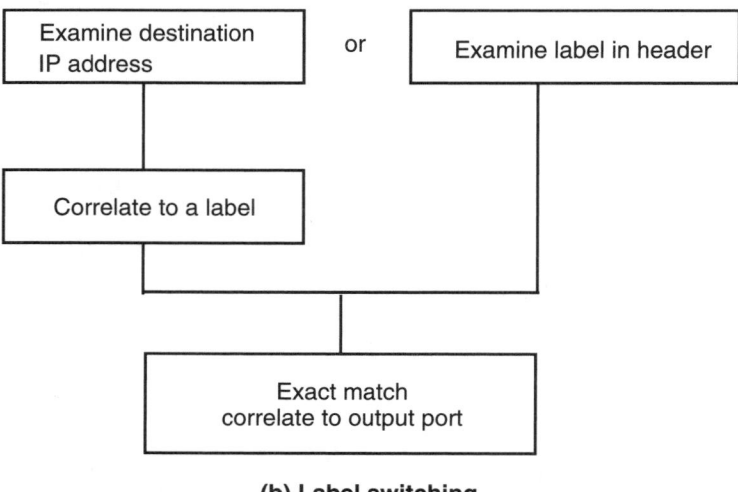

(b) Label switching

Figure 7–11   Relay methods.

est match. Many of these operations can be performed in hardware, which further speeds up the process.

LABEL SWITCHING

In the past few years, the concept of IP label switching (LS) has become a visible issue, and has sparked considerable controversy in the industry. The issue is visible, because label switching is designed to increase throughput and reduce latency in an IP router. It significantly improves performance in an internet. The issue is controversial because several different methods are used to achieve these goals, and all are called label switching in this book. The controversy arises when the methods are compared to each other, with some vendors claiming that their method is better than that of another vendor.

Regardless of the IP label switching method employed, IP label switching yields much better performance than the traditional IP routing. The conventional IP routing is software based and searches through potentially large routing tables to find a match of the IP destination address in the IP datagram with an entry in the routing table. As explained shortly, IP label switching may use hardware with application-specific integrated circuits (ASIC), as well as operations that are not employed in conventional IP routing.

This part of the chapter will explain the LS methods, first with a general introduction to the subject, and then to a more detailed examination.

DEFINITION OF A LABEL

A label is a short, fixed-length field residing in the header of a protocol data unit (PDU). It has no topological significance in regard to identifying a network or components within a network. Nor does it have any geographical significance, such as the identification of an area or an exchange within an area. In addition, it has no hierarchical attributes. For example, there is no means to identify a subnetwork within a network or a host attached to the subnetwork. In essence, it is a flat number.

Labels have been used in data communications networks for many years. Perhaps the earliest example is the label attached to X.25 packets, called the logical channel number (LCN). Another label is used for Frame Relay called the data link connection identifier (DLCI). ATM also makes use of the labels. The ATM label is called the virtual path ID/virtual channel ID (VPI/VCI).

LABEL SWITCHING: FORWARDING AND CONTROL

Forwarding Operations

The forwarding operations for a label-based switch are considerably simpler than a conventional routing operation discussed earlier in this chapter. Table 7–1 shows an example of a typical label switching table. Each row entry of the table is indexed by its label in the first column of this figure. When the incoming packet arrives at the switch, the label (n) in the header of the packet is used to index to the nth entry of the table.

The other entries in the rows for the table vary. For example, column 2 of Table 7–1 shows the primary route that the protocol data unit will take. This entry contains the label that will be mapped to the packet onto the outgoing interface. It also contains the identification of the outgoing interface, the outgoing label, as well as next hop address. The third column in the table may (or may not—it depends on the implementation) contain a secondary route and another column may contain yet another route. In addition, there can be entries in the table to define what services are to be provided for the packet and perhaps the outgoing queue in which the packet is to be placed before it is sent on to the outgoing link.

The end result of this approach is a very efficient table access mechanism. The table carries all the information needed for forwarding as well as the identification of any resources needed for the operation. Thus, unlike the IP-based routing discussed earlier in this chapter, LS routing (LSR) requires only one access to the table to obtain all the information it needs to forward the packet.

Table 7–1   The LS Table

Incoming Label	Primary Route	Secondary Route
Label 1	• Next hop address • Outgoing label • Output interface • QOS	• Next hop address • Outgoing label • Output interface • QOS
Label n	• Next hop address • Outgoing label • Output interface • QOS	• Next hop address • Outgoing label • Output interface • QOS

Figure 7–12 shows the entries in the LS table for one path between users XYZ and HIJ. The arrows are explained shortly. For this discussion, the path is identified with:

- Label 21:   Identifies the path between user XYZ and switch A
  - a: is the output interface at XYZ
  - b: is the input interface at switch A
- Label 30:   Identifies the path between switch A and switch B
  - d: is the output interface at switch A
  - a: is the input interface at switch B
- Label 21:   Identifies the path between switch B and switch C
  - c: is the output interface at switch B
  - d: is the input interface at switch C
- Label 55:   Identifies the path between switch C and user HIJ
  - a: is the output interface at switch C
  - b: is the input interface at HIJ

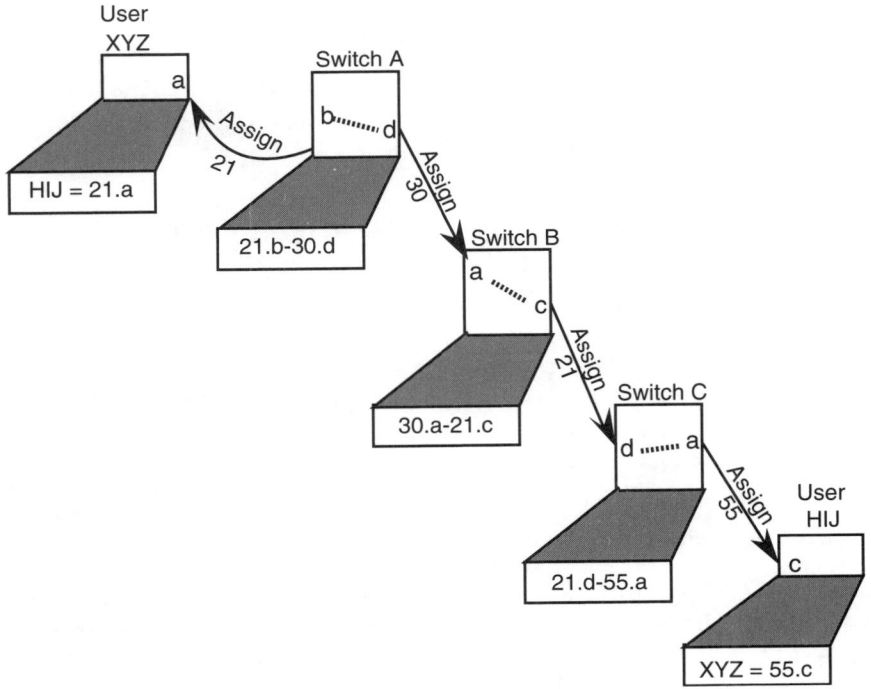

Figure 7–12   Cross-connect entries for the path from XYZ to HIJ.

Several observations are noteworthy about this figure. First, there must be some means to associate the labels with the source and destination addresses and the addresses of the switches that participate in the operation. And the association must be made at each machine that participates in the end-to-end connection. How it is done is decided by each vendor and network operator, but it must indeed be done. This aspect of label switching is discussed next in the section on LS control operations.

Second, in this example, the label is correlated with the sender's outgoing interface and the receiver's incoming interface. Since the labels are so associated, they can be reused at each interface on the switches or user machines. In a sense, the interface numbers in the switch act as *internal* "tags" for the connection.

Third, the selection of the labels is a matter between the user and its adjacent switch, or between adjacent switches. Consequently, there is no requirement to keep the labels unambiguous across interfaces, and through the network. For example, in Figure 7–12, label 21 is used twice, between XYZ and switch A, and then between switches B and C. Trying to manage universal label values across multiple nodes and different networks would not be a very pleasant task.

Fourth, I show the label "bindings" (the association of the labels between nodes) in one direction only. It is a straightforward task to use the LS table in a bidirectional manner. For example, if the traffic were flowing from switch C to switch B, the LS table would appear as:

- Label 21:   Identifies the path between switch C and switch B
     d: is the output interface at switch C
     c: is the input interface at switch B

Fifth, this example does not shows the next hop address, nor any QOS associated with the path. The next hop address is in the route columns in Figure 7–12, and it contains the IP address of the next hop. The QOS is subject to individual implementations.

Control Operations

Label switching control operations are responsible for the distribution of routing information and the implementation of the procedures to translate the routing information into the switching tables used at each node. Switching networks can use conventional advertising protocols such as OSPF and BGP, up to a point. However, these protocols do not contain sufficient information to support complete information exchange among LSRs. Specifically, the LSR needs information to allow it to bind its labels with other LSRs with the LSRs informing each other about these bindings.

Another option is to create another protocol for label distribution and develop this protocol to complement ongoing routing exchange protocols such as OSPF. This part of label switching is not fully defined in the industry. It is likely that more than one advertising/distribution protocol will be used, both a conventional OSPF/BGF protocol and a new label distribution protocol. These control operations are shown in Figure 7–12 with the arrows and the notation "Assign . . .".

The control component must create information permitting local binding and remote binding of the labels. Local binding entails the operations at the LSR to create the binding, assign it, and store it locally. Remote binding is the transmission of this information to another LSR or the reception of this information from another LSR.

The manner in which the labels are chosen can vary. The information can be chosen by the LSR that first transmits information or the LSR binding may occur by an LSR receiving information and then establishing the binding information back to the node that initially sent traffic to the LSR.

This concept is known as upstream binding where the LSR receives a packet, observes that binding is required, and sends the information back to the upstream node to create binding. See the binding in Figure 7–12 between XYZ and switch A. Downstream binding means that the packet arriving has label information contained in it from an upstream node. See the binding between A-to-B, B-to-C, and C-to-HIJ in Figure 7–12. Therefore, we refer to the upstream node as the node initially transmitting information and the downstream node as the node receiving that information.

Each node maintains a pool of labels. These labels are chosen and reserved for each binding. The size of the label pool varies depending on how many connections are needed, the size of the binding value itself (i.e., a label is restricted to a total length of 24 bits). I emphasize that the labels must be unique between two LSRs regarding a connection and perhaps an interface.

Creating the Label Binding

The label binding can be created in one of two methods. With the first method, the binding operations are initiated by a control operations such as a signaling message. For example, an ATM Q.2931 message could initiate the binding sent from an upstream node to a downstream node. Or a Resource Reservation Protocol (RSVP) Path Reservation message could affect the same operation. The second method for creating the label binding does not use any control signaling, rather it relies on the incoming packet flow into an LSR. In some literature this method is called "a data-driven label binding," and it deals with flow analysis of the packets. Davie et al. use this term. The LSR counts the number of packets going to a particular destination (perhaps as well as keeping records of quality-of-service indicators and perhaps the source address) and makes decisions that this traffic could benefit from the use of label switching.

ROLE OF THE EDGE DEVICE

The term edge device has been used in the industry for several years now. Typically, it describes a machine (usually a router) that sits at the "edge" of a specific network. One example of an edge device is a router positioned around the edge of an ATM network "cloud." In some networks the edge device connects conventional (legacy) networks to another network, once again such as an ATM network.

For label switching, the edge device operates with both conventional datagram forwarding (routing) and label forwarding (switching). Thus, the edge device receives conventional packets without any label information and implements procedures to determine if these packets are subject to label operations. If the packets are appropriate for label operations and/or if the next node to receive this traffic is an LSR, then the edge device institutes procedures to establish label bindings.

A GENERAL VIEW: YANKEE GROUP AND TOLLY GROUP CLASSIFICATIONS

For a general taxonomy of label switching, I have chosen two examples. The Yankee Group defines four switching methods: (1) flow classification, (2) layer 3 to layer 2 mapping, (3) route-server-based (with the ATM Forum's Multiprotocol over ATM [MPOA] as an alternative), and (4) layer 3 switching. The Tolly Group defines IP label switching in the context of cache-assisted routing and distributed routing. These classifications overlap and are summarized here.[6]

---

[6]For a more detailed explanation see: (a) K. Tolly, J. Curtis, and A. Hacker, "Straight Talk on Layer 3 Switching," *Business Communications Review*, September, 1997; (b) "IP Switching: Promise or Propaganda?", a white paper published by the Yankee Group as *White Paper*, *12*(7), June 1997. For additional information, see www.tolly.com and The Tolly Group Documents #7286 and #7250.

We now examine the methods for implementing label switching, starting first with the Tolly Group classification scheme (see Figure 7–13). First, with cache assisted routing, a cache is built for datagrams containing addresses for specific networks, as shown in Figure 7–13a. With this approach, each datagram is not subject to the conventional reliance on a central processor for the operation. For routes that change infrequently, this approach is very effective, and it is obviously not effective for routes that change frequently.

Second, with distributed routing, a separate processor is placed on each interface module, as shown in Figure 7–13b. The routing table is calculated by a central processor, but the processor does not become involved with the forwarding decisions for each datagram. Instead, the forwarding tables are downline loaded to the interface processors. In turn, these processors make the forwarding decisions.

In effect, the approaches described thus far are called layer 3 switching because the layer 3 IP addresses are used and not some other identifier or address.

The Tolly Group study shows a substantial increase in throughput. For example, a Rapid City router was configured with 16 ASICs, each serving four ports. The architecture is fully meshed of nearly 3,600 port pairs. This system routed almost 7 million datagrams per second. And these studies reveal that L_3 switching can achieve switching at wire speed.

The methods described by the Yankee Group include the methods described by the Tolly Group, as well as other techniques. The flow classification uses the idea that a long stream (flow) of datagrams is diverted to a faster ATM interface to an ATM backbone network, instead of a slower IP/router-based internet. Figure 7–13c shows the idea of the flow classification method.

The layer 3 to layer 2 method uses the same concept as the flow classification method in that it is flow-based. The mapping need not be to ATM, but to say Frame Relay. Also, the Yankee Group classification describes this method as software-based, as opposed to the next method, which is hardware-based.

The route-server-based method, again, is hardware-based (using separate processors) and maps the IP address to a layer 2 address or label. This method is similar to what the Tolly Group study calls distributed routing, except distributed routing does not map the IP address. Finally, the fourth method, layer 3 switching, is identical to distributed switching.

So, which is best? Vendors have different claims. Before you buy, do your homework, and these studies are a good place to start.

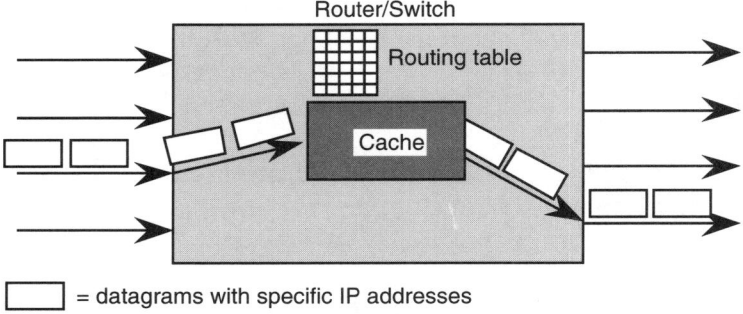

= datagrams with specific IP addresses

(a) **Cache-assisted routing**

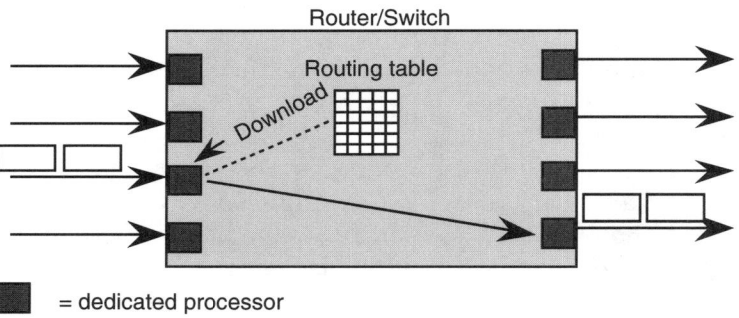

= dedicated processor

(b) **Distributed routing**

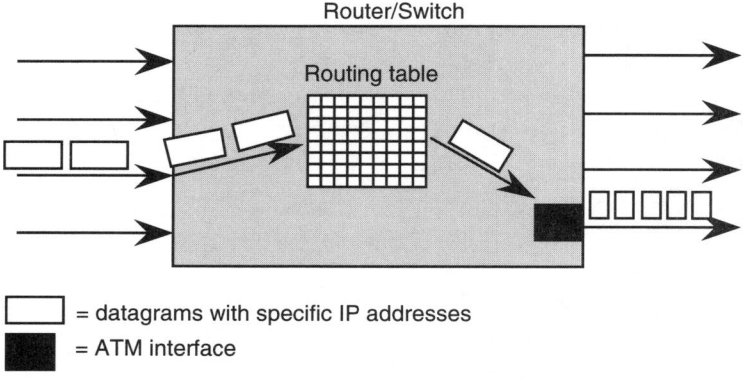

= datagrams with specific IP addresses

= ATM interface

(c) **Flow classification**

Figure 7–13   Switching operations.

THREE METHODS EXAMINED

For the remainder of the chapter, we focus on three approaches to label switching.

- IP switching
- Tag switching
- The cell switching router (CSR)

LOGICAL IP SUBNETS (LIS)

Before we discuss these approaches, it is necessary to introduce the topic of logical IP subnets (LIS). RFC 1577 defines the operations for encapsulating IP datagrams and ATM address resolution protocol (ATMARP) traffic over ATM and AAL5. Its principal concern is to specify the operation of IP over an ATM network and the resolving of IP addressees and ATM virtual channel IDs. The idea is to allow ATM to replace (1) a LAN backbone, such as FDDI; (2) dedicated links between routers; (3) LANs (such as Ethernet or Token Ring); or (4) Frame Relay and X.25 networks. The environment is established as a logical IP subnetwork (LIS).

As depicted in Figure 7–14, the LIS is configured with hosts and routers within a logical IP subnetwork. This concept means that IP hosts on different subnets are connected by a common ATM network. Each LIS communicates with each other through the same ATM network, although each LIS is independent. Communication occurs through an IP router, which is configured as an ATM endpoint connected both to the ATM network and to one or more LISs.

RFC 1577 requires that hosts operating on different IP subnets must communicate with each other through an intermediate router, so they cannot use a single ATM VC to communicate with each other! This rule is established even though it is possible to establish a direct virtual channel between the two IP members over the ATM network.

In retrospect, this restriction has proven to be unattractive. Indeed, the idea of an ATM-based backbone capable of connecting subnets contradicts this restriction. In any event, RFC 1577 uses ATMARP as the tool for IP nodes to learn about addresses needed for their communications with each other. Since ARP was designed for a broadcast LAN bus, ATMARP uses an ARP server, which provides a means to correlate an IP address to its associated ATM address (that is, the ATM address to reach the respective LIS).

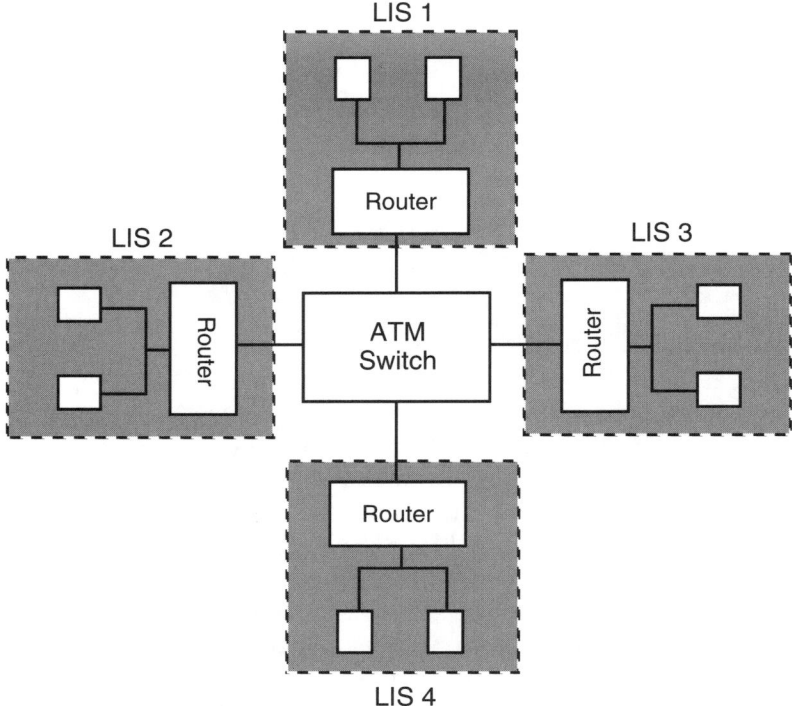

Figure 7–14   Logical IP subnets (LISs).

Given this basic scenario, the operations are established with the following rules:

1. All IP members (which consist of hosts and routers) are directly connected to the ATM network.
2. All members must use the same IP network/subnetwork number as well as address mask.
3. Any member that is outside the LIS must be accessed via a router.
4. All members must be able to resolve IP addresses to ATM addresses through ATMARP.
5. All LIS members must be able to communicate via ATM with other members within the same LIS (this means that within a list membership connection topologies are fully meshed).
6. Address resolution must be performed for both PVCs and SVCs.

Each IP station connected to the ATM network must be configured with an ATM address (which is the ATM address of the individual station) as well as an ATMARP request address. This value is the ATM address of an ATMARP server located at the LIS. The idea is to permit this server to resolve IP and ATM addresses. The server must be able to resolve all ATMARP requests for all IP members in the LIS. In addition, all operations must support the IEEE 802.2 LLC/SNAP encapsulation operations defined in RFC 1483.

IP SWITCHING

Several methods are employed to implement label switching. For this discussion, we examine the use of a high-speed ATM switch, co-located with IP. The approach described here is one used by Ipsilon (purchased by Nokia[7]) and called IP switching.

First, this approach uses the concept of a flow, which is a sequence of datagrams from one source machine or application to one or more machines or applications. For a "long" flow (many datagrams flowing between these entities), a router can cache information about the flow and circumvent the traditional IP routing mechanisms (subnet masking, search on longest subnet mask, and so on) by storing the routing information in cache, thus achieving high throughput.

Generally, the approach is to divert long flows, real-time traffic, or traffic with QOS requirements to an ATM connection, and use an individual ATM VPI/VCI for switching the traffic. For transaction-based traffic (database queries, such as a name server operation), the traffic is placed on a preassigned (default) ATM virtual circuit.

One of the difficulties of managing an ATM virtual circuit (VC) is that its "state" (up, down, inactive, active, etc.) must be maintained end-to-end, with all switches on the VC keeping state information about the VC. If a failure occurs on any part of the VC, extensive signaling is required to clear the VC and take remedial action, such as setting up the VC again. However, if the signaling software is removed and replaced with software that keeps state information only on a local basis, the operations are much more efficient and correlate more closely to IP's connec-

---

[7]For a more detailed description of this approach, see Newmand et al., "IP Label Switching—ATM under IP." *IEEE/ACM Transactions on Communications*, 6(2), April 1998.

tionless nature. The technique described here does not use end-to-end VCs; all are local to the two neighbor switches.

Architecture of the IP Switch

Figure 7–15 shows a simple view of the IP switch architecture. The switch contains the ATM switching fabric, the IP switch controller, the General Switch Management protocol (GSMP, see RFC 1987), and Ipsilon Flow Management Protocol (FMP, see RFC 1954).[8] The GSMP is used to provide the IP switch controller access to the ATM switching fabric. The FMP is used to associate IP flows with ATM VCs. The IP Switch Controller runs conventional IP routing and forwarding operations, in addition to GSM, FMP, and flow classification and control operations.

IP switching classifies a flow in two ways. The *host-pair flow* uses the source and destination IP addresses and time to live (TTL) to identify the flow. The *port-pair flow* identifies traffic flowing between the same source and destination ports, the same source and destination IP ad-

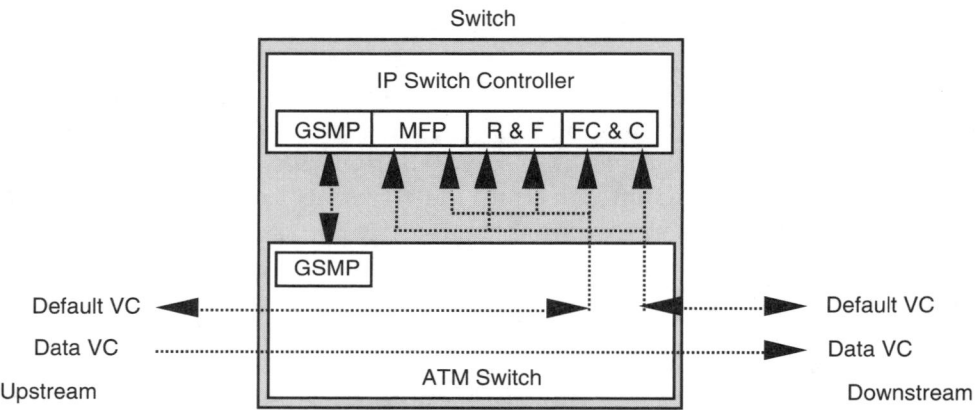

where:
  R&F   Routing and Forwarding
  FC&C   Flow Classification and Control

Figure 7–15   The IP switch architecture. (*Source:* B. Davie, P. Doolan, and Y. Rekhter, *Switching in IP Networks,* Morgan Kaufman Publishers, Inc., San Francisco, 1998.)

---

[8]Recent documents exclude Ipsilon's name from this protocol and use the initial FMP. I will follow this convention hereafter.

dresses, the same type of service (TOS), the same protocol ID (PID), and the same time to live (TTL). At first glance, one might question why all these fields are used. Why not just use the IP addresses? The answer is that identifying ports, protocols, and so on allows a switching decision to be made on the type of traffic (for example, a well-known port such as file transfer or the Domain Name System [DNS]). Thus, the file transfer traffic could be switched, and the DNS traffic could be routed. It makes little sense to build a VC for a one-time DNS query.

The host-pair flow is also called a type 2 flow. The port-pair flow is called a type 1 flow. So, the definition of a flow in IP switching depends on the type of flow, but it includes a set of packets whose header fields are identical.

To get things started, at system boot, a default VC is established between the switch (switch B) and all its neighbors (switches A and C). These VCs are used to forward IP datagrams on a hop-by-hop basis between switches. This VC is shown as the default VC in Figure 7–15, and is identified with a well-known ATM VPI/VCI value. Since this default VC is provisioned as an ATM PVC (permanent virtual circuit) there is no requirement to use the ATM signaling protocol Q.2931. The default VC is also used to transfer packets that do not have a label associated with them. These packets are routed by the switch controller routing and forwarding module.

The FMP Operations. In Figure 7–16, we assume that datagrams arrive at switch A from switch B on the default VC at port i. (Event 1 in the figure). The IP switch controller (executing AAL5) reassembles the datagram and forwards it with conventional IP routing operations. We further assume that the IP switch controller decides that the datagrams belong to a new flow. In event 2, the controller selects an unused VCI label (say, x') to operate between the ATM switch and the controller at port c (this port is some type of association between the controller and the switch and is not shown here). The controller selects an unused VCI (say, x) from a table associated with the input port (port i). Next, a switch driver is instructed to map VCI x on port i to VCI x' on port c. The value x' will be used as an index to cache that has stored the relay information for this VC. The entry is created with GSMP.

In event 3, the switch controller sends an FMP message to the upstream node that has been transmitting this flow. This message contains the label VC = x, a flow label and a lifetime value. The flow label contains the header fields that set up the flow to begin with. The lifetime states how long the flow is valid.

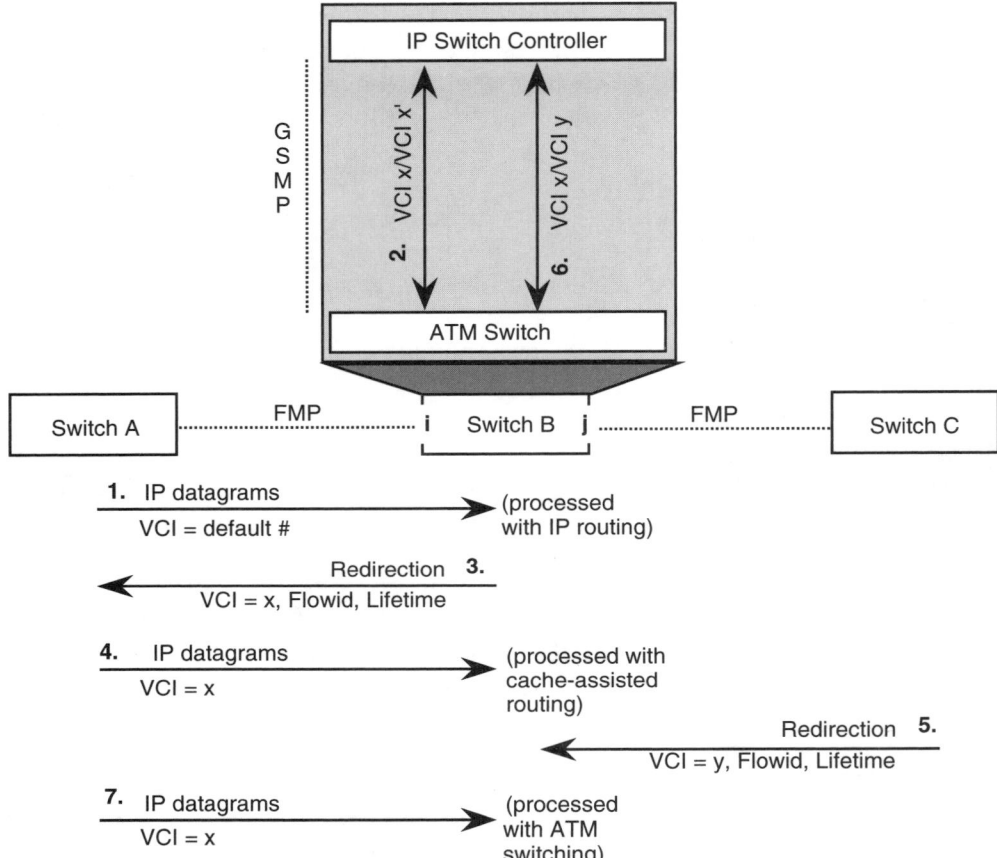

Figure 7–16   Flow redirection.

For a brief period, the cells will arrive at port i with VCI = x, shown as event 4. These cells are mapped to VCI x′, passed on port c to the controller, and forwarded to the next node. However, conventional routing table look-ups are not performed, because X′ is used an index into cache to obtain the forwarding information.

This intermediate step just described is needed until the next step occurs. Switch C has been receiving these datagrams, and (in event 5) sends a redirection FMP message to its upstream neighbor (switch B), instructing it to redirect this flow to another VCI; in this example VCI = y. This redirect is on port j. Upon receiving this message, the controller instructs the driver to map x.i to y.j, shown as event 6. Thereafter, the traffic on this flow is no longer processed by the IP switch controller and conventional IP routing. Rather, the traffic is processed directly through the ATM switch to the output port, as depicted in event 7 in the figure.

Overview of the General Switch Management Protocol

This section provides an overview of the general switch management protocol (GSMP, RFC 1987). The summary I am providing here is a general review; RFC 1987 is over 44 pages in length.

Switch ports are described by a 32-bit port number. The switch assigns port numbers, and it may choose to structure the 32 bits into subfields that have meaning to the physical structure of the switch (e.g., shelf, slot, port). In general, a port in the same physical location on the switch will always have the same port number. The internal structure of the port number is opaque to the GSMP protocol.

Each switch port also maintains a port session number assigned by the switch. A connection management message or a port management message with an incorrect port session number is rejected. This allows the controller to detect a link failure and to keep state synchronized. The port session number of a port remains unchanged while the port is continuously in the available state and the link status is continuously up. When a port returns to the available state after it has been unavailable or in any of the loopback states, or when the line status returns to the up state after it has been down or in test, or after a power cycle, its port session number will have changed. Port session numbers should be assigned using some form of random number.

GSMP also contains an adjacency protocol. The adjacency protocol is used to synchronize state across the link, to discover the identity of the entity at the other end of a link, and to detect when it changes.

GSMP packets are variable length and are encapsulated directly in an AAL-5 CPCS-PDU with an LLC/SNAP header. The default virtual channel for LLC/SNAP encapsulated messages is: VPI = 0 and VCI = 15.

GSMP is a master-slave protocol. The controller issues request messages to the switch. Each request message indicates whether a response is required from the switch and contains a transaction identifier to enable the response to be associated with the request. The switch replies with a response message indicating either a successful result or a failure. There are four classes of GSMP request-response messages: Connection Management, Port Management, Statistics, and Configuration. The switch may also generate asynchronous Event messages to inform the controller of asynchronous events. Event messages are not acknowledged by the controller. There is also an adjacency protocol message used to establish synchronization across the link and maintain a handshake.

For the request-response messages, each message type has a format for the request message and a format for the success response. Unless otherwise specified a failure response message is identical to the request message that caused the failure, with the Code field indicating the nature of the failure. Event messages have only a single format defined as they are not acknowledged by the controller.

Except for the adjacency protocol message, no GSMP messages may be sent across the link until the adjacency protocol has achieved synchronization, and all GSMP messages received on a link that does not currently have state synchronization must be discarded.

TAG SWITCHING

The tag switching procedure discussed in this section was developed by Cisco. The efforts by Cisco have resulted in the Multiprotocol Label Switching (MPLS) group, which is working to publish a "vendor-neutral" label switching protocol.

Tag switching consists of two components introduced earlier: forwarding and control. The forwarding component uses the tag information (tags) carried by packets and the tag forwarding information maintained by a tag switch to perform packet forwarding. The control component is responsible for maintaining correct tag forwarding information among a group of interconnected tag switches.

Forwarding Component

The forwarding operation employed by tag switching is based on label swapping. When a packet with a tag is received by a tag switch, the switch uses the tag as an index in its Tag Information Base (TIB). Each entry in the TIB consists of an incoming tag,[9] and one or more subentries of the form (outgoing tag, outgoing interface, outgoing link information).

---

[9]Not stated in RFC 2105 is the possibility of associating the tag with its incoming interface, thus allowing the labels to be reused at each interface. This method allows the use of fewer bits for the label, instead of using a pool of labels for all the interfaces. Also, multicasting requires the association of the incoming datagram to the incoming interface. However, as noted later in this chapter, associating the tag with the incoming interface entails additional overhead.

If the switch finds an entry with the incoming tag equal to the tag carried in the packet, it then replaces the tag in the packet with the outgoing tag. If appropriate, it also replaces the link information (e.g., MAC address) in the packet with the outgoing link level information, and forwards the packet over the outgoing interface.

The forwarding decision is based on the exact match algorithm using a fixed length, short tag as an index. This enables a simplified forwarding procedure, in comparison to longest match forwarding traditionally used at the network layer. The forwarding procedure is simple enough to allow a hardware implementation.

The forwarding decision is independent of the tag's forwarding granularity. For example, the same forwarding algorithm applies to both unicast and multicast—a unicast entry would just have a single (outgoing tag, outgoing interface, outgoing link information) subentry, while a multicast entry may have one or more (outgoing tag, outgoing interface, outgoing link information) subentries. (For multiaccess links, the outgoing link level information in this case would include a multicast MAC address.)

The forwarding procedure is decoupled from the control component of tag switching. New routing (control) functions can be deployed without disturbing the forwarding operation.

Tag Encapsulation.   Tag information can be carried in a packet in a variety of ways:

- As a small "shim" tag header inserted between the layer 2 and layer 3 headers
- As part of the layer 2 header, if the layer 2 header provides adequate semantics (e.g., ATM)
- As part of the header (e.g., using the flow label field in IPv6)

The tag forwarding component is L_3 independent. Use of control component(s) specific to a particular protocol enables the use of tag switching with different L_3 protocols.

Control Component.   The control component is responsible for creating tag bindings and then distributing the tag binding information among tag switches. The control component is organized as a collection of modules, each designed to support a particular routing function. To support new routing functions, new modules can be added. The following describes some of the modules, and is a brief summary of RFC 2105.

Destination-Based Routing. To support destination-based routing with tag switching, a tag switch (just like a router) participates in routing protocols (e.g., OSPF, BGP) and constructs its tag forwarding information base (TFIB) using the information it receives from these protocols.

There are three methods for tag allocation and TFIB management: (1) downstream tag allocation, (2) downstream tag allocation on demand, and (3) upstream tag allocation. In all three methods, a switch allocates tags and binds them to address prefixes in its TFIB.

In the downstream allocation, the tag that is carried in a packet is generated and bound to a prefix by the switch at the downstream end of the link (with respect to the direction of data flow). In the upstream allocation, tags are allocated and bound at the upstream end of the link. On demand allocation means that tags will only be allocated and distributed by the downstream switch when it is requested to do so by the upstream switch. The latter methods are most useful in ATM networks, for example, during a Q.2931 connection setup operation.

The downstream tag allocation scheme operates as follows: For each route in its TFIB the switch allocates a tag, creates an entry in its TFIB with the incoming tag set to the allocated tag, and then advertises the binding between the (incoming) tag and the route to other adjacent tag switches. When a tag switch receives tag binding information for a route, and that information was originated by the *next hop* for that route, the switch places the tag (carried as part of the binding information) into the outgoing tag of the TFIB entry associated with the route. This creates the binding between the outgoing tag and the route.

With the downstream tag allocation on demand scheme, for each route in its TFIB, the switch identifies the next hop for that route. It then issues a request (via a Tag Distribution Protocol [TDP]) to the next hop for a tag binding for that route. When the next hop receives the request, it allocates a tag, creates an entry in its TFIB with the incoming tag set to the allocated tag, and then returns the binding between the (incoming) tag and the route to the switch that sent the original request. When the switch receives the binding information, the switch creates an entry in its TFIB, and sets the outgoing tag in the entry to the value received from the next hop.

The upstream tag allocation scheme is used as follows. If a tag switch has one or more point-to-point interfaces, then for each route in its TFIB whose next hop is reachable via one of these interfaces, the switch allocates a tag, creates an entry in its TIB with the outgoing tag set to the allocated tag, and then advertises to the next hop (via TDP) the binding between the (outgoing) tag and the route. When a tag switch that is the next hop receives the tag binding information, the switch places the tag (carried as part of the binding information) into the incoming tag of the TFIB entry associated with the route.

Once a TFIB entry is populated with both incoming and outgoing tags, the tag switch can forward packets for routes bound to the tags by using the tag switching forwarding algorithm.

When a tag switch creates a binding between an outgoing tag and a route, the switch updates its TFIB with the binding information.

A tag switch will try to populate its TFIB with incoming and outgoing tags for all routes to which it has reachability, so that all packets can be forwarded by simple label swapping. Tag allocation is thus driven by topology (routing), not traffic—it is the existence of a TFIB entry that causes tag allocations, not the arrival of data packets.

Use of tags associated with routes, rather than flows, also means that there is no need to perform flow classification procedures for all the flows to determine whether to assign a tag to a flow.

Multicast. Essential to multicast routing is the notion of spanning trees. Multicast routing procedures are responsible for constructing such trees (with receivers as leafs), while multicast forwarding is responsible for forwarding multicast packets along such trees.

To support a multicast forwarding function with tag switching, each tag switch associates a tag with a multicast tree as follows. When a tag switch creates a multicast forwarding entry (either for a shared or for a source-specific tree) and the list of outgoing interfaces for the entry, the switch also creates local tags (one per outgoing interface). The switch creates an entry in its TFIB and populates (outgoing tag, outgoing interface, outgoing MAC header) with this information for each outgoing interface, placing a locally generated tag in the outgoing tag field. This creates a binding between a multicast tree and the tags. The switch then advertises over each outgoing interface associated with the entry the binding between the tag (associated with this interface) and the tree.

When a tag switch receives a binding between a multicast tree and a tag from another tag switch, if the other switch is the upstream neighbor (with respect to the multicast tree), the local switch places the tag carried in the binding into the incoming tag component of the TFIB entry associated with the tree.

When a set of tag switches are interconnected via a multiple-access subnetwork, the tag allocation procedure for multicast has to be coordinated among the switches. In all other cases tag allocation procedure for multicast could be the same as for tags used with destination-based routing.

Flexible Routing (Explicit Routes).   One of the properties of destination-based routing is that the only information from a packet that is used to forward the packet is the destination address. While this property enables scalable routing, it also limits the ability to influence the actual paths taken by packets. This, in turn, limits the ability to evenly distribute traffic among multiple links, taking the load off highly utilized links, and shifting it towards less utilized links. For Internet Service Providers (ISPs) that support different classes of service, destination-based routing also limits their ability to segregate different classes with respect to the links used by these classes. Some of the ISPs today use Frame Relay or ATM to overcome the limitations imposed by destination-based routing. Tag switching, because of the flexible granularity of tags, is able to overcome these limitations without using either Frame Relay or ATM.

To provide forwarding along the paths that are different from the paths determined by the destination-based routing, the control component of tag switching allows installation of tag bindings in tag switches that do not correspond to the destination-based routing paths.

Tag Switching with ATM.   Since tag switching is based on label swapping, and since ATM forwarding is also based on label swapping, tag switching technology can be applied to ATM switches by implementing the control component of tag switching.

The tag information needed for tag switching can be carried in the VCI field. If two levels of tagging are needed, then the VPI field could be used as well, although the size of the VPI field limits the size of networks in which this would be practical.[10] However, for most applications of one level of tagging the VCI field is adequate.

To obtain the necessary control information, the switch should be able to participate as a peer in L_3 routing protocols (e.g., OSPF, BGP). If the switch has to perform routing information aggregation, then to sup-

---

[10]This statement from RFC 2105 is open to question. If the VPI label is terminated at each interface, its size should not present a problem.

port destination-based unicast routing the switch should be able to perform L_3 forwarding for some fraction of the traffic as well.

Supporting the destination-based routing function with tag switching on an ATM switch may require the switch to maintain not one, but several tags associated with a route (or a group of routes with the same next hop). This is necessary to avoid the interleaving of packets that arrive from different upstream tag switches, but are sent concurrently to the same next hop. Either the downstream tag allocation on demand or the upstream tag allocation scheme could be used for the tag allocation and TFIB maintenance procedures with ATM switches.

Therefore, an ATM switch can support tag switching, but at the minimum it needs to implement L_3 routing protocols and the tag switching control component on the switch. It may also need to support some network layer forwarding.

Implementing tag switching on an ATM switch simplifies integration of ATM switches and routers—an ATM switch capable of tag switching appears as a router to an adjacent router.

Quality of Service (QOS).   Two mechanisms are needed for providing QOS to packets passing through a router or a tag switch. First, packets are identified as different classes. Second, appropriate QOS (bandwidth, loss, etc.) is provided to each class.

Tag switching provides a way to mark packets as belonging to a particular class after they have been classified the first time. Initial classification is done using information carried in the L_3 layer or higher layer headers. A tag corresponding to the resultant class is then applied to the packet. Tagged packets can then be handled by the tag switching routers in their path without needing to be reclassified.

Examples of Tag Switching Operations.   This section should piece together many of the concepts just discussed. Figure 7–17 is a redrawing of Figure 7–12 and the nodes are now called TSRs, for tag switching routers. Another node, TSR D has been added to the topology. The TSRs perform local binding (LB) of tags to interfaces. For example, TSR A has stored in its TFIB a binding of tag 21 to interface b. The other TSRs have stored bindings as follows:

TSR B	30.a
TSR C	21.d
TSR D	14.b

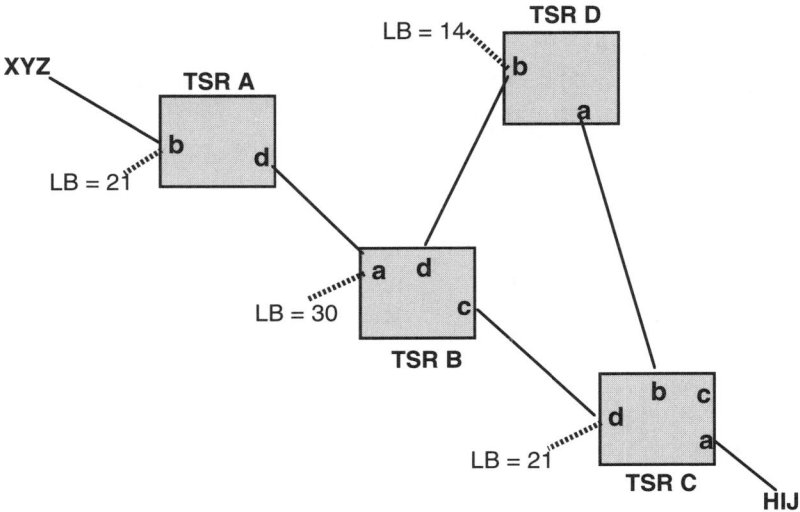

Figure 7–17   Tag switching routes (TSRs).

Through ongoing link state route advertising (such as OSPF), rout-ing information is flooded to the TSRs. Let us assume packets will be sent to address HIJ, so OSPF is used to build forwarding tables in each TSR to enable the TSR to forward traffic to a next hop, to reach HIJ.

Upon (say) TSR B finding a router (a next hop) to HIJ, it selects a tag from a pool of free tags. It uses the tag to index into its TFIB and up-dates this entry with (1) incoming tag of 30, (2) the associated incoming interface of a, (3) the address of the next hop, and (4) the outgoing inter-face to that next hop.

An important note: My description of this operation gets a bit tricky. It assumes that TSR B knows the incoming interface. Well, it may not. If the OSPF information came from (downstream) TSR C, TSR B cannot know the upstream interface, until it *actually* receives a datagram des-tined for HIJ on interface a. This approach of associating tags with outgo-ing *and* incoming interfaces requires extra bookkeeping and more steps in binding the two tags/interfaces together. A viable alternative is to not as-sociate a tag with an incoming interface, which means the tag pool is for all interfaces. This approach works if the length (in bits) of the tag is sufficient for all interfaces. Anyway, it requires some thought and I have shown the TFIBs in Tables 7–2 and 7–3 both ways: with an association to the incom-ing interface and without an association. Be aware that the Cisco tag switching specification does not populate the incoming interface.

Table 7–2(a)   TFIB: Initial Population with Correlation to Incoming Interface

TSR	Incoming Tag	Incoming Interface	Outgoing Tag	Outgoing Interface	Next Hop HIJ
A	21	b	—	d	TSR B
B	30	a	—	c	TSR C
C	21	d	—	a	HIJ (DIR)
D	14	b	—	a	TSR C

(Note: Row entries reflect an entry at each TSR)

Table 7–2(b)   TFIB: Initial Population with No Correlation to Incoming Interface

TSR	Incoming Tag	Outgoing Tag	Outgoing Interface	Next Hop to HIJ
A	21	—	d	TSR B
B	30	—	c	TSR C
C	21	—	a	HIJ (DIR)
D	14	—	a	TSR C

(Note: Row entries reflect an entry at each TSR)
where:
   DIR   means directly connected

Table 7–3(a)   TFIB: Final Population with Correlation to Incoming Interface

TSR	Incoming Tag	Incoming Interface	Outgoing Tag	Outgoing Interface	Next Hop to HIJ
A	21	b	30	d	TSR B
B	30	a	21	c	TSR C
C	21	d	—	a	HIJ (DIR)
D	14	b	17	a	TSR C

(Note: Row entries reflect an entry at each TSR)

Table 7–3(b)   TFIB: Final Population with No Correlation to Incoming Interface

TSR	Incoming Tag	Outgoing Tag	Outgoing Interface	Next Hop to HIJ
A	21	30	d	TSR B
B	30	21	c	TSR C
C	21	—	a	HIJ (DIR)
D	14	17	a	TSR C

(Note: Row entries reflect an entry at each TSR)
where:
   DIR   means directly connected

211

The results of the TFIB updates are shown in Table 7–2. Notice that the outgoing tag in the TFIB is not yet populated. Thus far, the local binding operations have only created information on incoming tags. The outgoing tags are populated by the TSRs distributing their local binding information, which is discussed next.

In Figure 7–18, TSR B distributes its local binding information to all TSRs in the routing domain (to simplify matters, I show TSRs C and D). Both TSR C and D ignore this information *because* TSR B is not the next hop to HIJ.

In Figure 7–19, TSR B receives binding information from TSR C and TSR D. It ignores the information for TSR D because this node is not the next hop to HIJ. It accepts the information for TSR C because C is the next hop to HIJ. This remote binding information is used to populate TSR B's TFIB, by using the tag of 21 from TSR C's message.

Eventually the TFIBs are fully populated as shown in Table 7–3. Note that the binding between TSR C and TSR D is shown in Table 7–3 because TSR C is TSR D's next hop to address HIJ.

Border TSRs. Tag switching is designed to scale to large networks. Its scaling capability is based on its ability to carry more than one tag in

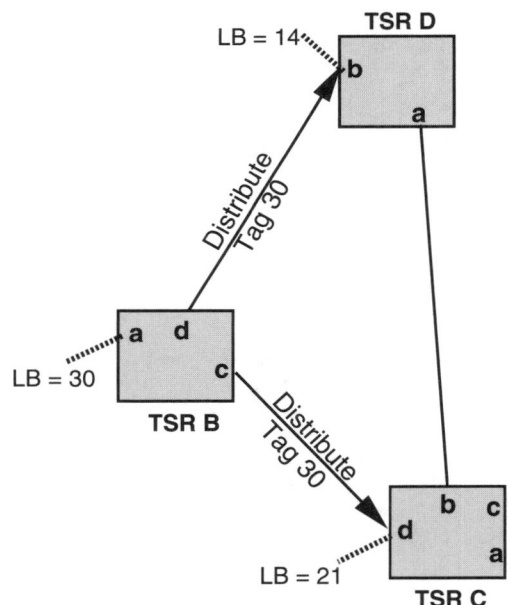

Figure 7–18   Tag information distribution.

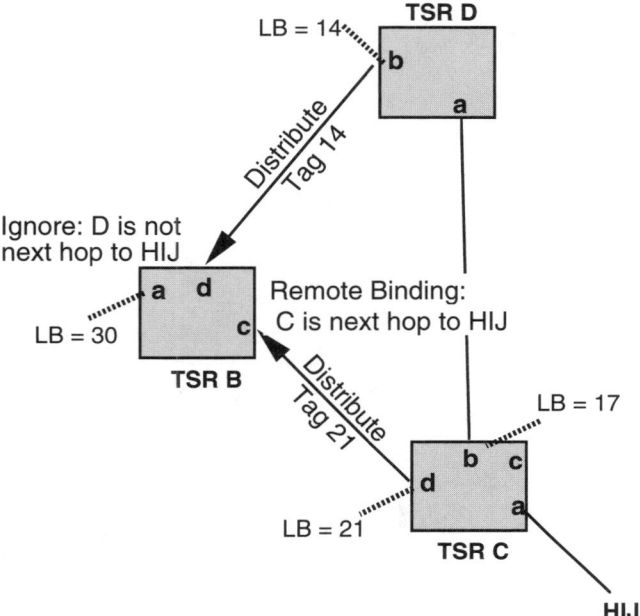

Figure 7–19 A remote binding.

the packet. As we will see, "tag stacking" allows designated TSRs to exchange information with each other and act as border nodes to a large domain of networks and other TSRs. These other TSRs are "interior" nodes to the domain and do not concern themselves with interdomain routes.

We will modify Figure 7–17 to Figure 7–20 in this discussion. Assume that three TSRs are members of the same domain (domain B) and TSR A and TSR C are border TSRs. This example also assumes that this domain is a transit domain (in which the packets traversing it neither originate nor terminate in this domain). It is certainly desirable to isolate the intra-domain TSRs from these operations. In fact, we will show that the interior TSRs only need to store in their TFIBs the routing information to reach their correct border router.

Border TSR X and TSR Y are the designated border routers for domains A and C, respectively. To advertise addresses from say, domain C, TSR Y distributes information to TSR C, which distributes it to TSR A, which then distributes it to TSR X. It is not distributed to TSR B because TSR B is an interior TSR.

We will dispense with the interface entries in Table 7–4, which shows the TFIP from domain B's perspective.

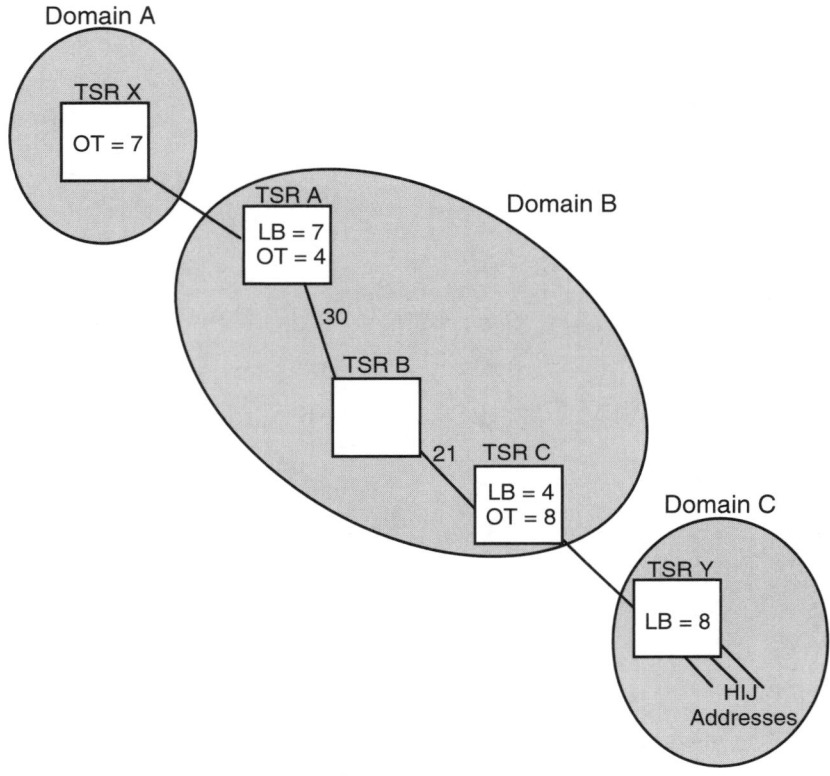

where
  LB   Local binding
  OT   Outgoing tag

Figure 7–20   Border TSRs and domains.

Assume the following (and see Figure 7–20): (1) TSR Y creates a local binding (LB) for the HIJ addresses in domain C using 8 as the local tag; (2) TSR C creates a local binding for the same HIJ addresses using 4 as the local tag; (3) TSR A does the same with a local tag of 7.

Table 7–4   TFIB for Domain B

TSR	Incoming Tag	Outgoing Tag	Next Hop
A	—	30	B
B	30	21	C
C	21	—	—

Using the tag distribution procedures discussed earlier, the following events occur: (1) TSR Y distributes its tag 8 to TSR C, which uses it as an outgoing tag (OT) to the HIJ addresses; (2) TSR C distributes its tag 4 to TSR A, which uses it as an outgoing tag to the HIJ addresses; and (3) TSR A distributes its tag 7 to TSR X.

In addition, when TSR A receives the tag binding message from next hop border TSR C, it notes that TSR C is not connected directly to TSR A. It must store this information and use it later for ongoing packet transfer, discussed next.

After all these activities have taken place, the label relationships are shown in Figure 7–21. Now, assume that a packet arrives at TSR X that is destined for one of the addresses in the aggregate HIJ address. TSR X sends this packet to TSR A with tag = 7. At TSR A, tag 7 is swapped for tag 4. Also, TSR A knows that this tag pertains to border TSR C, which is not connected directly to TSR A. In order to route the packet, TSR A pushes tag 30 onto the tag stack in the packet (on top of tag 7).

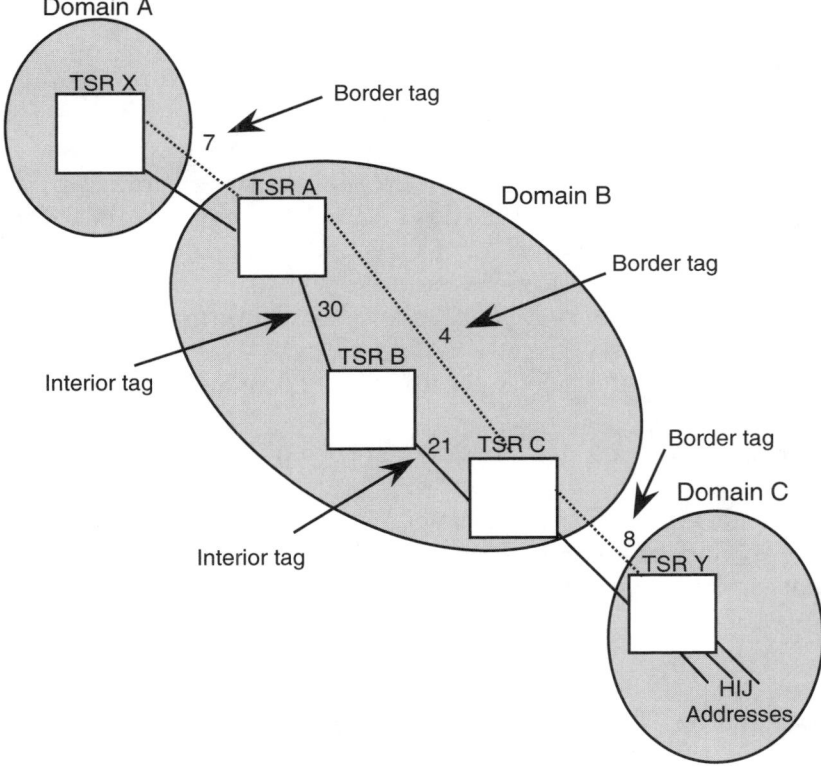

Figure 7–21   The label relationships.

Therefore, a packet will always contain two tags when transiting a routing domain. This approach keeps the internal TSRs isolated from interdomain routing.

To continue this example, TSR A sends the packet to TSR B, and TSR B swaps tag 30 for tag 21 (without disturbing tag 7), then sends the packet to TSR C.

TSR C's analysis of tag 21 must reveal that TSR C is to pop the tag stack in the packet, where tag 4 is found (placed there by border TSR A). TSR C then swaps tag 4 with tag 8 and sends the packet to TSR 2 and domain C where address HIJ can be found.

CELL SWITCH ROUTER

The Cell Switch Router (CSR) is an early label switching technique that has been published for public use.[11] CSR supports conventional IP datagram forwarding as well as cell switching. In addition, CSR maintains ATM signaling operations and the RFC 1577 operations. The following is a summary of RFC 2098.

In an ATM network composed of CSRs, VPI/VCI-based cell switching bypasses datagram assembly/assembly and IP header processing, at a CSR that lends itself to such (e.g., communications that require a certain amount of bandwidth and QOS). Additionally, conventional hop-by-hop datagram forwarding based on the IP header is also possible at a CSR.

CSR defines two different kinds of ATM VCs that exist between adjacent CSRs or between CSR and ATM-attached hosts/routers (Figure 7–22).

The default VC is a general purpose VC used by any communications that select conventional hop-by-hop IP routed paths. All incoming cells received from this VC are assembled into IP datagrams and handled based on their IP headers. VCs set up in the Classical IP Model are classified into this category.

The dedicated VC is used by specific IP that are specified by the destination IP address/port, the source IP address/port, or an IPv6 flow label. The dedicated VC can be concatenated with other dedicated VCs that accommodate the same IP flow and can constitute an ATM bypass pipe (a cut-through path) for those IP flows.

The bypass pipe is set up based upon a flow and bypasses conventional IP forwarding.

In Figure 7–22, host A checks an identifier in each IP datagram. The identifier could be (1) a source destination IP address, (2) source/destina-

---

[11]CSR was developed by Toshiba and presented to the IETF in 1994.

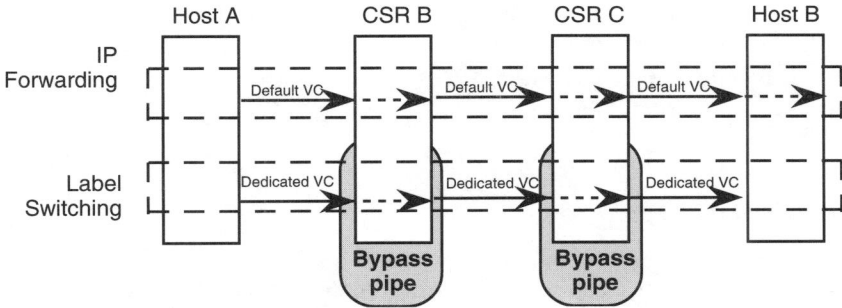

Figure 7–22   Default and dedicated VCs.

tion IP addresses, (3) source/destination IP address and source/destination port numbers, (4) IPv6 source IP address and flow label, and so on. If the identifiers indicate the datagram should be sent onto an ATM VC, the datagram is diverted to that VC, by using AAL to encapsulate the IP datagram into ATM cells.

At the CSRs, the cell's VPI/VCI is checked. If it matches an entry in the ATM switching table, it is relayed directly onto the outgoing ATM interface. If a match is not found in the table, or the table reveals that the outgoing interface is not ATM, conventional IP operations are invoked to route the datagram.

Figure 7–23 shows how the default and dedicated VCs are handled in a CSR. The IP datagram for a default VC is processed by AAL and the

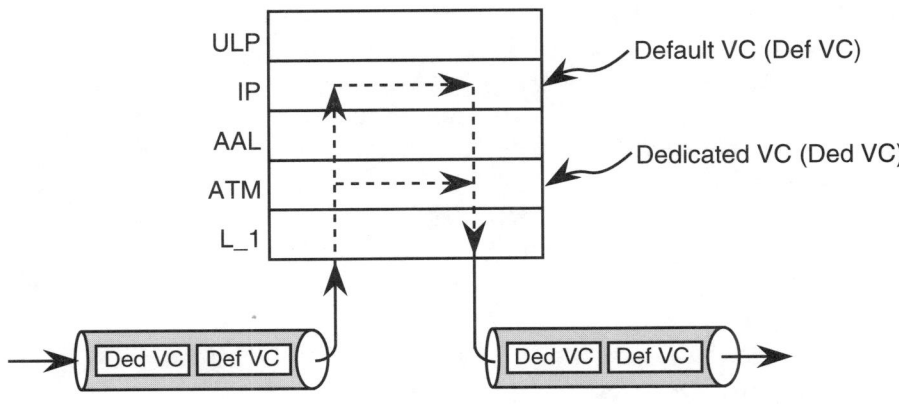

where:
   Ded   Dedicated
   Def   Default

Figure 7–23   A closer look at default and dedicated VCs.

IP forwarding module. The pieces of the IP datagram must be reassembled by AAL on the receive side and segmented by AAL on the transmit side. With a dedicated VC, the datagram is cut through the CSR in a bypass pipe.

MAJOR FEATURES OF CSR

CSR and the Next Hop Resolution Protocol (NHRP) provide direct ATM level connectivity beyond IP subnet boundaries, but several differences in the CSR-based architecture exist between the two. NHRP must manage two different routing protocols over the ATM cloud: network layer operations and ATM operations.

With CSR, IP layer routing determines an egress point of the ATM cloud and the intersubnet level path to the point that shows which CSRs it should pass through. ATM layer routing determines an intrasubnet level path for ATM VCs only between adjacent nodes (CSRs or ATM-attached hosts/routers). Since the roles of routing are hierarchically subdivided into intersubnet level (router level) and intrasubnet level (ATM SW level), ATM routing does not have to operate all over the ATM cloud but only in individual IP subnets independent from each other, which decreases the amount of information for ATM routing protocol handling.

A CSR-based network can dynamically change routes for bypass pipes when related IP layer routing information changes. Bypass pipes related to the routing changes do not have to be torn down or established from scratch since intermediate CSRs related to IP routing changes can follow them and change routes for related bypass pipes by themselves.

CSR keeps subnet-by-subnet internetworking with regard to any control protocol sequence and can provide multicast bypass pipes without requiring any modifications in IP multicast over ATM or multicast routing techniques.

In addition, since the CSR can handle RSVP messages that are transmitted in a hop-by-hop manner, it can provide bypass pipes that satisfy QOS requirements by the cooperation of the RSVP and the bypass pipe control protocol.

The Flow Attribute Notification Protocol

CSR uses a label distribution protocol called the Flow Attribute Notification Protocol (FANP). The FANP messages operate between LISs (and the router at the LISs) across an ATM cloud. RFC 2129 has more in-

formation than the FANP and I refer you to it for the details of the FANP
message exchanges between CSRs.

MPOA

MPOA is described in considerable detail in *ATM Volume III* of this
series. We review some of the major aspects of MPOA here, since it is one
approach to label switching, and leave the details to the other book.

The principal objective of MPOA is to support the transfer of intersubnet unicast traffic. MPOA allows the intersubnetwork traffic based on
layer 3 protocol communications to occur over ATM virtual channel connections (VCCs) without requiring routers in the data path. The goal of
MPOA is to combine bridging and routing with ATM in a situation where
diverse protocols and network topologies exist.

The job of MPOA is to provide this operation to allow the overlaying
of layer 3 protocols (also called internetwork layer protocols) on ATM.
MPOA is designed to use both routing and bridging information to locate
the optimal route through the ATM backbone.

MPOA supports the concept of virtual routing, which is the separa-
tion of internetwork layer route calculation and forwarding. The idea behind virtual routing is to enhance the manageability of internetworking
by decreasing the number of devices that are configured to perform route
calculation. In so doing, virtual routing increases scalability by reducing
the number of devices that participate in the internetwork layer route
calculations.

MPOA is responsible for five major operations:

1. *Configuration:* This operation obtains configuration information
   from the emulated LAN configuration servers (ELAN LECS).
2. *Discovery:* MPOA clients (MPCs) and MPOA servers (MPSs) dynamically learn of each others' existence. MPCs and MPSs discover each other by using minor additions to the LANE LE_ARP
   protocol. These messages carry the MPOA device type (MPC or
   MPS) and its ATM address.
3. *Target Resolution:* This operation uses a modified NHRP Resolution Request message MPCs to resolve the ATM address for the
   endpoints of a shortcut. Also, the mapping of a Target to an
   Egress ATM address is provided, as well as an optional tag (discussed later), and a set of parameters used to set up a shortcut
   VCC to forward traffic across subnet boundaries.

4. *Connection Management:* This operation controls the ongoing management of VCCs transfer control information and data.

5. Data Transfer: This operation is responsible for forwarding of internetwork layer traffic across a shortcut.

MPOA Operations

MPOA goes several steps further than LANE and NHRP. First, it incorporates the operations of LANE and NHRP, thus retaining the advantages of bridging, but it also supports the use of internetwork layer communications (L_3 routing). It continues to use ATM VCCs for the transfer of traffic and has schemes for bypassing routers. At the same time, intersubnet operations are supported (for unicast traffic). Furthermore, MPOA defines operations that enable an edge device to perform internetwork layer datagram *forwarding* operations without having to perform *route calculations*. This feature reduces the complexity and expense of these machines.

As a result of this extension, MPOA devices define shortcut interfaces for shortcut VCCs, as shown in Figure 7–24. Traffic coming from a bridge connected to an ELAN can be sent to another ELAN through a LEC service interface or to a shortcut VCC through a shortcut interface. Traffic coming from a shortcut VCC can be relayed to a local ELAN, or to another shortcut VCC.

Figure 7–24 illustrates the MPOA approach. Additional components are added to the system, and one is called the MPOA client (MPC). The MPC, say the MPC at subnet 192.168.1, is able to determine that a better path exists between subnets 192.168.1 and 192.168.3. The path is an ATM VCC and is used to provide the shortcut between the two systems. The MPOA resolution request protocol is used to obtain the information about the shortcut.

Companion Standards to MPOA

We must leave MPOA and point you to *ATM Volume III* of this series if you wish to pursue the subject in more detail. Other "companion" standards to MPOA are summarized here (see Table 7–5).

First, Classical IP over ATM is part of the Logical IP Subnet (LIS), and is published as RFC 1577. It defines the operations for encapsulating IP datagrams and the ATM address resolution protocol (ATMARP) traffic over ATM and AAL5. Its principal concern is to specify the operation of

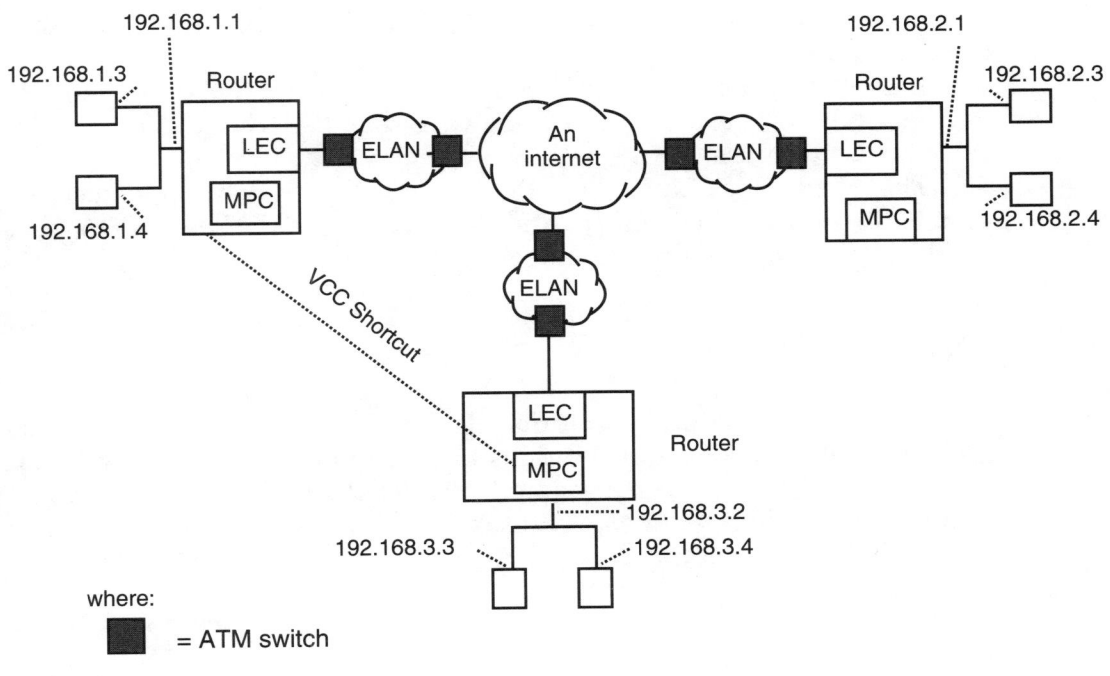

where:

■ = ATM switch

and:
ELAN   Emulated LAN
LEC   LANE client
MPC   MPOA client
VCC   Virtual channel connection

Figure 7–24   The VCC shortcut.

Table 7–5   Companions to MPOA

Classical IP over ATM
        Defines encapsulation and address mapping operations

Logical IP Subnetwork (LIS)
        Establishes methods for organizing IP subnets
        with ATM   backbones

LAN Emulation
        Defines how ATM emulates a LAN

Next Hop Resolution Protocol (NHRP)
        Establishes procedures to find routes to ATM backbones

Multiprotocol over ATM (MPOA)
        Embellishes Classical IP, LANE, and NHRP with additional capabilities

IP over an ATM network and the resolving of IP addressees and ATM virtual channel Ids.

LAN Emulation (LANE) is used when an ATM network connects multiple LANs. These LANs are unaware that LANE and ATM are involved in the process.

The Next Hop Resolution Protocol (NHRP) allows intermediate routers to be bypassed and traffic diverted to ATM. The MPOA uses NHRP and embellishes it with added features.

SUMMARY

The problem dictates a solution. The problem of IP routing has dictated a number of proposed solutions known as label switching. Without question, label switching is a good solution for the IP routing problem. As of this writing there is no *one* solution, but some form of tag switching will likely become a standard.

8

IPv6

T his chapter introduces the new IP, named IPv6 (IP, version 6). The rationale of the design of IPv6 is explained and the current version of IP (IPv4) is compared to this new version. We examine the new IP address and later in the chapter describe some migration (IPv4-to-IPv6) issues.

Earlier discussions in Chapter 2 explained the IPv4 address. Recall that it is 32 bits in length, and is organized around classes (see Figure 2–6, in Chapter 2). The inadequacies of the classed-based address has lead to classless addresses using a prefix to define the subnet mask. Even with classless addresses, it is clear that the present IP address scheme will not be adequate for the future. Consequently, the Internet authorities established a task force to come up with a solution to the problem—principally to devise a larger and more efficient IP address. At the same time, it was decided that IPv4 should be redesigned for reasons explained shortly. The result of this effort is IP version 6, or IPv6. It is published in RFC 1719 and revised in RFC 1883.

PROBLEMS WITH IPV4

IPv4 is an old protocol. It was conceived over twenty years ago and was designed to solve some very specific problems. It is remarkable that it has performed so well for so long a time. But with the changing technology, IPv4 now exhibits a number of deficiencies.

First, of course, is the limited IP address space. Various estimates have been made about when the 32-bit space will be used-up. Christian Huitema[1] provides an estimate that the 32-bit maximum address space (identifying 4 billion computers) will be exhausted between the years 2005–2015. Regardless of the exact time of IP address space exhaustion, it will indeed become exhausted. IPv6 stipulates an address of 128 bits.

Second, a number of operations in IPv4 are inefficient. Consequently, since the changing of IP's address requires the changing of the IP protocol, it makes sense to change other aspects of IP as well.

THE DESIGN PHILOSOPHY BEHIND IPV6

IPv6 is designed to overcome the limitations of IPv4. As we mentioned earlier, the major design philosophy behind IPv6 is to extend the IP address space. At the same time, the design philosophy of the IPv6 IP is to make the protocol simpler to use and more efficient in its operations. Clearly, its intent is to migrate from a data-specific protocol to a multimedia protocol. However, it was emphasized throughout the design process that IPv4 had been quite successful and most of its characteristics have been retained. Additionally, IPv6 is designed to be complementary to other related protocols that have been developed or are in development at the writing of this book. These protocols concern themselves with the support of either voice, video, data, or other traffic through an internet.

Before the analysis of IPv6 is undertaken, it is useful to pause and describe the rationale for the very large address of 128 bits. Many proposals pertaining to the size of the address were placed before the task force. These deliberations have continued since 1992 with the final completion of the specification in 1995. In essence, the IPv6 designers held fast to the notion that the Internet should be able to support anyone on earth who wishes to connect to it. Since IPv6 is positioned for the future, various estimates were made as to how many people would be on the planet in the next century. We just learned that one study projected the population growth to 2020. In addition, with the proliferation of comput-

---

[1]Christian Huitema, *IPv6: The New Internet Protocol,* Prentice Hall, 1996.

ers into many people's lives, it was essential that the IP address accommodate the probability that one person would utilize multiple computers. Some studies hypothesize that in the future perhaps 100 computers per person could occur. This may seem far-fetched to the reader but remember that computers are inculcating themselves into almost every facet of our lives. Computers operate our watches; computers run in our VCRs. LANs even run underneath our automobile hood. All these components need addresses in order to function properly. At any rate, the value of 2^{128} was believed to be sufficient for a long-term growth to accommodate approximately 10 billion people (projections to the year 2020). The final objectives were to provide an address that permitted 10^{15} computers connected through 10^{15} networks.

SUMMARY OF THE CHANGES

Table 8–1 provides a summary of the major changes made to IPv6 in relation to IPv4 and the reasons for the changes. The changes are significant, to the extent that IPv4 and IPv6 cannot interwork with each other unless conversions are made between the two. In some instances, conversions cannot be made, since IPv6 offers features that cannot be mapped to IPv4.

Table 8–1   IPv6

Reasons for a new IP

- Expand the IP address space
- Eliminate the cumbersome features of IPv4
- Add features for modern networks

Aspects of the Change

- Ethertype value is 86DD$_{hex}$
- These fields are eliminated: (a) header length, (b) TOS, (c) identification, (d) flags, (e) fragment offset, (f) header checksum
- These fields are renamed (redefined somewhat): (a) length, (b) protocol type, (c) time to live
- Options fields redone completely
- Two fields are added: (a) priority, (b) flow label
- Header is a fixed format
- Hop-to-hop fragmentation is not permitted

THE IPV6 ADDRESS

As stated earlier, the IPv6 address is 128 bits. The convention for writing the address is as 4-bit integers, with each integer represented by a hexadecimal (hex) digit. The address is clustered as eight 16-bit integers (four hex digits), separated by colons, as in this example:

68DA:8909:3A22:FA64:68DA:8909:3A22:FACA

It is unlikely that initial implementations will use all 128 bits, and some of them will be set to 0, as in this example:

68DA:0000:0000:0000:68DA:8909:3A22:FACA

This notation can be shortened by substituting four 0s in the hex 16-bit cluster as follows:

68DA:0:0:0:68DA:8909:3A22:FACA

In addition, if more one consecutive hex cluster of 16 bits is null, they can be replaced by two colons, as in this example:

68DA::68DA:8909:3A22:FACA

In order to determine how many hex clusters have been substituted by the colons, you must examine how many hex clusters are in the notation, and then simply fill in the 0000 sets to equal eight 16-bit integers. As another example, consider:

68DA::8909:3A22:FACA =   68DA:0:0:0:0:8909:3A22:FACA

Since four 16-bit integers are present, the double colon represents four null sets. This convention restricts the double colon from being used in an address only once. That is, an address of 0:0:0:FECA:68DA:0:0:0 can be coded as ::FECA:68DA:0:0:0 or 0:0:0:FECA:68DA::, but not ::0:FECA:68DA::.

Since the notation the IPv4 address is in decimal, dot form, IPv6 allows an IPv4 address to have the following notation:

::47.192.4.5

Hierarchical Addresses

We learned earlier in this book that hierarchical addresses are preferable to flat addresses, and IPv6 stipulates an hierarchical address format. The format of the address is coded with a prefix and five hierarchical subfields, in this order:

Prefix, Registry ID, Provider ID, Subscriber ID, Subnetwork ID, Interface ID

where:

Prefix: 010	Provider-based addresses
Registry ID:	Registry in charge of allocating
Provider ID:	Internet service provider (ISP)
Subnetwork ID:	Subscriber ID, which is obtained from the ISP
Subnetwork ID:	Subnetwork of the subscriber
Interface ID:	Host address on the subnetwork

Currently, the registry ID is set up to identify IP registration authorities. There are three registrations identified for North America, Europe, and Asia.

These registrations dole out provider IDS to ISPs. In the initial allocation, the ISPs assign the addresses (subnetwork ID and interface ID) to their subscribers, who can use these bits to their own preferences.

Special Addresses

Several special addresses are provided in IPv6 (which include the standard prefix of 010). The coding rules for these addresses are provided in Table 8–2.

An unspecified address consists of all 0s, can be coded in a source address, and is used in situations where a station has not been configured with an address. A loopback address is 0:0:0:0:0:0:0:1, and allows a node to send a datagram to itself; for example, when the source and destination application reside in the same node.

OSI network service access points (NSAPs) and Novell IPX addresses are supported in IPv6, due to their wide use in other systems.

The site local address prefix is used if an organization wishes to set up its own private addresses in its internet that cannot be employed in the Internet. Additionally, a node can be given a link local address if it has not been assigned a link local address or a provider-based address.

Table 8–2   IPv6 Special Addresses

Prefix	Allocation
0000 0000	Reserved
0000 0001	Unassigned
0000 001	ISO/ITU-T NSAP addresses
0000 010	IPX addresses
0000 011	Unassigned
0000 1	Unassigned
0000 10	Unassigned
0001	Unassigned
001	Unassigned
010	Provider- based unicast addresses
011	Unassigned
100	Geographic-based unicast addresses
101	Unassigned
110	Unassigned
1110	Unassigned
1111 0	Unassigned
1111 10	Unassigned
1111 110	Unassigned
1111 1110 0	Unassigned
1111 1110 10	Link local addresses
1111 1110 11	Site local addresses
1111 1111	Multicast addresses

Like IPv4, the IPv6 also supports unicasting and multicasting, and IPv6 adds additional functionality to multicasting. For example, the multicast address contains a field to limit the scope of the multicast operation to a local site, a local link, global, and so on.

I refer you to the Huitema text and RFC 1883 if you need more details on the IPv6 address syntax.

THE IPV6 DATAGRAM

Figure 8–1 illustrates the format of IPv6 datagram (also called a packet in some literature). This section provides a description of each

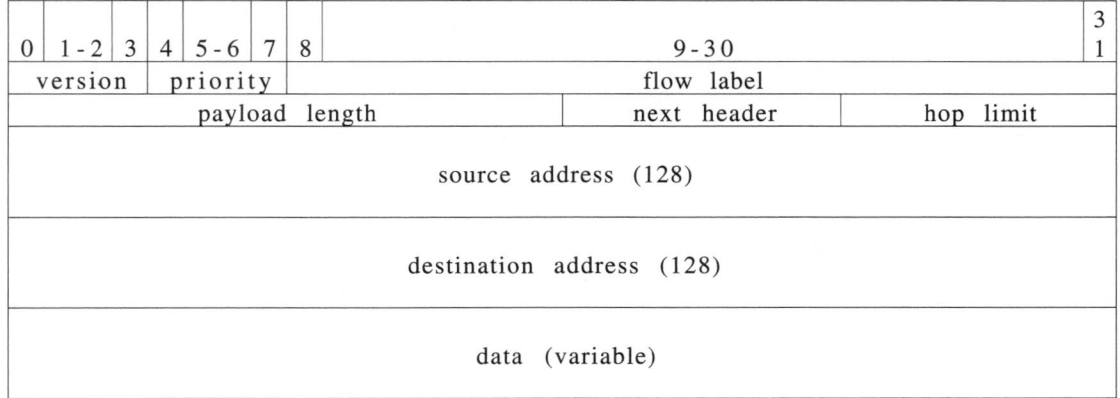

0	1 - 2	3	4	5 - 6	7	8	9 - 3 0	3 1
version		priority					flow label	
payload length							next header	hop limit

source address (128)

destination address (128)

data (variable)

Figure 8–1   The IPv6 datagram.

field in the datagram, and the next section compares the IPv6 fields with the fields in the IPv4 datagram.

The header consists of 64 bits of control field followed by a 128-bit source address and a 128-bit destination address. This initial 64 bits are:

- Version field, 4 bits
- Priority field, 4 bits
- Flow label field, 24 bits
- Payload length, 16 bits
- Next header type, 8 bits
- Hop limit, 8 bits
- Addresses, 128 bits each

The *version* field identifies the version of the protocol. For this implementation, the code is 6 (in decimal) or 0110 (in binary) for the 4-bit field.

The *priority* field is a new field. It can be coded to indicate sixteen possible values and is intended to play a similar role as the precedence field of IPv4. The IPv6 priority field will be used to support different types of traffic, from synchronous real-time video to asynchronous data.

Table 8–3 shows the permitted values for the IPv6 priority field and what types of traffic the priority values identify. The smaller numbers identify low-priority traffic, such as email and bulk-file transfers. The values 9–14 were set aside with the original publication of IPv6. The

Table 8–3   IPv6 Priority Field

0	Uncharacterized traffic
1	"Filler" traffic (news)
2	Unattended data transfer (e-mail)
3	Reserved
4	Bulk traffic (file transfer)
5	Reserved
6	Interactive traffic (...Telnet)
7	Control traffic (..OSPF,SNP)
8	High-fidelity video
9–14	Reserved
15	Low-fidelity video

standards groups are in the process of defining some of these values for traffic, such as voice.

RFC 1883 sets these rules for the priority field: Values 0 through 7 are used to specify the priority of traffic for which the source is providing congestion control. This type of traffic backs off in response to congestion, such as TCP traffic. Values 8 through 15 are used to specify the priority of traffic that does not back off in response to congestion, real-time voice or video packets being sent at a constant rate.

For non-congestion-controlled traffic, the lowest priority value (8) should be used for those packets that the sender is most willing to have discarded under conditions of congestion (e.g., high-fidelity video traffic), and the highest value (15) should be used for those packets that the sender is least willing to have discarded (e.g., low-fidelity audio traffic). There is no relative ordering implied between the congestion-controlled priorities and the non-congestion-controlled priorities.

The *flow label* field is also a new field in contrast to IPv4. Like the priority field, it is also designed to handle different types of traffic, such as voice, video, or data. The flow label field is a special identifier that can be attached to the datagram to permit it to be given special treatment by a router. It is called the flow label field because its intent is to identify traffic in which multiple datagrams are "flowing" from a specific source address to a specific destination address. The use of the flow label field can be used in place of the IP destination address fields, but its specific use is implementation-specific. Section 6 of RFC 1883 provides guidance on the use of flow labels. Some of this information has been "overtaking by events," and more recent information on flow labels is provided in Chapter 7.

IPv6 does not define the exact usage of the priority and flow label fields, their use will be defined further in subsequent RFCs and, of course, in many instances their use will be dictated by individual implementations.

The *payload length* field identifies the length of the payload. Since its length is 16 bits, the payload size is limited to 64 kbytes. However, the protocol does provide for the support of larger packets by utilizing the next header field.

Speaking of the *next header* field, this field represents one of the major changes in contrast to IPv4. First, it replaces the options field and, for normal implementations, it identifies the next header to be TCP or UDP. This simply means that the first part of the payload is carrying TCP or UDP traffic. However, other headers can be placed in the payload. They are called extension headers and reside between the IP header and the TCP or UDP header and payload. This approach simplifies the processing of a packet at a node, since the basic header is now a fixed length.

The *hop limit* field is a reflection of how many hops the datagram is permitted to traverse during its stay in an internet. This implementation is specific to the needs of the application.

The IP address fields are the last fields in the IP header. Each address is 128 bits in length, which allows for significant growth in the Internet.

COMPARISON OF IPV6 AND IPV4

This section is an extension to the previous discussion. It compares the headers of IPv4 and IPv6. This comparison will allow us to more into another level of detail about IPv6. The approach taken here is to start with the IPv4 header fields and to explain their fate in IPv6. To aid in this analysis, Figure 8–2 provides an illustration of the IPv4 datagram.

The version field is retained with the value of 6.

The IPv4 header length field is eliminated, and the IPv4 total length field is replaced by the IPv6 payload length. This latter field defines the contents of only the data (and not the header) field.

The IPv4 type of service (TOS) field is eliminated in IPv6, and parts of its contents (and functions) are placed in the IPv6 priority and flow label fields.

The identification, flags, and fragment offset fields in IPv4 are removed and similar functions are placed in an optional header extension.

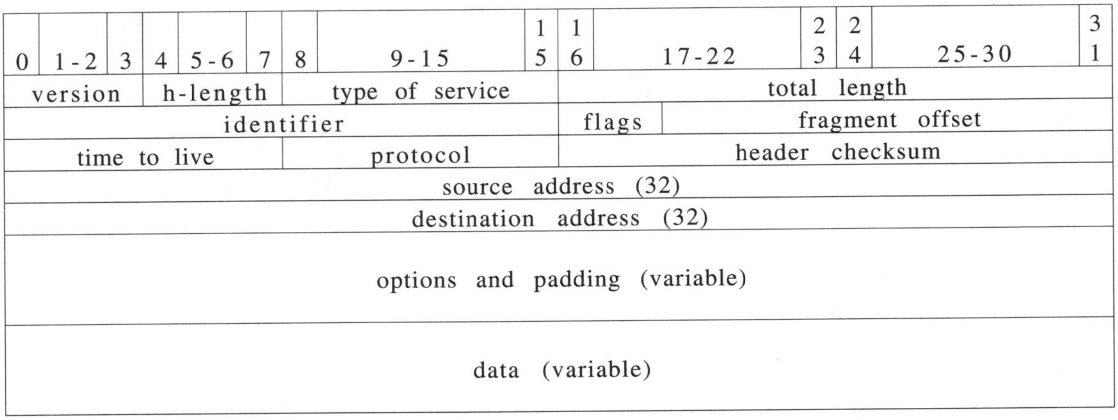

0	1-2	3	4	5-6	7	8	9-15	1 5	1 6	17-22	2 3	2 4	25-30	3 1
version			h-length			type of service				total length				
identifier								flags			fragment offset			
time to live				protocol				header checksum						
source address (32)														
destination address (32)														
options and padding (variable)														
data (variable)														

where: h-length header length

Figure 8–2   The IPv4 datagram.

The IP protocol field is removed and its function is retained in yet another extension header.

The IPv4 time to live (TTL) field is renamed the hop limit field in IPv6. But with the revision, the field's name is now accurate, because IPv6 uses it as a count of the number of hops the IP datagram has traversed.

The header checksum is eliminated in IPv6. This removal reflects the fact that the vast majority of communications systems in operation today perform error checks at the lower layers; that is, the layers below IP.

The options field in IPv4 is not used much. It is awkward to implement, and in some cases leads to considerable overhead in processing its contents because the field requires the execution of special routines in the IP software. It is replaced with IPv6 header extensions, discussed next.

THE IPV6 EXTENSION HEADERS

The approach in IPv6 is to use extension headers with each extension header stipulating what is in effect an option. As Figure 8–3 shows, the next header field describes a header that is inserted between the internet header and the user payload (data field). Indeed, there may be more than one header inserted here with the fields coded to identify each successive

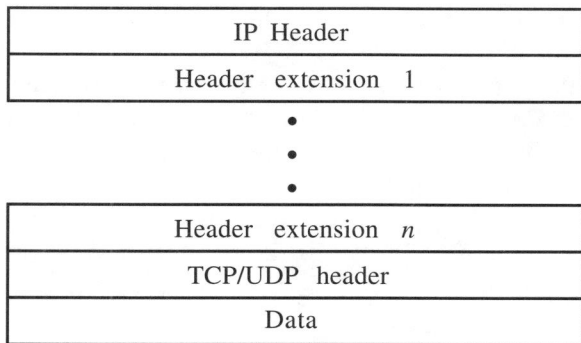

Figure 8–3   Example of headers.

header. In effect, a header is identified by its header type, which also carries a header type of the next header in the chain (if any exist).

The IPv6 RFC describes six extension headers:

- Fragment header
- Hop-by-hop options header
- Authentication header
- Encrypted security payload header
- Routing header
- Destination options header

With one exception, extension headers are not examined by any node along the delivery path. The node identified in the destination address of header examines the next header field to determine if an extension header is present, or if the upper layer header is present. The hop-by-hop options is the exception, and it is processed by every node on the path. The specification supports variable length extensions, if necessary.

Fragment Header.   IPv4 permits the fragmentation of large packets into smaller datagrams. This operation is useful, but it leads to considerable overhead in an internet. Consequently, IPv6 nodes will not fragment large packets once the traffic enters the network. In effect, the system reacts as if the IPv4 "don't fragment bit" is turned on. IPv6 does permit the packets to be fragmented before they are sent into the network. In addition, the fragments can be sent independently through an internet and arrive at different times and in different sequences at the receiver. The fragmentation operations of IPv6 are quite similar to IPv4, discussed in Chapter 2.

Fragmentation is performed only by the source node; intermediate nodes on the path are not allowed to fragment packets. If fragmentation is performed, the fragment header takes the form shown in Figure 8–4.

The fields in this header are as follows:

- *Next Header:* Identifies the initial header type of the fragmented part of the original packet. Uses the same values as the IPv4 Protocol field.
- *Reserved:* Reserved field.
- *Fragment Offset:* The offset, in 8-octet units, of the data following this header, relative to the start of the fragmentable part of the original packet. Parts of the packet cannot be fragmented if they are to be examined by nodes along the path (the routing header, and the hop-by-hop header).
- Res   Reserved field
- *M flag:* 1 = more fragments; 0 = last fragment.
- *Identification:* The source node generates an Identification value. The Identification must be different than that of any other fragmented packet sent recently with the same Source Address and Destination Address.

Hop-by-hop Options Header. The destination option header is used at the final destination. However, it may be important that intermediate nodes (hops) be able to exercise some operations to process the datagram. Functions come to mind such as ongoing debugging and network management operations. Therefore, the hop-by-hop options extension header is used for this purpose. The contents of the hop-by-hop options header must be defined based on the individual implementation but one service is defined in the current IPv4 RFC. It is the jumbo payload option. This option permits large PDUs to be sent whose length exceeds

0	1 - 6	7	8	9 - 14	1 5	1 6	17-27	2 8	29 - 30	3 1
Next Header			Reserved			Fragment Offset		Res	M
Identification									

Figure 8–4   The fragment header.

that encoded in the 16-bit length field. When this option is implemented, the IPv6 length field is set to all 0s. The processing node must then use a field in the hop-by-hop options to understand how to process the PDU. The format of the hop-by-hop options header is shown in Figure 8–5.

- *Next Header:* Identifies the type of header immediately following the Hop-by-Hop Options header. Uses the same values as the IPv4 Protocol field.
- *Hdr Ext Len:* Length of the Hop-by-Hop Options header in 8-octet units, not including the first 8 octets.
- *Options*: Variable length field, contents not defined

The IPv6 security features are provided by the authentication header and the encrypted security payload header. This section summarizes the IPv6 security features. More information is provided in RFCs 1825, 1826, 1827, 1828, and 1829.

Both authentication and encryption require that the sending and receiving parties agree on a key and a specific authentication or encryption algorithm. Other parameters are set up as well, such as the lifetime of the key.

Authentication Header. The authentication header is depicted in Figure 8–6. The format for the header is quite simple. It contains the next header indicator in the daisy chain of headers, the length of the header in multiples of 32 bits, a 16-bit reserved field that is currently set to 0s, the 32-bit security parameter index (SPI), and authentication data also coded in 32-bit word increments. The contents of the authentication data field depends on the specific encryption/authentication algorithm and the types of keys that are used.

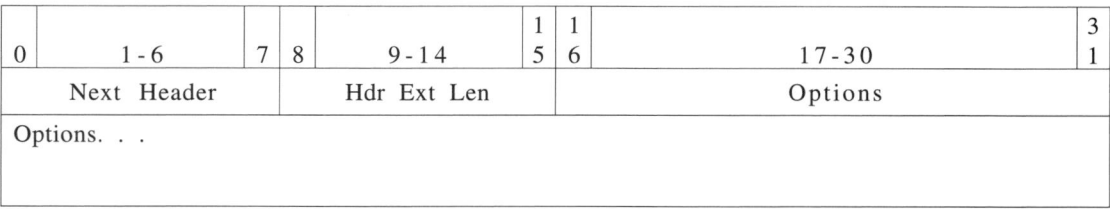

Figure 8–5 Hop-by-hop header.

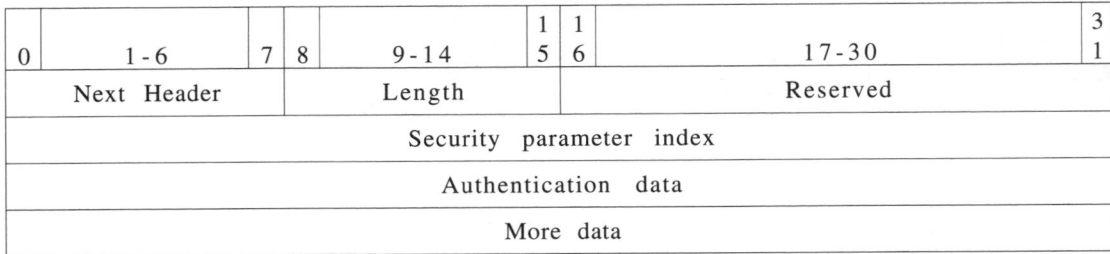

0	1-6	7	8	9-14	1 5	1 6	17-30	3 1
Next Header				Length			Reserved	
Security parameter index								
Authentication data								
More data								

Figure 8–6   IPv6 authentication header.

Encrypted Security Payload Header.   The encrypted security payload header is the last header in the daisy chain of headers. The format for this header is shown in Figure 8–7. The security parameter index (SPI) field is not encrypted; the payload (data) is.

Routing Header.   The routing header is quite similar in IPv6 to the source routing option in the options field of IPv4 (see Figure 8–8). Like its predecessor, the IPv6 routing header carries a list of intermediate IP addresses through which the datagram must be relayed. In IPv4, this option field stipulated either strict or loose source routing, IPv6 has a more efficient method of using source routing. The IPv6 node only examines the routing header if the node knows that one of its own addresses is in the destination IP field of the header. Otherwise, the node simply ignores this header extension. This will result in less overhead in processing the source routing feature.

- *Next Header:* Identifies the type of header immediately following the routing header. Uses the same values as the IPv4 Protocol field.
- *Hdr Ext Len:* Length of the routing header in 8-octet units, not including the first 8 octets.
- *Routing Type:* Identifier of a particular routing header variant.

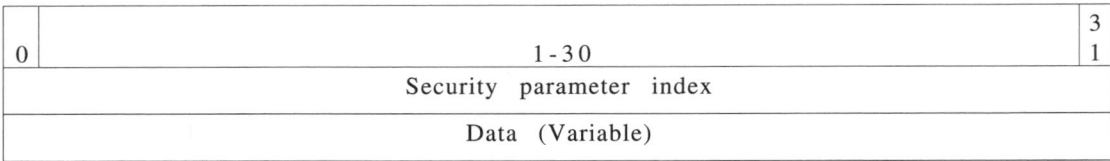

0	1-30	3 1
Security parameter index		
Data (Variable)		

Figure 8–7   Security payload header.

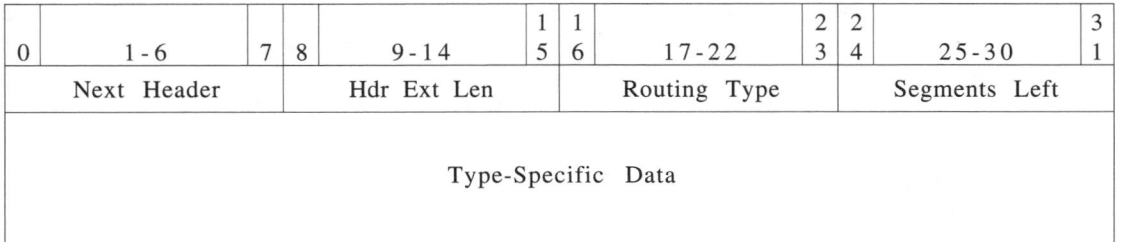

0	1 - 6	7	8	9 - 14	1 5	1 6	17-22	2 3	2 4	25-30	3 1
Next Header			Hdr Ext Len				Routing Type			Segments Left	
Type-Specific Data											

Figure 8–8   Routing extensions header.

- *Segments Left:* Number of intermediate nodes still to be visited before reaching the final destination.
- *Type-Specific Data:* Format determined by the routing type and length fields.

Destination Options Header.   In many systems, it is desirable to relay information transparently through an internet to be used only by the receiving end station. The IPv6 options destination options header provides for this service. Interestingly, it contains an options field within the header that is acted upon by the end user application. If the options field is not recognized by the destination, then this feature provides for the ability to generate an ICMP report stipulating the problem that has occurred by receiving an unrecognized options. The format for this header is shown in Figure 8–9.

- *Next Header:* Identifies the type of header immediately following the destination options header. Uses the same values as the IPv4 Protocol field.
- *Hdr Ext Len:* Length of the destination options header in 8-octet units, not including the first 8 octets.
- *Options*: Variable length field, contents not defined.

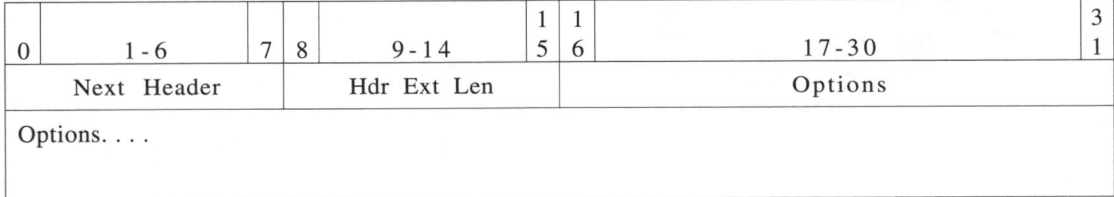

0	1 - 6	7	8	9 - 14	1 5	1 6	17-30	3 1
Next Header			Hdr Ext Len				Options	
Options. . . .								

Figure 8–9   Destination options header.

No Next Header. The value 59 in the next header field of an IPv6 header or any extension header indicates that there is nothing following that header.

SIZE OF THE PACKET

Here is some guidance from the IPv6 RFCs on packet sizes and fragmentation. IPv6 requires that every link in the internet have a maximum transmission unit (MTU) size of 576 octets or greater. On any link that cannot convey a 576-octet packet in one piece, link-specific fragmentation and reassembly must be provided at a layer below IPv6.

From each link to which a node is directly attached, the node must be able to accept packets as large as that link's MTU. Links that have a configurable MTU (for example, PPP links [RFC-1661]) must be configured to have an MTU of at least 576 octets; it is recommended that a larger MTU be configured to accommodate possible encapsulations (i.e., tunneling) without incurring fragmentation.

It is a good idea for IPv6 nodes implement Path MTU Discovery (RFC-1191), in order to discover and take advantage of paths with MTU greater than 576 octets. However, a minimal IPv6 implementation may restrict itself to sending packets no larger than 576 octets and omit implementation of Path MTU Discovery.

In order to send a packet larger than a path's MTU, a node may use the IPv6 fragment header to fragment the packet at the source and have it reassembled at the destination(s). However, the use of such fragmentation is discouraged in any application that is able to adjust its packets to fit the measured path MTU (i.e., down to 576 octets).

A node must be able to accept a fragmented packet that, after reassembly, is as large as 1500 octets, including the IPv6 header. A node is permitted to accept fragmented packets that reassemble to more than 1500 octets. However, a node must not send fragments that reassemble to a size greater than 1500 octets unless it has explicit knowledge that the destination(s) can reassemble a packet of that size.

In response to an IPv6 packet that is sent to an IPv4 destination (i.e., a packet that undergoes translation from IPv6 to IPv4), the originating IPv6 node may receive an ICMP Packet Too Big message reporting a Next-Hop MTU less than 576. In that case, the IPv6 node is not required to reduce the size of subsequent packets to less than 576, but must include a Fragment header in those packets so that the IPv6-to-IPv4 translating router can obtain a suitable Identification value to use in resulting IPv4 fragments. Note that this means the payload may have to be reduced to 528 octets (576 minus 40 for the IPv6 header and 8 for the fragment header), and smaller still if additional extension headers are used.

Path MTU Discovery must be performed even in cases where a host "thinks" a destination is attached to the same link as itself. Unlike IPv4, it is unnecessary in IPv6 to set a "Don't Fragment" flag in the packet header in order to perform Path MTU Discovery; that is an implicit attribute of every IPv6 packet. Also, those parts of the RFC-1191 procedures that involve use of a table of MTU "plateaus" do not apply to IPv6, because the IPv6 version of the "Datagram Too Big" message always identifies the exact MTU to be used.

IPV6 VERSUS ATM

There is considerable interest in the industry regarding the potential use of ATM or IP to support multiservice operations. The issues revolve around IPv6 (not IPv4) versus ATM, since IPv6 is designed to support different types of traffic.

The task force that developed the IPv6 specification believes that IPv6 can compete with ATM with the use of three fields in the IP header: (1) the priority field, (2) the flow label field, and (3) the routing extension header.

However, the use of IPv6 alone will not provide adequate support of multiservice applications. Consequently, partner protocols are designed to give IP a multiservice capability. These protocols are (1) the Real Time Protocol (RTP), (2) the Real Time Control Protocol (RTCP), and (3) the Resource Reservation Protocol (RSVP). In addition, another important partner to IP for multiservice operations is the Internet Group Management Protocol (IGMP). This protocol has been in service for several years and forms the basis for multicasting operations.

These protocols are covered in Chapter 10.

IPV6 AND ICMP

Since ICMP uses IP addresses, it too must be revised to operate with IPv6. In addition, the IPv4 Internet Group Membership Protocol (IGMP) was incorporated into ICMP.

The IPv6 ICMP messages have the same general format as the IPv4 ICMP messages including a type field, a code field, a checksum, and a variable length data part. The IPv6 ICMP also defines ICMP type messages that are similar to IPv4. Currently there are fourteen different types defined and they are listed here:

1 = destination unreachable
2 = packet too big
3 = time exceeded
4 = parameter problem
128 = echo request
129 = echo reply
130 = group membership query
131 = group membership report
132 = group membership termination
133 = router solicitation
134 = router advertisement
135 = neighbor solicitation
136 = neighbor advertisement
137 = redirect

IPV6 AND TCP/UDP

The implementation of IPv6 affects the TCP and UDP operations. The impact is not significant, but the following changes will be necessary. First, since TCP and UDP use the IP addresses, the operating system that interworks these programs with IP must be modified. Second, the error checking performed by TCP and UDP entails the use of a pseudo-header, which is the IP header. The idea is to include the IP source and destination address and checksum in order to detect delivery problems. Obviously, these upper layer checksums must be altered to account for the new IPv6 address base.

Since error checking with the checksum is deleted in IPv6, the TCP/UDP checksums become even more important and they are mandatory in both TCP and UDP operations.

IPV6 SUPPORT OF JUMBOGRAMS

IPv6 supports datagrams larger than 65535 bytes long (jumbograms), through use of the Jumbo Payload hop-by-hop option. The UDP protocol has a 16-bit length field that prevents it from supporting jumbograms. TCP does not have a length field, but both the maximum segment length (MSS) option and the Urgent field are constrained by 16 bits. This discussion explains how TCP and UDP can support jumbograms and is based on RFC 1883.

UDP Jumbograms

To allow UDP to make use of jumbograms, the UDP length field either needs to be extended, or it needs to be ignored. Since the size of the field cannot be changed, a length of zero is used to indicate that it is to be ignored, and the length in the "pseudo-header" is used to determine the length of the UDP header plus data.

Upon receiving a UDP packet with a length field of zero, the length of the UDP packet is computed from the length field in the Jumbo Payload option minus the length of all extension headers present between the IPv6 header and the UDP header.

TCP Jumbograms

If the maximum transmission unit (MTU) size of the directly attached interface is greater than 65535, the MSS value is set to 65535, and when an MSS value of 65535 is received, it is to be treated as infinity. Then MTU discovery, starting with the MTU of the outgoing interface, will be used to determine the actual MSS.

When a TCP packet is to be sent with an Urgent Pointer (i.e., the URG bit set), the following operations occur:

- Calculate the offset from the Sequence Number to the Urgent Pointer.
- If the offset is less than 65535, fill in the Urgent field and continue with the normal TCP processing.
- If the offset is greater than 65535 and the offset is greater than or equal to the length of the TCP data, fill in the Urgent Pointer with 65535 and continue with the normal TCP processing.
- Otherwise, the TCP packet must be split into two pieces.

The first piece contains data up to, but not including, the data pointed to by the Urgent Pointer, and the Urgent field is set to 65535 to indicate that the Urgent Pointer is beyond the end of this packet. The second piece can then be sent with the Urgent field set normally.

For TCP input processing, when a TCP packet is received with the URG bit set and an Urgent field of 65535, the Urgent Pointer is calculated using an offset equal to the length of the TCP data, rather than the offset in the Urgent field.

TRANSITION FROM IPV4 TO IPV6 ROUTING

As of this writing it is clear that people other than the IPv6 developers are aware that IPv6 must be dealt with. A number of organizations are now experimenting and shaking down IPv6 in test networks.

A key issue in the use of IPv6 is how to get there from IPv4. The Internet Working Groups have published RFCs to guide the network administrator through the transition maze. I refer you to RFCs 1933 and 2185, which are summarized here.

First, we define a few terms not used previously in this book or, if used, warrant iteration.

- *Border router:* A router that forwards datagram across routing domain boundaries.
- *Neighbors:* Nodes attached to the same link.
- *Routing domain:* A collection of routers that coordinate routing knowledge using a single routing protocol.
- *Routing region* (or just *region*): A collection of routers interconnected by a single internet protocol (e.g., IPv6) and coordinating their routing knowledge using routing protocols from a single internet protocol stack. A routing region may be a superset of a routing domain.
- *Reachability information:* Information describing the set of reachable destinations that can be used for packet forwarding decisions.
- *Routing information:* Same as reachability information.
- *Routing prefix*: Address prefix that expresses destinations that have addresses with the matching address prefixes. It is used by routers to advertise what systems they are capable of reaching.
- *Route leaking:* Advertisement of network layer reachability information across routing region boundaries.

Issues

As shown in Figure 8–10, during the extended Ipv4 to IPv6 transition period, IPv6-based systems must coexist with the installed base of

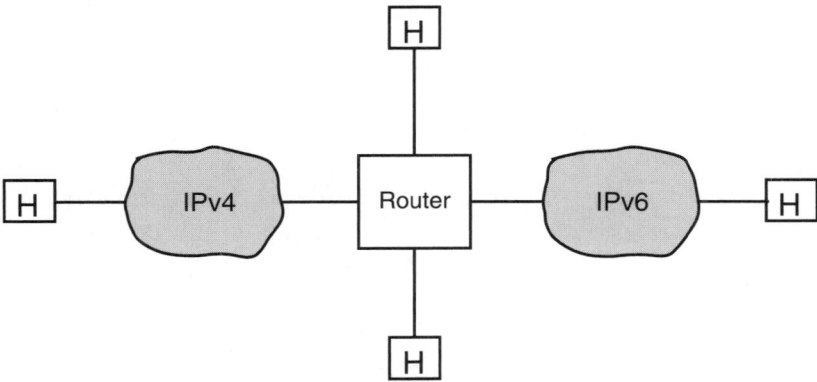

Figure 8–10   Dual IPv4–IPv6 environment.

IPv4 systems. Both sets of protocols will exist. It is certain that deployed IPv6 domains will not be completely interconnected together. They will need to communicate across IPv4-only routing regions. In order to achieve dynamic routing a mixed environment, there must to be mechanisms to distribute IPv6 network layer reachability information between dispersed IPv6 routing regions.

The IPv6 transition provides a dual-IP-layer transition, augmented by use of encapsulation where necessary and appropriate. The basic mechanisms required to accomplish these goals include: (1) dual-IP-layer route computation; (2) manual configuration of point-to-point tunnels; and (3) route leaking to support automatic encapsulation.

Tunnels and Configuration Alternatives

Tunnels (either IPv4 over IPv6, or IPv6 over IPv4) can be manually configured. For example, in the early stages of transition this approach will be used to allow two IPv6 domains to interwork over an IPv4-based domain. Manually configured static tunnels are treated as if they were a normal data link.

Use of automatic encapsulation, where the IPv4 tunnel endpoint address is determined from the IPv4 address embedded in the IPv4-compatible destination address of IPv6 packet, requires consistency of routes between IPv4 and IPv6 routing domains for destinations using IPv4-compatible addresses.

Basic Dual-IP-Layer Operation

In the basic dual-IP-layer transition scheme, routers may independently support IPv4 and IPv6 routing. Forwarding of IPv4 packets is based on routes learned through running IPv4-specific routing protocols. Similarly, forwarding of IPv6 packets (including Ipv6 packets with IPv4-compatible addresses) is based on routes learned through running IPv6-specific routing protocols. This implies that separate instances of routing protocols are used for IPv4 and for IPv6.

Automatic tunneling may be used when both the sending and destination nodes are connected by IPv4 routing. In order for automatic tunneling to work, both nodes must be assigned IPv4-compatible IPv6 addresses. Automatic tunneling can be especially useful where either source or destination hosts (or both) do not have any adjacent IPv6-capable router. With automatic tunneling, the resulting IPv4 packet is forwarded by IPv4 routers as a normal IPv4 packet, using IPv4 routes learned from routing protocols.

If both source and destination hosts make use of IPv4-compatible IPv6 addresses, then it is possible for automatic tunneling to be used for the entire path from the source host to the destination host. In this case, the IPv6 packet is encapsulated in an IPv4 packet by the source host and is forwarded by routers as an IPv4 packet all the way to the destination host. This allows initial deployment of IPv6-capable hosts to be done prior to the update of any routers.

Host-to-Router Configured Default Tunneling

In some cases configured default tunneling may be used to encapsulate the IPv6 packet for transmission from the source host to an IPv6-backbone. Configured default tunneling is useful if the source host does not know of any local IPv6-capable router (implying that the packet cannot be forwarded as a normal IPv6 packet directly over the link layer), and when the destination host does not have an IPv4-compatible IPv6 address (implying that host to host tunneling cannot be used).

Host-to-router configured default tunneling may also be used even when the host does know of a local IPv6 router. In this case, it is a policy decision whether the host prefers to send a native IPv6 packet to the IPv6-capable router or prefers to send an encapsulated packet to the configured tunnel endpoint.

The dual router that is serving as the endpoint of the host to router configured default tunnel must advertise reachability into IPv4 routing sufficient to cause the encapsulated packet to be forwarded to it.

In some cases, the source host may have direct connectivity to one or more IPv6-capable routers, but the destination host might not have direct connectivity to any IPv6-capable router. In this case, provided that the destination host has an IPv4-compatible IPv6 address, normal IPv6 forwarding may be used for part of the packet's path, and router-to-host tunneling may be used to get the packet from an encapsulating dual router to the destination host.

In this case, the difficult part is the IPv6 routing required to deliver the IPv6 packet from the source host to the encapsulating router. For this to happen, the encapsulating router has to advertise reachability for the appropriate IPv4-compatible IPv6 addresses into the IPv6 routing region. With this approach, all IPv6 packets (including those with IPv4-compatible addresses) are routed using routes calculated from native IPv6 routing. This implies that encapsulating routers need to advertise into IPv6 routing specific route entries corresponding to any IPv4-compatible IPv6 addresses that belong to dual hosts that can be reached in an neighboring IPv4-only region. This requires manual configuration of the encapsulating routers to control which routes are to be injected into IPv6 routing protocols. Nodes in the IPv6 routing region would use such a route to forward IPv6 packets along the routed path toward the router that injected (leaked) the route, at which point packets are encapsulated and forwarded to the destination host using normal IPv4 routing. Once again this is a general summary, and you should study RFCs 1993 and 2185 for fuller explanations on this important subject.

SUMMARY

IPv6's major feature is the expanded IP address. But, IPv6 is also represents enhancements to IPv4 and the inclusion of options for better security and the support of multimedia traffic. IPv6 is not yet in the marketplace, but many organizations have begun to test it and they are discussing migration plans to move from IPv4 to IPv6.

9

The Point-to-Point
Protocol (PPP)

The Point-to-Point Protocol (PPP) is really not a new or advanced Internet feature. It is included in this book because PPP is used with many other systems. For example, some residential broadband (RBB) systems are using PPP as part of the RBB protocol suite. This chapter introduces you to the architecture and major operations of PPP.

WHY PPP WAS DEVELOPED

The PPP was implemented to solve a problem that evolved in the industry during the last decade. With the rapid growth of internetworking, several vendors and standards organizations developed a number of network layer protocols. The Internet Protocol (IP) is the most widely used of these protocols. However, machines (such as routers) typically run more than one network layer protocol. While IP is a given on most machines, routers also support network layer protocols developed by companies such as Xerox, 3Com, and Novell. Machines communicating with each other did not readily know which network layer protocols were available during a session.

In addition, until the advent of PPP, the industry did not have a standard means to define a point-to-point encapsulation protocol. This term means that a protocol carries or encapsulates a network layer packet in its information (I) field and uses another field in the frame to identify which network layer packet resides in the I field. The PPP standard solves these two problems and provides an array of other features as well.

PPP is used to encapsulate network layer datagrams over a serial communications link. The protocol allows two machines on a point-to-point communications channel to negotiate the particular types of network layer protocols (such as IP) that are to be used during a session. It also allows the two machines to negotiate other types of operations, such as the use of compression and authentication procedures. After this negotiation occurs, PPP is used to carry the network layer protocol data units (PDUs) in the I field of an HDLC-type frame.

This protocol supports either bit-oriented synchronous transmission, byte-oriented, or asynchronous (start/stop) transmission. It can be used on switched or dial-up links. It requires a full duplex capability.

PPP AND HDLC

PPP operates over the High Level Data Link Control (HDLC) protocol, and consists of two major protocols, explained in the following material (see Figure 9–1).

The Link Control Protocol (LCP) is the first procedure that is executed when a PPP link is set up. It defines the operations for configuring and testing the link. As part of LCP, the authentication option (AUTH) can be invoked.

PPP uses the Network Control Protocol (NCP) to negotiate certain options and parameters that will be used by a L_3 protocol. This figure shows the IPCP (the IP Control Protocol), which is an example of an specific NCP, and is used to negotiate various IP parameters, such as IP addresses and compression.

The PPP PDU uses the HDLC frame as stipulated in ISO 3309–1979 (and amended by ISO 3309–1984/PDAD1). HDLC is beyond the scope of this book so this material is restricted to showing the HDLC frame format and its relationship to PPP. Figure 9–2 shows this format. The flag sequence is the standard HDLC flag of 01111110 (hex 7E), and the address field is set to all 1s (hex FF), which signifies an all-stations address. PPP does not use individual station addresses because it is a point-to-point protocol. The control field is set to identify a HDLC unnumbered information (UI) command. Its value is 00000011 (hex 03).

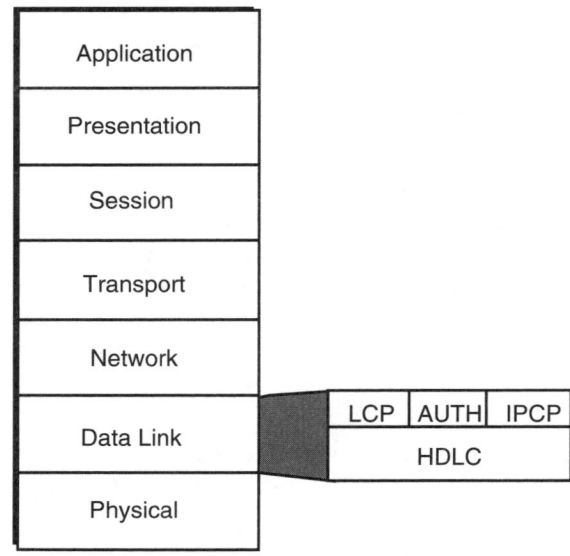

where:
AUTH   Authentication
LCP   Link Control Protocol
IPCP   Internet Protocol (IP Control Protocol)

Figure 9–1   The PPP entities.

The protocol field is used to identify the PDU that is encapsulated into the I field of the frame. The field values are assigned by the Internet, and the values beginning with a 0 identify the network protocol that resides in the I field. Values beginning with 8 identify a control protocol that is used to negotiate the protocols that will actually be used. Up-to-date values of the Protocol field are specified in the most recent "Assigned Numbers" RFC. This specification reserves the following values:

Value (in hex)	Protocol Name
0001	Padding Protocol
0003 to 001F	Reserved (transparency inefficient)
007D	Reserved (Control Escape)
00CF	Reserved (PPP NLPID)
00FF	Reserved (compression inefficient)
8001 to 801F	Unused
807D	Unused

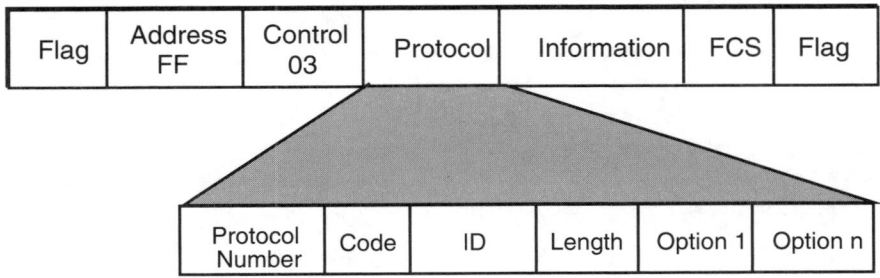

Figure 9–2   The PPP frame format.

80CF	Unused
80FF	Unused
C021	Link Control Protocol
C023	Password Authentication Protocol
C025	Link Quality Report
C223	Challenge Handshake Authentication Protocol

The PPP frame I field is used to carry the link control protocol packet. The protocol field in the frame must contain hex C021 to indicate the I field carries link control protocol information. The format for the field is shown in Figure 9–2. The code field must be coded to identify the type of LCP packet that is encapsulated into the frame. As examples, the code would indicate if the frame contains a configure request, which would likely be followed by a configure ACK or NAK. Additionally, the code could indicate (for example) an echo request data unit. Naturally, the next frame would probably identify the echo reply. Each of the packets discussed in the previous section are described with codes.

The identifier field is a value that is used to match the request and reply messages to each other. The length field defines the length of the packet, which includes code, identifier, and data fields. The data field values are determined on the contents of the code field.

LCP

LCP was introduced briefly earlier in this chapter. To iterate, its purpose is to support the establishment of the connection and to allow for certain configuration options to be negotiated. The protocol also maintains the connection and provides procedures for terminating the connection.

PPP requires that LCP be executed to open the connection between two stations before any network layer traffic is exchanged. This requires a series of packet exchanges that are called configure packets. After these packets have been exchanged and a configure acknowledge packet has been sent and received between the stations, the connection is considered to be in an open state and the exchange of traffic can begin. LCP confines itself only to link operations. It does not understand how to negotiate the implementation of network layer protocols. Indeed, it does not care about the upper layer negotiations relating to the network protocols.

Link quality determination is optional and allows LCP to check if the link is of sufficient quality to actually bring up the network layer. Although the link quality determination phase is defined in the standard, the actual implementation procedures are not specified. This tool exists to provide an LCP echo request and an LCP echo-type packet. These packets are defined within the protocol and exist within the state transition tables of the protocol.

After the link establishment (and if the link quality determination phase is implemented), the protocol configuration allows the two stations to negotiate/configure the protocols that will be used at the network layer. This is performed by the appropriate network control protocol (NCP). The particular protocol that is used here depends on which family of NCPs is implemented.

LCP is also responsible for terminating the link connection. It is allowed to perform the termination at its discretion. Unless problems have occurred that create this event, the link termination is usually provided by a upper layer protocol or a user-operated network control center.

GENERAL EXAMPLE OF PPP OPERATIONS

Figure 9–3 shows an example of how PPP can be used to support network configuration operations. Routers, hosts, and so on exchange the PPP frames to determine which network layer protocols are supported. In this example, two machines negotiate the use of the Internet Protocol (IP) and its OSI counterpart, ISO 8473, the Connectionless Network Protocol (CLNP). The LCP operations are invoked first to setup and test the link. Next, NCP operations are invoked to negotiate which network protocols (and associated procedures) are to be used between the machines. After this negotiation is complete, datagrams are exchanged. At any point, either node can terminate the session.

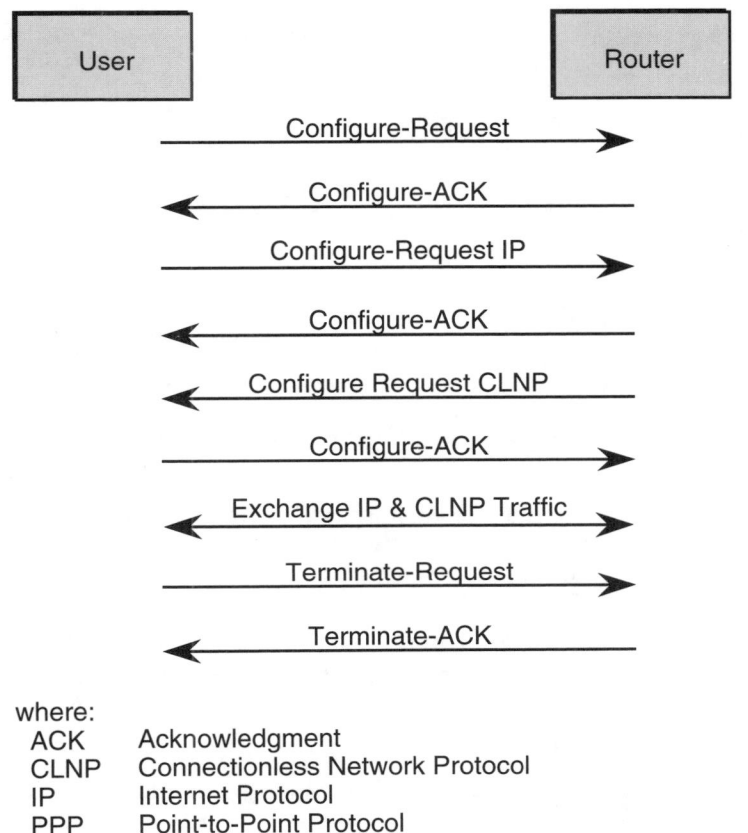

where:
  ACK   Acknowledgment
  CLNP   Connectionless Network Protocol
  IP   Internet Protocol
  PPP   Point-to-Point Protocol

Figure 9–3   Example of a PPP link operations.

PPP PHASE DIAGRAM

In the process of configuring, maintaining and terminating the PPP link, the PPP link goes through several distinct (phases), shown in Figure 9–4. This phase diagram is generalized for this explanation. Also, PPP (RFC 1661, Section 4) describes in considerable detail a state machine that explains the PPP events between PPP layers inside the machine. This chapter does not cover this aspect of PPP.

Link Dead (Physical Layer Not Ready)

The link begins and ends with this phase. When an external event (such as carrier detection or network administrator configuration) indi-

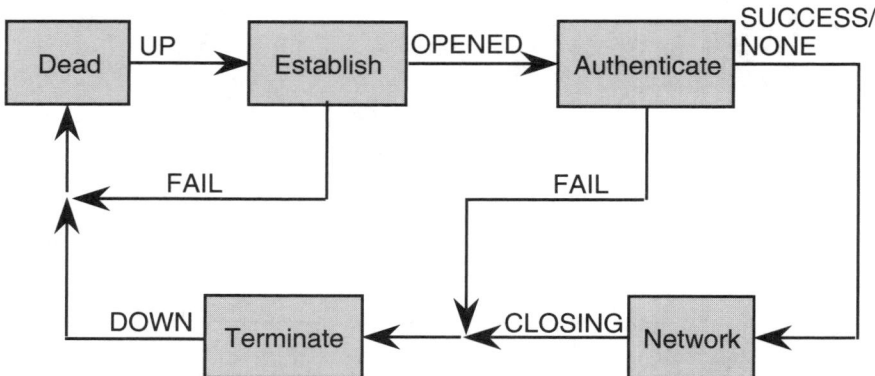

Figure 9–4   The PPP phase diagram.

cates that the physical-layer is ready to be used, PPP will proceed to the Link Establishment phase.

Typically, a link will return to this phase automatically after the disconnection of a modem. In the case of a hard-wired link, this phase may be extremely short—merely long enough to detect the presence of the device.

Link Establishment Phase

The Link Control Protocol (LCP) is used to establish the connection through an exchange of Configure packets. This exchange is complete and the LCP Opened state is entered once a Configure-Ack packet has been both sent and received. The receipt of the LCP Configure-Request causes a return to the Link Establishment phase from the Network-Layer Protocol phase or Authentication phase.

Authentication Phase

Authentication is not required. If an implementation desires that the peer authenticate with some specific authentication protocol, then it requests the use of that authentication protocol during Link Establishment phase. The method of authentication is implementation-specific.

Network Layer Protocol Phase

Next, each network layer protocol (such as IP, IPX, or AppleTalk) is separately configured by the appropriate Network Control Protocol (NCP).

After a NCP has reached the Opened state, PPP will carry the corresponding network-layer protocol packets. Any supported network-layer protocol packets received when the corresponding NCP is not in the Opened state MUST be silently discarded. During this phase, link traffic consists of any possible combination of LCP, NCP, and network-layer protocol packets.

Link Termination Phase

LCP is used to close the link through an exchange of Terminate packets. When the link is closing, PPP informs the network layer protocols so that they may take appropriate action. After the exchange of Terminate packets, the physical layer is usually notified to disconnect.

LCP PACKETS

This section describes the LCP packets, classified as follows (and some were introduced in Figure 9–3):

- Link Configuration packets are used to establish and configure a link (Configure-Request, Configure-Ack, Configure-Nak and Configure-Reject).
- Link Termination packets are used to terminate a link (Terminate-Request and Terminate-Ack).
- Link Maintenance packets are used to manage and debug a link (Code-Reject, Protocol-Reject, Echo-Request, Echo-Reply, and Discard-Request).

Each Configuration Option specifies a default value. This ensures that such LCP packets are always recognizable, even when one end of the link mistakenly believes the link to be open. Exactly one LCP packet is encapsulated in the PPP Information field, where the PPP Protocol field indicates type hex C021 (Link Control Protocol).

The Link Control Protocol packet format is shown Figure 9–5. The fields are transmitted from left to right.

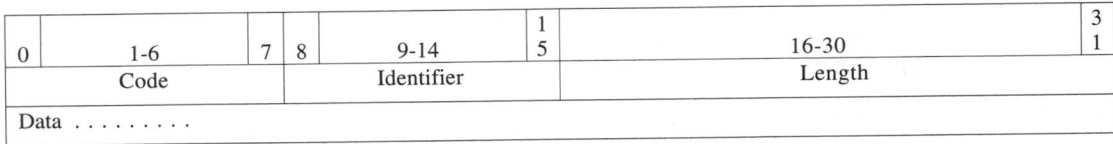

0	1-6	7	8	9-14	1 5	16-30	3 1
	Code			Identifier		Length	
Data							

Figure 9–5   Format of Link Control Packet (CP).

The fields in the LCP packet are as follows:

- *Code field*: Identifies the kind of LCP packet, currently defined in PPP for these codes:
  - 1 Configure-Request
  - 2 Configure-Ack
  - 3 Configure-Nak
  - 4 Configure-Reject
  - 5 Terminate-Request
  - 6 Terminate-Ack
  - 7 Code-Reject
  - 8 Protocol-Reject
  - 9 Echo-Request
  - 10 Echo-Reply
  - 11 Discard-Request
- *Identifier:* Used in matching requests and replies.
- *Length:* Indicates the length of the LCP packet, including the Code, Identifier, Length, and Data fields.
- *Data:* Format of the Data field is determined by the Code field.

The following section provides a brief explanation of the functions of each LCP packet.

Configure-Request

An implementation wishing to open a connection transmits a Configure-Request. The Options field is filled with any desired changes to the link defaults. Upon reception of a Configure-Request, an appropriate reply is transmitted.

Configure-Ack

If every Configuration Option received in a Configure-Request is recognizable, and all values are acceptable, then the receiver implementation transmits a Configure-Ack.

Configure-Nak

If every instance of the received Configuration Options is recognizable, but some values are not acceptable, then the receiver transmits a Configure-Nak. The Options field is filled with the unacceptable Configuration Options from the Configure-Request. All acceptable Configuration Options are filtered out of the Configure-Nak.

Each Configuration Option is modified to a value acceptable to the Configure-Nak sender. The default value can be used, when this differs from the requested value.

When a particular type of Configuration Option can be listed more than once with different values, the Configure-Nak includes a list of all values for that option which are acceptable to the Configure-Nak sender. This includes acceptable values that were present in the Configure-Request.

Configure-Reject

If some Configuration Options received in a Configure-Request are not recognizable or are not acceptable for negotiation, the receiver transmits a Configure-Reject. The Options field is filled with the unacceptable Configuration Options from the Configure-Request.

Terminate-Request and Terminate-Ack

PPP closes a connection by sending a Terminate-Request. Terminate-Request packets continue to be sent until Terminate-Ack is received, the lower layer indicates that it has gone down, or a sufficiently large number of these packets have been transmitted such that the peer is down with reasonable certainty. Upon reception of a Terminate-Request, a Terminate-Ack is transmitted.

Code-Reject

Reception of a LCP packet with an unknown Code indicates that the peer is operating with a different version. This information is conveyed in the unknown Code by transmitting a Code-Reject packet.

Protocol-Reject

Reception of a PPP packet with an unknown Protocol field indicates that the peer is attempting to use a protocol that is unsupported. This usually occurs when the peer attempts to configure a new protocol. Upon reception of a Protocol-Reject, the implementation stops sending packets of the indicated protocol at the earliest opportunity.

Echo-Request and Echo-Reply

LCP includes Echo-Request and Echo-Reply Codes in order to provide a data link layer loopback mechanism for use in exercising both directions of the link. This is useful as an aid in debugging, link quality determination, performance testing, and for numerous other functions.

Discard-Request

LCP includes a Discard-Request Code in order to provide a data link layer sink mechanism for use in exercising the local to remote direction of the link.

LCP Options

In addition to the operations just described, LCP supports a number of options. Table 9–1 provides a list of the LCP options and the associated RFC. Following the table, each is described briefly.

Table 9–1   LCP Options

Option Type	Name	RFC
00	Vendor extensions	2153
01	Maximum receive unit	1661
02	Asynchronous control character MAP	1662
03	Authentication protocol	1661
04	Quality protocol	1661/1989
05	Magic number	1661
06	Reserved	—
07	Protocol field compression	1661
08	Address and control field compression	1661
09	FCS alternatives	1570
0A	Self-describing PAD	1520
0B	Numbered mode	1663
0C	Multilink procedure	1663
0D	Call-back	1570
0E	Connect time	Obsolete
10	Nominal data encapsulation	Dropped
11, 13, 13	Multilink operations	1990
14	Proprietary	—
15	DCE identifier	1926
16	Multilink plus procedure	1934
17	Link discriminator	2125
18	LCP authentication option	Not assigned

Vendor Extensions

This option uses the well-known Ethernet Organization Unique ID (OUI) to identify vendor-specific information.

Maximum Receive Unit (MRU)

This option informs the receiving peer that the PPP can receive larger packets or requests that the peer send smaller packets. The default value is 1500 octets. If smaller packets are requested, an implementation should still be able to receive the full 1500 octet information field in case link synchronization is lost.

Asynchronous Control Character Map (ACCM)

This option allows an escape from the ASCII control characters 00–1F (the first two columns of the ASCII/IA5 code table).

Authentication Protocol

PPP sends the Configure-Request packet to indicate that it expects authentication from its peer. If an implementation sends a Configure-Ack, it is agreeing to authenticate with the specified protocol. An implementation receiving a Configure-Ack expects the peer to authenticate with the acknowledged protocol.

Quality Protocol

On some links it may be desirable to determine when and how often the link is dropping data. This process is called link quality monitoring.

The implementation sending the Configure-Request is indicating that it expects to receive monitoring information from its peer. If an implementation sends a Configure-Ack, then it is agreeing to send the specified protocol. An implementation receiving a Configure-Ack expects the peer to send the acknowledge protocol.

Magic Number

This option provides a method to detect looped-back links and other data link layer problems, such as echoes. The Magic Number is not negotiated, and zero is inserted where a Magic Number might otherwise be used.

PPP chooses its Magic Number in the most random manner possible in order to guarantee with very high probability that an implementation will arrive at a unique number.

When a Configure-Request is received with a Magic Number Configuration Option, the received Magic Number is compared with the Magic Number of the last Configure-Request sent to the peer. If the two Magic Numbers are different, then the link is not looped back, and the Magic Number is acknowledged. If the two Magic Numbers are equal, then it is probable that the link is looped back and that this Configure-Request is actually the one last sent. To determine this, a Configure-Nak is sent specifying a different Magic Number value. A new Configure-Request is not sent to the peer until normal processing would cause it to be sent (that is, until a Configure-Nak is received or the Restart timer runs out).

Reception of a Configure-Nak with a Magic Number different from that of the last Configure-Nak sent to the peer proves that a link is not looped back and indicates a unique Magic Number. If the Magic Number is equal to the one sent in the last Configure-Nak, the possibility of a looped-back link is increased, and a new Magic Number is chosen. In either case, a new Configure-Request is sent with the new Magic Number.

Protocol Field Compression (PFC)

This option provides a method to negotiate the compression of the PPP Protocol field. By default, all implementations transmit packets with two octet PPP Protocol fields.

PPP Protocol field number are chosen such that some values may be compressed into a single octet form that is clearly distinguishable from the two octet form. This Configuration Option is sent to inform the peer that the implementation can receive such single octet Protocol fields.

Address and Control Field Compression

This option provides a method to negotiate the compression of the Data Link Layer Address and Control fields. By default, all implementations transmit frames with address and Control fields appropriate to the link framing.

Since these fields usually have constant values for point-to-point links, they are easily compressed. This Configuration Option is sent to inform the peer that the implementation can receive compressed Address and Control fields.

FCS Alternatives

This option allows the use of a larger CRC for the PPP FCS field. The default value is 16 bits, which can be negotiated to 32-bits.

Self-Describing PAD

This option describes how padding octets are placed at the end of the PPP I field in order to place the field on a boundary convenient for processing.

Numbered Mode

This option uses X.25's L_2 LAPB, which provides for sequencing, ACKs, NAKs, and retransmissions of the PPP traffic.

Multilink Procedure

This option allows the grouping together of multiple single links. It is not needed now that multilink PPP (RFC 1990) is available.

Call-Back

This option is being reworked, and should not be used at this time.

Connect Time

This option is no longer used; it was part of the AppleTalk protocol suite.

Nominal Data Encapsulation

This option has been dropped.

Multilink Operations

As stated earlier, multilink operations permit multiple single links to be aggregated together.

Proprietary

This option is proprietary.

DCE Identifier

This option allows the identification of specific DCEs, such as DSU or CSU. It is used by these devices to negotiate a subset of PPP features.

Multilink Plus Procedure

This option is based on Ascend's proprietary protocol.

Link Discriminator

This option is used to identify a single link in a multilink group.

LCP Authentication Option

This option is not complete. If implemented, it will allow the incorporation of authentication into the LCP negotiation features.

NETWORK LAYER PROTOCOLS

PPP supports the encapsulation of several network layer protocols in the PPP I field. They are:

- IPv4
- IPv6
- Internet Packet Exchange (IPX)
- NetBIOS
- Systems Network Architecture (SNA)
- OSI's Connectionless Network Layer Protocol (CLNP)
- DECnet Phase IV
- Banyan Vines
- L_2 Bridges

Each network layer protocol usually has two PPP protocol numbers. The first is used by NCP to negotiate the options for the protocol. These PPP protocol numbers range from hex 8000-BFFF. The second number identifies the protocol itself and is the same value as the NCP value less 8000.

The Internet Protocol

The Internet Protocol (IPCP) is described in RFC 1332 and is identified with PPP protocol values of hex 8021 and 0021. The following IP features/options can be identified:

- *IP Compression Protocol:* Used to identify TCP/IP header compression (see RFC 1144 for more detail).
- *IP Address:* Used to configure IP addresses.
- *Mobile IPv4:* This option is discussed in Chapter 11.

IPV6 OVER PPP

With the increased interest in IPv6 and the increasing use of PPP, it is assured that IPv6 will run over PPP. This section describes these operations. A more thorough explanation is available in RFC 2023.

Basic Rules

Before any IPv6 packets are transmitted, PPP must reach the Network Layer Protocol phase, and the IPv6 Control Protocol must reach the Opened state. One IPv6 packet is encapsulated in the Information field of the PPP frame. The Protocol field indicates type hex 0057 (Internet Protocol Version 6). The maximum length of an IPv6 packet transmitted over a PPP link is the same as the maximum length of the Information field of a PPP frame. PPP links supporting IPv6 must allow at least 576 octets in the information field of a data link layer frame.

A PPP Network Control Protocol for IPv6

The IPv6 Control Protocol (IPv6CP) is responsible for configuring, enabling, and disabling the IPv6 protocol modules on both ends of the link. IPv6CP uses the same packet exchange mechanism as the Link Control Protocol (LCP). IPv6CP packets datagrams are not exchanged until PPP reached the Network-Layer Protocol phase. IPv6CP packets received before this phase is reached are silently discarded.

The IPv6 Control Protocol is the same as the Link Control Protocol with the following exceptions:

- One IPv6CP packet is encapsulated in the Information field of PPP frames where the Protocol field indicates type hex 8057 (IPv6 Control Protocol). Codes 1 through 7 are used. Other codes are rejected.
- The IPv6CP has a distinct set of Configuration Options, which are defined below.

IPV6CP CONFIGURATION OPTIONS

The IPv6CP Configuration Options allow negotiation of several IPv6 parameters. IPv6CP uses the same Configuration Option format defined for LCP, with a separate set of Options. Up-to-date values of the IPv6CP

Option Type field are specified in the most recent "Assigned Numbers" (RFC 1700). Current values are: assigned as follows:

- Interface-Token
- IPv6-Compression-Protocol

Interface-Token

The interface-token Configuration Option provides a way to negotiate a unique
32-bit interface token to be used for the address auto-configuration at the local end of the link. The interface token is unique within the PPP link[1] upon completion of the negotiation different Interface-Token values are to be selected for the ends of the PPP link.

IPv6-Compression-Protocol

The IPv6 Configuration Option supports the negotiation of the use of a specific IPv6 packet compression protocol. The IPv6-Compression-Protocol Configuration Option is used to indicate the ability to receive compressed datagrams. Each end of the link requests this option if bidirectional compression is used.

SUMMARY

The PPP is not a new protocol, but it has assumed a dominant position in the industry for L_2 implementations on non-LAN links. Its principal features are negotiation and encapsulation operations.

---

[1]RFC 2023 provides several suggestions on obtaining a unique value for the interface token. See RFC 2023, Section 4.1.

10

Internet Multimedia Protocols

This chapter introduces several protocols that are used to support multimedia Internet traffic. The first set of protocols deals with multicasting and the focus of attention is on IGMP and MBONE, which were introduced in Chapter 1. Next, the Real Time Protocol (RTP), the Real Time Control Protocol (RTCP), and the Resource Reservation Protocol (RSVP) are examined.

The discussions on RTP, RTCP, and RSVP are sourced from a variety of RFCs and the non-normative annexes to H.255.0, and my own thoughts and experiences.

DEFINITIONS

Before we examine these systems, we need to define several terms and concepts.

- *RTP session:* The association among a set of participants communicating through RTP and each other. For each participant, the session is defined by a particular pair of destination transport addresses (one network address plus a port pair for RTP and RTCP). The destination transport address pair may be common for all participants, as in the case of IP multicast; or may be different for each, as in the case of individual unicast network addresses and ports. In a multimedia session, each medium is carried in a separate RTP session with its own RTCP packets. The multiple RTP sessions are distinguished by different port number pairs and/or different multicast addresses.

- *Synchronization source (SSRC):* The source of a stream of RTP packets, the SSRC identifier is carried in the RTP header. All packets from a synchronization source form part of the same timing and sequence number space, so a receiver groups packets by synchronization source for playback.

- *Contributing source (CSRC):* A source of a stream of RTP packets that has contributed to the combined stream produced by an RTP mixer. The mixer inserts a list of the SSRC identifiers of the sources that contributed to the generation of a particular packet into the RTP header of that packet.

- *Mixer:* An intermediate system that receives RTP packets from one or more sources, possibly changes the data format, combines the packets in some manner, and then forwards a new RTP packet. Since the timing among multiple input sources may not be synchronized, the mixer will make timing adjustments among the streams and generate its own timing for the combined stream. All data packets originating from a mixer will be identified as having the mixer as their synchronization source.

- *Translator:* An intermediate system that forwards RTP packets with their synchronization source identifier intact. Examples of translators include devices that convert encoding without mixing, replicators from multicast to unicast, and application-level filters in firewalls.

- *Monitor:* An application that receives RTCP packets sent by participants in an RTP session and estimates the current quality of service for distribution monitoring, fault diagnosis and long-term statistics.

IP MULTICASTING

The IP multicast system is a one-to-many operation. The sender of the multicast traffic need only create one copy of the packet. This packet is sent to a multicast server (for example, a router), which is then responsible for creating as many copies as needed to send to the router's outgoing ports to reach the receiving nodes. This approach saves bandwidth at the sender since only one copy of the PDU is sent from the user. It also

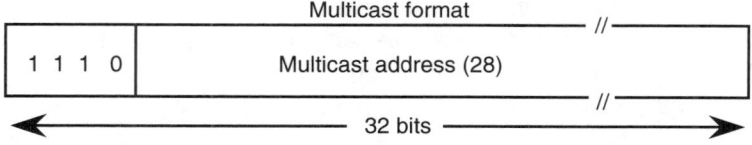

where: Range is 224.0.0.0–239.255.255.255

Figure 10–1   IP multicast.

saves bandwidth at the receiver if multiple multicast recipients are attached to the same shared bus network.

    IP multicasting is used in audio conferencing and video conferencing
environments and is also seeing use for remote distance learning, meetings, and interactive chalk talks.

    The format for the IP multicast address is shown in Figure 10–1.
This address is also known as a class D address, and the first four digits
of the address are set to 1110. The remaining 28 bits are set aside for the
multicast address. The IP address can take the values ranging from
224.0.0.0 to 239.255.255.255.

    Figure 10–2 shows a conventional unicasting operation where host
A is sending traffic to hosts B, C, and D. Since this example does not sup-

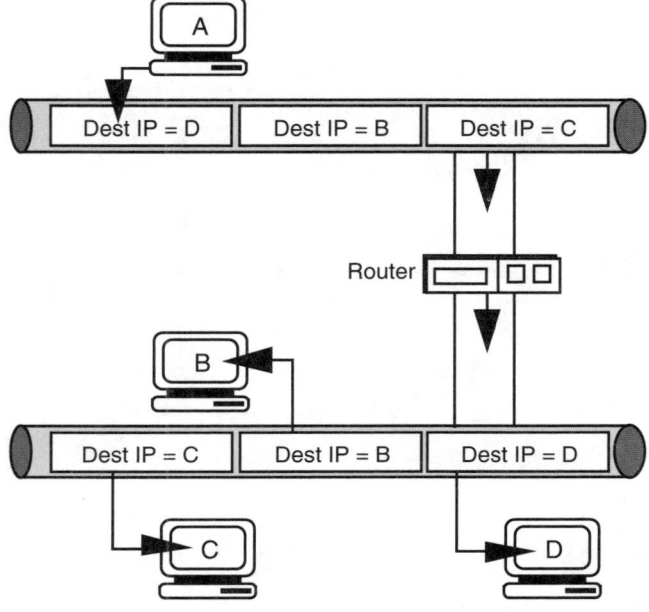

Figure 10–2   Unicasting concepts.

port multicasting, host A creates a datagram for each of the three destination hosts. These three datagrams are identical copies of each other, which, of course, translates into wasted bandwidth.

Figure 10–3 shows how multicasting saves bandwidth. Host A is required to create only one copy of the datagram and place the proper multicasting address in the destination address field of the multicast header. The datagram is routed to the router (which, of course, must be configured with the multicasting software). The routing table at the router reveals that the multicast datagram is destined for the egress port to a LAN that connects multicast hosts B, C, and D. Consequently, instead of generating three datagrams as in the previous example, only one datagram is generated.

The multicast traffic runs inside the data field of the IP datagram and relies on the conventional IP header for delivery of the traffic

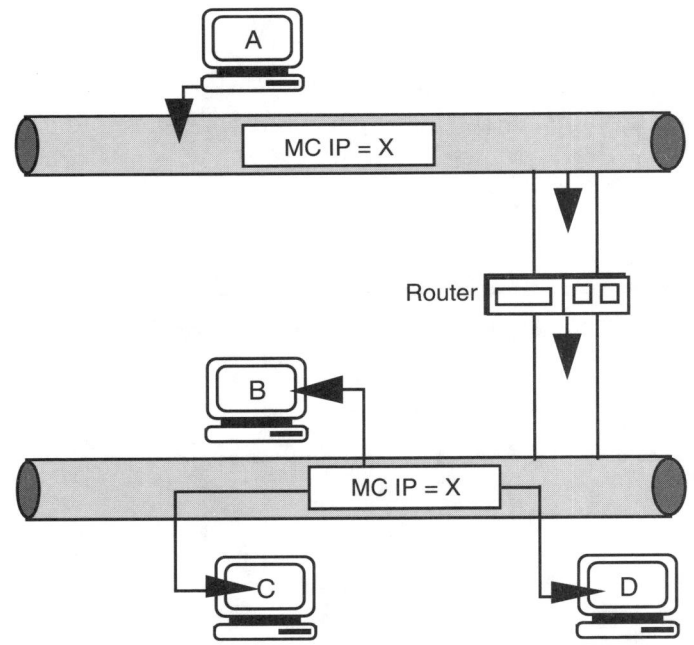

where:
  MC   Multicast
  X   32-bit IP MC address

Figure 10–3   Multicasting concepts.

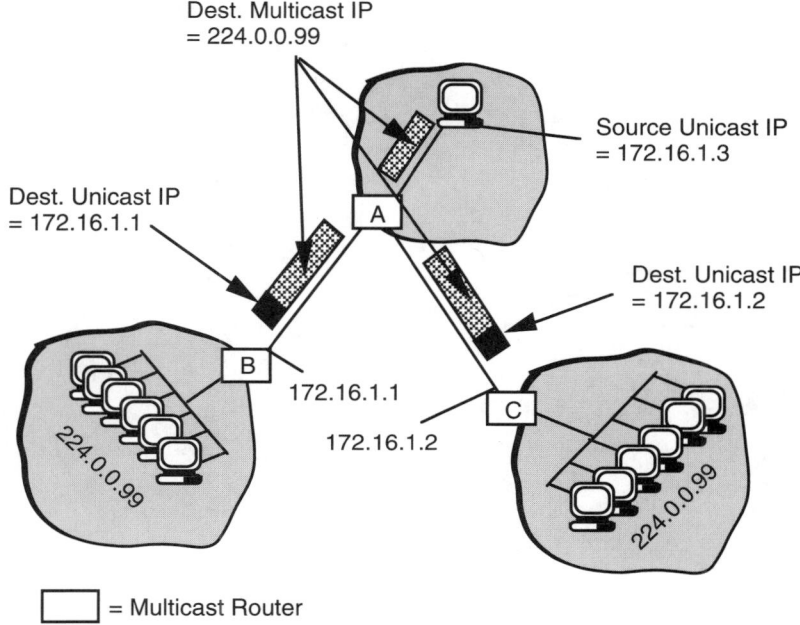

Dest. Multicast IP
= 224.0.0.99

Source Unicast IP
= 172.16.1.3

Dest. Unicast IP
= 172.16.1.1

A

Dest. Unicast IP
= 172.16.1.2

B

172.16.1.1

C

172.16.1.2

224.0.0.99

224.0.0.99

☐ = Multicast Router

Figure 10–4   Multicast tunnels.

through an internet. This concept is called multicast tunnels in the sense that the multicast traffic is tunneled through an internet by riding inside the IP datagram.

Figure 10–4 shows that multicasting traffic is destined to the hosts residing on the networks attached to routers B and C. The traffic emanates from a host attached to router A. The figure shows that the destination multicast IP address is 224.0.0.99. The figure also shows the unicast IP addresses of the sending host (172.16.1.3) and router B (172.16.1.1.), and router C (172.16.1.2).

IGMP OPERATIONS

As explained in Chapter 1, the IGMP permits a machine to advertise a multicast address to another machine. This advertisement is called an IGMP query. In Figure 10–5, router A is sending the IGMP query to a host. The addresses of the router and host are the same as in the previous example.

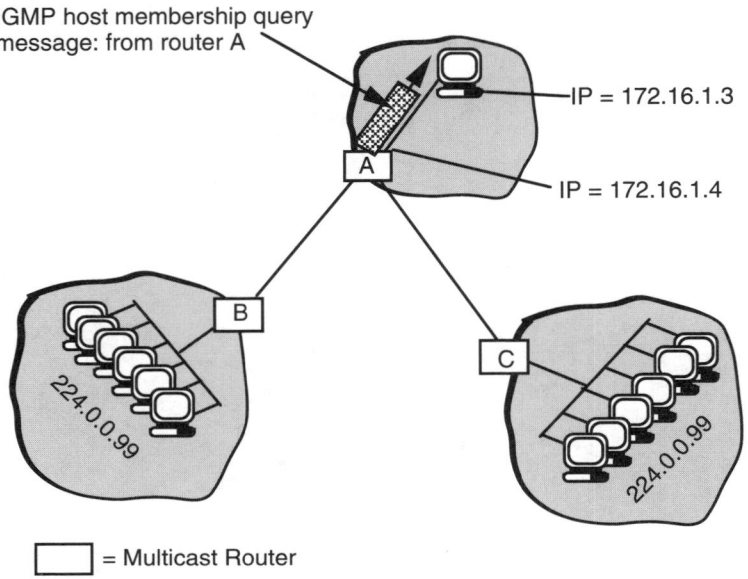

Figure 10–5   The IGMP query.

The IGMP report operation allows the host to inform the router as to whether it wishes to join the multicast group. In Figure 10–6, the message is returned from host 172.16.1.3 and sent to router 172.16.1.4.

MBONE

The Multicast Backbone (MBONE) was developed as part of experiments with the Internet Engineering Task Forces' multicasting their meetings. As explained earlier, MBONE is not a backbone network, but it runs on the Internet and is supported by those machines that are configured with MBONE software and routing tables.

The MBONE visual images are not of very good quality because they run at 128 kbit/s. Nonetheless, the system is popular because of its usefulness and simplicity.

For the reader who wishes more information on MBONE, here are some references. And for those of you who are thinking of implementing MBONE, here are a few helpful hints and references.

- IETF and some other audio/videocasts: Announced on IETF mailing list: ietf-request@cnri.reston.va.us

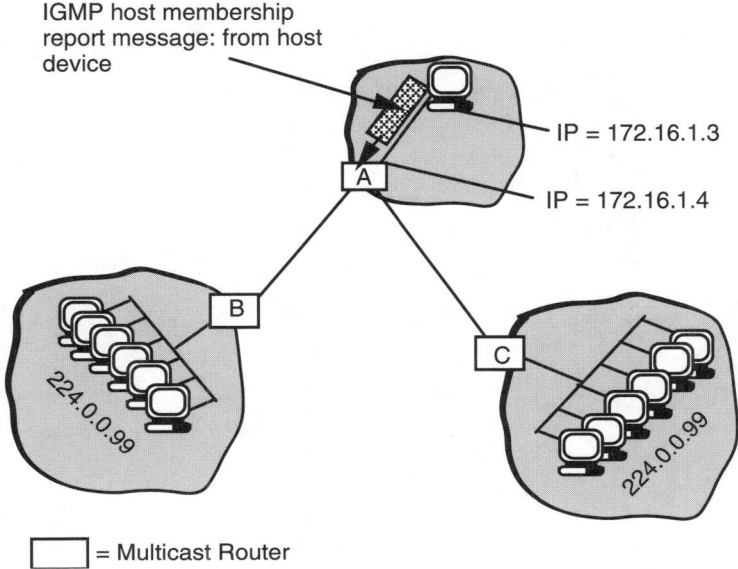

Figure 10–6   The IGMP report.

- Other events and information on protocols: rem-conf-request@es.net
- First, read the MBONE material first. Then you need the ability to install operating system kernels and the ability to choose a topology for multicast operations.

THE REAL TIME PROTOCOL

The Real Time Protocol (RTP) is designed to support real-time traffic, that is to say, traffic that requires playback at the receiving application in a time-sensitive mode. Typical real-time applications are voice and video systems. RTP supports both unicast and multicast applications.

RTP provides end-to-end delivery services for data with real-time characteristics, such as interactive audio and video. The services include payload type identification, sequence numbering, timestamping, and delivery monitoring. Applications usually run RTP on top of UDP to make use of its multiplexing and checksum services. RTP supports data transfer to multiple destinations using multicast distribution if provided by the underlying network.

The RTP does not provide any mechanism to ensure timely delivery or provide other quality of service guarantees, but relies on lower-layer

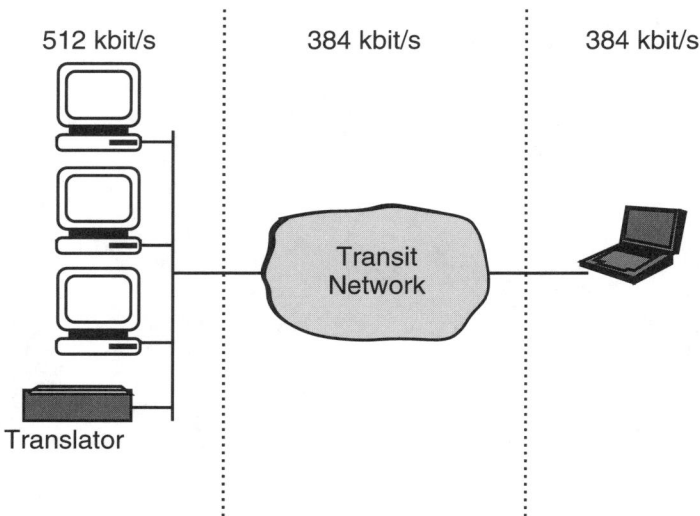

Figure 10–7   The RTP translator.

services to provide these services. It does not guarantee delivery or prevent out-of-order delivery, nor does it assume that the underlying network is reliable and delivers packets in sequence. The sequence numbers included in RTP allow the receiver to reconstruct the sender's packet sequence, but sequence numbers might also be used to determine the proper location of a packet.

RTP represents a new style of protocol following the principles of application level framing and integrated layer processing proposed by Clark and Tennenhouse.[1] That is, RTP is intended to provide the information required by a particular application and will often be integrated into the application processing rather than being implemented as a separate layer.

Unlike conventional protocols in which additional functions might be accommodated by making the protocol more general or by adding an option mechanism that would require parsing, RTP is intended to be tailored through modifications and/or additions to the headers as needed.

Figures 10–7 and 10–8 show two major features of RTP in how it supports traffic from senders to receivers. First, in Figure 10–7 the RTP system is acting as a translator.

---

[1]D. D. Clark and D. L. Tennenhouse, "Architectural Considerations for a New Generation of Protocols." *SIGCOMM Symposium on Communications Architectures and Protocols,* pp. 200–208, IEEE, *Computer Communications Review,* Philadelphia, PA, Sept. 1990.

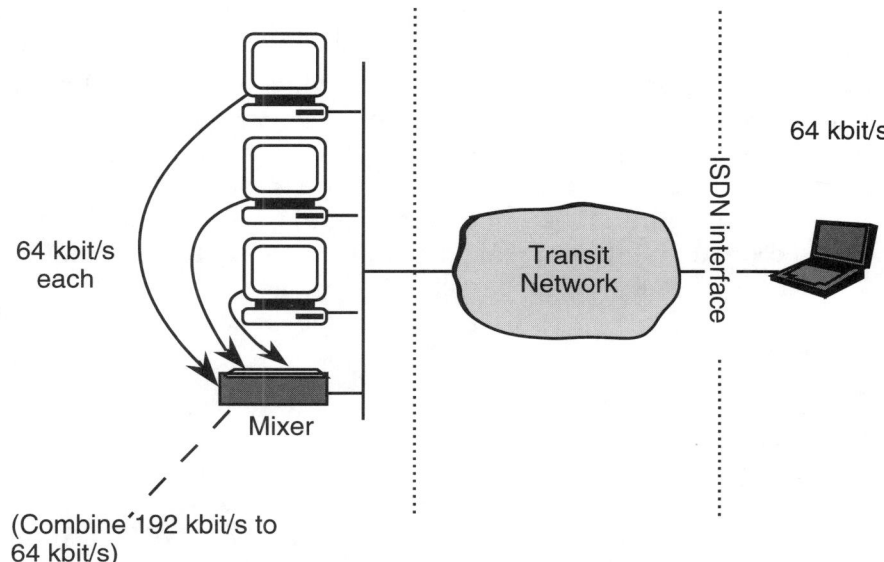

Figure 10–8   The RTP mixer.

The RTP translator translates (encodes) from one payload syntax to a different syntax. This figure shows how the RTP translator operates. The user devices on the left side of the figure are set up to use a 512 kbit/s video stream for their video application. The user device on the right side of the figure uses a 384 kbit/s video stream. As another possibility, the transit network may not be able to support the 512 kbit/s rate. So, whether from the user station on the right or the network in the middle, the users cannot communicate with each other.

The RTP translator allows these user stations to interact with each other. The job of the translator is to accept the traffic of the stations on the left side of the figure, translate (encode) that traffic into a format that is (1) in consonance with the bandwidth limitations of the transit network, and/or (2) in consonance with the bandwidth limitations of the user station on the right side of the figure.

Figure 10–8 shows an RTP server performing a mixer operation. Mixers combine multiple sources into one stream. Typically, mixers participate in audio operations and they do not decrease the quality of the signal to the recipients. They simply combine the signals into a consistent format. As I stated earlier, the RTP mixer operation is particularity suited to audio conferences. As a general rule, it does not work well with video conferences because it is quite difficult to combine multiple video sources into one syntax.

RTP mixers do not translate each source payload into a different format. The original format is maintained, and the various source payloads are combined into one stream. The mixer is used for audio conferences, but not for video sessions, since mixing video streams is not yet a commercial reality. On the other hand, if the audio streams are uncomplicated pulse code modulation (PCM) traffic, it is possible to arithmetically sum the values of each source payload and combine them into a single stream.

The RTP Message

The designers of RTP were careful to keep all messages in common format, which is shown in Figure 10–9. Before discussing the fields in the message, it should be noted that RTP does not have a well-known port (obviously, it operates on a UDP port). Its default port is 5004, if an application does not have a port setup. The reason for not having a well-known port is that RTP will be used with several-to-many applications, which themselves are identified with ports.

The message format for RTP is designed to support different types of payloads (operating in the application layer, L_7), such as the ITU-T

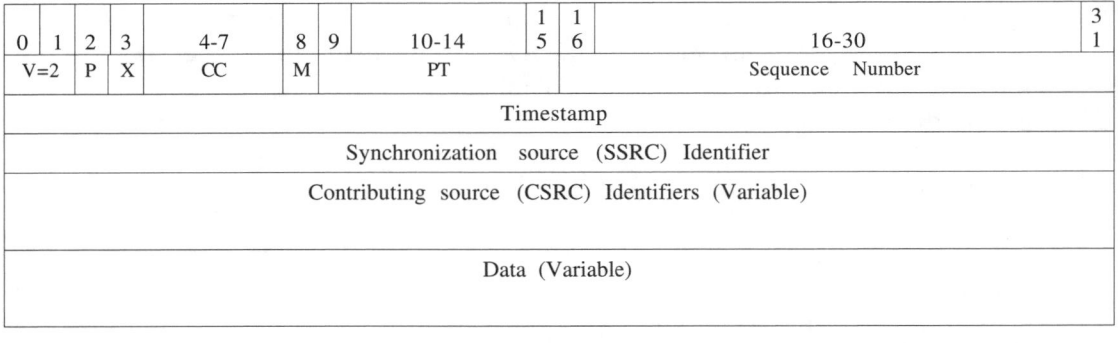

where:
CC   Contributor count
E   Extension
M   Marker
P   Padding
PT   Payload type
V   Version

Figure 10–9   RTP message format.

G.722 audio standard, and the JPEG video standard. The RTP protocol data unit (PDU) is carried in the User Datagram Protocol (UDP) and Internet Protocol (IP) PDUs, with these protocols' headers as part of the complete data unit.

This figure shows the format and contents of the RTP header. The fields are used in the following manner:

- *Version (v)*: Version 2.
- *Padding (P)*: Padding flag on, if padding bytes added to message.
- *Extension (X)*: To indicate a header after RTP header (not used yet).
- *Contributor count (CC)*: How many contributing source identifiers in message, which allows for 15 contributing sources.
- *Marker (M)*: Specific to application, typically used to set up demarcation boundaries in the datastream.
- *Payload type (PT)*: Type of traffic in the data field (G.722 audio, GSM, etc.).
- *Sequence number (SN)*: A number that increments by 1 for each RTP packet sent.
- *Timestamp*: Reflects the sampling instant of the first octet in the RTP data packet. The sampling instant must be derived from a clock that increments monotonically and linearly in time to allow synchronization and jitter calculations. The resolution of the clock must be sufficient for the desired synchronization accuracy and for measuring packet arrival jitter. If RTP packets are generated periodically, the nominal sampling instant as determined from the sampling clock is to be used, not a reading of the system clock. For example, for fixed-rate audio the timestamp clock would likely increment by one for each sampling period. If an audio application reads blocks covering 160 sampling periods from the input device, the timestamp would be increased by 160 for each such block, regardless of whether the block is transmitted in a packet or dropped as silent.
- *SSRC*: The SSRC field identifies the synchronization source. This identifier is chosen randomly, with the intent that no two synchronization sources within the same RTP session will have the same SSRC identifier.
- *CSRC list*: The CSRC list identifies the contributing sources for the payload contained in this packet. The number of identifiers is

given by the CC field. If there are more than 15 contributing sources, only 15 may be identified. CSRC identifiers are inserted by mixers, using the SSRC identifiers of contributing sources.

The sync source ID is the identifier of the original transmitter of the RTP message, which is responsible determining the values of the sequence number and the timestamp in the message. This identifier is preserved by RTP translators, but an RTP mixer becomes the sync source and the other (original) sources become contributing sources, and are identified in the contributing source ID fields in the message.

The sequence number and timestamp are used between the communicating parties to (1) make certain the traffic is in the proper sequential order, (2) see if any traffic is missing/lost, and (3) synchronize the traffic flow.

Note that RTP does not define the contents of the application data field, which, of course, is left to the application. Thus, RTP can carry various types of application traffic.

Table 10–1 shows the various payload types that are carried in the data field of the RTP PDU. Since this table was published, other stan-

Table 10–1   RTP Payload Types (Not All Inclusive)

Type ID	Type	Type ID	Type
0	PCMU audio	16–22	unassigned audio
1	1016 audio	23	RGV8 video
2	G.721 audio	24	HDCC video
3	GSM audio	24	CelB video
4	unassigned audio	26	JPEG video
5	DV14 audio (8 KHz)	27	CUSM video
6	DV14 audio (16 KHz)	28	nv video
7	LPC audio	29	PicW video
8	PCMA audio	30	CPV video
9	G.722 audio	31	H.261 video
10	L16 audio (stereo)	32	MPV video
11	L16 audio (mono)	33	MP2T video
12	TPS0 audio	34–71	unassigned video
13	VSC audio	72–76	reserved
14	MPA	77–95	unassigned
15	G.728		

dards have been defined that can be carried by RTP. As examples, H.324, H.263, and G.723 are more recent specifications for compressed audio and video traffic.

RTP Payload for H.263 Video

The IETF Audio-Video Transport (AVT) Working Group is in the process of defining the RTP payload format for ITU-T's H.263 Recommendation.[2] Our approach is to describe the RTP header usage and the video packet. The Internet draft cited in Footnote 2 has a wealth of information on this subject, which is beyond the summary explanations in this book.

Each RTP packet starts with a fixed RTP header. The following fields of the RTP fixed header are used for H.263 video streams:

- *Marker bit (Mbit):* The Marker bit of the RTP header is set to 1 when the current packet carries the end of current frame and is 0 otherwise.
- *Payload Type (PT):* The Payload Type shall specify the H.263 video payload format.
- *Timestamp:* The RTP timestamp encodes the sampling instance of the first video frame data contained in the RTP data packet. The RTP timestamp shall be the same on successive packets if a video frame occupies more than one packet. In a multilayer scenario, all pictures corresponding to the same temporal reference should use the same timestamp. For an H.263 video stream, the RTP timestamp is based on a 90 kHz clock, the same as that of the RTP payload for H.261 stream information. Both the RTP timestamp and the temporal reference (TR in the picture header of H.263) should carry the same relative timing information.

A section of an H.263 compressed bitstream is carried as a payload within each RTP packet. For each RTP packet, the RTP header is followed by an H.263 payload header, which is followed by a number of bytes of a standard H.263 compressed bitstream. The size of the H.263 payload header is variable, depending on the payload involved. The layout of the RTP H.263 video packet is shown in Figure 10–10.

---

[2]The Working Group has too many members to cite here. I refer you to draft-ietf-avt-rtp-h263-video-02.txt.

0	2-30	3 1
	RTP Header	
	H.263 Header	
	H.263 Compressed Datastream	

Figure 10–10   RTP H.263 video packet.

RTP Multiplexing Operations

RTP multiplexing is provided by the destination transport address.[3]
For example, a teleconference consisting of audio and video streams can
use two connections, each with a transport address (and different
SSRCs). The use of separate RTP sessions is recommended by H.225.0
(see Sections A.5.2) for the following reasons:

- If one payload type were switched during a session, there would be
  no means to identify which of the old values the new one replaced.
- An SSRC is defined to identify a single timing and sequence number space. Interleaving multiple payload types would require different timing spaces if the media clock rates differ and would require different sequence number spaces to tell which payload type
  suffered packet loss.
- The RTCP sender and recur reports can only describe one timing
  and sequence number space per SSRC and do not carry a payload
  type field.

Rosenberg and Schulzrinne have proposed an RTP payload format for
multiplexing traffic from multiple users into a single RTP packet.[4] These
authors cite the following inefficiencies with separate RTP sessions.

The audio payloads carried in each RTP packet are generally small.
For example, the ITU-G.729 speech coder generates a rate of 8 kbit/s in
frames of 10 ms duration. If packed three frames per packet, the resulting RTP payloads are 30 bytes long. The IP, UDP, and RTP headers add
up to 40 bytes, resulting in a packet efficiency of only 43%.

---

[3]Don't forget, the term transport address is an ITU-T term and refers to a network
layer address and a port number. In the Internet, this is known as a socket.

[4]From the AVT (Audio Visual Transport) Working Group, J. Rosenberg and
H. Schulzrinne. See draft-ietf-avt-aggregation-00.txt © The Internet Society.

On the other hand, suppose the payloads from two users are multiplexed into the same RTP session and packet. A multiplexing protocol is now required to delineate the packets. The protocol defined (by the authors and explained next) typically adds 16 bits of overhead per multiplexed user. In the two-subscriber example, this allows an RTP packet to be constructed with 60 bytes of useful payload and 41 bytes of header, and the efficiency improves to 59%.

A further benefit of multiplexing is a potential reduction in packetization delays. Most Internet telephony applications use fairly large packetization delays, mainly for the purpose of raising the size of the payloads to increase efficiency. However, if multiplexing is performed, the packet payload increases. This allows smaller packetization delays to be used as the number of multiplexed users increases.

This section of the chapter summarizes the Rosenberg/Schulzrinne draft pertaining to the RTP multiplexing packets. I refer you to their draft for more details as well as a discussion on these issues and operations: (1) QOS considerations, (2) security, (3) use of multiple packets, and (4) open issues, such as H.323 and MPEG-4 interworking.

Multiplexing Packet Formats. All fields of the RTP header except the timestamp, marker bit, and SSRC maintain their current definition. This format for the multiplexing packet is shown in Figure 10–11.

- *Payload type:* The payload type field designates the RTP packet as a multiplexed payload. The payload type value is chosen dynamically and the binding to this format is conveyed via non-RTP means.
- *Timestamp:* This protocol requires that all multiplexed streams in one packet have the same clock rate (i.e., sampling rate for audio) and generate media frames at integer multiples of a common frame duration. It is possible, for example, that a set of users generates a packet every 10 ms, while others generate packets at in-

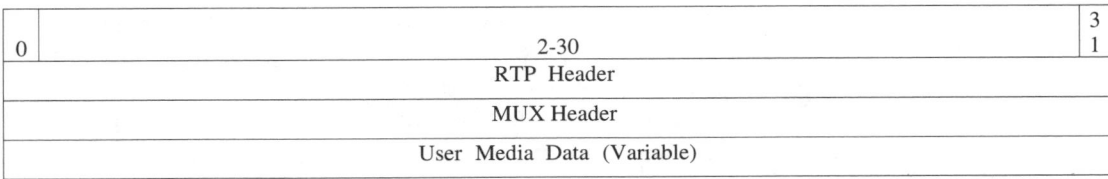

Figure 10–11   The RTP multiplexing packet.

tervals of 20 and 30 ms, but all frame generation instants must be multiples of this 10 ms interval.

- *Marker bit:* This field is not used for multiplexing and always has a value of zero. A marker bit is included for each user in the multiplexing header.
- *SSRC:* This field is used to identify groups of users (instead of a single user) whose frames are time synchronized.

The multiplexing (MUX) header contains information about each user that is part of the multiplexing operation. It contains information on the type of payload and an identifier value for each user payload.

THE REAL TIME CONTROL PROTOCOL

The Real Time Control Protocol (RTCP) is responsible for the management of the real time session between sending and receiving applications. The protocol is designed to allow senders to inform receivers about the RTP traffic that they should have received from the sender and it also allows the receiver of the traffic to generate reports back to the sender. This idea has been found to be quite useful in IP multicasting because it is used to troubleshoot faults in packet distribution.

Figure 10–12 shows the relationships of the RTP and RTCP message flows. The RTP traffic flows from the sender to their receivers, and the RTCP message flows in both directions.

The sender and receiver reports can generate a considerable amount of bandwidth use and RTCP contains provisions to define the frequency with which these reports can be sent. The concept is to keep the overall traffic flow for a session constant regardless of how many users are participating in the session. Since these reports are being multicast to all parties in the conference call, each application can keep track of the number of reports being disseminated and increase or decrease its reporting interval accordingly. In addition, RTCP provides procedures for the calculations of the reporting intervals to vary between the users in a session in order to prevent a heavy peak load with each user sending a message at the same time.

Each source of the RTCP packet sends source descriptions that provide information about the nature of the application sending the traffic. Within these messages are contained source description items that define attributes such as email addresses, geographic locations, phone numbers, and mailbox names. Participants in a conference call (video or

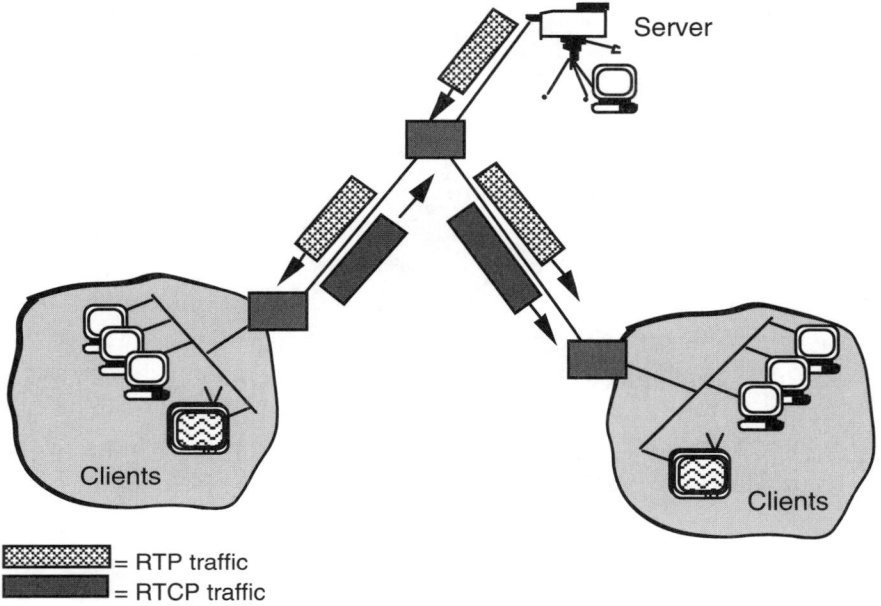

Figure 10–12   RTP and RTCP traffic flows.

audio) may leave the conference at any time they choose by sending a log-off message that is known as a *bye*. And then finally, RTCP messages can be coded specific to each application. RTCP really does not care about the contents of these messages, the RTCP operation conveys them transparently between applications.

The RTCP Packets.   A productive way to analyze RTCP further is to examine the packet types that are used for these operations. Five packet types are used and are summarized in Table 10–2.

Table 10–2   RTCP Packet Type

Number	Packet Type	Purpose
200	Sender report	Active senders send and receive statistics
201	Receiver report	Receivers only receive statistics
202	Source description	Source description items, including CNAME
203	Bye	End of participation
204	Application specific	—

Periodically, the sender in the session sends sender reports to the receiver, which are coded as shown in Figure 10–13. The contents of the fields are as follows:

- *Version (v)*: Version 2.
- *Padding (P)*: Padding flag on, if padding bytes added.
- *Receiver block count (RC)*: Indicates how many receiver blocks are contained in the message.
- *Packet type (PT)*: Set to 200 for a sender report message.
- *Length*: Length of the sender report message.
- *SSRC*: Sync source ID of sender (correlates RTP and RTCP PDUs) of a source.
- *Network Time Protocol (NTP)*: NTP time indicates the wallclock time when this report was sent, so that it may be used in combina-

0	1	2	3	4-6	7	8	9-14	1 5	1 6	16-30	3 1
V=2		P		RC			PT=SR=200			Length	
SSRC of sender											
NTP timestamp, most significant word											
NTP timestamp, least significant word											
RTP timestamp											
Sender's packet count											
Sender's octet count											
SSRC_1 (SSRC of first source)											
Fraction lost							Cumulative number of packets lost				
Extended highest sequence number received											
Interarrival jitter											
Last SR (LSR)											
Delay since last SR (DLSR)											
SSRC_2 (SSRC of second source)											
. . .											
Application-specific extensions (Variable)											

Figure 10–13   RTP message format.

tion with timestamps returned in reception reports from other receivers to measure round trip propagation to those receivers. A sender that can keep track of elapsed time but has no notion of wallclock time may use the elapsed time since joining the session instead. A sender that has no notion of wallclock or elapsed time may set the NTP timestamp to zero.

- *RTP Timestamp*: Corresponds to the same time as the NTP timestamp, but in the same units and with the same random offset as the RTP timestamps in data packets. This correspondence may be used for intra- and intermedia synchronization for sources whose NTP timestamps are synchronized and may be used by media-independent receivers to estimate the normal RTP clock frequency. This timestamp is calculated from the corresponding NTP timestamp using the relationship between the RTP timestamp counter and real time as maintained by periodically checking the wallclock time at a sampling instant.

- *Sender's packet and byte count*: Used to inform the receivers of how many RTP packets (PDUs) and the number of bytes that the sender has sent.

The next set of fields are used by the sender to report on the RTP traffic that it is has received. By use of the sequence numbers in the RTP message header, the sender can report of the percentage of PDUs lost (% lost), and total PDUs lost (cumulative packets lost) since the last reporting period. Here is a description of each of these fields.

- *Source identifier (SSRC_n)*: The SSRC identifier of the source to which the information in this reception report block pertains.

- *% lost:* The fraction of RTP data packets from source SSRC_n lost since the previous SR or RR packet was sent, expressed as a fixed point number. This fraction is defined to be the number of packets lost divided by the number of packets expected.

- *Cumulative packets lost:* The total number of RTP data packets from source SSRC_n that have been lost since the beginning of reception. This number is defined to be the number of packets expected less the number of packets actually received, where the number of packets received includes any that are late or duplicates. Thus, packets that arrive late are not counted as lost, and the loss may be negative if there are duplicates.

- *Extended highest sequence number received:* The low 16 bits contain the highest sequence number received in an RTP data packet from source SSRC_n, and the most significant 16 bits extend that sequence number with the corresponding count of sequence number cycles.

- *Interarrival jitter:* An estimate of the statistical variance of the RTP data packet interarrival time, measured in timestamp units and expressed as an unsigned integer. The interarrival jitter J is defined to be the mean deviation (smoothed absolute value) of the difference D in packet spacing at the receiver compared to the sender for a pair of packets. Equations for jitter calculation are provided in the RTP documents and the H.225.0 Recommendation.

- *Time of last sender report:* Middle 32 bits of the 64 bits in the NTP timestamp received as part of the most recent RTP sender report packet from SSRC_n.

- *Delay since last sender report:* Expressed as 1/65536 seconds, the delay between receiving the last sender report from SSCC_n and sending this reception report.

In many circumstances, the participant in multiconferencing operations does not send traffic, so it does not generate sender reports. However, it can generate receiver reports, which are depicted in this Figure 10–14. The contents of these reports are the same as the fields in the sender report.

0	1	2	3	4-6	7	8	9-14	1 5	1 6	16-30	3 1
V=2				SC			PT			Length	
SSRC or CSRC for first source											
SDES Items (Variable)											
SSRC or CSRC of second source											
SDES Items (Variable)											
SSRC or CSRC of last source											
SCES Items (Variable)											

Figure 10–14   RTCP source description packet (SDES).

Jitter Equation[5]

Interarrival jitter is the difference in relative transit time for two packets. It is the difference between the packets RTP timestamp and the receiver's clock at the time of arrival of the packet.

As shown in the equation below, this is equivalent to the difference in the "relative transit time" for two packets: The relative transit time is the difference between a packet's RTP timestamp and the receiver's clock at the time of arrival, measured in the same units.

If Si is the RTP timestamp from packet i, and Ri is the time of arrival in RTP timestamp units for packet i, then for two packets i and j, D may be expressed as:

$$D(i,j) = (Rj - Ri) - (Sj - Si) = (Rj - Sj) - (Ri - Si)$$

The interval jitter is calculated continuously as each data packet i is received from source SSRC_n, using this difference D for that packet and the previous packet i–1 in order of arrival (not necessarily in sequence), according to the formula:

$$J = J + (\ |\ D\ (i-1,i)\ |\ -J)/16$$

Source Description Packet (SDES). RTCP allows a source to provide more information about itself. This operation takes place through the transmission of the RTCP source description packet (SDES) (see Figure 10–4). These PDUs contain the sync or contributing source identifiers (SSRC or CCRC), and SDES items.

Table 10–3 shows the source description items that have been defined so far. As the table shows, the items simply provide more information about the source. How they are used is implementation-specific, and RFCs 1889 and 1996 provide additional information on this topic.

THE RESOURCE RESERVATION PROTOCOL

We have learned that RTP and RTCP are companion protocols that allow applications to control real-time, unicast, or multicast conferences for video or audio applications. We also learned that these protocols, while supporting unicast operations, are especially designed for multicasting. They

---

[5]See Annex A of H.225.0 and J. A. Caszow, *Foundation of Digital Signal Processing and Data Analysis*. Macmillan, New York, 1987.

Table 10–3   Source Description Items

CNAME	Unique and unambiguous name for the source
NAME	Real user name of the source
EMAIL	Email address
PHONE	Telephone number
LOC	Geographic location
TOOL	Name of application generating the stream
NOTE	Note about the source
PRIV	Private extensions
BYE	Goodbye RTP packet
APP	Application-defined RTCP packet

allow systems to provide translation or mixing functions, converting different payload syntaxes and changing high-bit rate streams to low-bit rate streams, if necessary. They also provide extensive feedback between the users in an audio-video conference to ascertain the quality of the signals that are receiving and to inform each other about their ongoing activities.

The Resource Reservation Protocol (RSVP), as its name implies, defines a reservation procedure for real-time multimedia conferences. RSVP is unique from some other systems that have been implemented in other technologies such as ATM and frame relay and X.25 because it is the recipient of the traffic that places the reservation. In contrast, other technologies allow the sender of the traffic to establish the requirements. The rationale for this approach is that it is the recipient of the traffic that has the best knowledge of its capacity and limitations. For example, a video server may be sending traffic out to its recipients at a very high bit rate, perhaps 100 Mbit/s for high-quality video. However, the various recipients (clients) may vary in their ability to receive this high-quality transmission. Consequently, they may send their reservation resource request to the server defining different types of throughput requirements. As an example, a device attached to an ATM network running an OC-3 line card might be unable to support the full 100 Mbit bandwidth transmission. Conversely, a personal computer attached to an Ethernet may only be able to support 10 Mbits of bandwidth. Therefore, these two devices can send to the server the reservation request noting what their capacity is (their bandwidth availability).

The RSVP uses the concept of a flow for its reserved traffic. Flows are somewhat similar to connection-oriented virtual circuits found in frame relay and ATM. They identify the traffic streams from the sending application to the receivers. This concept works well with IPv6 by using the IPv6 flow label field. It (in conjunction with the source address) will uniquely identify each flow. The idea of flow and flow label is to delineate between different kinds of traffic and to treat this traffic differently in the network depending on its timing and synchronization requirements. Indeed, the flow labels would most likely be used to place traffic in different queues at the intervening switches between the servers and the clients.

Path Operations

RSVP does not provide routing operations, but utilizes IPv4 or IPv6 as the forwarding mechanism in the same fashion as the Internet Control Message Protocol (ICMP) and the Internet Group Message Protocol (IGMP). RSVP operates with unicast or multicast procedures and interworks with current and planned multicast protocols. Like IP, it relies on routing tables to determine routes for its messages. It utilizes IGMP to first join a multicast group and then executes procedures to reserve resources for the multicast group. RSVP requires the receivers of the traffic to request QOS for the flow. The receiver host application must determine the QOS profile, which is then passed to RSVP. After the analysis of the request, RSVP is used to send request messages to all the nodes that participate in the data flow. As Figure 10–15 shows, the path message is used by a server (the flow sender) to set up a path for the session.

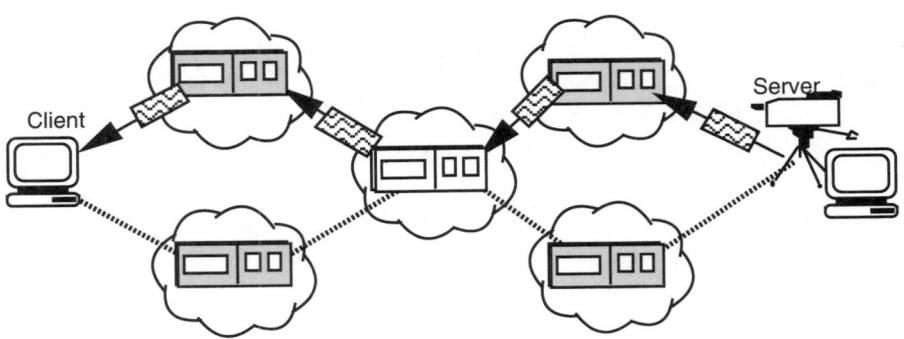

▨▨▨▨ = Path message flow

• Allows the receiver to learn the flow path
• Sets up the fixed path for the session
• Generated by flow's sender

Figure 10–15   RSVP path messages.

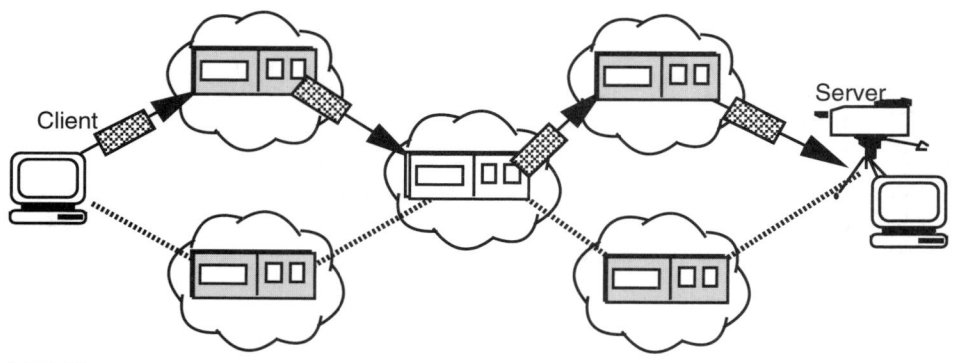

◼◼◼◼ = Reservation message flow

- Allows sender/routers to learn receiver's requirements
- Determines server and network requirements
- Generated by flow's receiver

Figure 10–16   RSVP reservation messages.

Reservation Operations

Figure 10–16 shows that the reservation messages are sent by the receivers of the flow, and they allow sender and intermediate machines (such as routers) to learn the receivers requirements.

Reservation Messages

All RSVP messages consist of a common header followed by a body. The body contains a variable number of objects. Figure 10–17 shows the format of the RSVP common header.

The fields in the common header are as follows:

- *Version:* Protocol version number. This is version 1.
- *Flags:* No flag bits are defined yet.

0	1-2	3	4	5-6	7	8	9-15	1 5	1 6	17-30	3 1
Version		Flags		Message type				RSVP checksum			
Send_TTL				Reserved				RSVP Length			

Figure 10–17   RSVP common header.

- *Message type:* Set to 1 = path, 2 = Resv, 3 = PathErr, 4 = ResvErr, 5 = PathTear, 6 = ResvTear, 7 = ResvConf.
- *RSVP checksum:* The ones complement of the ones complement sum of the message, with the checksum field replaced by zero for the purpose of computing the checksum. An all-zero value means that no checksum was transmitted.
- *Send_TTL:* The IP TTL value with which the message was sent.
- *RSVP Length:* The total length of this RSVP message in bytes, including the common header and the variable-length objects that follow.

Every RSVP object is coded in the message with one or more 32-bit words as shown in Figure 10–18.
The fields in this message are as follows:

- *Length:* The total length of the object field.
- *Class-Num:* Identifies the object class, discussed next.
- *C-Type:* Identifies the object type within the class-num, also discussed next.

RSVP Objects. The information in the RSVP messages is coded as objects that contain the information exchanged between servers, clients, and nodes on the reserved path.
The following object classes must be supported in an RSVP implementation.

- *NULL:* This object has a class-num of zero, and its C-Type is ignored. A NULL object may appear anywhere in a sequence of objects, and its contents will be ignored by the receiver.

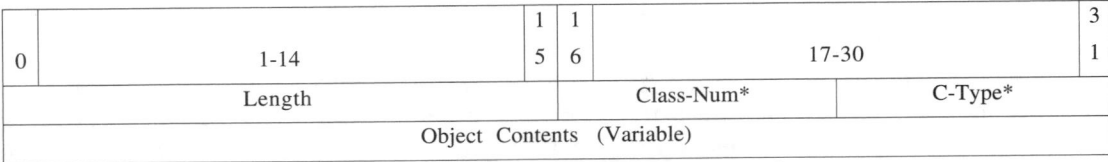

0	1-14	1 5	1 6	17-30	3 1
	Length		Class-Num*		C-Type*
		Object Contents (Variable)			

* Class-Num and C-Type together total 16 bits, but each field can vary in length.

Figure 10–18   RSVP objects in the message.

- *SESSION:* Contains the IP destination address, the IP protocol ID, and some form of generalized destination port to define a specific session for the other objects that follow.

- *RSVP_HOP:* Carries the IP address of the RSVP-capable node that sent this message and a logical outgoing interface handle (LIH). RFC 2005 refers to a RSVP_HOP object as a PHOP (previous hop) object for downstream messages or as a NHOP (next hop) object for upstream objects.

- *TIME_VALUES:* Contains the value for the refresh period R used by the creator of the message.

- *STYLE:* Defines the reservation style plus style-specific information that is not in FLOWSPEC or FILTER_SPEC objects.

- *FLOWSPEC:* Defines a subset of session data packets that should receive the desired QOS (specified by a FLOWSPEC object) in a Resv message.

- *SENDER_TEMPLATE:* Contains a sender IP address and perhaps some additional demultiplexing information to identify a sender.

- *SENDER_TSPEC:* Defines the traffic characteristics of a sender's data flow.

- *ADSPEC:* Carries OPWA data in a Path message.

- *ERROR_SPEC:* Specifies an error in a PathErr, ResvErr, or a confirmation in a ResvConf message.

- *POLICY_DATA:* Carries information that will allow a local policy module to decide whether an associated reservation is administratively permitted. The use of POLICY_DATA objects is not fully specified at this time; a future document will fill this gap.

- *INTEGRITY:* Carries cryptographic data to authenticate the originating node and to verify the contents of this RSVP message.

- *SCOPE:* Carries an explicit list of sender hosts towards which the information in the message is to be forwarded.

- *RESV_CONFIRM:* Carries the IP address of a receiver that requested a confirmation.

Table 10–4 lists the RSVP objects, and describes their purpose (in a general manner). The purpose of the objects is to describe the quality of service (QOS) needed by the conference nodes, and to provide information on the operations that will support the session.[6]

---

[6]See Stephen A. Thomas, *IPng and TCP/IP Protocols*. John Wiley & Sons, Inc., New York, 1996.

Table 10–4   RSVP Objects

#	Object	Type	Description
0	NULL		Ignored by recipient
1	SESSION	1	IPv4 session (destination of flow)
		2	IPv6 session (destination of flow)
3	RSVP_HOP	1	IPv4 previous or next hop address
		2	IPv6 previous or next hop address
4	INTEGRITY		Keyed MD5 authentication data
5	TIME_VALUES	1	Frequency of path or reservation refreshes
3	ERROR_SPEC	1	Error information from an IPv4 system
		2	Error information from an IPv6 system
7	SCOPE	1	List of IPv4 hosts to which reservation refresh messages apply
		2	List of IPv6 hosts to which reservation refresh messages apply
8	STYLE	1	Style of reservation
9	FLOWSPEC	1	Flow specification requiring controlled delay
		2	Flow specification: predictive quality of service
		3	Flow specification: guaranteed quality of service
		254	Flow specification: several, unmerged flows
10	FILTER_SPEC	1	IPv4-based filter to apply to flow
		2	IPv6-based filter using source port values
		3	IPv6-based filter using flow label values
11	SENDER_TEMPLATE	1	IPv4-based description of flow that sender is generating
		2	IPv6-based description of flow that sender is generating
12	SENDER_TSPEC	1	Upper bound on traffic that sender will generate
13	ADSPEC		Sender's advertised information for flow
14	POLICY_DATA	1	Policy information for flow
		254	Several unmerged policy data objects
20	TAG	1	Collection of objects to be associated with a given name

In the event of problems, RSVP provides for a number of diagnostics that are implemented with the error codes shown in Table 10–5.

A Summary of the RSVP Message Functions

We conclude this review of RSVP with a brief look at the functions of the RSVP messages. RFC 2205 contains the details, if you need them.

Path Messages. Each sender host periodically sends a Path message for each data flow it originates. It contains a SENDER_TEMPLATE object defining the format of the data packets and a SENDER_TSPEC object specifying the traffic characteristics of the flow. Optionally, it contains an ADSPEC object carrying advertising data for the flow.

A Path message travels from a sender to receiver(s) along the same path(s) used by the data packets. The IP source address of a Path message must be an address of the sender it describes, and the destination address must be the DestAddress for the session. These addresses assure that the message will be correctly routed through a non-RSVP cloud.

Each RSVP-capable node along the path(s) captures a Path message and processes it to create path state for the sender defined by the SENDER_TEMPLATE and SESSION objects. Any POLICY_DATA, SENDER_TSPEC, and ADSPEC objects are also saved in the path state. If an error is encountered while processing a Path message, a PathErr message is sent to the originating sender of the Past message.

Table 10–5   RSVP Error Codes

1	Admission failure, reservation could not be granted
2	Administrative rejection, reservation prohibited
3	No path information available for reservation
4	No sender for reservation
5	Ambiguous path
6	Ambiguous filter specification
7	Conflicting or unknown style
11	Missing required object
12	Unknown object class
13	Unknown object type
14	Object error
21	Traffic control error
22	RSVP system error

Periodically, the RSVP process at a node scans the path state to create new Path messages to forward towards the receiver(s). Each message contains a sender descriptor defining one sender, and carries the original sender's IP address as its IP source address. Path messages eventually reach the applications on all receivers; however, they are not looped back to a receiver running in the same application process as the sender.

Reservation (Resv).   Resv messages carry reservation request hop-by-hop from receivers to senders, along the reverse paths of data flows for the session. The IP destination address of a Resv message is the unicast address of a previous-hop node, obtained from the path state. The IP source address is an address of the node that sent the message.

The appearance of a RESV_CONFIRM object signals a request for a reservation confirmation and carries the IP address of the receiver to which the ResvConf should be sent. Any number of POLICY_DATA objects may appear.

Path Teardown Messages.   Receipt of a PathTear (path teardown) message deletes a matching path state. Matching state must have match the SESSION, SENDER-TEMPLATE, and PHOP objects. In addition, a PathTear message for a multicast session can only match path state for the incoming interface on which the PathTear arrived. If there is no matching path state, a PathTear message should be discarded and not forwarded.

PathTear messages are initiated explicitly by senders or by path state timeout in any node, and they travel downstream towards all receivers.

A PathTear message must be routed exactly like the corresponding Path message. Therefore, its IP destination address must be the session DestAddress, and its IP source address must be the sender address from the path state being torn down.

Deletion of path state as the result of a PathTear message or a timeout must also adjust related reservation state as required to maintain consistency in the local node. The adjustment depends upon the reservation style.

Resv Teardown Messages.   Receipt of a ResvTear (reservation teardown) message deletes a matching reservation state. Matching reservation state must match the SESSION, STYLE, and FILTER_SPEC objects. If there is no matching reservation state, a ResvTear message is discarded. A ResvTear message may tear down any subset of the filter specs in FF-style or SE-style reservation state.

ResvTear messages are initiated explicitly by receivers or by any node in which reservation state has timed out, and they travel upstream towards all matching senders. A ResvTear message must be routed like the corresponding Resv message, and its IP destination address will be the unicast address of a previous hop.

Path Error Messages.   PathErr (path error) messages report errors in processing Path messages. They travel upstream towards senders and are routed hop-by-hop using the path state. At each hop, the IP destination address is the unicast address of a previous hop. PathErr messages do not modify the state of any node through which they pass; they are only reported to the sender application.

Resv Error Messages.   ResvErr (reservation error) messages report errors in processing Resv messages, or they may report the spontaneous disruption of a reservation, for example, by administrative preemption.

ResvErr messages travel downstream towards the appropriate receivers, routed hop-by-hop using the reservation state. At each hop, the I destination address is the unicast address of a next-hop node.

Confirmation Messages.   ResvConf messages are sent to acknowledge reservation requests. A ResvConf message is sent as the result of the appearance of a RESV_CONFIRM object in a Resv message.

Rules for the Ports

An RSV session is normally defined by the triple: DestAddress, ProtocolId, DstPort. DstPort is a UDP/TCP destination port field. DstPort may be omitted (set to zero) if the ProtocolId specifies a protocol that does not have a destination port field in the format used by UDP and TCP.

RSVP allows any value for ProtocolId. However, end-system implementations of RSVP may know about certain values for this field, and in particular the values for UDP and TCP (17 and 6, respectively).

SUMMARY

The Internet multimedia protocols are partners. RSVP sets up the resources for the multimedia sessions. RTP transports the user traffic and manages the playback to the user application. RTCP provides a feedback mechanism to allow the users to ascertain the quality of the session. And IGMP provides the multicasting support, if needed.

11

Mobile IP

This chapter discusses Mobile IP (RFC 2002), of which this chapter provides a summary and the reasons for its deployment. The role of the Mobile IP node is explained as is the role of mobile routers. Since IP addresses are not designed to support a computer roaming from one network to another, we examine how Mobile IP keeps the node's IP address "intact" while allowing it to attach to another network.

TCP's timers and congestion control operations are affected by the movement of the IP-based machine and we look at some ideas on how to accommodate TCP to a mobile environment.

MARKET FORECASTS

Various studies predict a steady growth in the mobile PC user market. Figure 11–1 shows the forecasts for the worldwide market through the year 2000.[1] One might question the relatively small numbers, especially in light of the very large growth rate of the data communications market, but it is often inconvenient (and dangerous) to operate a data terminal in a moving vehicle. It is awkward to use with pedestrian mobility, as well.

---

[1]This forecast was provided by Intel at the IBC Data over GSM Conference (July 1 and 2, 1997), The Royal Garden Hotel, London.

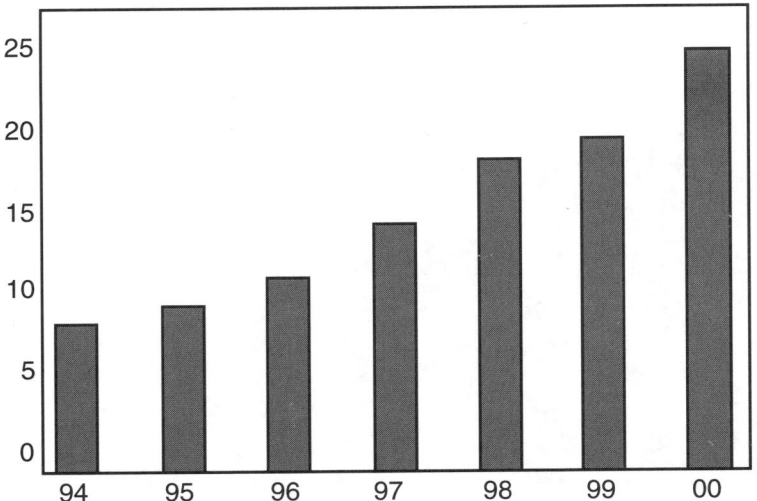

Figure 11–1   Worldwide mobile PC users (in millions).

Nonetheless, I think the forecast is too conservative. As keypads and notebook computers become more user-friendly and drop in price, and as the wireless phone reaches further into the population, the data market will be greater than this study predicts. But the very nature of user-network interaction with a data terminal will always limit the deployment of data communications applications in mobile, cellular networks.

On another note, data over wireless represents an attractive market for the service provider. One reason for this statement is the long holding times for many data-related calls, which translates into more revenue for the network operator.

The data over wireless market is limited in its bandwidth, and current techniques limit most transmissions to only 9.6 kbit/s. But products are emerging and the GSM standards bodies are putting together specifications that provide more throughput across the air interface.

CONNECTION OPTIONS

As the data over wireless market emerges, several connection options are becoming available to users and are shown in Figure 11–2 as options 1, 2, and 3. These options may not be available in some countries, due to regulations and the state of the data communications technology.

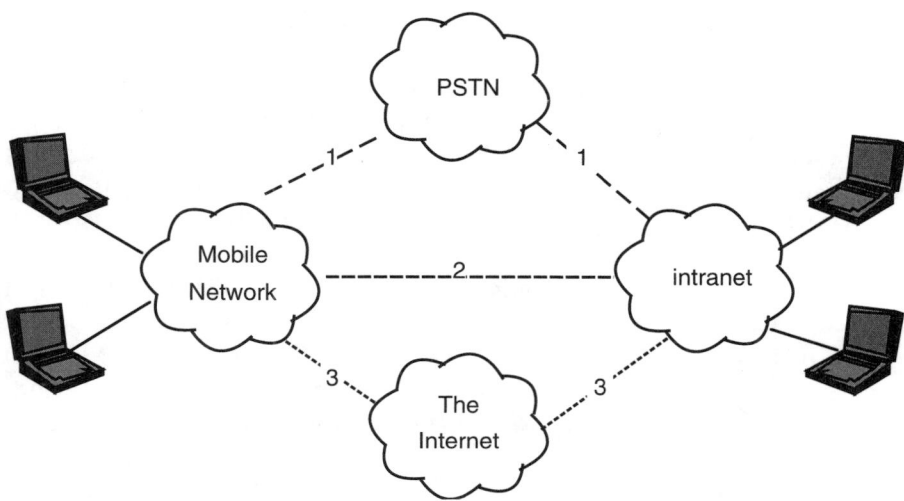

Figure 11–2   Connection options.

The first option is to use the telephone network for the transit system between the mobile user and the user's home network (an intranet), although the session could just as easily be a session to a server in the Internet. In the long run, this option is the least desirable, because it consumes resources of a network (the telephone network) that is not designed for data transport. I say "in the long-run," because this approach is certainly effective, but until the telephony infrastructure evolves to an asynchronous, statistical multiplexing architecture, this option will remain suboptimal. But in some locations in the world, the only way to do data over wireless is through the telephone system.

Option 2 is the bypassing of the telephone network with a direct access to the mobile user's communicating partner. Examples are private microwave systems and satellite systems. In some instances, this option takes the form of using non-telephone service providers. For example, in the United States, using the Ardis and RAM service providers or the Cellular Digital Packet Data (CDPD) network that is deployed in most large U.S. cities.

Option 3 makes use of the Internet. In many installations, this option still takes the traffic through the public telephone network, at least through a local end office. At this end office, a "front-end processor" may be installed to divert data traffic from the conventional voice-oriented circuit switch to a packet switch and/or directly to an Internet Service Provider (ISP). This option is only as effective as the ISP's capabilities.

REASONS FOR THE DEPLOYMENT OF MOBILE IP

TCP/IP will play a big role in data communications systems operating with mobile-wireless technology. One of the principal challenges in applying TCP/IP to a mobile-wireless environment is accommodating the user's IP address. This address is a fixed address designed to identify the point-of-attachment of a user device (host) to a specific subnetwork. Consequently, when the mobile station host and its user roams into another network, some technique is needed to properly identify the roaming host that is now attached to a different network.

The purpose of Mobile IP is to enhance the conventional Internet protocols to support the roaming of nodes wherein the mobile station can receive datagrams no matter where they are located. Without the use of Mobile IP, a mobile station node would have to change its IP address whenever it moves to a new network (that is, whenever it changes its point of attachment). Additionally, without the use of Mobile IP, routes specific to the host would have to be propagated into the networks that are concerned with supporting this host. Obviously, these two operations are not efficient and would create tremendous housekeeping problems for the network. In addition, due to the nature in which IP addresses are used to identify higher-layer connections (sockets to the applications themselves), it becomes an impossible task to maintain this relationship if the IP address changes.

The requirements for any type of system that supports the mobility of an IP node, are summarized here:[2]

- The mobile station must be able to communicate when it moves to another point of attachment without having to change its IP address.
- The mobile station must be able to communicate with non–mobile-IP nodes. This should require no enhancements to conventional hosts or routers.
- Authentication must be provided to protect against security breaches.
- Overhead traffic flowing across the air interface must be kept to a minimum in order to reduce complexity and cut down on the

---

[2]For a more thorough description, I recommend Charles E. Perkins, *Mobile IP: Design Principals and Practices*. Addison-Wessley, 1998.

power requirements for "continuous" transmission of overhead messages.

- The IP address must be the conventional IP address currently used in internets.
- There must be no additional requirements for these procedures (for example, the allocation of special addresses).
- Mobile IP supports mobility in wireless as well as wire-based networks.

Hereafter, the term mobile node is used to describe any device that changes its point of attachment from one network to another network. The mobile node is typically a mobile station but it could be a more elaborate device, such as a router. Home network refers to the original point of attachment, the mobile node has made when it received its IP address. At the home network the home agent (typically a router) is responsible for sending traffic to the mobile node when it is away from the home network. This home agent is also responsible for maintaining location information on the mobile node. Another device involved in the process is called the foreign agent. This device is typically a router attached to the visited network and acts as a conduit of traffic coming from the home agent to the mobile node.

Let us use these concepts to show an example of how Mobile IP operates. In Figure 11–3, a mobile node (node A) has moved from its original point of attachment (its home address) to another subnetwork. The operations involved to support this movement require that two IP addresses are made available. One IP address is used to locate the mobile node and another is used to identify the endpoint of the mobile node.

If the mobile node is attached to its home network, then the IP operations are the same as with any internet routing. However, if the mobile

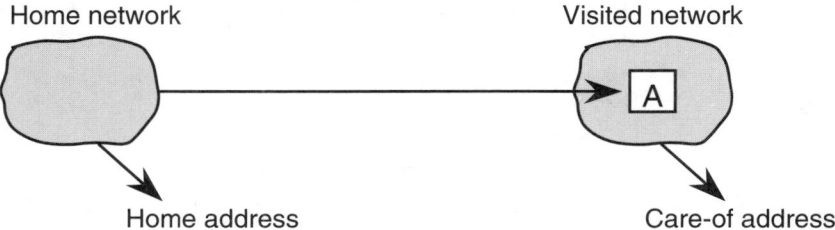

Home network   Visited network

Home address   Care-of address

Figure 11–3   The Mobile IP concept.

node has roamed to another network, then the datagram that is sent to this node is tunneled inside another datagram. This datagram has a different address in its header called the "care-of address."

The changing of the address of the datagram for routing to the other network is known as readdressing. In addition, once the traffic has arrived at the mobile node's point of attachment, an operation called inverse readdressing occurs. Inverse readdressing entails the transformation of the datagram so that the care of address is replaced by the original address in the datagram.

MOBILE IP ENTITIES, ADDRESSES, AND OPERATIONS

The following entities, addresses, and operations are part of Mobile IP. They are not the total Mobile IP picture, but sufficient for us to understand Mobile IP. For more detailed explanations, I refer you to RFC 2002.

- *Mobile Node*: A host or router that changes its point of attachment from one network or subnetwork to another without having to change is IP address. The mobile node can continue to communicate with other Internet nodes using its conventional IP address, assuming link-layer connectivity to a point of attachment is available.
- *Home Network*: A network having an address prefix matching a mobile nodes home address.
- *Home Agent:* A router on a mobile node's home network that tunnels (encapsulates) datagrams for delivery to the mobile node when it is away from home. The home agent also maintains current location information for the mobile node.
- *Foreign Agent:* A router on a mobile node's visited network that provides routing services to the mobile node while the mobile node is registered with the foreign agent. The foreign agent detunnels (decapsulates) and delivers datagrams to the mobile node that were tunneled by the mobile node's home agent. For datagrams sent by a mobile node, the foreign agent can serve as a default router for registered mobile nodes. As a general rule, the foreign agent provides a care-of address (which can be its IP address) to the mobile node at the mobile node's home agent. This address is

used to route the datagram to the foreign agent, who then uses the conventional IP address (that is also in the datagram) to deliver the datagram to the mobile node.[3]

- *Foreign Network:* A network other than the mobile node's home network.
- *Care-of Address:* A mobile node is given an IP address on a home network. This home address is administered in the same way as a conventional IP address is provided to a stationary host. When away from its home network, a care-of address is associated with the mobile node and reflects the mobile node's current point of attachment to a subnet. As a general practice, the mobile node uses its home address as the source address of all IP datagrams that it sends (some exceptions deal with mobility management operations, not discussed in this overview).
- *Agent Advertisement*: A message sent by attaching a special extension to an ICMP router advertisement message.
- *Tunnel:* The path taken by an IP datagram from one entity to another. While in the tunnel, the datagram is encapsulated into another protocol data unit (another datagram) whose purpose is to deliver the original datagram (unaltered) to the receiver.

THE MOBILE IP SERVICES

Mobile IP requires an array of operations to be executed if the users are to exchange messages with each other. These services require two processes: discovery and registration.

- *Agent Discovery:* Home agents and foreign agents advertise their availability on each link for which they provide service. A newly arrived mobile node can send a solicitation on the link to learn if any prospective agents are present to provide services to the mobile node.
- *Registration:* When the mobile node is away from home, it registers its care-of address with its home agent. Depending on the

---

[3]It is possible for the care-of address to be obtained from other means besides the foreign agent. For more details on this aspect of the care-of address (called a co-located care-of address) see Section 1.7 of RFC 2002.

method of attachment to the agent, the mobile node will register either directly with its home agent, or through a foreign agent which forwards the registration to the home agent.

OVERVIEW OF PRINCIPAL OPERATIONS

Figure 11–4 shows the principal events that are invoked in a typical Mobile IP operation.

Mobility agents (i.e., foreign agents and home agents) advertise their presence via Agent Advertisement messages. In event 1 in Figure 11–4, mobile node A receives an advertisement message from foreign agent B. Although not shown in this figure, a mobile node can solicit an Agent Advertisement message from any locally attached mobility agents through an Agent Solicitation message.

A mobile node receives these Agent Advertisements and determines whether it is on its home network or a foreign network. In this example, node A detects that it has moved to the foreign network on which foreign agent B is attached. Therefore, it obtains a care-of address on the foreign network that is in the advertisement message. The care-of address can be determined from this message (a foreign agent care-of address), or by another assignment mechanism such as the Dynamic Host Configuration Protocol (DHCP) (a co-located care-of address).

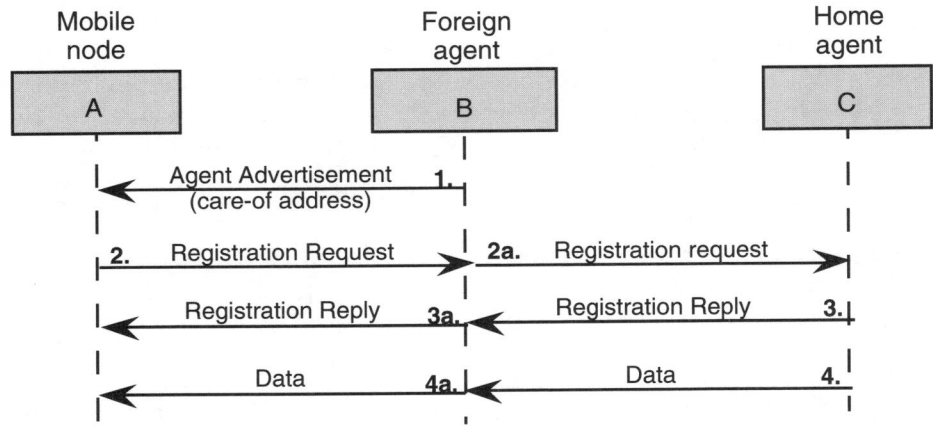

Figure 11–4   Advertising and registration.

In events 2 and 3, the mobile registers its new care-of address with its home agent (C) through the foreign agent with the exchange of a Registration Request and Registration Reply messages.

After these registration procedures are completed, datagrams can now be exchanged with the mobile node, as shown in event 4. Other IP nodes are not aware that mobile node A is no longer attached to its known "permanent address." So, these nodes continue to send datagrams to the home address. These datagrams are intercepted by the home agent, and tunneled by the home agent to the mobile node's care-of address. The care-of address must be such that it can be used to route the datagram through an internet to the tunnel endpoint. When the datagram arrives at the tunnel endpoint at the foreign agent (although the tunnel endpoint can also be the mobile node), the datagram is decapsulated and presented to the mobile node.

Several other points are noteworthy here. First, when the mobile node is located on its home network, it operates without mobility services. If returning to its home network from being registered elsewhere, the mobile node deregisters with its home agent, through exchange of a Registration Request and Registration Reply messages. Second, the datagrams sent by the mobile node are generally delivered to their destination using conventional IP routing mechanisms and do not have to pass through the home agent. For example, the foreign agent (the local router) to the mobile node simply uses the destination IP address in the datagram to determine the next node, which may or may not be the home agent.

NEW MESSAGES AND PROTOCOL EXTENSIONS

Mobile IP's messages use three arrangements. First, new messages are defined to run on UDP using well-known port number 434. Second, Mobile IP uses the existing Router Advertisement and Router Solicitation messages defined for the ICMP Router Discovery. Third, Mobile IP defines a general extension mechanism to allow optional information to be carried by Mobile IP control messages or by ICMP Router Discovery messages. Using well-known port number 434. Two message types are defined: Registration Request, and Registration Reply

Two separately maintained sets of numbering spaces, from which extension type values are allocated, are used in Mobile IP.

The first set consists of those extensions which appear in Mobile IP control messages (those sent to and from UDP port number 434). The following types are defined for extensions appearing in Mobile IP registration messages:

    32 Mobile-Home Authentication
    33 Mobile-Foreign Authentication
    34 Foreign-Home Authentication

The second set consists of extensions that appear in ICMP Router Discovery messages. Mobile IP defines the following types for extensions appearing in ICMP Router Discovery messages:

    0   One-byte Padding (encoded with no length nor data field)
    16 Mobility Agent Advertisement
    19 Prefix-Lengths

The general extension mechanism to allow optional information to be carried by Mobile IP control messages or by ICMP Router Discovery messages. Each of these extensions (with one exception) is encoded in the type-length-value format shown in Figure 11–5.[4] The three fields are the type, which indicates the type of extension; the length, which indicates the length of the data field (in bytes); and the data (value) field associated with this extension.

AGENT DISCOVERY

Agent Discovery is the method by which a mobile node determines whether it is currently connected to its home network or to a foreign network. This method allows a mobile node to detect when it has moved

0	1-6	7	8	9-14	15	16	17-30	31
	Type			Length			Data	

Figure 11–5 Type, length, and data format.

---

[4]The type-length-value notations in this discussion have nothing to do with the type, length, value notations used in many presentation layer (layer 6) protocols.

from one network to another. When connected to a foreign network, Mobile IP allows the mobile node to determine the foreign agent care-of address being offered by each foreign agent on that network.

Mobile IP uses the ICMP Router Discovery procedure as its primary mechanism for Agent Discovery. An Agent Advertisement is formed by including a Mobility Agent Advertisement Extension in an ICMP Router Advertisement message. The Agent Solicitation message is identical to an ICMP Router Solicitation, except that its IP TTL must be set to 1.

Agent Advertisement

Agent Advertisements are transmitted by a mobility agent to advertise its services on a link. Mobile nodes use these advertisements to determine their current point of attachment to the Internet. An Agent Advertisement is an ICMP Router Advertisement that has been extended to carry a Mobility Agent Advertisement Extension and an optional Prefix-Lengths Extension.

Within the Agent Advertisement message, ICMP Router Advertisement fields in the message are required to conform to the following additional specifications:

- Link-Layer Fields
  Destination Address: The link-layer destination address of a unicast Agent Advertisement is the same as the source link-layer address of the Agent Solicitation that prompted the Advertisement.
- IP Fields
  TTL: The TTL for all Agent Advertisements is set to 1.

  Destination Address: As specified for ICMP Router Discovery, the IP destination address of an Agent Advertisement is either the "all systems on this link" multicast address (224.0.0.1) or the "limited broadcast" address (255.255.255.255).
- ICMP Fields
  Code: The Code field of the agent advertisement is interpreted as a 0 or 16:

  0 Means the mobility agent handles common traffic; that is, it acts as a router for IP datagrams not necessarily related to mobile nodes.

  16 Means the mobility agent does not route common traffic. However, all foreign agents will forward to a default router any datagrams received from a registered mobile node.

- *Lifetime:* The maximum length of time that the Advertisement is considered valid in the absence of further Advertisements.
- Num Addrs
  The number of Router Addresses advertised in this message.

ROUTER DISCOVERY PROTOCOL

A relatively new ICMP operation is the router discovery feature (RFC 1256). It entails a host, upon being installed and bootstrapped onto a network, sending an ICMP router solicitation message. It is sent as a broadcast or multicast message. Any router on the same subnet responds with a router advertisement message. This message contains the router's IP address (or addresses) and a preference level for which address the host should use when sending traffic to that router. The preference level field can be set to hex 80000000 to indicate that an address is not to be used as a default router address. The lifetime field in the advertisement informs the receivers how long (in seconds), the addresses are valid. If an interface is down, the advertisement's lifetime field is set to 0.

Obviously, this ICMP operation allows the host to discover the routers on its subnet. And when the host is first brought up on the subnet, it usually sends solicitation messages three seconds apart. When it receives an advertisement, it stops sending the solicitations.

A router transmits router advertisements on all its interfaces that are configured as broadcast or multicast. These advertisements are sent by the router every 450 to 500 seconds. Since some systems have multiple routers on a subnet, the messages must be set up such that the preference levels are indicative of the network administrator's intents with regard to primary routers, backup routers, and so on. Figure 11–6 shows how the router discovery messages are exchanged.

Figures 11–7 and 11–8 show the formats for the Router Advertisement and Router Solicitation messages.

The fields in the Advertisement message are:

- *Type*:   9
- *Code*:   0
- *Checksum*: An error-check field
- *Num addrs:* The number of router addresses advertised in this message

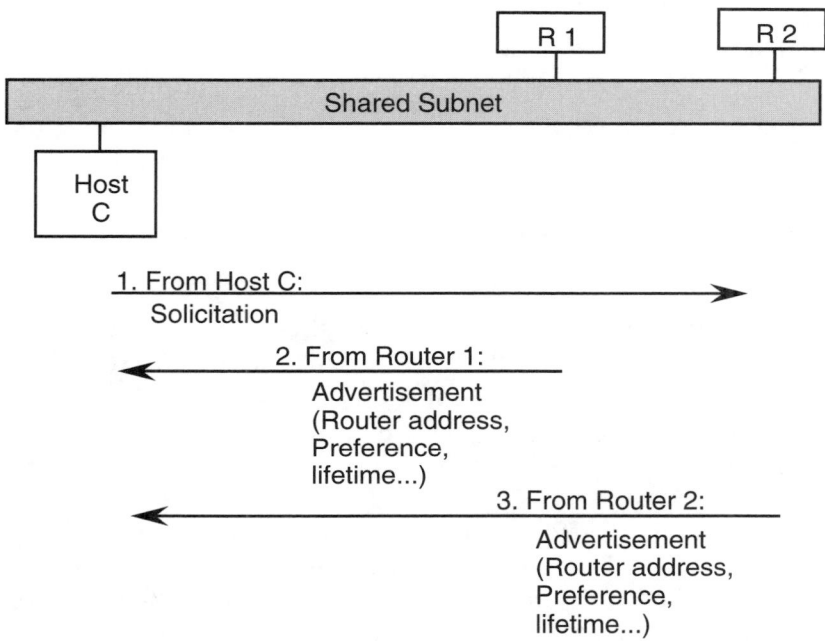

Figure 11–6   Router discovery operations.

- *Addr entry size:* The number of 32-bit words of information for each router address
- *Lifetime:* The maximum number of seconds that the router addressees are considered valid

0	1-6	7	8	9-14	1 5	1 6	17-22	2 3	2 4	25-30	3 1
Type				Code			Checksum				
Num Addrs				Addr Entry Size			Lifetime				
Router Address (1)											
Preference Level (1)											
				│							
				│							
				│							
				│							

Figure 11–7   Router Advertisement message.

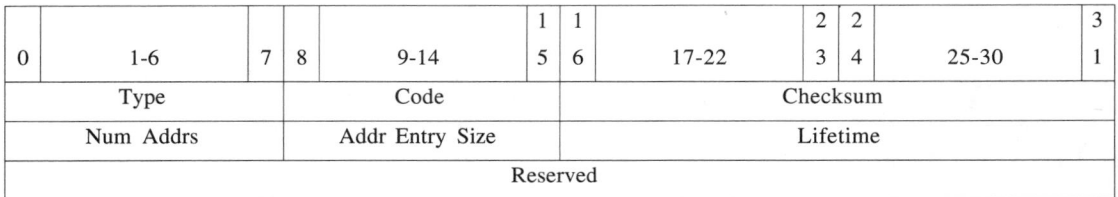

0	1-6	7	8	9-14	1 5	1 6	17-22	2 3	2 4	25-30	3 1
Type			Code				Checksum				
Num Addrs			Addr Entry Size				Lifetime				
Reserved											

Figure 11-8   Router Solicitation message.

- *Router Address (i):* i = 1...Num Addrs, the sending router's IP addresses on the interface from which this message is sent
- *Preference level(i):* i = 1...Num Addrs, the preferability of each corresponding router address as a default router address relative to other router addresses on the same subnet

Since this is an ICMP message, it is preceded by an IP header. In the IP header, the fields are set to mostly natural values. If the destination address is chosen to be the multicast address 224.0.0.1 (the all-systems multicast address), then the TTL (time to live) field is required to be set to 1.

The fields in the Solicitation message are:

- *Type:*   10
- *Code:*   0
- *Checksum:* An error-check field
- *Reserved:* Sent as 0

A host sending a solicitation is required to set the TTL field to 1. The only permissible values for the IP destination are the all-routers multicast address, 224.0.0.2, or the limited-broadcast address, 255.255.255.255.

AGENT ADVERTISEMENT

An Agent Advertisement is an ICMP Router Advertisement that has been extended also to carry Mobility Agent Advertisement Extension. A mobility agent transits Agent Advertisements to advertise its services on a link. Mobile nodes use these advertisements to determine their current point of attachment to the Internet. The advertisement may also carry other extensions, notably the Prefix-Length Extensions, one-byte padding extension, or other extensions that might be defined in the future. Unquestionably the most important extension is the mobility agent extension. Within an agent advertisement message, ICMP Router Advertisements include the following link-layer, IP, and ICMP header fields:

- Link-layer fields
  Destination address: The link-layer destination address of a unicast agent advertisement is required to be the same as the source link layer address of the agent solicitation that prompted the advertisement.
- IP fields
  TTL: The TTL for all agent advertisements is required to be set to 1.

Mobility Agent Advertisement Extension

The Mobility Agent Advertisement Extension follows the ICMP Router Advertisement fields. It is used to indicate that an ICMP Router Advertisement message is also an Agent Advertisement being sent by a mobility agent. The Mobility Agent Advertisement Extension is defined in Figure 11–9.

The fields in this message are as follows:

- *Type:* 16.
- *Length:* (6 + 4*N), where N is the number of care-of addresses advertised.
- *Sequence Number:* The count of Agent Advertisement messages sent since the agent was initialized.

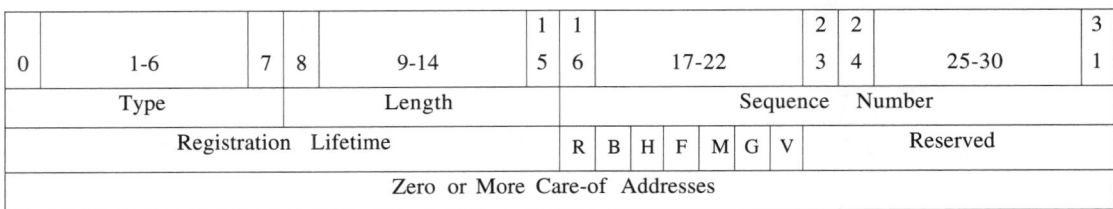

0	1-6	7	8	9-14	15	16	17-22	23	24	25-30	31
Type			Length				Sequence Number				
Registration Lifetime						R	B	H	F	M	G	V	Reserved
Zero or More Care-of Addresses											

Figure 11–9   Mobility Agent Advertisement Extension message.

- *Registration Lifetime:* The longest lifetime (measures in seconds) that this agent is willing to accept in any Registration Request. A value of hex FFFF indicates infinity.
- *R:* Registration required. Registration with this foreign agent (or another foreign agent on this link) is required rather than using a co-located care-of address.
- *B:* Busy. The foreign agent will not accept registrations from additional mobile nodes.
- *H*: Home agent. This agent offers service as a home agent on the link on which this Agent Advertisement message is sent.
- *F:* Foreign agent. This agent offers service as a foreign agent on the link on which this Agent Advertisement message is sent.
- *M:* Minimal encapsulation. This agent implements receiving tunneled datagrams that use minimal encapsulation.
- *G:* GRE encapsulation. This agent implements receiving tunneled datagrams that use GRE encapsulation.
- *V:* Van Jacobson header compression. This agent supports use of Van Jacobson header compression (RFC 1144) over the link with any registered mobile node.
- *Reserved:* Sent as zero; ignored on reception.
- *Care-of Address(es):* The advertised foreign agent care-of address(es) provided by this foreign agent. An Agent Advertisement should include at least one care-of address if the 'F' bit is set. The number of care-of addresses present is determined by the length field in the extension.

Prefix-Lengths Extension

The Prefix-Lengths Extension, as shown in Figure 11–10, can follow the Mobility Agent Advertisement Extension. It is used to indicate the number of bits of network prefix that applies to each Router Address listed in the ICMP Router Advertisement portion of the Agent Advertisement.

0	1-6	7	8	9-14	1 5	1 6	17-22	2 3	2 4	25-30	3 1
Type				Length			Prefix Length			. . . . . .	

Figure 11–10   Prefix-Length Extension message.

- *Type:* 19 (Prefix-Lengths Extension).
- *Length:* N, where N is the value of the Num Addrs field in the ICMP Router Advertisement portion of the Agent Advertisement.
- *Prefix Length(s):* The number of leading bits that define the network number of the corresponding Router Address listed in the ICMP Router Advertisement portion of the message.

One-Byte Padding Extension

Some IP protocol implementations insist upon padding ICMP messages to an even number of bytes. If the ICMP length of an Agent Advertisement is odd, this Extension may be included in order to make the ICMP length even. Unlike other Extensions used in Mobile IP, the One-Byte Padding Extension is encoded as a single byte, with no "Length" nor "Data" field present. The One-Byte Padding Extension is shown in Figure 11–11.

Agent Solicitation

An Agent Solicitation is identical to an ICMP Router Solicitation with the restriction that the IP TTL Field must be set to 1.

Foreign Agent and Home Agent Considerations

A mobility agent that cannot be discovered by a link-layer protocol sends Agent Advertisements. An agent that can be discovered by a link-layer protocol also implements Agent Advertisements. However, the Advertisements need not be sent, except when the site policy requires registration with the agent (i.e., when the "R" bit is set), or as a response to a specific Agent Solicitation. All mobility agents respond to Agent Solicitations.

The same procedures, defaults, and constants are used in Agent Advertisement messages and Agent Solicitation messages as specified for ICMP Router Discovery, with these exceptions:

- A mobility agent must limit the rate at which it sends broadcast or multicast Agent Advertisements; a recommended maximum rate is once per second.

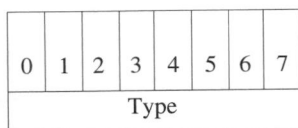

Figure 11–11   One-Byte Padding Extension.

- A mobility agent that receives a Router Solicitation does not require that the IP Source Address is the address of a neighbor (i.e., an address that matches one of the router's own addresses on the arrival interface, under the subnet mask associated with that address of the router).
- A mobility agent may be configured to send Agent Advertisements only in response to an Agent Solicitation message.

Advertised Router Addresses

The ICMP Router Advertisement portion of the Agent Advertisement contains one or more router addresses. Thus, an agent includes one of its own addresses in the advertisement. A foreign agent discourages use of this address as a default router by setting the preference to a low value and by including the address of another router in the advertisement (with a correspondingly higher preference). Nevertheless, a foreign agent routes datagrams it receives from registered mobile nodes.

Sequence Numbers and Rollover Handling

The sequence number in Agent Advertisements ranges from 0 to hex 0000 to hex 0FFF. After booting, an agent must use the number 0 for its first advertisement. Each subsequent advertisement must use the sequence number one greater, with the exception that the sequence number hex FFFF is to be followed by sequence number 256. In this way, mobile nodes can distinguish reductions in sequence numbers that result from reboots, from reductions that result in rollover of the sequence number after it attains the value hex FFFF.

MOBILE NODE CONSIDERATIONS

Every mobile node implements Agent Solicitation. Solicitations are only sent in the absence of Agent Advertisements and when a care-of address has not been determined through a link-layer protocol or other means. With some minor exceptions, the mobile node uses the same procedures, defaults, and constants for Agent Solicitation as the for ICMP Router Solicitation messages.

The rate at which a mobile node sends Solicitations is limited by the mobile node. The mobile node sends three initial Solicitations at a maximum rate of one per second while searching for an agent. After this, the rate at which Solicitations are sent is reduced so as to limit the overhead on the local link. Subsequent Solicitations are sent using a binary exponential back-off mechanism, doubling the interval between consecutive Solicitations, up to a maximum interval.

While still searching for an agent, the mobile node must not increase the rate at which it sends Solicitations unless it has received a positive indication that it has moved to a new link. After successfully registering with an agent, the mobile node increases the rate at which it will send Solicitations when it next begins searching for a new agent with which to register. The increased solicitation rate reverts to the maximum rate, but then is limited in the manner described above.

Registration Required

When the mobile node receives an Agent Advertisement with the "R" bit set, the mobile node registers through the foreign agent, even when the mobile node might be able to acquire its own co-located care-of address.

Move Detection

When the mobile node detects that it has moved, it registers with a suitable care-of address on the new foreign network. However, the mobile node does not register more frequently than once per second on average.

Returning Home.   A mobile node can detect that it has returned to its home network when it receives an Agent Advertisement from its own home agent. If so, it deregisters with its home agent. Before attempting to deregister, the mobile node configures its routing table appropriately for its home network. In addition, if the home network is using ARP, the mobile node follows the procedures with regard to ARP, Proxy ARP, and gratuitous ARP.

Sequence Numbers and Rollover Handling.   If a mobile node detects two successive values of the sequence number in the Agent Advertisements from the foreign agent with which it is registered, the second of which is less than the first and inside the range 0 to 255, the mobile node registers again. If the second value is less than the first but is greater than or equal to 256, the mobile node assumes that the sequence number has rolled over past its maximum value (hex FFFF), and that reregistration is not necessary.

REGISTRATION

Mobile IP registration provides a mechanism for mobile nodes to communicate their current reachability information to their home agent. It is the method by which mobile nodes:

- Request forwarding services when visiting a foreign network.
- Inform their home agent of their current care-of address.
- Renew a registration which is due to expire.
- Deregister when they return home.

Authentication

Each mobile node, foreign agent, and home agent is able to support a mobility security association for mobile entities, indexed by its SPI and IP address. In the case of the mobile node, this must be its Home Address. Registration messages between a mobile node and its home agent are authenticated with the Mobile-Home Authentication Extension.

Registration Request

A mobile node registers with its home agent using a Registration Request message so that its home agent can create or modify a mobility binding for that mobile node (e.g., with a new lifetime). The Request may be relayed to the home agent by the foreign agent through which the mobile node is registering, or it may be sent directly to the home agent in the case in which the mobile node is registering a co-located care-of address. The IP and UDP fields are coded as follows:

- IP fields
  Source Address: Typically the interface address from which the message is sent.
  Destination Address: Typically that of the foreign agent or the home agent.
- UDP fields
  Source Port: variable
  Destination Port: 434

The UDP header is followed by the Mobile IP fields shown in Figure 11–12.
The fields in the message are:

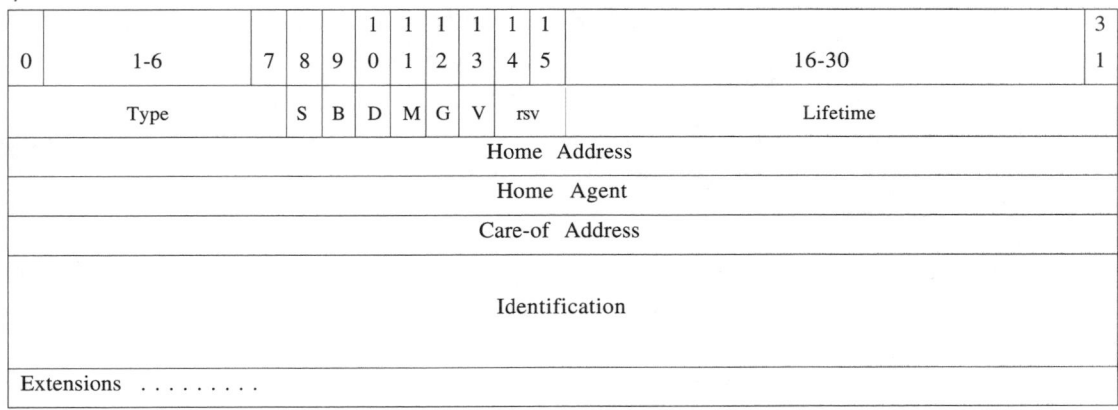

0	1-6	7	8	9	1 0	1 1	1 2	1 3	1 4	1 5	16-30	3 1
Type		S	B	D	M	G	V	rsv			Lifetime	
Home Address												
Home Agent												
Care-of Address												
Identification												
Extensions												

Figure 11–12   Registration Request message.

- *Type:* 1 (Registration Request).
- S = *Simultaneous bindings:* If the "S" bit is set, the mobile node is requesting that the home agent retain its prior mobility bindings.
- B = *Broadcast datagrams:* If the "B" bit is set, the mobile node requests that the home agent tunnel to it any broadcast datagrams that it receives on the home network.
- D = *Decapsulation by mobile node:* If the "D" bit is set, the mobile node will itself decapsulate datagrams that are sent to the care-of address. That is, the mobile node is using a co-located care-of address.
- M = *Minimal encapsulation:* If the "M" bit is set, the mobile node requests that its home agent use minimal encapsulation for datagrams tunneled to the mobile node.
- G = *GRE encapsulation:* If the "G" bit is set, the mobile node requests that its home agent use GRE encapsulation for datagrams tunneled to the mobile node.
- V = *Van Jacobson Header Compression:* The mobile node requests that its mobility agent use Van Jacobson header compression over its link with the mobile node.
- *rsv = Reserved bits*: Sent as zero.
- *Lifetime:* The number of seconds remaining before the registration is considered expired. A value of zero indicates a request for deregistration. A value of hex FFFF indicates infinity.

- *Home Address:* The IP address of the mobile node.
- *Home Agent:* The IP address of the mobile node's home agent.
- *Care-of Address:* The IP address for the end of the tunnel.
- *Identification:* A 64-bit number, constructed by the mobile node, used for matching Registration Requests with Registration Replies, and for protecting against replay attacks of registration messages.
- *Extensions:* The fixed portion of the Registration Request is followed by one or more of the Extensions.

Registration Reply

A mobility agent returns a Registration Reply message to a mobile node that has sent a Registration Request message. If the mobile node is requesting service from a foreign agent, that foreign agent will receive the Reply from the home agent and subsequently relay it to the mobile node. The Reply message contains the necessary codes to inform the mobile node about the status of its Request, along with the lifetime granted by the home agent.

The IP and UDP fields are coded as follows:

- IP fields
  Source Address: Typically copied from the destination address of the Registration Request to which the agent is replying.
  Destination Address: Copied from the source address of the Registration Request to which the agent is replying
- UDP fields
  Source Port: <variable>
  Destination Port: Copied from the source port of the corresponding Registration Request

The UDP header is followed by the Mobile IP fields shown in Figure 11–13.

The fields in the message are:

- *Type:* 3 (Registration Reply).
- *Code:* A value indicating the result of the Registration.
- *Request:* A value indicating the result of the Registration Request.
- *Lifetime:* If the Code field indicates that the registration was accepted, the Lifetime field is set to the number of seconds remain-

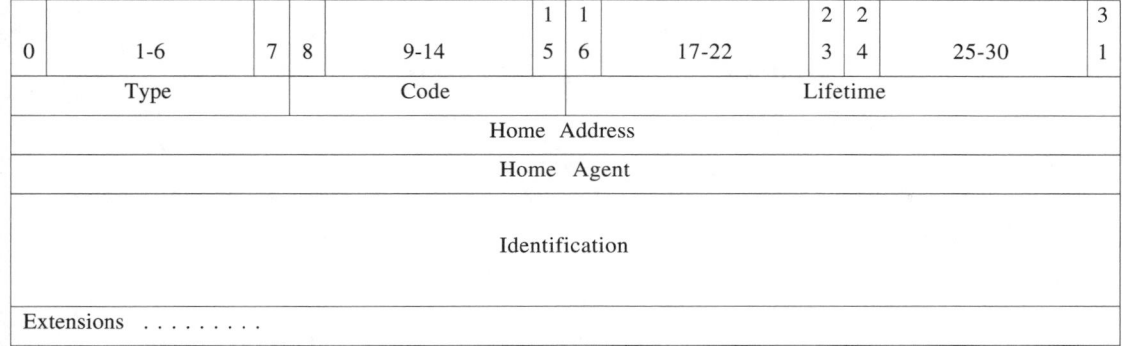

0	1-6	7	8	9-14	1 5	1 6	17-22	2 3	2 4	25-30	3 1
Type			Code				Lifetime				
Home Address											
Home Agent											
Identification											
Extensions											

Figure 11–13   The Registration Reply message.

ing before the registration is considered expired. A value of zero indicates that the mobile node has been deregistered. A value of hex FFFF indicates infinity.

- *Home Address:* The IP address of the mobile node.
- *Home Agent:* The IP address of the mobile node's home agent.
- *Identification:* A 64-bit number used for matching Registration Requests with Registration Replies and for protecting against replay attacks of registration messages.
- *Extensions:* The fixed portion of the Registration Reply is followed by one or more of the Extensions.

THE SECURITY PARAMETER INDEX

The Security Parameter Index (SPI) within any of the authentication Extensions defines the security context that is used to compute the Authenticator value and that is used by the receiver to check that value. The SPI selects the authentication algorithm and mode and secret (a shared key, or appropriate public/private key pair) used in computing the Authenticator.

One Mobile-Home Authentication Extension is present in all Registration Requests and Registration Replies.

Figure 11–14 illustrates the Mobile-Home Authentication Extension message.

The contents of the message are:

0	1-6	7	8	9-14	1 5	1 6	17-22	2 3	2 4	25-30	3 1
Type			code				SPI				
. . . . SPI continued						Authenticator					

Figure 11–14   Mobile-Home Authentication Extension message.

- Type: 32.
- *Length:* 4 plus the number of bytes in the Authenticator.
- *SPI = Security Parameter Index (4 bytes):* An opaque identifier.
- *Authenticator:* (variable length).

A mobile node is configured with its home address, a netmask, and a mobility security association for each home agent. In addition, a mobile node is configured with the IP address of one or more of its home agents; otherwise, the mobile node discovers a home agent using the procedures.

For each pending registration, the mobile node maintains the following information:

- The link-layer address of the foreign agent to which the Registration Request was sent, if applicable.
- The IP destination address of the Registration Request.
- The care-of address used in the registration.
- The Identification value sent in the registration.
- The originally requested Lifetime.
- The remaining Lifetime of the pending registration.

FOREIGN AGENT CONSIDERATIONS

The foreign agent relays Registration Requests between mobile nodes and home agents, and, when it provides the care-of address, decapsulates datagrams for delivery to the mobile node. It also sends periodic Agent Advertisement messages to advertise its presence.

A foreign agent does not transmit a Registration Request except when relaying a Registration Request received from a mobile node to the mobile node's home agent. A foreign agent cannot transmit a Registration Reply except when relaying a Registration Reply received from a mobile node's home agent, or when replying to a Registration Request received from a mobile node in the case when the foreign agent is denying service to the mobile node.

Configuration and Registration Tables

We know that each foreign agent is configured with a care-of address. In addition, for each pending or current registration, the foreign agent maintains a visitor list entry containing the following information obtained from the mobile node's Registration Request:

- The link-layer source address of the mobile node
- The IP Source Address (the mobile node's Home Address)
- The IP Destination Address
- The UDP Source Port
- The Home Agent address
- The Identification field
- The requested registration Lifetime
- The remaining Lifetime of the pending or current registration

Receiving Registration Requests

If the foreign agent accepts a Registration Request from a mobile node, it relays the Request to the indicated home agent (as shown in Figure 11–2). Otherwise, if the foreign agent denies the Request, it sends a Registration Reply to the mobile node with an appropriate denial Code.

If the foreign agent accepts the mobile node's Registration Request, it relays the Request to the mobile node's home agent as specified in the Home Agent field of the Registration Request. The foreign agent cannot modify any of the fields beginning with the fixed portion of the Registration Request up through and including the Mobile-Home Authentication Extension.

HOME AGENT CONSIDERATIONS

Home agents play a reactive role in the registration process by receiving registration requests from the mobile node (perhaps relayed by a foreign agent). This message allows the Home Agent to update its record of the mobility bindings for this mobile node. The Agent issues a suitable Registration Reply in response to each registration request.

Configuration and Registration Tables

Each home agent is configured with an IP address and with the prefix size for the home network. The home agent is configured with the home address and mobility security association of each authorized mobile node that it is serving as a home agent. When the home agent accepts a valid Registration Request from a mobile node that it serves as a home agent, the home agent creates or modifies the entry for this mobile node in its mobility binding list containing:

- The mobile node's care-of address
- The Identification field from the Registration Reply
- The remaining Lifetime of the registration

Receiving Registration Requests

If the home agent accepts an incoming Registration Request, it updates its record of the mobile node's mobility binding(s) and sends a Registration Reply with a suitable code. Otherwise, it sends a Registration Reply with an appropriate code specifying the reason the Request was denied.

IP/UDP FIELDS

This section provides the specific rules by which mobile nodes pickvalues for the IP and UDP header fields of a Registration Reply.

- *IP Source Address:* Copied from the IP Destination Address of Registration Request, unless a multicast or broadcast address was used. If the IP Destination Address of the Registration Request was a broadcast or multicast address, the IP Source Address of the Registration Reply is set to the home agent's (unicast) IP address.
- *IP Destination Address:* Copied from the IP Source Address of the Registration Request.
- *UDP Source Port:* Copied from the UDP Destination Port of the Registration Request.
- *UDP Destination Port:* Copied from the UDP Source Port of the Registration Request.

BROADCAST DATAGRAMS

When a home agent receives a broadcast datagram, it cannot forward the datagram to any mobile nodes in its mobility binding list other than those that have requested forwarding of broadcast datagrams. A mobile node can request forwarding of broadcast datagrams by setting the "B" bit in its Registration Request message. For each such registered mobile node, the home agent forwards received broadcast datagrams to the mobile node. The home agent decodes as to which specific categories of broadcast datagrams will be forwarded to such mobile nodes.

If the "D" bit was set in the mobile node's Registration Request message, indicating that the mobile node is using a co-located care-of address, the home agent tunnels appropriate broadcast IP datagrams to the mobile node's care-of address. Otherwise, the home agent encapsulates the broadcast datagram in a unicast datagram addressed to the mobile node's home address, and then tunnels this encapsulated datagram to the foreign agent.

MULTICAST DATAGRAM ROUTING

In order to receive multicasts, a mobile node joins the multicast group in one of two ways. First, a mobile node may join the group via a (local) multicast router on the visited subnet. This option assumes that there is a multicast router present on the visited subnet. If the mobile node is using a co-located care-of address, it uses this address as the source IP address of its IGMP messages. Otherwise, it uses its home address.

Alternatively, a mobile node that wishes to receive multicasts can join groups via a bidirectional tunnel to its home agent, assuming that its home agent is a multicast router. The mobile node tunnels IGMP messages to its home agent and the home agent forwards multicast datagrams down the tunnel to the mobile node. The rules for multicast datagram delivery to mobile nodes in this case are identical to those for broadcast datagrams.

A mobile node that wishes to send datagrams to a multicast group also has two options: (1) send directly on the visited network or (2) send via a tunnel to its home agent. Because multicast routing in general depends upon the IP source address, a mobile node that sends multicast datagrams directly on the visited network uses a co-located care-of address as the IP source address. Similarly, a mobile node that tunnels a multicast datagram to its home agent uses its home address as the IP source address of both the (inner) multicast datagram and the (outer) encapsulating datagram. This second option assumes that the home agent is a multicast router.

ARP, PROXY ARP, AND GRATUITOUS ARP

The use of ARP requires special rules for correct operation when wireless or mobile nodes are involved. The requirements specified in this section apply to all home networks in which ARP is used for address resolution. In addition to the normal use of ARP for resolving a target node's link-layer address from its IP address.

For a gratuitous ARP, the ARP packet is transmitted as a local broadcast packet on the local link. Any node receiving any ARP packet (Request or Reply) updates its local ARP cache with the Sender Protocol and Hardware Addresses in the ARP packet, if the receiving node has an entry for that IP address already in its ARP cache.

While a mobile node is registered on a foreign network, its home agent uses proxy ARP to reply to ARP Requests it receives that seek the mobile node's link-layer address. When receiving an ARP Request, the home agent examines the target IP address of the Request, and if this IP address matches the home address of any mobile node for which it has a registered mobility binding, the home agent transmits an ARP Reply on behalf of the mobile node. After exchanging the sender and target addresses in the packet, the home agent sets the sender link-layer address in the packet to the link-layer address of its own interface over which the Reply will be sent.

When a mobile node leaves its home network and registers a binding on a foreign network, its home agent uses gratuitous ARP to update the ARP caches of nodes on the home network. This causes such nodes to associate the link-layer address of the home agent with the mobile node's home (IP) address. When registering a binding for a mobile node for which the home agent previously had no binding (the mobile node was assumed to be at home), the home agent transmits a gratuitous ARP on behalf of the mobile node. This gratuitous ARP packet is transmitted as a broadcast packet on the link on which the mobile node's home address is located.

When a mobile node returns to its home network, the mobile node and its home agent use gratuitous ARP to cause all nodes on the mobile node's home network to update their ARP caches to once again associate the mobile node's own link-layer address with the mobile node's home (IP) address. Before transmitting the (de)Registration Request message to its home agent, the mobile node transmits this gratuitous ARP on its home network as a local broadcast on this link.

When the mobile node's home agent receives and accepts this (de)Registration Request, the home agent also transmits a gratuitous ARP on the mobile node's home network. This gratuitous ARP also is used to associate the mobile node's home address with the mobile node's own link-layer address. A gratuitous ARP is transmitted by both the mobile node and its home agent, since in the case of wireless network interfaces, the area within transmission range of the mobile node will likely differ from that within range of its home agent.

While the mobile node is away from home, it cannot transmit any broadcast ARP Request or ARP Reply messages. While the mobile node is away from home, it cannot reply to ARP Requests in which the target IP address is its own home address, unless the ARP Request is sent by a foreign agent with which the mobile node is attempting to register or a foreign agent with which the mobile node has an unexpired registration. In the latter case, the mobile node uses a unicast ARP Reply to respond to the foreign agent. Note that if the mobile node is using a co-located care-of address and receives an ARP Request in which the target IP address is this care-of address, then the mobile node replies to this ARP Request.

TCP CONSIDERATIONS

RFC 2002 states that most hosts and routers that implement TCP/IP do not permit easy configuration of the TCP timer values. When high-delay or low-bandwidth links are in use, the default TCP timer values in many systems may cause retransmissions or timeouts, even when the link and network are actually operating properly.

Mobile nodes often use media that are more likely to introduce errors, effectively causing more packets to be dropped. This introduces a conflict with the mechanisms for TCP congestion management found in modern versions of TCP. Now, when a packet is dropped or an ACK arrives late, the correspondent node's TCP implementation is likely to react as if there were a source of network congestion, and initiate the slow-start (closing its window to one) mechanisms designed for controlling that problem. However, those mechanisms are inappropriate for overcoming errors introduced by the links themselves and have the effect of magnifying the discontinuity introduced by the dropped packet. And repeated errors will ensure that the send window remains small.

Error prone links are not the only problem. When a mobile station roams to another all traditional hand-offs (not IS-95, but AMPS- and TDMA-based systems) necessitate the breaking of the mobile stations connection with the base station. Furthermore, it is possible that the new cell may not have bandwidth immediately available for the handoff. This situation can result in more lost TCP segments, more retransmissions, and often the loss of the TCP socket connection.

Traffic Management and Integrity Issues

Figure 11–15 shows one approach to providing data integrity in a mobile wireless system. As suggested by the solid arrow operating at the data link layers, error detection, acknowledgments, and retransmissions are provided at the air interface itself. Therefore, conventional layer 2

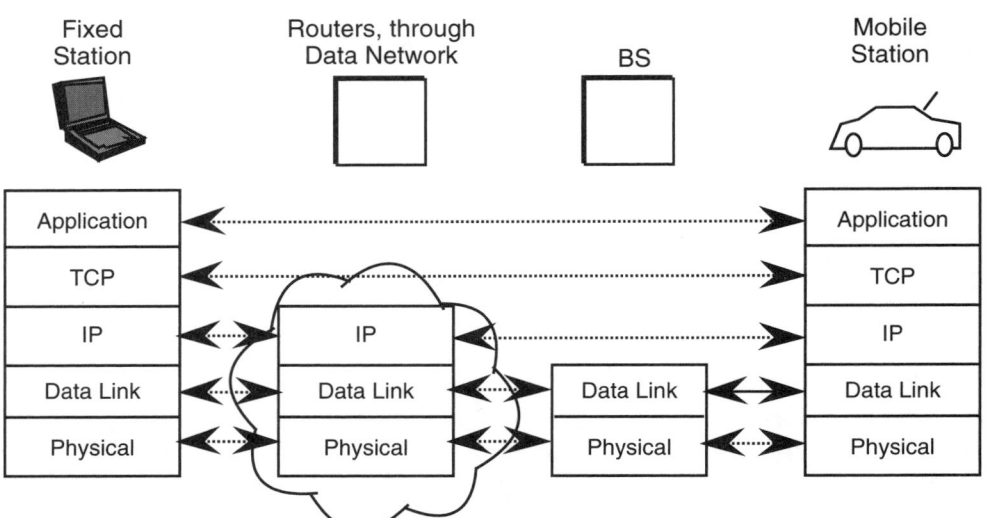

Notes: Dashed lines = traffic flow
         Solid arrows = traffic flow and ACKs
         UDP not invoked if ACKs needed

Figure 11–15   Approaches to data integrity: Option 1.

protocols such as LAPB or PPP can be utilized.[5] The advantage to this option is that it corrects the problem shortly after it is detected. In addition, retransmissions, if needed, occur only on the RF channel. Consequently, duplicate data units are not introduced into other components and links in the overall system.

The disadvantage to this approach is that traffic integrity is provided only at the air interface and there is no assurance that the traffic arrives correctly at the remote host. Link layer operations are capable only of error control measures on a specific link. If the traffic is delivered safely to the node attached to the link and is acknowledged by that node, then the original transmitting station deletes its copy of the traffic. Subsequently, if the acknowledging node fails (software bug, memory hit, etc.), then the traffic is lost from the standpoint of the data link (L_2) protocol.

Another option for providing data integrity is to execute acknowledgments and retransmissions between the host machines themselves. Figure 11–16 shows the approach is performed through the layer 4 protocol, the Transmission Control Protocol (TCP). The advantage to this approach is that it provides end-to-end integrity since the acknowledgments and possible retransmissions are performed by the TCP modules that reside in the two host machines.

The disadvantages to this approach are as follows. First, the retransmission timers are more difficult to manage in a mobile network than in a fixed network due to increased variability in the transmission schemes. The second disadvantage results from the fact that while an error might occur at one specific node or specific link, the retransmitted traffic is reintroduced on each link and through each node. If errors are frequent, the retransmissions through the entire system will affect throughput and performance.

TCP Split Connection. Another option, depicted in Figure 11–17, for providing data integrity is to place TCP at the base station and map two TCP connections. The first connection exists between the base station and the mobile station, and the second connection exists between the base sta-

---

[5]PPP would be a good choice for layer 2 because of its negotiation and encapsulation features. However, it would have to be modified if retransmissions of errored traffic are required. Currently, PPP uses the unnumbered information operation, which does not support retransmissions. However, it is a straightforward task to run PPP over another retransmission layer two protocol, such as a LAPB (a subject covered in Chapter 9).

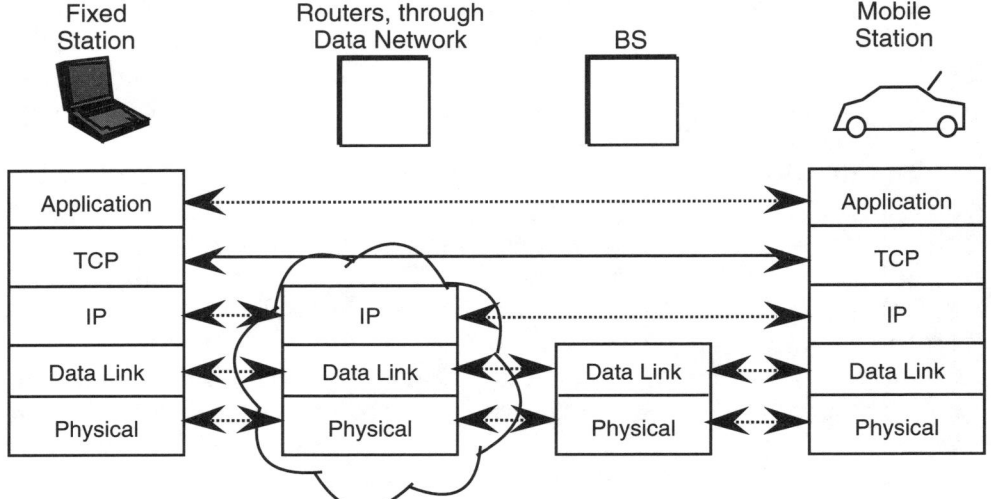

Figure 11–16   Approaches to data integrity: Option 2.

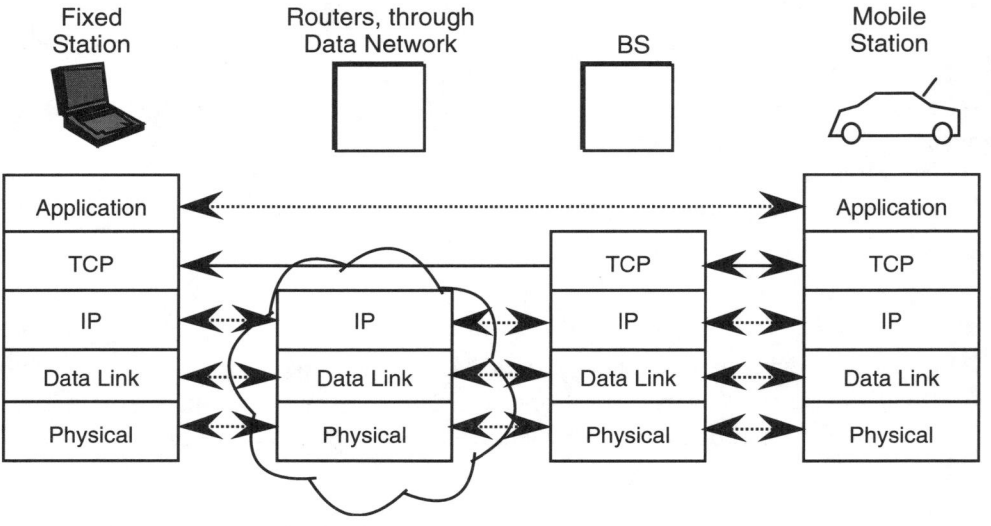

Figure 11–17   Approaches to data integrity: Option 3.

tion and the other host. This approach does not eliminate the problems associated with the option just discussed (option 2), but the initial implementations of this option indicate that overall performance is improved in comparison to option 2. This concept is known by several terms in the industry. One of its original descriptions was data link switching (DLS). Some implementations call this approach packet interceptions.

However, the base station (BS) split connection approach does not work well if the mobile system is subject to frequent disconnections. For this type of an environment, a split connection[6] can still be used, but the TCP operations are modified (see Figure 11–18):

- TCP is moved away from the BS to a machine that controls multiple cell sites (such as the mobile switching center [MSC]). This site is called the Supervisor Host (SH).
- The SH passes the segment from the fixed station to the MS, but does not ACK until the MS ACKs. The M-TCP module informs the SH-TCP module of the ACKs.
- The fixed station is choked when the MS is temporarily disconnected.
- When the MS is reconnected, the fixed station can send a full window of segments.

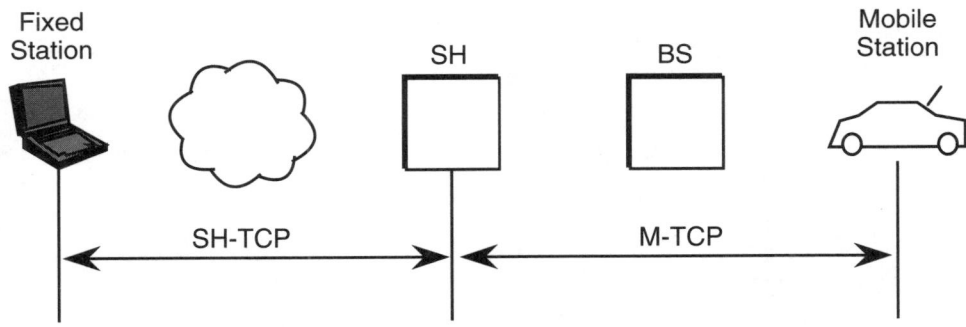

where:
  BS   Base station
  M   Mobile
  SH   Supervisor host

Figure 11–18   Option 3 layout.

[6]See Kevin Brown and Suresh Singh, "M-TCP: TCP for Mobile Cellular Networks," NSF Grant NCR-94/0357.

Also, the packet interception approach isolates the stream transmissions in the mobile cells from those in an internet and does not affect the overall operations of the internet traffic. This approach also simplifies and optimizes buffer management and reduces computational overhead in the mobile station.

The Brown/Singh algorithm operates as follows (from which this description is abstracted):

- Assume that W denotes the currently advertised receive window at SH-TCP, and the window contains $w \leq W$ bytes. Assume that the MH as ACK'ed bytes up to $w' \leq w$. SH-TCP sends and ACK for bytes up to $w' - 1$ in the normal way. When the MH ACKs more data, more ACKs are generated but one last byte is always left unacknowledged (to prevent the TCP client from going into the persist mode).

- Now assume that MS disconnects after having ACK'ed bytes up to w'. The M-TCP client assumes that the MS has been temporarily disconnected because it stops receiving ACKs for bytes transmitted after w'. M-TCP sends an indication of this fact to SH-TCP who then sends an ACK for the $w'th$ byte to the sender. This ACK will also contain a TCP window size update that sets the sender's window size to zero. When the TCP sender receives the window update, it is forced into persist mode. While in this state, it will not suffer from retransmit timeouts and will not exponentially back off its retransmission timer, nor will it close its congestion window.

- If the MS has not disconnected but is in a cell with very little available bandwidth, SH-TCP still sends an ACK for byte w' with a window size set to 0. SH-TCP estimates the round trip time (RTT) to the TCP sender and estimates the RTO interval. It uses this information to preemptively shrink the sender's window before the sender goes into exponential back off (to implement this scheme Brown/Singh define a timer at the SH that is initialized to this estimated RTO value).

- When the MS regains its connection, it sends a greeting packet to the SH. M-TCP is notified of this event and it passes on this information to SH-TCP that, in turn, sends an ACK to the sender and reopens its receive window (and hence, the sender's transmit window). The window update allows the sender to leave the persist mode and resume data transmission.

For the reader who wishes more information on pros and cons of traffic integrity in a mobile environment the following paper is an excellent introduction: "Reliable Stream Transmission Protocols in Mobile Computing Environments," by Kevin Houzhi Xu, from *BellLabs Technical Journal on Wireless, 2*(3), Summer 1997.

Brown/Singh tested M-TCP against end-to-end TCP by running data on a emulated 32 kbit/s wireless link and placing the traffic on 5 and 15 hops between the fixed station and the MS. They plotted the transfer time for a 500 kbyte and 1 Mbyte files against the disconnection length from 0.5 to 4.5 seconds. Figure 11–19 shows the results of one of their 500 kbyte tests where latency and disconnection length were normally distributed random variables and the end-to-end path was 5 hops.

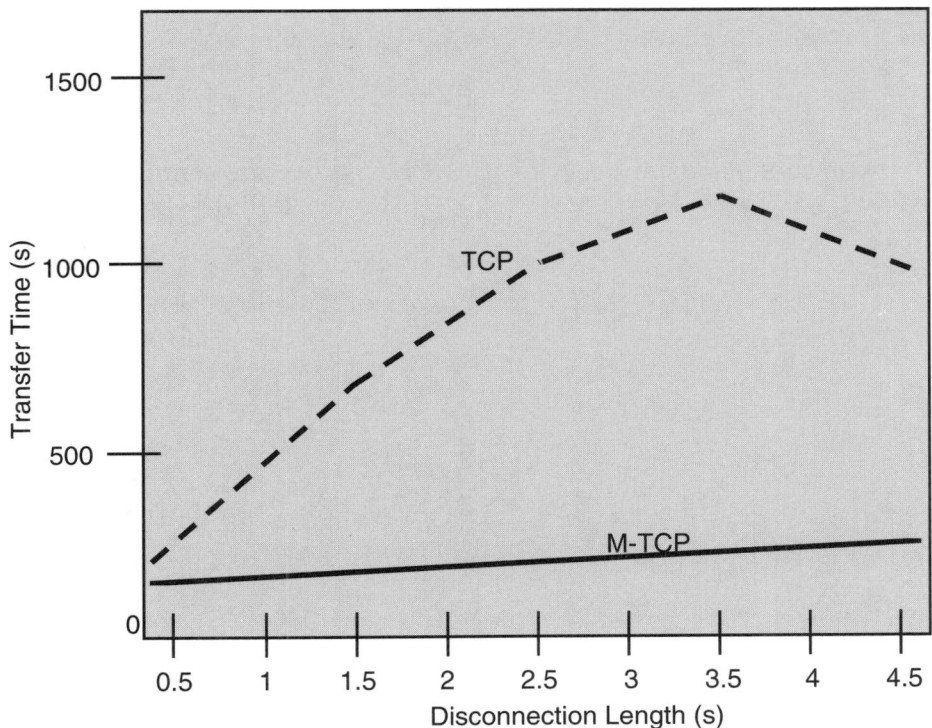

Note: M-TCP vs. TCP (5 hops, 500k file, normal means)

Figure 11–19   M-TCP. (*Source:* See footnote 6.)

Clearly, M-TCP outperforms TCP. Indeed, their tests revealed that M-TCP was quite consistent in comparison to end-to-end TCP's behavior.

So, it looks as if this approach will work. The authors describe other aspects of their M-TCP. I refer you to the referenced paper if you are interested.

SUMMARY

Mobile IP is the first industry-wide effort to define how the IP can be moved from one network to another. The key to the Mobile IP operations is the use of a care-of address and the concept of IP tunneling.

While most of the issues surrounding Mobile IP are resolved, those surrounding TCP are not. However, considerable progress has been made in defining how TCP can be made to operate effectively over a mobile environment.

12
Conclusions

PROBLEMS AT THE LOCAL LOOP

For today's voice requirements, the present structure on the local loop provides adequate capacity, but that capacity is insufficient for other applications, such as data and video. Voice has a modest bandwidth requirement, and the local loop is designed to support voice bandwidths.

The problem is that many applications that are now in the marketplace, or are being developed, are significantly handicapped by local loop bottlenecks. As one example, file transfer and database accesses take too long with current technology. As another, Internet access and browsing is often a chore, due to the limited bandwidth of the local loop.

The present structure is not conducive to building multimedia networks, because voice, video, and data are difficult to run concurrently on the local loop. Regardless of what happens in the Internet, if the local loop is not upgraded, multimedia is a dead technology for the mass marketplace.

PROBLEMS IN THE INTERNET

Of course, there are significant problems in the Internet as well. They were discussed in earlier chapters, so we need not revisit them here. The only additional point I would like to make about the Internet is that in its embryonic stages, it is not very efficient in allowing users to browse across many sites and access large chunks of information in a real-time mode. The current technologies are largely text-oriented, with very limited audio and video display capabilities.

THE ETERNAL CIRCLE

Since the inception of the computer, there has existed the eternal circle, illustrated in Figure 12–1. The triangle represents a symbiotic relationship between computer capacity needs, the bandwidth needs of applications, and the bandwidth capacity of communications links and networks.

In the simplest terms, the increasing sophistication of applications (large file transfers, browsing, video, etc.) acts as a driving force for "larger pipes" to transfer the applications' traffic. Yet, in order for the applications to generate these large data flows, the supporting computer must have fast processors and fast memory. Consider how difficult it would be to do Web browsing on a 5 MHz processor.

The term "symbiotic" is appropriate; the elements in the circle—processors, channels, and applications—feed each other, support each other (and sometimes, become bottlenecks to each other).

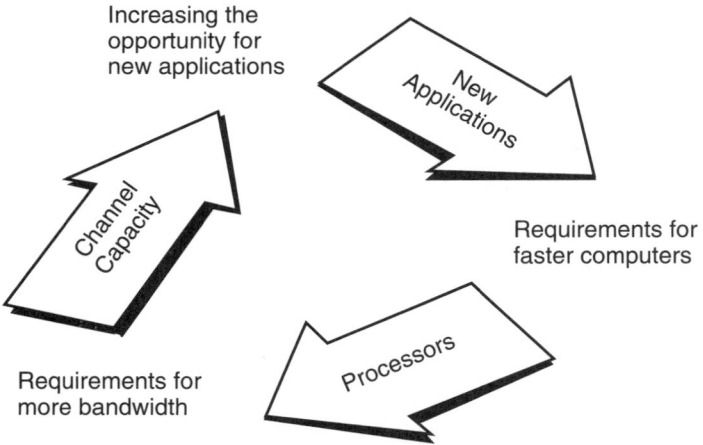

Figure 12–1   The eternal circle.

Where is the bottleneck today? It is at the local loop. In the future, it could very well be in the Internet, if the Internet service providers are not able to keep pace with the growing user base.

But the eternal circle is just that, eternal. The industry struggles continuously to achieve a balance, but so far, we have never attained an equilibrium. As soon as it appears that enough bandwidth is available, the next generation of chips appear, and the processor's output overwhelms the communications links' capacity. Just as soon as the new gigahertz processors are installed, then someone develops an application that requires even faster processors.

WHAT IS NEXT?

So, what is next? Next is the migration to a complete multimedia, real-time culture. One that, among other things, will make the current Internet seem archaic. Can you imagine what second generation browsers running with MPEG-7, and artificial intelligence (AI) software will be able do? Can you imagine how speech-activated inquiries, also supported with AI, will transform our Internet browsing?

I am convinced that one our biggest challenges (perhaps the biggest challenge of all) is the ability to store and identify terabytes of information in such a way to make it available in a real-time fashion (with audio and video displays) to anyone who has a terminal.

The multimedia, real-time culture depends on bandwidth to be sure, but it equally depends on the ability to store and manage information.

HOW DO WE GET THERE?

How do we get to the multimedia, real-time culture? We are already on the way and have been for some time. For the next few years, we must make significant strides in four areas.

I can summarize the areas as follows: To move to a true multimedia, real-time culture, (1) the telephone network has to behave more like a data network, (2) the Internet has to behave more like a telephone network, (3) the Internet has to become much more intelligent (the browsers and the data base repositories), and (4) the local loop has to support multimedia bandwidth rates.

THINGS WILL GET MESSY

Many of the subjects in this book have focused on deploying technologies that compensate for the asynchronous, long-delay behavior of the Internet (label switching, fixed routing) and the limited capacity of the local loop (low-bit rate codecs).

Yet it is reasonable to state that these technologies may not be as important in the future as they are now. As cable modems and ADSL (asymmetrical digital subscriber line) modems become consumer items, the local loop bandwidth will be increased to support almost any known application's requirements. Further in the future are optical-based switches, and in the near future is the availability of unprecedented bandwidth with the deployment of wave division multiplexing networks, some of which are now being installed.

The inculcation of these technologies into current systems will change the systems online today. This is certainly the case for the local loop technologies. For example, the ADSL technology defines several conventions for framing the signals into messages. It remains to be seen how these conventions will interwork with current systems, such as codecs. Even the emerging cable modems must be able to interwork with say ATM. All in all, things are going to get messy as we move from one generation technology to the next, try to overlay the new with the old, and achieve a balance in the eternal circle.

In 1975, I read an article in *Fortune* magazine, written by Max Ways. He said, "Democracy is like a raft: You never sink, but damn it, your feet are always in the water." We can paraphrase Mr. Ways' statement as, "The eternal circle is like a raft: You never sink, but damn it, your feet are always in the water." But if you don't mind the wet feet, the journey in this leaky raft can be an interesting one.

Abbreviations

A audio
AAL adaptation layer
ACCM asynchronous control character map
ACELP Algebraic-Code-Excited Linear-Prediction
ACF Admission Confirmation message
ACKs positive acknowledgment
A/D analog-to-digital
ADPCM Adaptive differential pulse code modulation
AI artificial intelligence
ANS Advanced Network Services
API application programming interface
ARIS aggregate route-based IP switching
ARJ Admission Reject message
ARP Address Resolution Protocol
ARPA Advanced Research Projects Agency
ARQ Admission Request message
ASN.1 Abstract Syntax Notation One
ASIC application-specific integrated circuits
ATM Asynchronous Transfer Mode
ATMARP ATM address resolution protocol
AUTHU authentication option
AVT Audio-video Transport

BECN Backward explicit congestion notification
BER bit error rate
BGP Border Gateway Protocol
BIND Berkeley Internet Name Domain
BS base station
C client
C control
CBR Constant Bit Rate
CC contributor count
CD Compact disc
CD Constant delay
CDPD Cellular Digital Packet Data
CDV constant delay value
CELP Code excited predictive linear coding
CIDR Classless Interdomain Routing
CLNP Connectionless Layer Network Protocol
CN Congestion notification
CRC cyclic redundancy check
CSR cell switching router
CSRC Contributing source
D data
D bit delay bit
DCA Defense Communications Agency

DCF Disengage Confirmation

DHCP Dynamic Host Configuration Protocol

DIRECT directly attached to router

DLC data link control

DLCI data link connection identifier

DNS Domain Name System

DOD Department of Defense

DRJ Disengage Reject

DRQ Disengage Request

DSP digital signal processing

E extension

EOT end-of-transmission

ESN electronic serial number

ES elementary stream

FANP Flow Attribute Notification Protocol

FCS frame clerk sequence

FDDI Fiber Distributed Data Interface

FEC forward error correction

FECN forward explicit congestion notification

FM Frequency modulation

FMP flow management protocol

FTP File Transfer Protocol

GCC Generic Confernce Control

GCF Gatekeeper Confirmation message

GRJ Gatekeeper Reject message

GRQ Gatekeeper Request message

GSMP General Switch Management Protocol

GSTN General Switched Telephone Network

HDLC High Level Data Link Control

IACS Integrated Access and Cross-Connection System

ICMP Internet Control Message Protocol

ID identifier

I/G individual/group

IGMP Internet Group Management Protocol

IMP interface message processors

IMTC International Media Teleconferencing Consortium

IP Internet Protocol

IPX Internet Packet Exchange

IRQ Information Request

IRR Information Request Response

IS international standard

ISDN Integrated Services Digital Network

ISP Internet Service Provider

ISS initial send sequence

IWU internetworking unit

kbits large bandwidth

LAN local area network

LANE LAN Emulation

LB Local binding

LCF Location Confirm

LCN logical channel number

LCP Link Control Protocol

LD-CELP Low delay code excited linear prediction

LIH logical outgoing interface handle

LIS logical IP subnetwork

LPAS Linear prediction analysis-by-synthesis

LPC linear predictive coding

LRQ Location Request

LS label switching

LSR label switching routing

M marker

mbit marker bit

MAC media access control

MAE Metropolitan Area Exchanges

MBONE Multicasting backbone

MC multipoint controller

MC multicast

MCS Multipoint Communication Service

MCU Multipoint Control Unit

MELP mixed-excitation LPC

MOS Mean Opinion Scores

MP multipoint processor

M/P more/poll bits

MPCS MPOA clients

MPEG Motion Pictures Expert Group

MPEG-2 Motion Pictures Experts Group-2

MPLS multiprotocol label switching

MP-MLQ Multipulse Maximum Likelihood Quantization

MPOA multiprotocol over ATM

MPSs MPOA servers

MRU maximum receive unit

ms milliseconds

MSC mobile switching center

MSS maximum segment size

MT mobile termination

MTU maximum transmission unit
N ISDN narrowband-ISDN
NA "not applicable"
NAK negative acknowledgment
NAPs Network Access Points
NCP Network Control Protocol
NHRP Next Hjop Resolution Protocol
NSAP network service access points
NSF National Science Foundation
NSP Network access point
NTP Network time protocol
OPCR original program clock reference
OSI Open Systems Interconnection
OSPF Open Shortest Path First
OT Outgoing tag
P padding
PARC Palo Alto Research Center
PC personal computer
PCM Pulse code modulation
PCR program clock reference
PDU protocol data unit
PES packetized elementary stream
PFC Protocol Field Compression
PID protocol ID
PM program stream
PPP Point-to-Point Protocol
PS program streams
PSVQ predictive split vector quantizer
PT payload type
PUP Universal Packet Protocol
QCIF Quarter Common Inermediate Format
QOS quality of service
RARP Reverse Address Resolution Protocol
RAS Registration, Admissions, and Status
RBB residential broadband
Rbit reliability bit
RCF Registration Confirmation message
REMOTE reached through another router
RFCs Request for Comments
RPC Remote Procedure Call
RRJ Registration Reject message
RRQ Registration Request message
RSVP Resource Reservation Protocol
RTCP Real-time control protocol
RTP Real Time protocol
RTT round trip time

S server
SAP service access point
SCN switched circuit network
S/D signal to distortion
SDES source description packet
SDLC Synchronous Data Link Control
SEQ sequence
SH Supervisor Host
SMTP Simple Mail Transfer Protocol
SN sequence number
SNA Systems Network Architecture
SNMP Simple Network Management Protocol
SPI Security Parameter Index
SRI Stanford Research Institute
SSRC Synchronous Source
SSRC_n Source identifier
STC system time clock
Sync Source ID
TASI imte-assigned speech interpolation
T bit throughput bit
TCH traffic channels
TCP Transmission Control Protocol
TDM time division multiplexing
TDP Tag Distribution Protocol
TFIB fkorwarding information base
TFTP Tivial File Transfer Protocol
TIB Tag Information Base
TIP Terminal IMP
TOS type of service
TS timestamp
TS transport stream
TSAP Transport Service Access Point
TSI time slot interchange
TTL time to live
UCF Unregister Confirm message
UDP User Datagram Protocol
UI unnumbered information type
UIH unnumbered information with header check
U/L local or universal bit
ULP Upper layer protocol
UNI user-to-network interface
URJ Unregister Reject message
URQ Unregister Request message
V video
V version
VBR Variable Bit Rate

VC virtual circuit
VD variable delay
VLSM variable length submask
VoIP Voice over IP
VPI/VCI virtual channel identifier/virtual
  path identifier

V/UV voiced/unvoiced
WAN Wide area network
WD working draft
XBNS Very High Speed Backbone Net-
  work Service

Index

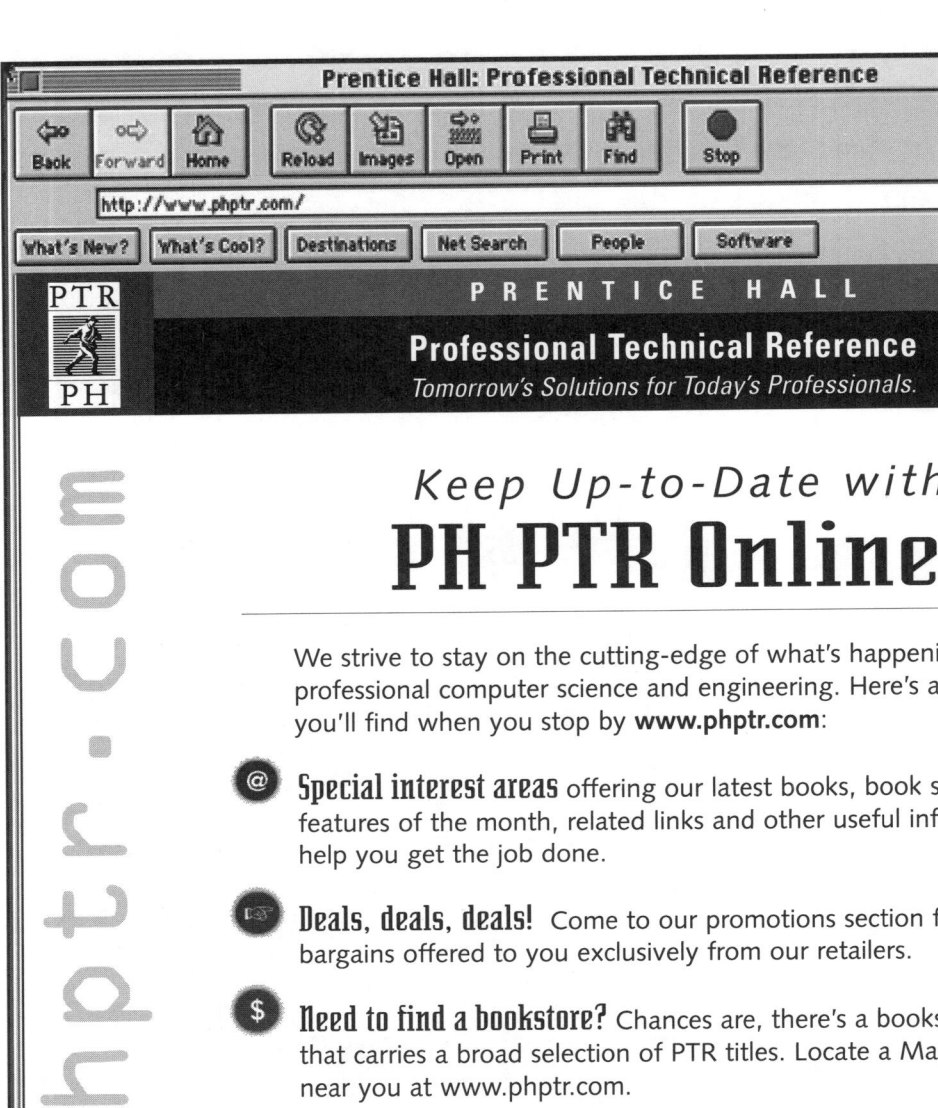